FRESH BLOOD

FRESH BLOOD

THE NEW AMERICAN IMMIGRANTS

SANFORD J. UNGAR

University of Illinois Press
Urbana and Chicago

Illini Books edition, 1998
© 1995, 1998 by Sanford J. Ungar
Manufactured in the United States of America
P 5 4 3 2 1

This book is printed on acid-free paper

Previously published in hardback (ISBN 0-684-80860-9) by
Simon & Schuster

Excerpts from "Truth or Dare," by Debbie Hakimian, in the
January 1994 edition of *Megillah,* are reprinted with the permission
of the author.

"This Is My Country," by Al Jacobs and Don Raye, © 1940
(renewed) by Shawnee Press, Inc. (ASCAP) and Warock Corporation.
International Copyright secured. All rights reserved.
Reprinted by permission.

Library of Congress Cataloging-in-Publication Data

Ungar, Sanford J.
Fresh blood : the new American immigrants / Sanford J. Ungar.—
Illini Books ed.
p. cm.
Originally published: New York : Simon & Schuster, 1995.
Includes bibliographical references and index.
ISBN 0-252-06702-9 (pbk. : alk. paper)
1. Immigrants—United States. 2. United States—Emigration and
immigration. I. Title.
JV6455.U57 1998
325.73—dc21 97-37568
CIP

TO BETH

CONTENTS

A NOTE TO THE READER

THIS BOOK is based primarily on interviews that I conducted around the United States, and in some cases in other countries, over a period of more than four years. Unless there was a specific objection by the source or some unusual logistical difficulty, whenever possible the interviews were taped and later transcribed. Some of the conversations took place in Spanish or French or, through interpreters, in other languages; a few were translated after the fact. In quoting the immigrants and refugees I interviewed, where necessary I have tended to render their comments into standard, grammatical English, for ease of reading and comprehension. In doing so, however, I have made every effort to be faithful to their original meaning.

Most of the people who appear in this book are given the age, and identified by the affiliation or title, they had at the time I met them. Except where a change was germane to a particular anecdote or chronology, or otherwise of special interest, I have not attempted to update that information. Similarly, I have not revised the U.S. dollar equivalents of foreign currency amounts cited in the text; they were correct at the time of the research and reporting.

PROLOGUE:
THE ROAD TO TUSICE

THIS IS A BOOK of immigrant stories, and so it seems only appropriate to start with my own, which took almost as much effort to piece together as any of the others that follow.

In the first decade of the twentieth century, both of my parents arrived in America from eastern Europe, each from a small village in a different part of the old Austro-Hungarian Empire.

According to her official papers, my mother, Tillie Landau, was from "Austria," but more precisely, her village—named Chrenif, or somesuch—was in Galicia, near present-day Lvov (sometimes in Poland, now part of Ukraine). She came in 1908, at the age of seven, with her parents, Manuel and Miriam Landau, and several siblings. Escaping the grinding poverty of a classic Jewish *shtetl*, they sailed as "steerage," she always told me, and came with great wonderment through Ellis Island into what seemed to them a magnificent land of opportunity. The oldest brothers in her family of seven children had preceded them and found a promising spot to live, a booming coal town in northeastern Pennsylvania named Wilkes-Barre, where many other immigrants were settling at the time. My grandfather, whom I never met, was in the "dry goods" business. What that meant in the early days, I later learned, was that he was a peddler, complete with horse and buggy. Eventually he opened a shop of his own, and several of his sons—my uncles—became prosperous small-town furniture and jewelry dealers. Another became an insurance agent, a legend in his time for his extraordinary ability to convince humble people to insure their lives. Before he could read or write English, we were told, Uncle Herman could sell insurance.

My father, Max Ungar, who was born in 1895, immigrated as a teen-ager, on his own. He, too, came ashore in New York City, probably at the age of fifteen (but almost certainly pretending to be older), and stayed at first with an aunt and uncle in Far Rockaway. Welcoming as they might have been, my father's relatives spoke only Hungarian and Yiddish, so when he heard that cousins who had made their way from Europe to a tiny place near Scranton, Pennsylvania (not far from Wilkes-Barre), had apparently begun to master English, he quickly went to join them there. (His older brother, Joe, had actually come to America and spent time with this family a few years earlier but had already moved on to a different small town.) For a time, my father worked in the cousins' grocery store in the daytime and went to school at night, but before long he was drafted. The United States Army shipped him back to Europe in the infantry, and he passed a year or two as a gung-ho American GI fighting on behalf of freedom in the trenches in France.

As a child, I found it fascinating that my father had spent World War I on the opposite side of the conflict, yet not many miles, from his native country, where his parents and other family members still lived. I never figured out whether he actually marched down the Champs-Elysées in Paris with the Yanks, but he certainly knew all the songs they had sung. ("Three German officers crossed the line, *parlez-vous* . . ." and all that.)

Back from the war, my father met my mother—some say the match-making was done by one of my mother's brothers—and they eloped to New York City in 1920. The marriage was performed by the uncle my father had originally stayed with, a butcher who also had religious credentials that authorized him to preside over weddings, along with circumcisions and the humane slaughter of animals to produce kosher meat. My parents bought a house in Kingston, a smaller town just across the Susquehanna River from Wilkes-Barre, and soon opened their own grocery store. They were upstanding citizens, charter members of the local Conservative synagogue. At least until the Great Depression ruined their prospects of collecting the large amounts of money their credit customers owed them, they lived a modest version of the American Dream.

As a young couple, Max and Tillie Ungar were responsible for helping several members of my father's family come to America. Despite my father's pleading, however, his parents refused to leave their village in Upper Hungary (by then part of the interwar state of Czecho-slovakia). The story was later told that they feared the United States would not be clean enough, that they did not expect to like it here and did not even care to visit. Besides, at the time the issue was first raised, they still had a son who was subject to the draft. They had no way of getting him out of it and did not want to leave him behind.

My grandfather on my father's side, Philip Ungar, himself a grocer, was apparently the kind of Old-World figure who totally dominated his wife, Rose, and had the unquestioned authority to forbid some of his children, even married daughters who lived in distant cities, to leave. As a result, several of my father's siblings never emigrated but stayed behind near their parents. Indeed, in the 1920s, all of the children who did live in America made pilgrimages home to see their parents and other members of the family. My father's older sister took her two children in 1926; my father himself went with a friend in 1927; and two of his brothers traveled back to Czechoslovakia together in 1929 on the occasion of their brother Paul's wedding. (One of them, it was whispered in private moments, actually skipped the ceremony and went to take the waters in Carlsbad instead, hoping for a cure for his bad back.)

By the time I was born in 1945, the youngest of five children, all of this seemed like ancient history. My father's parents had perished in the Holocaust, along with Paul and his family, two of my father's sisters, and various other relatives. But no one knew when, exactly—communication with them ceased abruptly after the war began—and these matters were not discussed much in front of me. Closer to home was the fact that my parents' older son, my brother Calvin, had died fighting for his country in World War II. A patriotic volunteer and an air force navigator, he was shot down over Italy in 1944. I arrived, as consolation, just eleven months later.

The important thing was that we were Americans, good Americans, typical products of the melting pot. Truthfully, I grew up with only the dimmest sense of where my people had come from, and I had but a vague idea of what it must have felt like for my parents to be uprooted as youngsters from their home and culture in Europe and transplanted to another land. Perhaps I was tuning out the bad stuff. But my parents, old as they were compared to most, had no "foreign accent"—at least none discernible to me—and they said often that they felt lucky to have been liberated at an early age from the actual and potential horrors of these European villages. Occasionally my father would speak glowingly of Budapest, which he had visited more than once as a child. But especially after he died, when I was eleven years old, I felt little awareness of, or connection with, my family's past or my personal roots.

Surely, no place could have been more all-American than Kingston and Wilkes-Barre and the "Wyoming Valley" in which they were situated. This was particularly true during the period of steep economic decline suffered by the region in the 1950s and 1960s, when people seemed instinctively to pitch in and help one another. Ours was the kind of small-town life where we seldom locked our front doors and, in the summer, rarely even closed them. There were, of course, families with many different kinds of names and ethnic origins—including an especially rich mix of East Europeans, Irish, and Italians. We were all minorities, but we all lived together harmoniously, and somehow our upbringing emphasized the similarities more than the contrasts. In retrospect, perhaps this was made simpler by the fact that my class at Kingston High School had just one black male (whose family was from the Virgin Islands, it was reassuringly explained) and a young woman whose parents were from the Philippines. (There was a primarily black section of Wilkes-Barre, and those kids were mostly concentrated in one of the city's three public high schools.) Our community was often cited for its successful interfaith efforts, and in my generation, we actually learned a bit about one another's religions and customs. We were not completely assimilated, by any means, but we got along fine, the way Americans were supposed to.

Some cousins who were Holocaust survivors came through our house when I was a young child, and I found the way they talked strange and frightening. They, and other people who occasionally arrived in our midst from Europe with tales and scars of a troubled past (even, in some cases, tattooed numbers on their arms), were "refugees," a designation that seemed to imply something undesirable, or at least unfortunate. Indeed, for my peers, immigrants and refugees were *other* people, maybe the ones you read about in the newspaper in connection with some distant crisis. Whatever our families' histories might be, my friends and I were normal, fully adjusted Americans, growing up in a cozy place that seemed unlikely ever to change. Television came late, and for the longest time, we did not even have Chinese restaurants to prod us into thinking that there might be other ways of living daily life.

Still, on some level, I quietly, almost secretly, treasured my mysterious, eccentric status of being a first-generation American. This was a rather unusual thing for someone my age, both in my small town and in most of my future worlds. At some point, I actually began to enjoy telling people that my parents had both been born in Europe, and watching as their faces registered surprise. But I did not really know what this meant, and anyway, it all seemed very far away.

•

MY PRINCIPAL INFORMANT about the old country, as an adult, was my Uncle Leo, my father's baby brother, who died in November 1994 at the age of ninety-one. By the time I was ready to ask questions, he took particular pleasure in giving the answers. Whenever I found myself in the Los Angeles area, where he lived, I would sit with him for hours. He would tell me stories of his own quasi-illegal exit from Czechoslovakia in 1921 as a young man with somewhat irregular documents (he had paid a bribe of a thousand crowns to get them), and of his nervous wait in cosmopolitan Prague—hundreds of miles west of his home village in eastern Slovakia—for an American visa. He would draw me maps of that village, Tusice, locating it in relationship to the old Hungarian market town of Kassa (now Kosice), and he would explain which relatives had once lived in nearby places with exotic names like Secovce, Michalovce, and Hriadky.

In 1988, while working on a public television documentary about Czechoslovakia, to commemorate the twentieth anniversary of "Prague Spring" and the Soviet invasion that put an end to it, I knew our production team would be researching and filming in eastern Slovakia; and so before I left the States, I called Uncle Leo. Although he had not been there since his brother's wedding fifty-nine years earlier, he gave me precise instructions on how to find Tusice—where to leave the highway just outside of Secovce and follow the twists and turns of a road along a small, meandering river.

For some years I had looked for Tusice, without success, on every map of eastern Europe that I could get my hands on, and I had begun to wonder whether the village had actually survived all the turbulence in the region during and after World War II. But now, in the course of a long, gray day at a gigantic steel mill in Kosice, I came upon a detailed map of Slovakia that seemed to confirm my uncle's recollections. Tusice was there, right where it was supposed to be. While the producer looked for camera angles, I went off with our car and driver and Romana, our young Slovak interpreter. Following Uncle Leo's instructions, we were in Tusice within forty-five minutes.

It turned out to be a quiet place in a little valley between low mountains, with neat, albeit modest, houses; one of their most striking characteristics was that many of them had outdoor ladders, instead of internal stairways, as the means of reaching their second floor. The storm drains were aboveground, not below, and some houses seemed to have their water supply and plumbing outdoors. Unlike most Slovak villages that I had traveled through in the previous days, Tusice had no factory at its edge, belching acrid smoke into the air. Rather, to my surprise, it seemed to be an agricultural place; the fields were very green, and some families had farm animals on their premises. The town hall and the Communist Party headquarters (this was still a year and a half before the "Velvet Revolution" hit Czechoslovakia, and several years before the country split in two) looked freshly painted. In front of them was an intercity bus stop.

Romana, a college student from Bratislava, had lived in America with her diplomat father (actually an employee of the Interior Ministry). She seemed to regard my quest for my father's birthplace as impulsive and improbable, yet probably a more interesting way to spend the afternoon than hearing about whether production quotas at the steel mill had been met. As we arrived on the outskirts of the village, she got out of the car and approached a woman tending some chickens alongside a large house. Dressed in black, she appeared to be in her seventies, and so we thought she might know something. Had she ever heard of a family named Ungar and did she have any idea where they might have lived, Romana asked. "But of course," the woman replied with a shrug. She was actually only in her fifties, she said, but she had heard about this family long ago. They had once lived on one of the main streets, at number 38 or 40, she could not remember which. She pointed us in the right direction.

Off we went, following the woman's instructions. My heart was pounding. I felt a great sense of urgency, as if, after all these years, my father's childhood home might disappear any minute if I did not locate it right away. The first house we tried was the wrong one, but an elderly woman who lived there, also dressed in black, told us she had known my grandparents. She did not remember my father (who had, after all, left in 1910), but as a teenager, she thought, she had helped my grandmother take care of her youngest children or some of her grandchildren. There had been only two Hungarian Jewish families in Tusice, she recalled: one that ran the local tavern and the other, the Ungars, who operated their grocery business out of the front of the house next door to her family. My bearded grandfather, she said, used to go to Secovce, the nearest city, for his supplies and bring them back by horse-drawn cart.

We knocked at the house next door. A tall, burly man in his seventies answered and, once we had explained ourselves, invited us in. We sat around his kitchen table, and as his wife, who seemed frightened, looked on skeptically, he eventually told this story:

A native of Tusice, he had gone off as a young Slovak soldier to fight in the war—on the German side, of course, because Hitler had broken up Czechoslovakia, occupied the Czech part, and set up a puppet state in Slovakia (which, at the time, feared being swallowed up again by Hungary). One day, probably in 1943, when he came home on leave from the Russian front, he said, he was startled to find that my grandparents and their family were gone. Neighbors told him that they had been taken away one night, presumably by the Gestapo or its Slovak equivalent. The wartime government of Slovakia, led by the fascist nationalist priest Josef Tiso, had not merely cooperated with the Nazis' policies, but had actually paid the Germans by the head to deport the country's Jews to the concentration camps. Everyone in the village felt very sad, he said, because the citizens of Tusice had all gotten along well with each other. The Ungars had been kind, honest people. No one ever heard from them again.

After the war, this man reminded me, one of the grandchildren in the Ungar family, a first cousin of mine named Kalman, emerged from a displaced-persons camp. Because he was able-bodied, Kalman had been sent not exactly to a concentration camp, but to some kind of German work camp, where he had been assigned to the kitchens and befriended an SS guard. When his friend warned him that he was about to be killed, Kalman somehow managed to escape and go into hiding. In 1946 he made his way back to Kosice, where he had lived as a child, and there he saw his grandparents' home on a list of unclaimed, abandoned property in the region. He promptly took over the house and tried living in Tusice for a year or so, but this obviously did not work out well. It was too hard to overlook what had happened, and he simply did not fit in. In 1947 he decided to sell the property—to the man I was now meeting—and to use the proceeds to make his way to the Jewish homeland that was emerging amidst great struggle in the Middle East. (I later learned that when my parents found out that Kalman was alive, they had tried unsuccessfully to locate him and persuade him to come to America instead.)

"Tell me," asked the Slovak man, looking me straight in the eye, "did Kalman ever make it to Palestine?" Forty-one years after they had last seen each other, I was the unwitting messenger who was able to answer his question: Yes, Kalman had managed to get there, I reported, and, while not in the best of health, he still lived in Israel. I had met him only once, fourteen years earlier, at the wedding in Belgium of one of his sons, now a physician in France and my good friend. Would I, he asked, please give Kalman his regards.

It was an emotional, transforming moment. I was astounded—and have remained so ever since—by the ease with which I had found my roots, or at least one half of them. It was as if this place had been sitting there, just waiting for me, or for one of my sisters or a cousin, to come and rediscover it. My host, himself quite amazed by the encounter, became steadily more animated and gave the impression that although he was slightly wary of me, he would have been willing to talk all night. He liked Americans, he said. In fact, his daughter had emigrated to Chicago, and he had gone once to visit but decided he would not like to live amongst all the hustle and bustle of the United States.

There were endless issues that could be raised and explored. The house I was visiting, it turned out, was not actually the one where my father had been raised. That one had been torn down in the 1950s, the man said, and replaced with this new one by the communists, who were trying to develop Slovakia at the time. I learned some more about the village and its recent history. We stayed away from politics, but it was clear to me that my host was not so happy with his country's stodgy, hard-line Marxist regime, which at the time was more orthodox even than its Soviet sponsors.

The hour grew late, and we had to get the car back to the steel mill in Kosice. But I also grew uneasy. I began to wonder whether some of the people I had met, or their parents or friends, might have been the ones who denounced my frail old grandparents to the Gestapo. I thought about how frightened they must have been as they were taken away. I could not help but speculate whether some of the lovely silver and glass items I now saw in this house had once been theirs and been looted after they were gone. I turned over in my mind the questions of what could have been avoided, and what might have been, if only they had agreed to leave for America as my parents had urged them to do. There were other opportunities to return to Tusice later, as we completed our documentary, but I decided not to go. A little knowledge felt safer than a lot might be.

But something very important had changed for me. I knew now, really, where my father was from. I had stood where once he had played, and I had a feel for the village from which he had set out, three-quarters of a century earlier, on his own bold journey to America. I had mental, and actual, photographs of the place as it was today. I was no less American than ever before, of course, but now, in middle age, I had discovered my own immigrant consciousness. Indeed, in that sense, I could now feel even more authentically American.

And that is how I came to write this book.

INTRODUCTION

TOWARD THE END of a 1992 conference in Washington on Environmental Challenges and the Global South, a young black man in the audience rose to speak. He was tall and slight, well dressed, and had a rich, thick accent from West Africa, probably Nigeria. It seemed natural to presume that he wanted to say something on behalf of "the South"—the Third World, which many Americans would now consider "the other side" in a new, post–Cold War global struggle. But the first words out of the man's mouth contained a simple clarification of who he was. "I call myself an American," he said, in a tone of notification, and then went on to join the discussion.

Although the man might superficially have looked and sounded like an outsider to many of the other people in the room, with those few introductory words he was serving notice that he took seriously his status as a naturalized U.S. citizen. As I listened, it occurred to me that he was buying in to some very old rhetoric about how easy it is for anyone to become an American. There was a time—and not so long ago, at that—when this rhetoric was honored mostly in the breach, when it was difficult for an Italian or someone from China, let alone a West African, to be regarded as a "real" American. But now, notwithstanding whatever lamentable discrimination he might still encounter in his daily life, it was utterly plausible for this man to call himself an American and to speak as one in an open forum. Indeed, he could venture forth into the mainstream of American life as a fully qualified player and hope to be measured, like anyone else, on credentials and performance.

That's just the point: Since World War II, a much broader range of people have come to live in the United States than ever before. The laws have changed, and the doors have opened wider once again—at least temporarily. But now the variety of people seeking economic or political refuge and human fulfillment has grown dramatically. Many of these immigrants look different, sound different, and may dress and eat differently from what we have come to regard as typically "American." At first, some immigrant groups may seem far more difficult to assimilate into America's daily routine than most of us think our own ancestors must have been. (Actually, the same was said about every group at one time or another; those who had come somewhat earlier invariably treated each wave of new arrivals as outsiders.) Despite whatever American customs they begin to observe, once these newcomers reach critical mass, they may try to hold on to and cherish their cultural distinctness and separateness as long as possible. They may choose to remain quietly apart from the crowd, to resist being smothered by the materialism and high-tech consumerism they see on television and their children bring home from school. Often, this means that they continue to speak the language they brought with them and make a special effort to pass it on to their children and grandchildren.

In most cases, however, the idea of America that we have sold the immigrants—the dream of economic success and financial independence, the concept of participating in civil society and gaining some control over one's own destiny without fear of arbitrary power—still takes effect rather quickly. The newcomers are not all enduringly or unanimously happy with the lives they carve out in America, and their presence may at first seem threatening to those who have been here longer. Yet, however distinct they may try to remain, they soon come to consider themselves Americans, and, by definition, once they complete a few formalities, they—and especially their children—have just as much claim to being American as anyone else.

The overall effect on the United States of this new and different immigration, although only gradually played out, has been profound. The great ethnic, racial, and linguistic diversity among the new immigrants is probably the main factor causing the old, sacred melting-pot image of America finally to give way to something more realistic, like a mosaic or a salad bowl. The concept is no longer advanced that we must all somehow become the same eventually, but rather that we should be able to learn to live peacefully and respectfully with one another. In fact, it may be easier to fulfill this more realistic national myth than the old one. And so, in the context of shared community goals and values, a benign multiculturalism, seen by some conservatives as such a threat to American life, may make simple sense after all. We can, it turns out, live with many languages, skin colors, cuisines, and seemingly exotic religions in our midst. They may even make us stronger—more interesting and dynamic—as a society.

The new immigrants are, in effect, changing old notions about what it takes to be an American and helping revise the standard of how much deviation from the average is acceptable. As they grow in number, it becomes increasingly difficult to pretend that we are all of English origin, or would be if we could be. Indeed, few Americans seemed to get hung up on the fact that the army general who became chairman of the Joint Chiefs of Staff in 1993 was named not Taylor or Jones, but Shalikashvili. On the contrary, it was regarded as a fascinating story, even a point of pride that the United States could hold up to the rest of the world, that his origins could be traced to the Georgia in the Caucasus, not the one north of Florida, and that he had immigrated as a child from Poland to Peoria. It is difficult to imagine such a thing occurring in Great Britain, France, or Japan.

But it is easy enough now to encounter a university professor in America, or even a disc jockey on the radio, with an Australian or a South African accent. Best-selling novels tell more openly the painful stories of the displacement and adjustment of immigrants from China, the Dominican Republic, and India. Big-city taxi drivers are quite likely to be from Ethiopia, Israel, Russia, Bangladesh, or Afghanistan. Even the smallest town in the heartland is liable to have not just a Chinese and an Italian restaurant, but also a Thai, a Greek, or a Caribbean one. The radiologist or anesthesiologist at the local hospital could easily be from Pakistan or the Philippines, and the corner grocery store may well be run by Palestinians or Koreans. Everyone, it seems—not just big-city people—meets immigrants in his daily life.

Our children are getting used to the fact that many of their friends speak a language other than English at home; there is no shame attached to it. At the same time, it is ever more commonplace to come across young people who *look* like "foreigners" but sound and move and react like any other American. They are the children of immigrants, but all they carry with them to prove it is the color of their skin or the spelling of their names. This can be very confusing to people who grew up accustomed to a more uniform, homogenized, perhaps simpler America.

LIKE ALL THOSE who came before them, today's immigrants are occasionally controversial, but they are transforming—and constantly improving—America. That transformation, begun soon after World War II but still very much underway, is the subject of this book. It is, if you will, an anthology of recent immigrant stories, a collection of individual and group experiences, good and bad, ordinary and profound, realistic and romantic, meant to reveal sides of life in the United States that do not often make it into the news and cannot be easily captured in pithy sound bites or quick turns of phrase. This is the new Americana—every bit as American as apple pie and bagels and egg rolls and fajitas and gyros and pizza and sushi.

Previous generations of immigrants have long since had their stories recorded and enshrined in modern American history. We have a grip on them. Oscar Handlin, Irving Howe, Nathan Glazer, Daniel Patrick Moynihan, and others have told of the early tribulations of the Irish in Boston and the Jews on New York's Lower East Side, among others. We know about the Germans in Chicago and Saint Louis, the Chinese laborers who built the great railroads across the continent, and the Swedes and Norwegians who fled starvation in their own countries to establish themselves gratefully in Minnesota and other parts of the Upper Midwest in the nineteenth century. (Quite a few of these people and others, by the way, were "illegal" at one end of their journey or another, but we have tended not to dwell on that issue.) We have all watched the Italian immigrants' struggle not to be tarred with the reputation of a minority of the Sicilians among them who became enmeshed in organized crime syndicates, and we have learned, albeit belatedly, about the indignities visited on Japanese Americans in detention camps in the Western United States during World War II. All of this has now become the stuff of fiction, film, and television series.

But what of those who came more recently, who did not have a Little Italy or a Chinatown where they could settle, who had no relatives or friends or Hebrew Immigrant Aid Society waiting to receive them? What happened to the waves of refugees and immigrants who fled communism in various parts of the world during the Cold War and came to the United States with great expectations? Where have the survivors of America's disastrous involvement in the withering battles of Southeast Asia taken refuge, and what have they found to do here? Who are these ostensibly uncountable Mexicans and Central Americans who flood across the southern border of the United States and provoke political crises in California? Why do they keep coming, when so many people try to make them feel unwelcome? And how about the victims of famine in Africa and turmoil in the Middle East and the Persian Gulf?

Most of these new immigrants, of course, like those who came before them, are self-selected. Legal or not, they tend to be the adventurers, the risk takers, the strong of mind and body who can cope with being uprooted and landing in a totally new environment. Some, especially those who arrive with familiar middle-class values and habits, settle into America quite smoothly; they are models of entrepreneurship and vitality. Others, survivors of turmoil in the mountains or the villages of a distant land, feel utterly bewildered; they may seem hopelessly dependent, and it can take years until they get on their feet. Those in another category come to work but cross the border to go back home and share their limited wealth whenever they think they can get away with it. But however different their adaptations may be, all of these immigrants bring us something. And once again, the whole, thankfully, is indisputably greater than the sum of its disparate parts.

Admittedly, there are important differences between today's immigration and earlier waves. The United States is now a wealthy, fully developed, powerful country, unique in its hemisphere, if not the world. It is far from being a perfect place, and more than a bit cynical about itself; the standard of living and the quality of life are now actually higher elsewhere, the studies tell us. Yet America still feels like the most open place on earth, where anything is possible. It is more than ever a magnet for those who seek to improve themselves economically, even if it is less obvious by far than it was at the beginning of the twentieth century where and how they will be able to do so. There may still be a labor shortage in America, but it is harder to define, and no one wants to recognize it as a permanent feature of the national landscape, especially not while there is still substantial unemployment and underemployment among native-born Americans of many different backgrounds. It is uncomfortable, perhaps, to acknowledge publicly that in many cases, immigrants are taking the jobs that more established Americans refuse to do.

Meanwhile, there is an odd coalition of forces—trade union members, the urban underclass, and assorted elites—who see the new immigrants, legal and illegal alike, as a threat to the social, economic, and political fabric of the land. They worry about being outnumbered, outvoted, outmaneuvered, and outperformed by people they do not even know . . . yet.

Look beyond appearances and scratch just a bit below the surface, and you will find that every one of the newcomers has a story worth telling. Unless some of those stories are heard and written down soon, both within each family and for the larger public, they risk being lost.

Posterity will never fully appreciate what it has inherited, and an important part of America's recent history will be skipped over.

Through the stories I tell here, I hope I have managed to introduce some of the newest Americans to one another and to their compatriots. At best, I will have shed light on a phenomenon that is still underway, while the country is still trying to figure out what, if anything, to do about it and how to appreciate its newest, sincerest recruits. With luck, I will also have damaged, or at least diluted, some stereotypes and easy assumptions. Not all illegal immigrants, for example, are Hispanics who come across the southern border. There are undocumented workers in the United States—in large numbers—from Ireland, Italy, Poland, Canada, Taiwan, and many other places, too. More than half of today's illegal immigrant population, in fact, flew in as tourists or students or on business trips or family visits and simply stayed, without great fear of being caught. The Hispanics who do come, most of them legally, are of varied backgrounds and may have plenty of trouble understanding one another's cultures. What makes the biggest difference, and is most instructive about the immigrant experience, is not how and in what status people arrive, but the atmosphere and the opportunities they find and develop once they get here. The reception in New York, Minnesota, or Texas, these days, may be vastly warmer than in California or Florida.

Above all, I hope I will convince many of my readers that the news is better than they think, that immigration is still an extraordinarily positive feature of American life—that immigrants invariably contribute at least as much as they take, that they help the United States maintain its place as an international leader by changing, adapting, and evolving. This is a point easily lost amid the regional and national hysteria that has led to California's Proposition 187 and other such anti-immigrant measures.

The individuals, the groups, and the events I have focused on are not necessarily representative or typical. They are, in fact, an eclectic bunch, chosen not scientifically but serendipitously, because they caught my eye or ear or I somehow crossed their paths. Inevitably, many have been left out. But in the end, the struggles and the joys of the immigrants I met seem to me at least as significant as political polls and economic statistics as a means of understanding what is happening and where we are headed in America.

PART ONE

IMMIGRATION TODAY

About a million people are now immigrating to the United States every year, at least 70 percent of them legally. That is one hundred thousand more than came during the average year between 1901 and 1910—the previous peak decade, when a total of nine million people arrived. But today a million people obviously represent a much smaller percentage of the American population overall than they did in the first decade of the twentieth century. Hard as it may be for some to imagine, the economic and social impact of immigration is much milder now than it was then.

Apart from a much more elaborate network of laws and regulations governing immigration and a vigorous but largely unsuccessful effort to police the border, what is different today is who is coming. There is astonishing diversity among the people who have arrived in the United States since World War II. Ever greater and more widespread turbulence around the world has caused the variety—along with the volume—of immigrants to increase steadily. Anyone is liable to come to America at any time and could wind up as the next-door neighbor of an average, all-American white-bread family that has never consciously thought about immigration. And although four states—California, New York, Florida, and Texas—accounted for two-thirds of the immigrants in 1990, the new arrivals settle in many other places, too, and they are not all concentrated in the big cities.

In Chapter I, I tell seven individual stories, as recounted to me by immigrants I encountered from India, Vietnam, Haiti, Poland, Syria, Hong Kong, and Zambia. They live in major urban centers, smaller towns, and rural areas. It is highly unlikely that any of these people will ever meet each other. The only thing they have in common is that each came into my life while I was working on this book and made an indelible impression on me. They are typical only for the differences of background and experience among them, and for their individual, unheralded struggles to figure out for themselves the meaning of becoming "an American."

Still, many Americans of longer standing, though they may meet and come to appreciate individual immigrants or refugees, think about immigration issues only through the vehicle of random events that impinge quite accidentally on their daily lives. Some of those events receive broad national—even international—attention, like the grounding near New York City early one morning in June 1993 of the *Golden Venture,* a rusting old freighter that was being used to smuggle illegal Chinese immigrants into America. Ten people drowned that morning, and hundreds more were rescued, only to face deportation proceedings.

In Chapters II and III, I look in on two other crises, at opposite ends of the country—in Temecula, California, and Revere, Massachusetts—that made people suddenly aware of an immigration drama unfolding in their midst. They were not the kind of incidents that shock the world, like the fate of the *Golden Venture.* The events I describe here were, if you will, smaller-scale tragedies that affected a more limited audience; they received mostly local and regional attention. But for those who lived through them on the front lines, immigration, for better or worse, will mean something different for the rest of their lives.

I
WE CALL OURSELVES AMERICANS

PENSACOLA, FLORIDA

ALAN PATEL, who was thirty years old when I met him, is not the first person one would expect to encounter in this old, very Southern military port at the western end of the Florida Panhandle on the Gulf of Mexico. He grew up in the small town of Vhamaiya, near Bardoli, in the Surat District on the west coast of India, about 225 miles north of Bombay. His father was a professor of history at a nearby university, and his mother was a high school teacher. Vhamaiya is in an agricultural area where there seemed to be few long-term opportunities for an ambitious young man like Alan. He became restless at an early age, dreaming of greener pastures and a more interesting life.

In 1984 Patel's parents packed up and brought Alan and his sister and brother for an extended visit to their uncle in San Francisco. It was an experiment: If they liked it, perhaps they would all stay. The uncle, Alan's father's brother, was the adventurous member of the family. He had long since left India, migrating in 1952 to England, where for years he ran a laundromat and a dry cleaning business. But, like many other Indians, he had become fed up with England and its social problems in the mid-1970s; he decided that the real opportunities awaited him in America. Before long, he was running a motel in San Francisco, and every two years he came back to India and regaled the family with stories about his wonderful life in Northern California. They had no idea what they were missing, he said; so now they were going to find out. A few weeks into the family visit, however, Patel's father declared that he was not so impressed with San Francisco. He was bothered by the fact that Americans kept such a distance from one another and barely knew their neighbors; after just two months, he took everyone home to India.

But a little more than a year later, more restless than ever and imbued with an entrepreneurial spirit common to Indians, Alan and his wife were back in San Francisco, helping his uncle run the motel. In his spare time, he went to school in order to improve his English, and soon he and his wife were on their own, managing a different motel for its Indian owner. But they decided they did not like the San Francisco weather—it exacerbated Alan's allergies—and they moved to Florida at the end of 1986. In Tallahassee, the state capital, Patel initially worked for his wife's brother-in-law, who had also immigrated from India, until he had saved enough money to go into business for himself. First he ran several stalls in a flea market, then he managed hotels in Tallahassee and Panama City, some one hundred and twenty miles to the west, and finally he took over a grocery store. Despite the sixteen-hour days he put in, his venture into the grocery business was a bust. When he and the brother-in-law heard in 1991 about a Quality Inn on the outskirts of Pensacola whose mortgage had been foreclosed on, they bought it from the bank.

That 120-unit modern motel on Pensacola Boulevard north of town, on the road to Alabama, is now both business and home for the Patel family—Alan, his wife, and their four-year-old daughter. However difficult Pensacola's transition away from dependence on the military may be, there is a lot of tourist traffic through here all year round. Many Canadians, among others, are drawn to spend the winter in this still-quiet stretch of Florida that has come to be known affectionately as the "redneck riviera." The Quality Inn is clean and neat and seems to be successful with overnight guests and the banquet trade, too. Increasingly involved in local business organizations, Patel has become an avid community booster and, with his citizenship papers imminent, a patriotic American. Whereas he often felt uneasy and occasionally experienced discrimination in San Francisco, Patel feels that he fits in well in Florida, getting along easily with the great variety of people here.

He proudly recalls an unusually cold winter in Tallahassee when the city ran out of funds to help the homeless. He agreed to house them in his hotel for only ten dollars a night each, and fifty or sixty people who could not pay at all stayed free. Eventually, Patel remembers, after he had put them up without compensation for more than two weeks, "the city recognized what I had done and they paid me."

"Everything has worked out pretty good for us here," Patel says in his thick, singsong Indian accent, "and I love this country. I like the freedom. We're proud of America." In their household, the family speaks its original Gujarati language, but his little girl attends parochial school nearby, where she is perfecting her English. "When she goes to college," Patel says, as if the moment were just around the corner, "she must speak fluently."

By now, Patel's sister and brother have also returned to America. She is running a hotel in Merced, California, and he in Dallas, Texas. And Patel knows of other families from the Surat District who are doing the same—for example, a fifty-year-old couple who had arrived just a few weeks before our conversation and were already working happily in the housekeeping department of a California property, saving up money to buy their own. "They are making a thousand dollars a month, and their living quarters are free," he says, still capable of amazement over the opportunities available to immigrants. Patel has heard stories about Indians who are so desperate to come that they are paying five or ten thousand dollars each to be smuggled into the United States through Mexico or Panama. Once they establish themselves, perhaps through fraudulent marriages, they will begin sending for other relatives from home. And the chances are quite good that many of them will work in the hotel industry.

Indeed, for reasons that remain obscure to most people, the small hotels and motels of America—in particular, the franchise operations along the highways—are increasingly owned, managed, and staffed by Indian or Pakistani immigrants. Legend has it that the first motel taken over by an Indian in the United States was in San Francisco in the 1950s, but no one really knows for sure. It is clear, though, that the number has been growing steadily every year, and the phenomenon is well enough recognized to have been the subject of a popular film, *Mississippi Masala.*

Michael Leven, a longtime executive in the hotel and travel business, recognized the trend soon after he became president of Days Inn hotels in 1985. When, a short time later, he helped launch the Asian-American Hotel Owners Association, to bring together franchise operators with a common background and mutual interests, Leven says he suddenly "discovered hundreds and hundreds of hotels owned by Indians. I found that they were just like everyone else, except they worked harder." Now president of Holiday Inn Worldwide, based in Atlanta, Leven has crusaded to eliminate discrimination against Asians in the industry. Today, he says, they own about seventy-five hundred properties, worth billions of dollars, and "they are being wooed by every major chain" to buy or build more.

It is not that the Indians have particular experience in the hotel business—there are many fewer hotels and motels in India than in the United States—but that they, like other enterprising immigrants, are seizing an opportunity. "Back in the seventies and eighties," says Patel, "more people started to come from India. We like to help each other. There were very low down payments on the properties, and 85 or 90 percent of them were financed by the previous owners. That made it very easy for us. The mortgages were fifteen or twenty years, and now they are getting paid off. So Indians are buying more hotels and motels, and we are having a big success. Now all the franchises like us, because they know we believe in working hard. Seventy or 80 percent of us were small farmers in India, and we are committed to work."

Even more remarkable than the concentration of Indians working in the hotel and motel industry in the United States is the fact that, according to Patel, the majority of them are from his home district of Surat. "Indians just love to talk about America," he says. "The young generation in Surat hear about their family in America, and all the youngsters are wanting to move here. Some of the villages are getting empty." Furthermore, a very substantial number of those in the hotel business happen to have the family name Patel. They are not necessarily related to each other. "It's just a coincidence. Patel is a very common name in Gujarat state, just like Smith here," Alan explains, "but Patels do tend to be businesspeople. We don't engage in illegal activities. We are very calm, and we try to live in peace." He pauses and smiles, about to utter a slogan with which he has had great success: "We say our business in this country is 'Hotels, Motels, and Patels.' "[1]

The only drawback to his life here, says Alan Patel, is that he misses his father, who still refuses to immigrate. "He doesn't like the way we talk about money here. He thinks that every time you go somewhere in this country, the bottom line is money. For everyone. But I realize that this is good. This is money—this is the way it is in America."

RITTMAN, OHIO

THE HOUSE is a modern rambler, and it could be anywhere in Middle America. But perched on top of a hill at the center of a three-acre plot on the edge of this rural town of 7,000 about forty-five minutes south-

---

[1] *One of the best-known Indian hotel operators in America, H. P. Rama, who owns at least fifteen properties in the southeastern states, was originally named Patel, but he changed his name, so as not to be confused with others. He selected his new surname, it is said, because of his success with a Ramada Inn that he owned.*

west of Cleveland, it looks as if it belongs in an update of a classic Grandma Moses painting. Even in the gray of winter, it seems to have a certain sparkle. It is tidy on the outside, spotlessly clean and meticulously organized on the inside. The photographs on the walls are of three well-groomed all-American children, two girls and a boy, in their mid- and late teens.

It is quiet here. There are very few people in evidence during the day, and if there were more, there would be little industry in the vicinity to employ them, or to pollute the air. The epidemic of drug-related crime and violence that has transformed so many parts of the United States seems to have passed Rittman by. For local entertainment, there is not much beyond the Amish livestock market in Kidron or the museum at the Smuckers plant in Orrville. But the law-abiding, church-attending people of this region invariably go elsewhere for adventure and come back to lead peaceful, outwardly contented lives in a community they count upon not to change drastically anytime soon. That is the pattern Roger Bartram followed when he went off to fight in Vietnam in the late 1960s and, several years later, brought home what used to be known as a "war bride" to live amongst his family and friends in the house he would build on the hill.

My Le Bartram first met her American Prince Charming in 1969, when she was still a young teenager. She came from the small town of Van Vieng, but attended high school in Vung Tau, where she also worked part time as a cashier at the Palace Hotel. He was stationed nearby as an army communications specialist at a satellite ground station. She spoke no English, and he no Vietnamese. "It was kind of hard," she remembers, but adds romantically that "when two people love each other, they don't care what language they speak." She had an older colleague who sometimes interpreted for them on important matters. Roger wanted to whisk her right off to America with him when his tour of duty ended, but My Le, warned by her aunt and others against trusting the lonely and impetuous American soldiers, insisted, as she now retells it, that "if you really care for me, you will come back for me." To her surprise, that was exactly what he did, landing a private-sector job with ITT doing the same things he had done in the military. He returned to Vietnam in February 1971. With the enthusiastic blessings of her well-established, Westernized parents—her father had fought in the French army in World War II—they were married in June, when Roger was twenty-two years old and My Le was not quite eighteen. He agreed to a big Catholic family wedding, although he had grown up as a Baptist.

The war was going badly for the Americans and the anticommunist government in Saigon at the time, but Roger's pay was decent and life was still comfortable and carefree enough for the expatriate community in South Vietnam, especially in a provincial city like Vung Tau. Within three years, the Bartrams had two children and a third was on the way. But after her husband nearly died in a motorcycle accident, My Le began to worry how she would ever manage to support her family in Vietnam without him, especially if the communists took over the south, as seemed increasingly likely. A visit to Ohio in 1973 went well—"everybody just loved me and treated me like someone they knew for years," she says— and so she agreed to immigrate to the United States the next year. The Bartrams got out of Vietnam about ten months before the fall of Saigon.

From the start, life was difficult for My Le in Rittman. Her husband was only sporadically employed, until he went back to school under the GI bill to study advanced electronics, and they and their three children lived in cramped quarters in her mother-in-law's nearby house for a year until their own place was ready. Even after they moved, she was stuck at home in the countryside almost all the time, with no car or driver's license and still only rudimentary English-language skills. Taking a special summertime English class designed for the refugees who began arriving in 1975 helped her get oriented; but as her children went off to school, learning more English and gradually forgetting or rejecting what little Vietnamese language and culture they knew, My Le began to feel intensely isolated. "I was just here all day long," she tells me in her living room during a long conversation punctuated with tears, "cooking, cleaning, ironing, and sweeping. I just cleaned constantly. I felt like a prisoner." After she got word from Vietnam that her mother had died, she became acutely depressed and finally persuaded her husband that it would be better for everyone if she could get out of the house more often and spend her time more productively. Soon he bought her a car and she obtained a driver's license.

Thus began My Le Bartram's career in the restaurant world. For several years, she got up at five o'clock every morning and drove into Rittman to work as a housekeeper at the local hotel and then serve as the lunchtime cook at the restaurant attached to it, returning home to greet her children after school. Next she became assistant manager of an Italian restaurant in Wadsworth, about seven miles away in the next county, where she supervises both the waitresses and the kitchen. There were lots of jokes at the beginning about the fact that she did not exactly look Italian, but she was a great success. Her income not only made it easier to begin sending her children to college for the education she never had herself but also gave her an opportunity to send money home to her father and brother, who My Le felt were being persecuted by the communist government because she and her sister had both gone off to live in America. She tried repeatedly to bring them over, but they refused to leave. Her father, she says, "doesn't want to die in Ohio."

My Le, a U.S. citizen since 1981, has returned to Vietnam only once, for a somewhat controlled three-week trip that included four intense days with her surviving family members there. She was appalled by many of the changes the communists had made, and she felt distant and different from the Vietnamese. Suddenly she was an American who found it surprisingly difficult to express herself in the country of her birth. Still she harbors the hope that improved relations between Washington and Hanoi might make it possible for her to go back more often and for longer periods. Indeed, for all the material comforts she has enjoyed in America, Bartram says, she often feels that "if I could have a decent job, I would want to go back to live [in Vietnam]. It's still my country. But I don't think I would want my children to live there; there's nothing in Vietnam for them."

Is this idea of returning a typical immigrant fantasy, or a real possibility? Would it not imply a painful separation from her children, much like the one she endured from her own parents? Bartram reflects quietly and then replies, with tears in her eyes, as if she knows she is expressing forbidden, heretical thoughts: "Well, the thing is, children here, when they get married, usually leave their parents and don't really think much about them. Some of them have too much, and they don't really appreciate what their parents have done for them. In Vietnam, when you marry, you still respect your parents and you do what they tell you. I like that better."

As her own, highly Americanized children grew up and began to leave home, Bartram found a new focus for her longing to be connected to Vietnam—an incorrigible Amerasian teenager known only as "Mickey," ostensibly the son of a Vietnamese woman and an African American serviceman. Mickey began life as a typical casualty of the war, but he had been twice abandoned, first at an orphanage in Ho Chi Minh City (formerly Saigon) and then in small-town Ohio by a cynical Vietnamese couple who had adopted him from the orphanage and used him as their excuse for priority immigrant visas to America. (Amerasian children, maliciously taunted in Vietnam as an unwelcome reminder of U.S. intervention, were being brought over in large numbers at the time as a humanitarian gesture.) Mickey spoke no English at all, and he was clearly a street kid from the big city who was totally out of place in small towns or the countryside. Even his age was in doubt, his Vietnamese adoptive parents claiming that he was eighteen (and thus eligible to be set loose on his own) when others thought he could be no more than fifteen. Shunted from one foster home to another, especially after he had surgery for a brain tumor, Mickey attracted My Le Bartram's attention when he was written about in the local newspapers.

As one of the few people in the area who could speak Vietnamese with him, Bartram took on Mickey as a cause. At one point, she bailed him out of jail, where he had been sent after fighting with one set of foster parents, and she took him into her home. That lasted only a month, until his habit of watching television well into the night disrupted her family's life and her children began to resent the attention he required. Soon he was back in foster care, receiving various government benefits but unable to attend school because of repeated incidents of inappropriate behavior toward young women.

Bartram and I drove together to Medina, another small town about fifteen miles north, where Mickey was now living with a different Vietnamese immigrant couple and working in the kitchen of their Chinese restaurant, supposedly for twenty dollars a day. He had an enthusiastic, almost silly, manner about him; he walked clumsily and seemed to have some trouble speaking. But when he saw Bartram walk in, Mickey smiled broadly and came running up to her, chattering in Vietnamese about the latest intelligence testing being done on him and the driver's education course he was hoping to take. The proprietors complained to her that it was hard to keep him focused on his work but acknowledged that they were expecting him to put in six long days a week. Once we had left the restaurant, Bartram confided her fear that Mickey was being treated like a servant by this couple but said she could not figure out how to help him further. As long as he could not conduct any conversation in English, nor read or understand the most basic numbers, she concluded, he was doomed to be exploited.

As we returned to Rittman, My Le Bartram's face was grim. She philosophized about immigrant life in America, particularly for people from Southeast Asia, speaking mournfully of the many struggles and hardships, physical and emotional, that are so often hidden from public view. She was writing a book about her life and her experiences, she said, and she shared with me her dream to get her own saga—and the tale of her effort to help Mickey—onto *20/20* or some other popular television program. That would somehow validate her suffering and her efforts to build a meaningful life in a new world. "A lot of people look up to me, because of what I have done," she said proudly.

SOMERVILLE, MASSACHUSETTS

THE POPULAR IMAGE of Haitians in the United States since the early 1980s has been of tragic boat people—rural, poverty-stricken, semiliterate, angry characters who will do anything to escape the political chaos and economic deprivation in their Caribbean homeland. Nearly everyone has seen videotape on the news of Haitians building small, rickety wooden craft along their country's coast, and then of Haitians being washed ashore, dead or alive, in South Florida or the Bahamas.

What many Haitian refugees have endured in between those moments is almost unimaginable. To make things even worse, most of those who survive the ordeal are soon processed by the Immigration and Naturalization Service, to be quarantined until it can be established that they are not HIV-positive or to be sent back to Haiti, to the U.S. naval base at Guantánamo Bay, at the eastern tip of Cuba, or to another country that has agreed to be a temporary "safe haven." The situation was especially insulting to Haitians during the years when Cuban refugees, some of whom may even have been picked up at sea and arrived in the same boats, were welcomed as heroic escapees from one of the world's last communist despots.

But there have been many previous Haitian immigrants to America in the post–World War II period, and Alix Cantave is a prime example. He is a certified member of the modern-day "second wave" of professionals, businessmen, politicians, and intellectuals who came to the United States from Haiti's urban areas during the 1970s to escape the brutal, corrupt regime of President-for-Life Jean-Claude "Baby Doc" Duvalier. (The first wave, composed even more so of well-educated people from the cities, had come in the mid- to late-1960s, running from Duvalier's father and predecessor, François, or "Papa Doc." The third wave has been made up primarily of economic migrants who poured out of the rural areas during the 1980s and early 1990s.)

Cantave was only fourteen years old when he arrived in New York in 1974 from Port-au-Prince with his stepmother and his three siblings. They were catching up with his father, an electrician, who had, in time-honored immigrant fashion, come to Brooklyn four years earlier to test the economic waters in America (and, after a period of adjustment, found them relatively welcoming). Alix's personal transition into his new life was generally smooth. Although there were few people around him who spoke Creole, the French-derived tongue that is Haiti's first language, he had the luxury of going through public high school in New

York City with virtually all of his instruction in French, Haiti's colonial language, and of learning English at his own speed. When he graduated from John Jay High School, he went on to the State University of New York at Buffalo, where he studied environmental design, and later he completed a master's degree in urban planning at the Pratt Institute.

Today, Cantave is a project manager in the Office of Housing and Community Development in this mostly blue-collar suburb of Boston, where he works on old-fashioned urban renewal projects. At the same time he tries to persuade big companies in the city to take an interest in the smaller entrepreneurs and the general economic well-being of some of the region's struggling communities, which are undergoing rapid demographic and social change.

Somerville, for example, where housing costs have gone up more slowly than in Boston itself or in nearby Cambridge or Medford, nonetheless saw a major shift in its population between the 1980 and 1990 censuses. As white working-class families vacated neighborhoods where they and previous generations had lived for much of the twentieth century, a rainbow of minorities gradually moved in—including Asians, Hispanics, and the Portuguese-speaking immigrants who used to be concentrated in Brockton and other parts of lower Massachusetts. The black population of Somerville alone more than doubled during the 1980s, and most of the newcomers turned out to be Haitians.

After a disappointing stop in Miami or New York, Cantave explains, many Haitian immigrants from the third wave—those who got in before the Bush and Clinton administrations began turning them away—were drawn to the Boston area by the hype about the new opportunities being created in the so-called economic miracle put in place by former governor Michael Dukakis. The old manufacturing jobs, which had attracted previous waves of immigrants from Europe, were now being replaced by positions in the high-tech and service industries. At the peak of this trend, somewhere between 60,000 and 75,000 Haitians were thought to be living in the Boston area.[2] The high-tech world was initially beyond their reach, but a substantial number did find semiskilled and maintenance work in hospitals, nursing homes, hotels, and other service facilities in the suburbs. They moved into Somerville and similarly situated towns to take advantage of the

[2] *Approximately 290,000 Americans cited Haitian ancestry in the 1990 census, but this figure omits undocumented immigrants who probably were not counted and second- or third-generation Haitian Americans who now identify themselves simply as black or African American. Michel S. Laguerre, an anthropologist at the University of California who is himself of Haitian origin, estimates that there are about 1.2 million people of Haitian ancestry in the United States.*

relatively cheaper apartments and efficient public transportation to their jobs. Some of the apartments became very crowded, as new arrivals packed in with friends or relatives for six months or more, until they could establish themselves on their own.

One early result of this rapid transformation of Somerville, says Cantave, was "a number of incidents" in the public schools, including sometimes violent confrontations between white students and their new Haitian classmates. (Many immigrants from the more well-to-do first and second waves, in Boston as elsewhere, had previously been able to send their children to parochial schools, where they received special attention, so the phenomenon was a new one.) Before long, Cantave was being asked to consult with the Somerville Housing Authority on how to ease tensions and to hold a seminar on Haitian culture for teachers at the local high school. Creating bilingual classrooms with teachers who could work in French was not an option this time around, he notes, "because these students cannot read in any language," and the only one they can really speak well is Creole. (There is a substantial body of Creole literature, but very few, if any, textbooks have been published in the language.) "There was also a cultural shock," says Cantave, surrounded by census printouts, maps, and charts during our conversation in his office in Somerville's old city hall. "People who had never before left their village [in Haiti] all of a sudden found themselves in a huge metropolis." And it often seemed like a cold, harsh metropolis, in attitude as well as climate.

Relations between the newly arrived young Haitians and the local indigenous African American community also got off to a shaky start, in part because they knew so little about each other. Cantave points to the poor performance statewide by black high school students in Massachusetts on a scholarship examination administered by TransAfrica, a lobbying group in Washington that promotes greater U.S. awareness of, and generosity toward, the countries of Africa and the Caribbean. Few students even bothered to try answering the questions about Haiti—or, for that matter, the ones about Angola and South Africa.

"When you've grown up in the black community here," Cantave says, "your view of what's going on in Haiti, if you have one, is violence, AIDS, and poverty." (At an earlier stage, he suggests, voodoo and "black magic" might have been on the list, too.) Meanwhile, newly arrived Haitian parents tend to warn their children against becoming involved with the black youths they meet in school or on the street, who they believe will lead them into trouble. Not many people today remember the history of Haitians' and African Americans' involvement in one another's liberation and civil-rights struggles, Cantave points out. Indeed, most Americans are surprised when they learn that Haitians began immigrating to the United States as early as the 1790s (during the slave revolt at home), and that Frederick Douglass, the American abolitionist orator, at one point traveled to Haiti for a look at the world's first black republic.

As young Haitian immigrants become educated, many reject their parents' preoccupation with the arcane politics in their native country and "go American," says Cantave. But another faction, especially those attending college or university in the northeastern United States, searches for its cultural roots and becomes "very militant," he says, embracing Pan-Africanism and demanding an end to American influence and intervention in Haiti. These students were an important element in the hard-core exile support for Jean-Bertrand Aristide, a Roman Catholic priest popular among Haiti's poorest people, who assumed office as the first democratically elected Haitian head of state in February 1991. After he was overthrown by the military seven months later, he took refuge in Venezuela and then the United States. The militant exiles did not object when the Clinton administration sent troops in 1994 to restore Aristide as president.

Cantave's personal mission, when he is not dealing with crises in Somerville, is to try to explain Haitian immigrants and the larger American society to one another. He helped launch the Haitian Studies Association, a quasi-academic organization that has sponsored several conferences at Tufts University dealing with historical, political, and cultural themes. It has also published a series of research papers on scholarly topics and launched a study of Haitian immigrants' problems in American cities. In the long run, Cantave predicts, even if stability comes to their homeland, Haitians will be no more likely than Italian, Irish, or Polish immigrants to stage "a mass exodus" from the United States. But no matter how long they stay, they will, he believes, reserve the right to "see themselves as refugees. Always."

He himself seems to have settled in, however. A U.S. citizen since 1987, Cantave lives with his wife, also a Haitian immigrant, and their two young sons in an old gray-and-white clapboard house in the Roslindale section at the southwestern edge of Boston. The family speaks both English and Creole at home and, according to Cantave, makes every effort to maintain its Haitian identity. But he and his wife have repeatedly postponed their project of visiting Haiti to introduce the children to their roots, because of the political violence there. In the meantime, Fadil, their six-year-old, who was born in the United States, has taken matters into his own hands: For reasons that his parents are at a loss to explain, he has repeatedly told his teachers in school that he has "two homes, one in Haiti and one in Africa."

DUBOIS, WYOMING

DOWN TOWARD the end of Ramshorn Street in this old sawmill town, where the Louisiana Pacific Company once logged the forests, just before the road goes around the bend and disappears into the Western wilderness, there is a spiffy new little shop called Two Ocean Books. Across the street from the Rustic Pine steak house, nestled between the Dubois Drugstore and the Sew What? sewing supply store, it is approached on a covered wooden sidewalk that looks straight out of the movies and resonates well to proper cowboy boots. The bookstore is owned and run by a proudly Polish American woman named Anna Moscicki, who is gambling that she can make a living by serving the intellectual needs of the Northern Rockies and of the people who pass through town on their way to or from Yellowstone National Park, eighty miles to the northwest.

Not so many years ago, after the local logging operations shut down, Dubois, on the east side of the Togwotee Pass and the Continental Divide, at the edge of the Wind River Range, was virtually abandoned for dead. But then in 1988, there were twelve new phone installations in town, a sure sign that the rebirth—indeed, the gentrification—of Dubois was underway. By 1992 the population had reached 1,000 (with another 1,500 or so in the surrounding area) and was still climbing.

It was in January of that year that Moscicki arrived from Jackson, the fashionable ski resort on the other side of the mountains. For most of her seventeen years there, her official job was as a clerk in a bookstore, but politics became her nearly full-time hobby. First she was a member of the local planning commission, and then she was appointed, and later elected, to the Jackson town council. But everyone knew that Moscicki had another specialty: She was the only known Polish-speaker in Jackson. Once, when a Polish visitor had a heart attack, she was tracked down and brought in to interpret between him and his doctors. And when the Moscow String Quartet came to perform, with no one around who spoke or understood Russian, she was the only one in town who had any hope of being able to communicate, however imperfectly, with the musicians.

Moscicki, two years old and seasick, had a dramatic arrival in New

York Harbor on the Fourth of July, 1952. Customs and immigration facilities were closed for the holiday, and so her family and the other weary travelers had to spend an extra night on their boat as fireworks exploded overhead. They were awed and impressed. But ever since, Moscicki has been grappling with her ethnic identity, trying to decide whether to wave an American flag or a Polish one.

She is the second of three daughters of a Polish couple whose lives were ravaged by World War II. Her father, an engineer, was in a German prison hospital when the Nazis towed its patients out into the Baltic Sea on barges and left them to die; he somehow survived and ended up in a sanatorium in Sweden with tuberculosis. There he met his wife, who had been a courier of documents for the Polish underground, before being captured and sent to Auschwitz. After surviving for two years working in the infirmary there, she was on a trainload of people headed for the gas chambers that was turned around and swapped for medical supplies by the Swedish Red Cross. The couple married in Stockholm in 1947 and, having heard from his uncle in Detroit that there were great job opportunities in America, they applied immediately as Polish nationals, under the quota system then in effect, for immigrant visas to the United States.

Five years later their number finally came up, and they settled in Detroit, where Anna Moscicki's parents were determined to preserve their Old World culture in the midst of New World influences. Like typical immigrants, they worked hard at multiple jobs to save for a house and a car. But there was to be no automatic assimilation for them. Only when she was twelve years old did Anna discover, at a grocery store, that her mother spoke any language other than Polish and Swedish. Occasionally, she remembers, her father would insist, "Okay, we're going to be Americans and speak English now. We can't speak Polish in front of strangers; they'll think we're talking about them." The three Moscicki girls (one born in the United States, who suffered from polio) went to public school, "only because my mother felt suspicious of the nuns" at the local parochial school, Anna says. Yet they were Polish Girl Scouts and attended Polish language and cultural school every Friday afternoon. They ate traditional Polish food at home and had a Polish-speaking pediatrician.

The family's politics also strictly followed the conservative Polish émigré line. There was a book about the war—*We Have Not Forgotten*, in English, French, Polish, and Russian—on the coffee table in the living room, and Anna vividly remembers a conversation during high school, when her mother flatly branded President Franklin D. Roosevelt a communist for conspiring with British Prime Minister Winston Churchill to "sell out" Poland to Stalin at the Yalta conference.

Moscicki studied education at Michigan State and then resisted the entreaties of her friends and family to go visit Poland or Sweden. "Everyone told me, 'Oh, you should go, because they love meeting Americans,' " she recalls. "But I said, 'What can I tell them about America? I grew up in a Polish-speaking family in a Polish community in Detroit. I've never been west of Chicago or east of Niagara Falls.' " To her parents' dismay, in 1972 she set out instead to see more of her own adopted country, hitchhiking and camping around the West and finally settling more or less permanently in northwest Wyoming three years later.

"I broke away from the mold," Moscicki says with a certain relish, "by not marrying a nice Polish boy and settling into a nice house two or three miles away from my family." In Jackson, she felt "different" from almost everyone else, and yet at home: "It was a small town where we had a core group of people who helped each other." Whenever her mother visited, "she was always impressed by the number of people I knew. She said it was just like living in the Polish community in Detroit."

Moscicki moved to Dubois with a boyfriend, a late-blooming entrepreneurial spirit, a nostalgia for the book business, and a desire once again to break away from a routine, predictable life. Her shop specializes in Western writers, children's books, and material of special interest to women. It instantly became the place where the intelligentsia came out of the woodwork to reminisce and talk politics. One day when I visited, a woman had come down from the hills to pick up her copy of a new biography of President Harry S Truman; lingering in the store, she recalled lying on the floor of her nearby childhood home in 1948, listening to election returns on the radio, feeling slightly uncomfortable with the knowledge that her parents were the only ones in the local precinct who had voted Democratic.

With a new group of people to teach how to pronounce her name, Moscicki (mose-chich'-kee) still feels a bit like the odd person out in Dubois. "I've thought of myself for many years as an American," she says. But when her mother, now widowed, comes to visit, she is transported back into her intensely ethnic childhood. Her mother recites Polish poetry she remembers from her own youth and ruthlessly corrects Anna's Polish grammar. Anna's thoroughly assimilated older sister, who lives in Washington, D.C., speaks only Polish to her children.

HOUSTON

IT TOOK Mohamed Arabi two tries to find success and happiness in the United States. He was born in 1948 as the son of a Damascus tailor who had once become wealthy making high-fashion custom clothing for government officials, military officers, and the French and English occupiers of his country, but had long since fallen on hard times. Restless and dissatisfied with his lot in life, young Mohamed had trouble convincing his parents to let him come to America "for a short time" to pursue his education. They, like the people who issued visas at the U.S. consulate, feared that he had no intention of returning home. They were right.

When Arabi finally left Syria in 1973 as a twenty-five-year-old high school graduate "looking for freedom," he first settled in Austin, where he enrolled at the University of Texas. He was dazzled by what he found there. Compared to the closed, restrictive, Old World atmosphere of Damascus and Beirut, where he had spent all of his life, in the Texas capital "the streets were superclean, and people were really nice and friendly. Everything was completely different, and I was very excited."

Inexperienced and lacking anyone who could give him reliable advice, Arabi was confused about how to focus his studies—he dabbled in economics and business administration—but even more perplexed over issues in his personal life. The "freedom of sex" that he found in America was particularly shocking to him. Because of his strict Islamic upbringing, he says, "I just couldn't go out with a girl I wasn't married to. It was something very shameful. So I had to get married in order to fulfill my needs." But his marriage, after just a few years in Austin, to one of the first young American women he had encountered, was an almost immediate failure. It did help him regularize his immigration status in the United States, after living in a twilight zone of uncertain legality on a questionable student visa. Within a year of getting married, Arabi had a green card, but he also had an ex-wife. He moved to Houston at the end of 1977, "running away from my bad feelings."

Here he started a new life and established a completely different lifestyle, rooted in Houston's substantial Arab-American community.[3] He returned to school, this time studying political science with the hope of

[3] According to the 1990 census, only about 15,000 of the 870,000 Arab Americans counted in the United States were living in Houston, but most are concentrated in one neighborhood there. Detroit, New York, and Los Angeles are the three cities with the largest Arab American populations. Activists in the community contend that there was a serious undercount in the census and that their true number is closer to three million nationwide.

eventually becoming politically active himself. To earn a living, he went to work in a restaurant but soon was promoted to be food and beverage manager at a large Holiday Inn. After two years, Arabi went into business for himself, opening a specialty grocery store on Hillcroft Avenue, in the southwestern section of the city, that catered to the local Arab clientele. "I offered the types of food we eat back home. It was an attractive service," he says. "I got involved with the Arabian society here, and now almost all the Arabs in Houston know who is Mohamed Arabi."

That gave Arabi the opportunity to launch his Arab American Communication Service around the corner on Richmond Avenue, in a neighborhood of Middle Eastern restaurants. Officially, he provides translation and interpretation between English and Arabic, especially in court cases. But his real goal, says Arabi, is to help immigrants from various Arab countries—particularly the elderly and the poor—learn how to settle comfortably in the United States. Located on the fourth floor of an office building that houses Kuwaiti trading companies and a collection of photo studios, insurance agents, and private detectives, he shares a small suite with the publisher of an Arabic-language newspaper. "Sometimes I get lucky and I get some business that I can charge for," says Arabi, but often he pays his half of the rent from his own pocket. This is made possible by the fact that he has a full-time job at night, in charge of quality control at a nearby Procter & Gamble factory that produces instant coffee.

Arabi teaches Arab immigrants how to obtain driver's licenses and the other necessities of daily life in Houston, and he shows senior citizens how to apply for their Social Security benefits. Occasionally, he helps someone exploit the loopholes in the system and obtain legal documentation to stay in the United States without going through an immigration lawyer. (When he discovered that his service could qualify for official status as a nonprofit organization representing people before the INS only if he had a lawyer on his staff, he decided to enroll part time in law school, too.)

A short, thin, intense man, Arabi knows where he stands on most of the issues of the day. In a universe where there are plenty of fly-by-night organizations offering citizenship classes and get-rich-quick schemes to immigrants, he has some unconventional free advice for his informal constituency. "I tell Arabs who are trying to understand American society that they should make their kids watch *Sesame Street*," he says. "And for older people I recommend family shows and game shows, like *Family Feud* and *The Price Is Right*. They pick up words that way. *The Price Is Right* teaches you how to say the names of the things you use, the things you buy every day." Other Arab immigrants have more serious problems, for which he cannot recommend easy solutions: "When I came here in 1973, America had a great society, but now I can tell the difference. When some people come here now, especially teenagers, they are left on their own and they get lost. They ask the wrong people, and then they do the wrong stuff. Some of them wind up in jail for committing some foolish, stupid crime, like shoplifting. I try to guide people where they can meet other Arabs instead."

At the same time, Arabi worries that the established Arabs in Houston are segregating themselves too much, holding themselves aloof particularly from Hispanics and black people. "Arabs will only associate with Arabs," he complains. "They don't want to associate with anyone else, if it's not necessary. They're afraid of contracting AIDS, or being exposed to drugs, or being shot. You hear about all these shootings! But by doing this, they're isolating themselves from the entire society and they're not being recognized. This is something I'm trying to break through, by offering this communication between Arabs and Americans."

In his own personal life, meanwhile, Arabi has retreated to a very traditional, devout Islamic perspective. He has never been back to Syria, because of his disapproval of the repressive regime of President Hafez el-Assad. But he did make a trip to Egypt in 1987, long after his divorce was final, for a prearranged marriage to a Syrian woman known by his family there—the sister of his brother's wife. This union, he says, is much more successful, in part because it has not been tainted by the absurd extremes of "freedom" that have taken root in America in recent years. Rather, it is governed by religious rules that everyone in his world can understand and accept. His wife keeps her head and neck covered, for example, as a matter of propriety. "There's nothing wrong with a woman having her hair and neck visible or touched by strangers, but it's a step in the wrong direction," Arabi says. "Once you have your hair and neck visible, why not have your breasts visible? And then why not wear a bikini, and why not take your underwear off? If you're not going to go all the way, then why start down that road?"

Soon after he became a citizen in 1986, Arabi began encouraging other members of his family to come to the United States. First he sponsored his mother, who by then had been widowed. "My mother brought my brother, and my brother brought his wife," Arabi explains. "Then my mother brought my other brothers, and my other brothers brought their wives. And my wife brought her mother, and her mother brought her father. My sister and her husband migrated to Canada, but soon my baby sister is coming to the U.S. Now we are a big family here, about twenty-two individuals."

Arabi's son and daughter are being raised in the midst of this old-fashioned extended family, most of whom live in the same area and see each other every day. He hopes that his children will learn "the American way of life" but at the same time "keep the good from our culture." Indeed, his ideal is to "try to take both cultures and mix them, and come up with a new life for my kids. I do believe in freedom, and I want my kids to grow up free. But I believe there has to be a limit on the freedom; I don't think our family, or any American family, thinks freedom of sex is desirable. I want them to have the freedom of the mind, not the animal freedom. It's something you feel inside, and it's like a light you turn on." If one could just combine the freedom of thought prevalent in America with the family values practiced in Syria, Arabi says, "then you would have a perfect society."

SAN FRANCISCO

"When I was still living in Hong Kong, I would watch American movies to learn about this country," says Po Wong, executive director of the Chinese Newcomer Service Center in America's largest Chinatown. "The people in China do the same thing now. You can see nice homes, nice cars, nice scenery. Everything is a beautiful dream. Even the air seems to smell sweet in these movies."

During the first few months after his arrival with his wife and three children (then aged twelve, ten, and eight) in 1969, Po Wong had no reason to be disappointed. "We saw the beautiful scenery, the cars, the shops, and the people who dress nicely. We felt the sweetness," he says. "There is a honeymoon period. All your friends and relatives welcome you. They take you to dinner several times, one by one, and you feel good. But then they have their own jobs to do and their own problems to take care of. After all these nice gatherings and the chatting, you are suddenly alone with your family, and you feel lost. It is the second phase. You feel frustrated and you realize, 'I need to get a job and a place to live. I have to pay my daily bread and send my kids to school.' You can't go back to your friends who fed you the first few days. That's when you know you're on your own and have to make the adjustment. Maybe the success story will come later on."

Born in the village of Shiqi, in Guangdong province in south China, Po Wong went to high school in the town in the Portuguese colony of

Macao where Sun Yat-sen was born. He was taken to British-controlled Hong Kong by an aunt early in World War II, before the Japanese occupation could overwhelm his life. He always hoped to immigrate to the United States, he says, but that seemed impossible until after the old U.S. quota system was abolished in 1965 and Asians began to be welcomed in greater numbers. When the opportunity finally came four years later, Po Wong, who had been educated as an aircraft engineer, found himself totally lacking in the practical knowledge he would need to begin life in a new country.

"I sent a letter to an old schoolmate who had graduated from M.I.T.," he remembers. "I told him, 'I need some information from you. I am going to leave Hong Kong and come to San Francisco as an immigrant. How do you think I can survive from day one to day three hundred and sixty-five? What do I have to know?' Maybe he was busy, but he sent me just a short note, saying, 'You can survive after the first two months. I have confidence in you.' That's all. I didn't even know whether I should bring long-sleeve or short-sleeve shirts! In Hong Kong it's hot, but I didn't know about San Francisco."

Po Wong had learned to speak English in Hong Kong, with a pronounced British accent, but the woman assigned to sponsor his family in Chinatown, with whom they would live at first, spoke only Chinese, and she was even less helpful in response to a similar letter. For several months after their arrival, he says, his wife cried herself to sleep every night, taking care not to let the sponsor know of her unhappiness but asking her husband repeatedly, "How could we come to a place where we can't survive?"

When he applied for his first job in America, answering the newspaper ad of an insurance company looking for a bookkeeper, Po Wong had no idea how to proceed. He easily passed the simple mathematical test that the company gave him and next, as required, he went to a designated doctor for a physical examination. Then he went home and waited . . . and waited. "Nobody called, for more than a week," he says. "They never told me the next step. Finally I called, and the person said, 'Where have you been? Why didn't you come back to talk to us?' So I did, and they asked me to start the next week."

It was to save other new arrivals from China some of this same anguish that Po Wong eventually started his social service agency. Its counselors now handle tens of thousands of inquiries a year, many of them repeat calls from the same clients, about long-term problems as well as the mundane issues of daily life. But the center has been overwhelmed recently by the steady influx of people into San Francisco, where at least a fifth of the Chinese immigrants to the United States tend to settle every year. In 1989 alone, for example, according to official INS figures, 12,000 people immigrated to the San Francisco Bay area from China and Taiwan, and that number does not include anyone who slipped in illegally or overstayed a tourist or student visa. However many there were altogether, nearly all of them tried at first to find housing and work in the already hopelessly overcrowded Chinatown.

"I don't think our community is equipped to welcome this large a number," says Po Wong. He has seen much hardship and unhappiness, even tragedy, from up close. "It is especially difficult to find employment for those who speak only Chinese, who have very little education, or who never have acquired a skill to compete in this new job market. It's very depressing to see so many people come here looking for work." The problem was exacerbated, he says, by the 1988 earthquake in Northern California, which temporarily made public and private transportation into and out of Chinatown more difficult. As more and more of the immigrants are forced to find their opportunities in the outlying suburbs, Po Wong notes, the essential character of Chinatown is changing. Increasingly, he says, it is populated by "the old-timers who've been here for their entire lives." As a result, its internal economy suffers and a decreasing percentage of its residents are fluent in English. It comes to life, and takes on its traditional character as a center of Chinese American culture, Po Wong says, primarily on the weekends.

As for his own family, Po Wong has watched his children succeed on American terms but remains convinced that "if you are Chinese, your chances of moving up in this country are not as great as the white people. Even if your language is good, your skin is yellow, and you will always look different." Nonetheless, he is distressed that he sees the next generation drifting too far from its Chinese traditions. His oldest child is a lawyer in New York who, to his dismay, "speaks only English at home" with her two children, abandoning any hope that they will grow up bilingual. His second child, a son, who he says was the most aggressive about trying to move into the mainstream quickly, is now a senior vice president in San Francisco for a Japanese corporation. And his youngest, another daughter, works as a nurse in San Francisco.

"All her friends at school were Caucasian girls," he says of his youngest child. "That's fine while you're growing up. But Caucasian girls marry Caucasian husbands and observe western customs. Then you start to feel the differences between you, but it is too late. When you pay too much attention and spend too much time with your Caucasian friends, you tend to ignore your own group. And Chinese people don't come to you as a friend unless you stretch out your hand first. That is one of the handicaps she is facing. But this is a free world, and maybe that's why her English, among the three, is the best."

SILVER SPRING, MARYLAND

THE STARS AND STRIPES flutter in the Labor Day breeze in front of the tasteful red-brick home with white pillars at the far end of this close-in suburb of Washington, D.C. The house was built in the 1960s in a middle-class subdivision where it was not considered a good idea for all families to live in identical units and where ostentation was not in style. It is easy to imagine the days not so long ago when this was an all-white, hostile, segregated neighborhood, but now it appears to be fully integrated by race, age, and lifestyle. On a table inside the front door, the colorful Maryland state flag is still neatly folded in its box, but by the next public holiday, I am assured, it will be flying out front, too.

Until a year or so earlier, Charles and Munira Mwalimu thought they were temporary residents of the United States, just waiting for the right moment to go back to Zambia, in southern Africa. Indeed, they were among the organizers of the Washington Office for Democracy in Zambia, which argued that Kenneth Kaunda, the country's leader since independence from Britain in 1964, should finally step aside and let a new generation try to solve its intractable economic problems. A few months after the Mwalimus' candidate, trade union activist Frederick Chiluba, came to power through a fair and open election in October 1991, Charles actually went back to have a look. He bought a small farm on the outskirts of Lusaka, the capital, and planned the construction of a new house there. But the job he had been promised as a presidential aide did not materialize—there were too many other people demanding rewards for helping the new leader—and he rejected an offer to become Zambia's deputy ambassador to Japan. He was disappointed by the corruption that emerged under the new regime, as well as the reports that circulated of severe human rights violations. "Besides," he says now, "my colleagues [his wife and three daughters] were not very keen" on leaving the United States. The children, in particular, were entrenched; they thought this scheme of "returning" to a country they had never seen, or could not remember, was ridiculous.

So it is that the Mwalimus, as they approach the age of forty, have become very serious Americans. They accepted citizenship, for which they had long since qualified, and took their oath, in glorious fashion, in

1993 in a massive ceremony at Camden Yards, the Baltimore Orioles' new baseball stadium. "We have a commitment to the United States," says Charles, a large, robust man with a forceful personality, "and our participation is going to be full and effective." Munira, in fact, promptly registered to vote; Charles, still uncertain which party deserves his allegiance, has delayed taking that step.

They moved out of the rental house where they had been living for some years and took out a mortgage to buy this one, with a big backyard. Munira was promoted to a management position at the research firm where she works, which has a major contract with the U.S. Department of Education, and he advanced in the hierarchy at the legal division of the Library of Congress, while continuing to publish his own articles on human rights and constitutionalism. They became more intensely involved in their Catholic church, where Charles already taught a Bible-studies class, and he found a new cause: working with the handicapped.

The Mwalimus are the first to acknowledge that they have come a long way since they arrived in Seattle with two babies in 1980, in order that Charles could study for his master's degree in law librarianship at the University of Washington. While there, to help make ends meet, Munira provided day care in their small apartment for six children besides her own.

When they moved to Washington, D.C., a year later, so that she could pursue a doctorate in legal studies at Georgetown University, they lost the Zambian government scholarships they had originally brought with them. (The Ministry of Education suspected—correctly, it turned out—that they might not be coming back home to share the benefits of their advanced education.) Until they managed to adjust their visas so that Charles could accept a job at the Library of Congress, where he had already done an internship, they went through a period of severe hardship, using furniture from the Salvation Army and living on money borrowed from friends several thousand dollars at a time. Even after their visa problems had been worked out, they remember none too fondly, they had to endure what Charles calls a "winter of discontent," during which he went to work in a harsh climate without a warm coat and with a single pair of shoes that never had a chance to dry between wearings.

The couple had rejected the United Kingdom as a place to go, says Munira, because they were looking for a more "free and open country." For his part, Charles says that he had dreamed of coming to America ever since he watched a film of President John F. Kennedy's funeral as a child. Already, at the university in Lusaka, they had been a controversial interracial couple: he a high-achieving student and an altar boy from a family of nine in a traditional Bemba village in a northeastern province, who had spent two years in the seminary[4]; she the third child of ten in a wealthy Asian family that had come to dominate the transportation and retail business in Zambia's eastern province after prior sojourns in South Africa and Malawi. Shunned by her friends and disinherited by her Muslim family for marrying outside its circle—her mother refused even to get out of her car to say good-bye when they left—Munira was especially eager to go far away to a place where she expected greater acceptance and tolerance. "I have been able to live here without worrying about those things," she says, even though, sometimes, "you can feel that you are not white."

Charles cites "the freedom of the individual" and "the comforts we enjoy" as the major assets of life in America. He still preserves many of his original customs—for example, eating the traditional Zambian dish, *inshima,* made from cornmeal, with his hands at the dinner table—but he enjoys wearing elegant, natty western clothes. In 1983, when he and Munira got tired of taking public transportation to go grocery shopping, he took out a loan from the Library of Congress credit union to buy a car—not just any car, but a Mercedes-Benz that cost $25,000 at the time. "I was flabbergasted," Munira says. But Charles had an explanation: Well aware of the tendency among the African elite to buy luxury automobiles with funds that were corruptly obtained, he says, "I wanted to be sure I got my Mercedes early but honestly." That one, paid for long ago, still works, but now there is another, second-hand Mercedes in the driveway, and a Honda, too.

The Mwalimu children, including a much doted-upon little boy named Charlie, born in 1992, are thoroughly American. The oldest girls, now in high school, have excellent academic records and a great variety of friends. Still the issue comes up often of whether the entire family will stay permanently in America. "The only hesitation I have," says Munira, "is that life for old people in this country is really terrible, because nobody cares about you. Back there [in Zambia], you stay with your family or with relatives, and there's always somebody to watch over you. You're not denigrated, and you're not ill treated." She pauses and laughs. "So maybe we will retire there."

---

[4] *The name* Mwalimu, *Swahili for teacher, comes from Charles's great-great-grandfather, a mailman who traveled among Tanzania, Malawi, and Zambia with the missionaries and was thought to impart great wisdom to those he met.*

II
LIFE ON THE FRONTLINES
OF IMMIGRATION:
PARADISE LOST

TEMECULA, CALIFORNIA

SEVENTY-FIVE MILES north of the Mexican border and thirty miles inland from the Pacific Ocean, this community of some 36,000 people is almost a caricature of Southern California—a dreamland of endless summer and carefree prosperity, where material and spiritual well-being seem to have become intertwined as a single quality at the core of daily life. At first glance, landscaping appears to be the most important local industry, and water to keep the lawns a deep green and the pools and ponds full and sparkling the town's most abundant resource. Most of the houses are behind walls, in tasteful, modern developments with names that are virtually indistinguishable from one another. No one seems to go anywhere on foot, and every car that is not a convertible has its windows closed tight to keep the air-conditioning inside.

Temecula is split by a busy north-south freeway, Interstate Highway 15. On the west side there is a small historic district, with a few ersatz old-time trading posts and a profusion of antique shops. But spread across the commercial districts on both sides is every imaginable variety of fast-food outlet and hotel or motel, several large look-alike shopping malls, and endless rows of low-rise office buildings, each more modern than the last, their environmentally correct dark windows concealing what might be going on inside. Here and there an automobile sales lot or a supergrand service station features a gigantic American flag of the type familiar in political commercials on television.

The city streets—particularly the narrow bridge that carries Rancho California Road over the freeway in the heart of town—are clearly inadequate for the traffic they must bear and so are chronically under construction. But the sun beats down beneficently, and there is not a cloud in the sky. A typical day here is quiet, smooth, and peaceful. As if to fulfill the stereotype, nearly everyone a visitor encounters on arrival looks young, blond, tan, and healthy, without any sign of a serious worry.

Temecula does have a rich history, insists Patricia Birdsall, a book-keeper and the wife of a retired marine, and also the mayor at the time of my visit. There is archaeological evidence, she points out, that the site was first occupied by the Luiseño and Diequeño Indians as early as seven thousand years ago. The Mexican government established Rancho Temecula with a land grant in the early 1800s, and the rancho was in turn officially recognized by the United States government in 1850, when California was admitted to the Union. Early on, the township of Temecula became a railroad shipping center for granite cut from nearby quarries. As the quarries were depleted and the rail line abandoned in the mid-1930s, it settled into an unobtrusive, unexceptional rural life. Avocados, grapes, and citrus fruit were shipped out in plentiful quantities, but hardly anyone ever bothered to look in to see what, if anything, was happening here.

As recently as 1964, Temecula was still home to only 5,000 souls. Tucked into the quiet southwestern corner of Riverside County, they were occasionally visited by a lone sheriff's deputy whose bailiwick covered about five hundred square miles. But otherwise, the community's modest law-enforcement needs were handled by the California Highway Patrol or, more likely, by the local contingent of the U.S. Border Patrol, which had established a checkpoint back in 1924 out on the northbound side of the nearby road (the sleepy predecessor to I-15), south of town and just over the line in San Diego County. On the rare occasion when there was trouble, a Border Patrol agent would respond to any emergency call and swing by to make a provisional arrest. In recent years, the suspects would be held at the Border Patrol's small branch office and lockup on Rancho Way near Diaz Street, until the sheriff's department in Riverside, forty-two miles to the northwest, could dispatch someone with proper authority to deal with the problem. It was an arrangement that allowed Border Patrol officers, who suffered from low status at the bottom of the law-enforcement pecking order, to play real-life cops-and-robbers occasionally, and it seemed to suit everyone else just fine.

Then came the boom. As the roads improved, more people moved in. Temecula was one of hundreds of new communities that were sprouting up in rural California, within easy commuting distance of the major cities. For the upwardly mobile, essentially rootless white middle class, it seemed like a splendid alternative to the megalopolis around Los Angeles, eighty-seven miles north, which was becoming far more crowded and expensive as a place to live. Here, housing costs and taxes were only a fraction of what they were in L.A., and everything was new and pristine. Temecula was "all-American," free of any obvious racial tension or moral ambiguity. The nearby canyons were still green and unpopulated, and there were excellent equestrian trails and fishing streams. The mountains, the ocean, and the desert were all close by.

For employers of every kind, there was a large supply of relatively cheap labor around Temecula, but this was especially true in the fields, where Mexican immigrants, legal or not, seemed willing to work for a pittance. And the growers had an exemption from the usual concerns; by long-standing arrangement, the Border Patrol would not go onto private agricultural property to search for undocumented aliens.[1] The local vineyards turned out to be very productive and profitable indeed, and Temecula became the center of a burgeoning Southern California wine industry, producing chardonnay, cabernet, and zinfandel that began to challenge their equivalents from the more famous wineries north of San Francisco. In a spot where a few years earlier there had been almost nothing, by the 1980s Temecula emerged as a very rich community indeed. Its official average annual family income was soon $43,000, higher even than that of Palm Springs.

Soon the need for a proper infrastructure loomed large. What had seemed like a certain Wild West charm, laid-back California style, evolved into a kind of mild, but potentially risky, suburban lawlessness. First there was the issue of nonexistent traffic control, as well as a growth in minor incidents of vandalism. In the absence of a regular police presence, "crimes of opportunity" (including burglary and random thefts) flourished, and people running drugs from San Diego to Los Angeles began to perceive Temecula and its vicinity as a safe transit zone. It was. On some occasions, it took the deputies from Riverside as long as six hours to show up and investigate the report of a crime.

Temecula finally incorporated itself as a city on December 1, 1989,

[1] *The Immigration Reform and Control Act of 1986 formalized the arrangement, requiring Border Patrol agents to obtain a warrant before searching any private property, including farms. An exception to the rule permits agents to pursue suspected undocumented aliens onto and through farms when they are within twenty-five miles of the border.*

and its residents elected a rookie municipal government, a city council composed of five people who had never been in politics before. As one of their first official acts, after establishing themselves in city hall on Business Park Drive, the councillors contracted with the Riverside County sheriff's department to provide the community with appropriate law enforcement. For a cost that worked out to $115 per citizen per year, Temecula got its own tailor-made police force, with a right to handpick the chief and each individual officer. Next the council started working on fixing and expanding the streets, and then began negotiating with the state transportation department to move an existing weigh-station on I-15 north into the city limits, so that Temecula could get a cut from any fines that might be levied on heavy trucks passing through. The city's new official seal featured a golden sun whose rays shine in every direction from a blue sky over green hills, the profile of a long-haired Native American, and a stagecoach being pulled by a team of horses. Around the outer rim were two bunches of grapes and the motto OLD TRADITIONS, NEW OPPORTUNITIES.

THERE WAS, of course, a predictable downside to the economic growth of Temecula and the I-15 corridor—or "Southern California's new frontier," according to a data sheet welcoming guests to the Doubletree Suites Hotel beside the freeway. It is a frontier in more ways than one. Quick access to the Los Angeles basin for residents of the Temecula Valley and their agricultural goods and other products also brought an improved route for Mexicans and other would-be immigrants crossing the U.S. border near Tijuana. L.A., like New York City, is a mecca for people entering the United States without a visa or other required documents—a place filled with kindred spirits and a guaranteed, well-organized support system for almost any ethnic group; a place to disappear into the crowd.

Temecula's geographic location, and the topography of the surrounding area, make it a choke-point—a "second line of defense" for the INS—that is regarded as one of the last places to catch "illegals" on their way to Los Angeles. The old Border Patrol station just outside of town, along with a similar one twenty-eight miles northwest, near Camp Pendleton and south of San Clemente on I-5 (which was established in 1969, after Richard Nixon was elected president and began visiting the area often), began to take on new importance. During periodic political uproars over illegal immigration, the INS had to try to prove that it really did have some control over the flow of people from Mexico into the United States. Riding these freeways is not the only way north from the border for those who must travel furtively—some people get on a train or a plane in San Diego, take a boat, or even walk—but it is certainly the most common method.

Today, at each of the freeway checkpoints, northbound traffic must slow to a crawl as Border Patrol agents, many of them Hispanic themselves, try to glance inside every car in search of suspicious-looking characters. At night, they often shine powerful, bright flashlights into the faces of the drivers and their passengers and demand proof of identity and legal status. Some cars are pulled over, so that their trunks and any other compartments can be searched. At the same time, pale-green Border Patrol vehicles of various shapes and sizes ply the freeways and the side roads, sometimes at very high speed, looking for "illegals" whose drivers might have gotten through the checkpoints undetected or known just where to turn off the highway, and where to get back on, in order to avoid them. Other agents actually hide their cars in the bushes and avocado groves along the country roads, waiting for potential suspects to come by, and then shine their headlights into oncoming cars. For young Border Patrol agents, staffing the checkpoints or riding the roads can be a difficult, frustrating, and often demeaning assignment, with a low rate of success and a lot of abuse from people accustomed to driving fast and arriving at their destination quickly. At the same time, for a Mexican-looking man driving a beat-up car belching exhaust on this stretch of I-15, or on the rural roads that feed into it, life can be very dangerous indeed, especially toward the end of the officers' shift. Citizen or not, he is almost certain to be stopped and questioned, and possibly severely mistreated.

There is, in fact, a great deal of tension on the road and in the air around Temecula. The Border Patrol, as Rick Sayre, the city's new police chief, euphemistically puts it, had come to feel "autonomous" in the area, as a result of its long-standing "significant role in the community." Because they were relied upon for so much for so long, many Border Patrol agents working in this area do not necessarily feel the usual need to coordinate their actions with the city government or other law-enforcement agencies, and they see Temecula as turf that they are entitled to control. At the same time, the shrewd "coyotes," who promise to smuggle Mexicans and others across the border and all the way to Los Angeles for $300 or more a head, can be ruthless. They are notorious, for example, for packing an unsafe car or van with a large number of migrants and then compelling the youngest one to drive at top speed, even if he has no license. The hazards to everyone on the road are obvious, and at any sign of trouble, the coyote himself is usually the first to jump out of the car and run away. For the unsuspecting motorist who happens to drive through on I-15 or I-5 at the wrong time and gets caught between the lawbreakers and the law, the consequences can be lethal.

Representative Ron Packard, the Republican congressman who represents Temecula in Washington, tells the emblematic story of a constituent who struck and killed an "illegal" who was trying to run across I-5 to safety—such accidents occur on the average of once a week—and then was sued in the American courts by the dead man's family. "It has become a physical and legal obstacle course to drive down I-5 or I-15," complains Packard. "This is absurd."

GLORIA MURILLO had just seen her children off to school on the morning of June 2, 1992, when she reported for work shortly before nine o'clock at *El Remate*, a local Spanish-language community newspaper where she was a reporter. A thirty-eight-year-old Mexican American woman, she had grown up in Indio, in the California desert eighty-five miles to the east, where families arbitrarily divided by the border historically treated it as an inconvenient formality and moved easily back and forth across the line as their daily lives required. But after traveling widely with her military husband, from whom she was now divorced, Murillo found something of a niche in the larger Anglo world, and she had moved recently from Anaheim, in Orange County, to share a cousin's apartment in Temecula.

Here she struggled as a single mother to run a complicated household that included the baby boy born eighteen months earlier to her unmarried, oldest child, also named Gloria. The family did not have much, sometimes scraping by between paychecks with a less than adequate diet. The younger Gloria, now seventeen, had recently returned to high school as a junior and was determined to graduate and go on to a community college. Along with her brother José Tomás ("Tommy")—a year younger and said to be an astute, ambitious teenager who intended to go places—she would walk every morning to Temecula Valley High School, while her mother drove the third child in the family, Ricardo, eleven years old, to his middle school and dropped off the toddler, Anthony, with his baby-sitter, before going to work.

When she arrived that morning at her office, on the west side of the freeway, Murillo did not even have a chance to sit down or have a cup of coffee before her editor came up and said they must run out. The police radio was reporting a major accident on the other side of town, involving "illegals" and the Border Patrol. They had to go cover it for the paper.

It would be some time before all the facts could be pieced together, but according to a subsequent internal INS inquiry, the incident began with a 5:00 A.M. stakeout by two plain-clothes agents from an antismuggling unit of the Border Patrol at a hotel in San Ysidro, a largely Hispanic town south of San Diego that sits just on the American side of the border. When the agents saw two men get into a dark-green Chevrolet Suburban truck in the hotel parking lot shortly after 6:00 A.M., they followed it in the government-owned, unmarked red Chevrolet Cheyenne pickup truck they were using. After spotting what looked like several other people through the Suburban's tinted windows—there would turn out to be twelve altogether—and watching the driver buy gas on the outskirts of San Diego and then head north on I-15, they decided they were on to something serious. The agents radioed for a marked vehicle to help stop the Suburban (which turned out to have been stolen) and arrest its occupants, whom they presumed to be undocumented aliens, before they could travel very far. Meanwhile, the Suburban and the Cheyenne moved along the freeway at normal speeds.

After a number of snafus, including the dispatch of a car from the Border Patrol station in Chula Vista that could not catch up with the Suburban and several mistaken or unclear radio contacts with the Border Patrol communications center for the area, the agents in the pickup truck saw the Suburban leave the freeway on Rainbow Canyon Road, south of Temecula, ostensibly to evade the usual immigration checkpoint. But shortly after 7:30, other agents in a marked car from the Temecula Border Patrol Station finally spotted the Suburban back on I-15, north of the checkpoint. As it speeded up, they began to chase it at between eighty to eighty-five miles an hour.

When the Suburban left the freeway again at Rancho California Road, the agents followed it into and through the parking lot of a shopping mall, then onto city streets filled with commuter traffic, using their siren and red flasher lights only intermittently. At no point did the Border Patrol attempt to advise the Temecula police about what they were doing or ask for their help. Much of the action occurred with the Suburban driving on the wrong side of the road, while bystanders watched in horror. As the siren, lights, and radio of the original pursuit vehicle inexplicably failed, several other Border Patrol cars converged on the area and tried to join the chase.

But the Suburban broke away at about eighty miles an hour. It passed through an elementary school zone, and then as it sped downhill and around a curve on Rancho Vista Road and reached the intersection of Margarita Road, just near the high school, it ran a red light and careened out of control. Still moving at a reckless speed, it sliced through a black Acura Legend that had been approaching the school, throwing its two halves eighty feet apart. The Suburban then rolled onto its side and slid through the intersection onto the sidewalk, hitting two pedestrians before it came to a stop at 7:39 A.M. Several Border Patrol cars screeched immediately to the scene; leaving it to their office to advise the Temecula police about the accident, the agents jumped out and began controlling traffic and administering first aid to the people who lay inside or staggered out of the Suburban, all of them injured. They apparently did not notice at first that five other dead bodies lay in the street, on the sidewalk, or in the wreckage of the Acura.

Gloria Murillo and her editor arrived at the scene of the accident at 9:15. "We heard that it was another Rambo situation with the Immigration people," she recalled later; "that they were going at excessive speeds and being careless . . . that there were several injuries and fatalities." Murillo fought her way through the crowd and argued with a police officer, who did not want to let her get closer. "I said, 'I'm with the press. Can you give me some information?' And part of my motherly instinct said, 'Well, was it a boy and a girl?' He wouldn't say anything. I said, 'Would you please tell me the names?' And he says, 'We can't tell you until we notify the next of kin, so go sit down with the rest over there.' I said, 'But I'm a mother, my kids go to this school. I could be one of the parents.' I just said it, simple as that. And he turned around and said, 'Well, what is your full name?' My press pass had turned over, so he couldn't see my name, and I said, 'Gloria Gómez Murillo.' And then he walked towards me, and, you know, with his eyes he told me that they were my kids. At that moment, I lost it. I screamed and I yelled and I cried. I couldn't believe it."

Young Gloria and Tommy Murillo had been killed instantaneously when the Suburban hit them just as they were arriving at school, a few minutes late. Also dead were the three passengers in the Acura: John Davis, forty-six, a prominent banker who had raised money for a local home for abused children; his son Todd, eighteen, whom he was driving to school; and Monisa Emilio, the fourteen-year-old daughter of a white working-class contractor (and the younger sister of Todd's girlfriend), whom they were also giving a ride. If the accident had occurred ten or fifteen minutes earlier, when the sidewalks and streets were packed before the high school's 7:30 opening, dozens of students and family members might have died.

One of the passengers in the Suburban, Eniceforo Vargas Gómez, twenty-two years old, died five days later of injuries sustained in the accident; according to the Mexican consulate in San Bernardino, he was

from a poor, remote village in central Mexico called San Antonio Ami-
alco. Little more is known about him, except that he had set out from
his parents' home to try—illegally, along with hundreds, if not thousands, of other people that same day—to come to live and work in the
United States. Instead, his body was sent home for a government burial.

THE REACTION in Temecula was extraordinary. Perhaps because the
random victims of this tragedy represented such a broad socioeconomic
cross section of the community, the anger was unanimous, and it was
directed largely at the Border Patrol. There had been serious accidents
before: Two years earlier, a thirty-two-year-old pregnant woman and
her unborn child were killed during a similar high-speed chase near
Temecula, and at one point a van full of undocumented aliens had
plunged into a nearby duck pond while being pursued. Another time,
several Border Patrol agents prowled the grounds of a local elementary
school with their guns drawn, looking for "illegals" who had evaded
them on the road; the principal reacted by calling an earthquake drill
and protected the children by ordering them to stay under their desks.

The Border Patrol had a reputation for indifference in such circumstances, preferring to leave local communities to pay the costs and
deal with the consequences of the incidents, even to the point of dropping off at hospitals suspected "illegals" who were injured in accidents
and never returning to check on them or take them into custody. But
now the conservative leaders of Temecula were united with their community in demanding greater accountability from a federal agency that
seemed unconcerned about the collateral dangers of its work. Neither
the undocumented immigrants pouring in from Mexico nor the citizens
of Temecula had designated this well-heeled, still-growing city as the
perfect place to draw the line and have a confrontation. It was the
unilateral, if unconscious, choice of the INS that idyllic Temecula would
become a more-dangerous-than-average place to live.

At a special town meeting, tempers flared. Past victims of less well
known accidents involving the Border Patrol came out to tell their own
tragic stories. "This town belongs to us, not to the federal government,"
screamed one man, demanding immediate action by the city council to
protect the citizens from high-speed chases. "Tomorrow is too late," he
said. The wife of a Border Patrol agent, meanwhile, accused the residents of behaving like a "lynch mob." She urged that the outrage be
directed toward policy makers in Washington, rather than the men and
women on the firing line—local citizens, too—who were simply trying
to do their job.

Thousands of people signed a petition demanding that the checkpoint on I-15 be permanently closed, and the city council filed a lawsuit in Los Angeles federal court, proposing that the Border Patrol be banned from entering the Temecula city limits without explicit permission. With broad bipartisan support from around the state, the local representative to the California State Assembly introduced a resolution in Sacramento condemning the INS for its high-speed chase policies. The agency acknowledged seventy-five chases in and around Temecula in 1989 alone, the last year for which it appeared to have kept a record. An investigation by the *Orange County Register*, however, revealed that at least 35 people had been killed and 225 injured over a ten-year period in accidents related to high-speed pursuits by the Border Patrol in the region. The resolution, which passed overwhelmingly in August 1992, said that "no high-speed chase is worth a human life" and pressed Congress and the president to take up the issue at the national level.[2]

The community also mounted an assault on a provision of the California legal code that allowed, and even encouraged, law enforcement officers to pursue, by whatever means seemed reasonable in a moment of crisis, any suspected offender who failed to yield or comply with an order; it seemed wide open to abuse, especially by the Border Patrol. Why, wondered the people of Temecula, could the Border Patrol not use helicopters or various other high-tech methods for surveillance and pursuit, rather than endangering the lives of innocent citizens, including children? Do the agents receive training that permits them to react subtly when challenged, they asked, or are they under intense pressure to improve their apprehension figures, and thus not care how they go about it?

In the first days after the accident, the Border Patrol was silent, presumably worried about the possible legal fallout from the accident and concerned to protect individual agents who had been involved in the chase, some of whom, understandably, were emotionally distraught themselves. By late June, however, INS was aggressively defending itself. An internal review by an auditor sent to California from Washington concluded that the agents from the Temecula station had "exercised good judgment," except when they traveled at high speed on I-15 without using their emergency lights and siren. "All other INS employees" involved, said the report, "were in compliance with current policy." The Border Patrol claimed to have abandoned the chase almost a mile away from the high school. For his part, then-INS Commissioner

---

[2] *The bill was vetoed by Governor Pete Wilson.*

Gene McNary declared, "I am deeply saddened at the deaths of six people caused by the appalling and reckless act of an uncaring smuggler of illegal aliens, but I am convinced that the INS officers involved acted responsibly." He promised only to continue "a routine examination" of the agency's pursuit policies, which had already been underway before the accident.

In early July another accident occurred in nearby Lake Elsinore, when a Border Patrol car collided with a pickup truck in the midst of its pursuit of a station wagon thought to contain illegal immigrants. The California Highway Patrol declared the next day that the Border Patrol agent who was driving was at fault, because he "failed to proceed safely" through a busy intersection. No one was seriously injured this time, but another community became enraged. An INS spokesman in San Diego said that "the smugglers are very aware of the community sentiment" after the uproar over the Temecula tragedy. "They are taking advantage of that. We are seeing an increase in the number of vehicles failing to yield. The smugglers are making a run for it now."

For Gloria Murillo, who had no intention of keeping quiet, the INS position could be translated to mean that "there's a price to pay to keep the illegal aliens out of our country. . . . My children were the price that had to be paid? . . . No one can tell me it's justifiable. If any judge can tell me that, I hope they can sleep at night."

The most startling recognition of all for the people of Temecula was that illegal entry into the United States is a misdemeanor, not a felony. Most of those caught committing this infraction are punished only with detention, sometimes for just a few hours, followed by deportation (unless they are entitled to an asylum hearing). "This is not a high-crime thing, not a guy threatening us with an Uzi," notes Karel F. Lindemans, a retired accountant who was "mayor pro tem," or the second-ranking member of the city council, at the time. "So, as a misdemeanor, it is the same as stealing a candy bar from a grocery store. Now, for that you do not chase through our urban areas, and especially through school zones, and kill our kids who are walking on the sidewalk."

Some of the recent efforts to tighten enforcement of the immigration laws, Lindemans complains, have actually made things worse. For example, one revision of the law required that any car being used by a coyote to transport undocumented aliens into the United States—much like a car used to bring in illegal drugs—be confiscated. The usual result? "The coyote will steal another car. Crime increases."

•

THE COLORFUL, goateed Lindemans became something of a point man in Temecula's improbable struggle with the system, ready at a moment's notice to talk with a reporter or go on television to defend what he thought was right. A Dutch immigrant himself, he had arrived in New York from Rotterdam in 1954, at the age of twenty-three, with seven dollars in his pocket. "I was bombed by the Germans when I was eight years old," he says. "When the war was over, I was fourteen. I needed air, and I was in love with the Americans; they liberated us." He soon gravitated to California. After ten years of study, Lindemans became a CPA and then began speculating in real estate, often putting together deals that required him to return to Holland. Now he is a rich man.

"America today is no longer the America of 1954," says Lindemans with a cultivated sneer, launching into his assessment of the country's serious ills. "We had chances and freedom and liberty. Now all that has changed. . . . We're being depleted. Every year we get a huge bill for our taxes. We don't make TVs, CDs, or cars anymore." Not surprisingly, Lindemans has identified immigration as one of the causes of the problem. "We are facing a crisis. We in North America, in Canada and the U.S., have to brace ourselves for an invasion from the south. Unless we make a buffer zone, like Mexico, and give them the proper aid, we have seen nothing yet. This is not immigration, this is an invasion."

Until something more fundamental can de done, Lindemans suggests, instead of bothering with ineffective regulations and dangerous high-speed chases, "either you close the border or you open it. All it takes to close it is an electric fence, with a thousand or ten thousand volts, with another fence in front of it which says, 'Don't climb over this fence, because you will get electrocuted.' Put in minefields, for all I care. Then you will have closed the border."

Listening to this tirade over lunch, the equally troubled mayor, Patricia Birdsall, blanches. She is embarrassed by her flamboyant associate. "Mexico is an independent country. You have to look at the ramifications," she protests, somewhat meekly.

Well then, Lindemans replies, not about to be stymied, "let's say we do want these people to come in, because we do want them to pick lettuce, we do want them to pick grapes. Three to four dollars an hour to them is a lot of money, because they only make four dollars a day down there. They send their money home—it's a form of foreign aid. In Holland, there is not a soul who picks up a garbage can. That's for Turks, and Turkish people do that. We could do the same. Instead of having [the people trying to enter the United States illegally] pay the coyotes three hundred dollars each, let's have the Border Patrol collect three hundred dollars. You give them a work permit, which is good for six months, and then they get out. But they cannot bring their wife and kids. . . . It's workable. And you have a low-maintenance border, because it's deadly."

Rick Sayre, Temecula's thirty-nine-year-old intellectual police chief (actually on temporary assignment from his job as a sheriff's captain in Riverside County), is often on the firing line with respect to the local impact of immigration control. He is cautiously critical of the Border Patrol—"they're tight-lipped; they don't come out to talk"—but thinks that law-enforcement officials generally must be more selective in the techniques they use. In his own police department, "we have a standing, unwritten rule that says that any supervisor who calls off a pursuit will never be asked why he or she called it off." In other words, young officers are encouraged to exercise sophisticated judgment and think broadly about their responsibility for public safety, rather than just measuring their immediate "performance" by how many criminal suspects they have caught and arrested.

Sayre, who is short, stout, and bespectacled and seems permanently bemused by the dilemmas of his work, points to parallels between the enforcement of drug laws and immigration laws, but he takes a very different view from Lindemans about how to solve the problems. Freely conceding that he smoked marijuana when he was young, Sayre advocates decriminalizing "non-mind-altering" drugs. In fact, he says, many public officials are unrealistic or hypocritical on this issue. "In half of Northern California, marijuana's the major local product. We have this state eradication program that all the law-enforcement agencies are supposed to be a part of. But a lot of the little counties up there don't want the program to come in, because that's how the local hardware store and the restaurants make it. It's crazy, because the demand is there . . . and I'd rather have a person around me under the influence of marijuana than someone flashing down the Budweisers in a bar and then going out to his car and killing people on the road."

As for illegal immigration, Sayre compares the efforts to control it to the ineffective American bombing of the Ho Chi Minh trail during the Vietnam War. "We were dropping five-hundred-pound bombs, but [the Vietcong] kept coming south, and the supplies kept coming, too. The problem here is, no matter what kind of barrier you put up at the border, even if you try to seal it, [the undocumented workers] are going to keep coming, one way or the other. They need to come, because they're tired of not being fed, tired of a miserable work environment."

What has happened in Temecula, Sayre says, is that "people who live in the housing tracts see these green cars from the Border Patrol zipping around. They see these guys jump out with their pistols drawn and hop over fences and run through their backyards. Then they see this poor old Hispanic guy running away from them, who's trying to make ends meet. There's an imbalance. There's a need for some of this [border enforcement]—don't misunderstand me—but the bottom line is that the way they're applying themselves does not seem right."

The net effect, according to Sayre, is that to their own surprise, many ordinary citizens have found themselves sympathizing with the underdog immigrants against the intrepid forces of law and order. Now, he worries whether the public will really learn to live more comfortably with these new arrivals. "I hate to hear the term racist, but that's probably what it boils down to," says the police chief with a sigh. "In America, maybe we don't like the fact that so many brown people are coming in. They're Hispanics, they stand out, and they can't just go into their back room and do their thing the way the German immigrants did, who never spoke German in public."

ON A QUIET Sunday morning in July, about six weeks after the accident, John Ruffner takes me on a tour of the outskirts of Temecula in his car. He moved here with his family in 1989 from the Bay Area, seeking more space and some peace and quiet. At the time of our meeting, he is a hospital administrator in Riverside and, incidentally, a member of the newly formed "Citizens' Committee for the Removal of the U.S. Border Patrol from Temecula." At about 9:00 A.M., at the corner of Rancho California Road and Butterfield Stage Road, just outside the new Vintage Hills development, we spot four Mexican-looking men huddling together and glancing around warily. One appears to be in his fifties, the other three in their twenties, and one of the latter is sitting on a motorcycle. According to Ruffner, this is one of several unofficial street-corner labor markets in town, where undocumented workers gather seven mornings a week, sometimes as many as twenty or thirty on a corner, looking for a day's work. Typically, potential employers—growers, construction foremen, or just ordinary citizens digging in their gardens—will cruise by, roll down their car or truck windows, and negotiate a daily or hourly rate, usually quite low. The laborers "don't know what kind of work they'll have to do. They don't know whether they'll really get paid at the end of the day, or what exactly is going to happen to them, but they're willing to risk it," says Ruffner.

An avid runner and cyclist, Ruffner has occasionally witnessed impromptu chases through the nearby canyons—Border Patrol vehicles zooming along bicycle paths and forestry roads in pursuit of "illegals" who have eluded them elsewhere, almost as if they were engaged in a sporting event in which there can be no winner. From time to time, a friend who works in the California Department of Forestry has told him, there are accidents on the back roads in which vehicles are damaged but no one is hurt, so they go unreported by the media. From this and other local evidence—including an apparent reluctance by INS to apply for warrants and raid business places where a large number of aliens may be working illegally—it sometimes seems as if the Border Patrol prefers chasing people to catching them. The new Citizens' Committee has been formed, Ruffner says, because "from the taxpayers' standpoint, we want to know what we're getting for our money [from the Border Patrol]. So we're going to ask that the General Accounting Office, or whoever, conduct that kind of analysis."

We return to Ruffner's home, a rambling one-story modern structure with glass on every side, in an area called Meadow View in the hills above Temecula. The birds are chirping, and there is a cool breeze moderating the effect of the warm sun. It is easy to see why newcomers think of this as paradise. At the kitchen table, Ruffner and his wife, Gloria (herself the daughter of a Chilean woman who immigrated to California as a young girl in 1923 with questionable documents that had been written out by her own grandmother), discuss why they are uncomfortable with current U.S. immigration policy and enforcement. "On the one hand, we have been encouraging countries to adopt a democratic model, to open the borders and tear down the walls, as in East Germany," he says. "Yet when people are trying to come to this country because they see the advantages of what we espouse, they are chased away with guns. Doesn't that seem paradoxical? I wonder how other countries in the world view this."

The Ruffners have just returned with their daughter from a camping trip deep into the Mexican peninsula of Baja California, and they are struck by the fact that the economic activity along the Pacific coast is continuous and consistent and does not happen to respect the frontier. "The political and economic reality," says Ruffner, "is that the communities on both sides of the border are symbiotic." Again a familiar analogy arises: "I was in Vietnam, and I saw what determined people can do. I am convinced that you cannot stop determined people from coming here."

AT 11:00 A.M. on the next-to-last day of July 1992, in room 2203 of the Rayburn House Office Building on Capitol Hill, the Government Information, Justice, and Agriculture Subcommittee of the House Committee on Government Operations, prodded by California congressmen who were feeling the heat about Temecula, convened a public hearing on the mission of the INS and the Border Patrol's pursuit policies. Representative Robert E. Wise, a Democrat from West Virginia and the subcommittee chair, was presiding.

For some, this seemed a lame way to deal with a tragedy that had affected so many people's lives so profoundly, but scheduling the hearing implied at least a recognition that impersonal immigration policies and procedures might have to be calibrated to take account of human factors. The rhetoric flew furiously, as the legislators tripped over one another to deplore what had happened and, in the case of the Southern Californians on hand, to bemoan Washington's "indifference to the problem of illegal immigration."

Patricia Birdsall, Temecula's mayor, testified that the city's severe emotional trauma after the accident—more than 600 "grieving and hysterical students" had required psychological counseling—was compounded by substantial financial costs, including $33,000 for emergency services. She complained that the INS pursuit policy was "an outdated throwback to the Old West 'posse' mentality" and argued that "unless the occupants of a fleeing vehicle are suspected of committing a serious felony, or are known to pose a serious threat to the lives or safety of the public (aside from any threat posed by the high-speed pursuit itself), then a high-speed pursuit should not be undertaken." She was backed up by Geoffrey P. Alpert, a professor at the University of South Carolina and an academic expert on police pursuit, who pointed out that a high-speed chase is a form of "deadly force" that must be used cautiously and only after all the risks have been evaluated.

McNary, a former Republican county executive from Saint Louis whose questionable credentials for the job of running INS combined with his scrappy political instincts to create a stormy tenure for him there, was a key witness. He testified to the enduring value of the highway checkpoint near Temecula, saying that agents working there had apprehended 23,320 people and seized $2.9 million worth of drugs in fiscal year 1991 alone. (The checkpoint at San Clemente, he said, had even more impressive results.) He defended the training given to Border Patrol agents and insisted that the 81 men and women assigned to the Temecula station were themselves sensitive citizens of the community and shared its sorrow over the accident. "Legitimate public anger about this violence," he concluded, "should be directed toward those who violate the law."

By the time of the House hearing, reports had begun to circulate that the Border Patrol pursuit policy was under review and about to change. But in his own appearance before the subcommittee, T. J. Bonner, president of the National Border Patrol Council, the agents' union, warned against placing "impractical restrictions" on Border Patrol officers. "The real danger to the public," he testified, "lies in the reluctance of government to protect its citizenry through the enactment and enforcement of strict prohibitions against reckless driving by criminals attempting to elude law-enforcement officers." Bonner pointed to the low pay, stressful working conditions, and unreliable equipment available to Border Patrol agents as additional problems preventing them from doing their job well.

A SHORT TIME later, with little fanfare, the INS formally revised the guidelines governing Border Patrol pursuits of vehicles suspected of containing illegal immigrants, sharply restricting them and theoretically requiring the approval of a supervisor before they can be initiated. According to the new rules, only a supervisor may authorize a "high-speed/high-risk" chase or even one of the "low-speed/low-risk" variety. In effect, said one Border Patrol agent, who asked that his name not be used, supervisors do not like to give approval for a controversial action that may come back to haunt them, and, therefore, the high-speed chases are now much less likely to occur. The result, he complained, is that officers working in the border region may feel obliged to allow large numbers of undocumented aliens to proceed north toward Los Angeles, even if they suspect they are transporting illegal drugs such as cocaine.

An expert on a congressional subcommittee staff, however, said he doubted the effectiveness of the policy change, especially with respect to agents working beyond radio contact with their headquarters. In any event, for a time there appeared to be fewer accidents in Southern California involving the Border Patrol, but little discernable impact on the flow of "illegals" into the United States.

Temecula's lawsuit against the INS was dismissed by a federal judge in Los Angeles, who ruled that under the doctrine of sovereign immunity, the city did not have the right to bring legal action against a federal agency. California filed homicide charges against the sixteen-year-old undocumented immigrant who was driving the Suburban, Jesús Macias. In initial hearings, he claimed to be a hired hand and said that someone else forced his foot down hard on the gas pedal during the effort to escape the Border Patrol. He was convicted of vehicular manslaughter and sentenced to serve twenty-five years to life in prison.

Alfredo Flores, identified as the coyote trying to get the group to Los Angeles, went free, however, and was deported to Mexico. But no disciplinary action was taken against any of the Border Patrol agents involved in the chase, and the federal government offered no apology or compensation to the families of those killed in the accident.

Gloria Murillo, grief stricken, moved back to Indio with her surviving son and grandson to live with her extended family. She won her lawsuit in state court against Macias, but the $5 million default judgment granted by the judge in the case seemed unlikely ever to be paid, unless he won the lottery from prison. Meanwhile, her federal suit against the INS was still pending in the summer of 1995. Her lawyers were taking depositions in the case, but estimated that it would be "extremely difficult" for her to prevail. Linda Davis, whose husband and son were killed in the Acura, filed a similar suit in federal court, as did the family of the girl killed in the Davis car, with no expectation of better results.

In the aftermath of the accident, the people of Temecula rallied to help the families whose lives had been torn apart that June morning. Mobilized by a bank and a local car dealer, they raised more than $30,000, some of which helped pay the costs of burying the Murillo children. Funds left over were used to erect a bronze plaque, surrounded by roses, at the corner of Margarita and Rancho Vista Roads, in memory of the victims.

III
LIFE ON THE FRONTLINES
OF IMMIGRATION:
TROUBLE ON THE BEACH

REVERE, MASSACHUSETTS

IF THERE IS anyplace in America that was built and shaped by immigration, it is this middle-class city of nearly 43,000 people on Boston Harbor. It is named for Paul Revere, the patriot of the midnight ride during the American Revolution, but few if any of the city's current residents can trace their roots back to the aristocracy or the political leadership of colonial New England. On the contrary, in the middle years of the twentieth century, Revere, having split off from nearby Chelsea, grew and prospered primarily as a place where immigrant Italian, Irish, and Jewish communities lived separately but peacefully and more or less equally, where "neighborhood" was an all-American concept that implied stability, continuity, and generally peaceful coexistence among minorities. To be sure, there were also a certain number of people in town who were known generically as "Protestant Americans," but as the old-timers remember it, they too seemed to accept the notion that they were but one part of a complex yet comfortable mosaic. Eventually the Irish came to dominate the police force, the Jews the business sector, and the Italians the political structure. But there seemed to be enough of everything to go around in Revere.

"There was never any great problem in this city," says George Colella, who was elected to ten two-year terms as mayor of Revere during a twenty-six-year period that ended in 1991. "We came out of different sections of the city, but everyone met at Revere High School.

That's how everybody got to know one another, and got to live and work and play and have fun together." Colella's paternal grandparents had arrived from Italy to live in the North End of Boston in the late 1800s, and as they prospered, they moved out to Revere around the turn of the century. His father was the city's first "Italo-American" firefighter and, Colella recalls, "he had a tough time at first" gaining acceptance. But with each succeeding generation, things became easier. Colella himself "intermarried," as he puts it, "with the Irish girl I took to the junior prom, June Murphy." After graduating from Boston University, he became an insurance agent and later a politician.

Bill Waxman, the longtime principal of Garfield Elementary School, has similarly sentimental feelings. His family had come directly to Revere from Germany in the early twentieth century, and he grew up in the cozy, protective Shirley Avenue neighborhood. "It was a Jewish ghetto," he says. "But when I use the word *ghetto,* I think of it in positive terms, because it was a happy place. It was like being in the old country. We grew up when nobody had a key to the house. And you had a hundred mothers. Any house was your house." Waxman's wife happens to be from Medford, about five miles away on another side of Boston, but, he says, "I don't think there's another community in the country where so many people married within a mile of their home as they did in Revere. I think I'm the only one of all my friends who didn't marry someone from Revere." In fact, Waxman moved on up the North Shore to live in Peabody years ago, but he left his heart in Revere. Although he is now retired, he comes back almost every day.

BUT IF THERE is anyplace in America that has, in recent years, been nearly torn apart by immigration, it is also Revere. Since the early 1980s, a large number of Cambodian refugees have come to live in the city—at least 2,000 at any given time, by the most reliable count—and their presence has tested all the ideals of tolerance and goodwill that had been taken for granted, and boasted about, before. A series of incidents in the early 1990s served to dramatize the tension.

On December 14, 1990, for example, a huge fire ravaged several city blocks in the run-down Shirley Avenue neighborhood, where the large apartments in old two- and three-story, wood-frame, multifamily buildings had now come to be occupied primarily by immigrant Cambodians and Hispanics (plus a few blacks and working-class whites). The fire itself was not the first to hit the neighborhood since it had changed, but it was by far the biggest. Fire departments from thirty-six communities in Massachusetts and New Hampshire responded, as heavy winds helped the flames jump across streets and cut a broad swath. It took forty hours to put out the fire completely, and many months later one could still see charred remains and smell the smoke damage on several blocks. Five buildings were totally destroyed, and six others damaged; at least 130 poor people were driven out of their homes, and the overall losses were estimated at $3 million.

In a gesture that was seen as symbolic, the 150 or so people left homeless by the blaze were temporarily taken in by the local Jewish Community Center, which was about to close its doors because most of its membership had moved away. As Amy Sessler, who covers the area for the *Boston Globe,* puts it, "Besides being a devastating event, this was a defining event. It made people take a look at who was living in Revere and what the special problems are that they face."

The first instinct was to suggest that the fire was caused by the Cambodians' careless use of electricity, their notorious and reckless overloading of circuits in their often overcrowded apartments. "They think all you have to do is plug everything into one [extension cord] and it will work," says one local official. "I've been in homes where you couldn't touch the wire, it was so hot." Others insisted they had seen Cambodians set small fires on top of the wooden floors in their apartments for ceremonial reasons or while preparing exotic medical potions. One person told me he had even heard that it was traditional in Khmer (Cambodian) culture to build a fire under the bed right after a woman has given birth to a baby at home.

In reality, few people in Revere know very much about Cambodian culture. And few doubted that the 1990 fire was caused by arson, as they believe several earlier and smaller ones had been. But there were differing theories as to motive. "It was either for fun or profit," insists the Reverend Nick Granitsas, pastor of the First Congregational Church of Revere, pointing out that the primary target this time appeared to be an empty building, whose absentee owner may have wanted to collect the insurance on his unprofitable investment. "Revere has a long history of fun arsons," he adds, including fires in vacant school buildings that had been shut down, presumably set by teenaged troublemakers. "I'm sure that this fire was not racially motivated. The one in 1986, perhaps, but not this one," says Granitsas.

Others were not so sure. From the moment the Cambodians began to arrive in Revere, there had been serious language barriers and communication problems. Few of the traditional residents of the city had any idea what their new neighbors were doing or how they lived. Although it appeared to the casual observer that many were on welfare—

and a minority of them actually were—some of the Cambodians tried to become successful quickly on American terms. "They were very industrious to begin with, maybe working two or three jobs," says Mayor Colella, who admits that he himself took a long time to understand these new constituents. "If there were a number of working people in one apartment, that added to the income of that apartment. And as a result, they were soon able to make purchases that some other people could not. So you had white Americans, who had financial problems, saying, 'Oh, look, the government is buying cars for them. They're getting everything. The government's taking care of them.' It wasn't true at all. These people were out there working and pooling their money. But it brought on antagonism."

There were frequent incidents along Shirley Avenue and the hilly residential streets that intersect with it—random fights, muggings, thefts, and, eventually, a steady stream of unprovoked assaults against Cambodians of all ages by young, otherwise unoccupied white toughs. A number of mischievous small fires were set; one Cambodian family put out a mysterious fire in their own home on three different occasions. Often these incidents went unreported by the Cambodians, who have a traditional distrust of authority that was reinforced by the recent history of official brutality when the Khmer Rouge ruled their country. In any event, the problems rarely warranted mention in the local newspapers or otherwise attracted much attention. A fire that is put out before it does any major damage is hardly news, and it contributes nothing to raising community consciousness.

No one could prove that the Great Fire of 1990, as it came to be known locally, was connected to anything else, yet for many it fit a new pattern. For more than a year, an investigation into its cause led nowhere, but that almost did not matter. It seemed plausible to interpret the incident as one more way of saying that the Cambodians and other newcomers were not so welcome in Revere.

Then on June 1, 1991, shortly before midnight, two white men in their twenties left a party at a house near Revere Beach to walk home. They were immediately set upon by a group of Asian men—somewhere between ten and thirty of them, depending on whose version you believe—presumed by neighbors and the police to have been Cambodians. One of the intended victims escaped, but the other, twenty-two-year-old Michael Guarino, himself an immigrant from Italy, was brutally beaten with pipes and baseball bats before being stabbed several times and left to die in the street. By the time the police arrived, the attackers had long since sped away in their cars.

It was a crime that baffled the authorities. One theory was that the attack grew out of a brawl the night before in a nearby bar, in which several Asian men had been severely injured by whites, presumed to be Italians or Italian Americans. According to that theory, the assault on Guarino amounted to massive retaliation and a warning that the Cambodians were not to be messed with. But no one seemed clear as to whether Guarino had been personally involved in (or even present at) the barroom fight, physically resembled someone else who had, or was merely a random victim, singled out because of his skin color, age, and ethnic background, who happened to be in the wrong place at the wrong time.

After months of investigation, the Revere police could not even be certain whether some, or all, of the attackers were local people or if they had converged from somewhere else—perhaps from Lowell, an old mill town about twenty-five miles away with a significantly larger Cambodian population and, according to some, an East Coast base for some tough Asian gangs operating across the United States. The leads were thin and confusing. If the Revere police had valuable contacts in the Cambodian community, they were not talking, and the investigators were left to sort out unsubstantiated rumors, including one that some of the attackers had fled to California, where they could easily disappear amongst other Cambodian refugees. "It's not a typical case you'd work on," says Detective William Gannon of the Revere Police Department, shaking his head. "It's very unusual for an Asian group to attack a white male. It's not uncommon for one gang to attack another gang, but it is unusual for them to attack just one white person."

"This was a very isolated incident," insists Granitsas, ever the optimistic pastor. "From my street-level perspective, things had been getting better. We had not even had any assaults, Asian on white. There was one kid who was shot a year earlier by an Asian, but the kid was himself involved in a lot of different things; he could have easily been shot by a white. It was not particularly racial. But the June first incident—it just struck people as being racial."

Certainly the Italian American community thought so, and it wanted prompt action. Guarino's family was from nearby East Boston—where justice can sometimes be swift and unofficial—and they were furious when the police did not make an immediate arrest in the case. Family members began to hold weekly Thursday night rallies and candlelight vigils in front of the Revere City Hall and police headquarters, after which they and their growing support group would march down Shirley Avenue, through the Cambodian neighborhood, demanding more attention to the murder from the city authorities.

Revere's Cambodians, who felt collectively and unjustly accused of complicity in the Guarino killing, found all of this intimidating. "The old people were scared," remembers Chanta Svay, a high school student who says she has many friends outside the Cambodian community. "They wouldn't even go out of the house. One day [the Italian American demonstrators] threatened that they were going to send for a gang from New York" to solve the problem. "They wanted revenge," says Darith Chhith, another Revere High School student. "I don't think it's right for them to do all that. If some black dies in Roxbury, you don't hear much about it. They just die—they're a minority. But when a white person dies, there's a big problem," he adds.

Frustrated by their inability to make progress on the case and faced with new pressures growing out of rumors that big trouble was coming over the Fourth of July weekend—possibly even firebombings of Cambodians' homes and businesses—the Revere police made a sweep through the Shirley Avenue neighborhood on a weekday afternoon in late June 1991. Accompanied by representatives of other law-enforcement agencies, including the Massachusetts State Police and the INS, they conducted an old-fashioned lockdown, blocking off streets and ordering that no one leave the area until an extensive search had been completed. According to Gannon, it was all well intentioned. The officers went into the neighborhood with an assortment of about a hundred arrest warrants covering a variety of offenses allegedly committed by people on five or six different blocks. Their real goal, of course, was to develop evidence or intelligence relating to the Guarino murder.

What the police got, in the end, were just three of the people for whom they had warrants. They obtained no meaningful information on the Guarino case, but a great wave of trouble over their investigative tactics. "I think it was controversial only because Cambodians don't understand our system of justice, and they thought we were trying to infringe upon their rights," says Gannon with the wonderment of a public servant who feels unappreciated. "It wasn't that we were picking people out randomly to target. We had a very specific plan as to who we were looking for and where we were going. We did it on a very limited basis. We only went there for two hours, and we did it early in the afternoon to lessen the inconvenience. It was as peaceful as can be."

But that was not how the raid came across to the Cambodian community or in the media. The way Regina Lee, director of the Massachusetts Office for Refugees and Immigrants, had it reported to her state agency, "They stopped every single Cambodian and asked them to produce identification, to show that they were here in the U.S. legally.

In some instances, Cambodian youths were searched. And that really escalated racial tension in the neighborhood."

Bill Waxman, who has long enjoyed a cordial working relationship with the police, goes further: "They violated civil rights, no question about it. It was stupid. They would walk by an Anglo or a black or a Hispanic on the street, but grab a Southeast Asian and frisk him. They went into homes. I was talking to one of the high school girls who had been sick in bed that afternoon, and she told me they went into her bedroom, searching. We asked them to justify it in some way and they couldn't." Indeed, at a public meeting to confront community anger over the sweep, the Revere police chief acknowledged that the immigration authorities had been brought in to look for "illegal aliens" in the neighborhood, and Waxman upbraided him. "I said, 'When was the last time you ever heard of a Southeast Asian illegal alien around here? Either you're very stupid, or you think we're very stupid.' I don't think he understood anything of what I was saying."

The result was that various law-enforcement agencies issued public apologies to the Cambodian population of Revere. "I think what they really wanted to do was frighten some people into giving them information" about the Guarino killing, says Waxman. "But they didn't accomplish that, because I don't think anybody knew anything to tell them in the first place. [The murder] happened at night, it was quick— two or three carloads of people jumped out and killed this kid, and it was all over within seconds. What can they expect to come out of this sweep?"

"It set us back a long way," says Granitsas of the police raid. "It was a very, very unwise move. They got nothing that led to any indictments, arrests, or anything, and the price that was paid was high. Cooperation of the Asian community on this case, I would say, was lessened as a result." Regina Lee, herself a Chinese immigrant who was raised in Boston's Chinatown, adds, "We need to spend some real effort to promote a more cooperative relationship between the Cambodian community and the police and the political leadership in Revere. Unfortunately, in that one afternoon of the police blockade, all the effort we've spent in the last ten years to build up that relationship has been destroyed."

Not so, says Detective Gannon. "The media got a lot of mileage out of this, but it really wasn't the way they portrayed it. If we had wanted to get maximum results, we could have gone in at five o'clock in the morning, and I'm certain we would have gotten half of those people on our list."

Fourth of July weekend, 1991, ironically, was one of the quietest Revere had seen in years.

THE BEST—and the truest—thing that can be said for Revere is that it has seen better days. It was never a wealthy town. But at its peak, it became a highly desirable close-in suburb where young, hardworking couples from immigrant families settled down soon after getting married or proudly moved later from more crowded, declining Boston neighborhoods. At the same time, Revere had the first public beach in America—a great egalitarian contrast with the exclusive and exclusionary beaches further up along Boston's North Shore. In summer, it was a grand resort for every social class, easily accessible just a few stops from downtown on the MTA (Boston's subway system), and full of bright lights, snack shacks, and a seaside amusement park with scary rides that put your heart in your throat. People who grew up during the postwar years in Brookline or Newton, upper-middle-class suburbs west of Boston, remember that after the school year ended, they would pack up and move out to beach cottages or apartments in Revere with their family for all or part of the season. It was only a few miles from home, but they had the time of their lives, year after year.

Revere's glory days finally dwindled in the 1970s. The buildings along the beach had steadily deteriorated, as the more well-to-do summer patrons moved on to other, fancier resorts and different pursuits, and the most delapidated structures were condemned and torn down one by one. "The finishing touch," as Colella puts it, came from a massive blizzard that struck the Boston area in the winter of 1978. "That destroyed the rest of the buildings—the stands, the rides, and the games. The wrecking crews came in and just cleared it all out." Suddenly he was mayor of a very different, and somewhat depressed, place.

Today Revere Beach is still a fine spot to look at Boston Harbor, and an especially good vantage point to observe the pollution that has made it one of the dirtiest bodies of water in the United States. Along with a great concentration of ominous-looking algae, quite a lot of unidentifiable waste material washes up on the sand every day. The view—and the roar—of airplanes taking off from Logan Airport, across the harbor, is now totally unobscured. The beach itself is barren and quiet. A multimillion-dollar physical rehabilitation project is under way, and city leaders hope it will soon be designated a national historic landmark or even a national park, making it once again an attraction for visitors, albeit a calmer one. But Revere will clearly never regain its past glory.[1] Across the beachfront road, where there used to be amusements and summer lodging, there are now tall, modern, dull gray condominium buildings, where mostly retired people have taken up residence.

Shirley Avenue and its environs could be a location for a film about changing neighborhoods in America. On a gray, rainy fall afternoon, it is a bleak landscape. Many of the older shops are boarded up, but others have been taken over by Cambodian merchants. Directly across the street from the old-line Revere Elks Lodge is an Asian grocery store, the Khmer script on its sign unintelligible to any of the traditional residents of the city. Phnom Penh Jewelry Sales and Repair is totally empty every time I pass it, but Angkor Services and other similar establishments—catering to passport photos, visa processing, and other immigrant-oriented needs—seem to have a few customers. There is a credit union and a dreary laundromat. Lieberman's Bakery is closed, but Meyer's kosher butcher shop is still in business (it is said to be one of only two remaining kosher butcher shops on the North Shore and a particular specialist in knishes); it has a sign prominently displayed in its glass door: WE WELCOME YOUR FOOD STAMPS. A coffee shop near the MTA station serves bagels, but spells them "baigels."

A number of the street corners along Shirley Avenue, in Massachusetts style, still bear commemorative signs with a little star at the top, designating them as "squares," in memory or in honor of someone who has been important here before but now may be scarcely remembered. Sumner, Highland, Thornton, Hitchborn, and the other residential streets running uphill from the avenue are littered with large quantities of trash. Banged-up cars are parked bumper-to-bumper, and bilingual signs, in English and Khmer, warn that they will be towed away if they are left in a spot that interferes with Tuesday-morning street cleaning. Hardly anyone is outside, but a few young Cambodian children play in the street in front of the old wood-frame apartment buildings, pretending to dance. Some of the smallest run around half-clothed, with no evidence that anyone is paying attention to them. At the top of the hill is the start of an old Italian American neighborhood, where the houses look to be freshly painted and have manicured lawns

---

[1] *In 1992 President George Bush vetoed a bill, which had been approved by both the House and the Senate, to earmark $200,000 toward turning Revere Beach into a national park. Representative Edward Markey, Democrat of Massachusetts, vowed to keep trying, but he persuaded only the House to go along with him in 1993, and the effort died before the Republicans won control of Congress in the 1994 midterm elections.*

surrounded by low wrought-iron fences; some of the lawns are adorned with holy statues.

"You don't know if [the Cambodian neighborhood] is dirty because the town doesn't give it the same attention as some of the better neighborhoods, or if the people are making it dirty, or a combination," says Amy Sessler, who has struggled with the duty to provide a fair but realistic picture of Revere for her newspaper. But the contrast in the streets is of great concern to local Cambodian leaders like Kieng Kim, a social worker with the Massachusetts welfare department. "The kids do not behave. They have no discipline," he complains during a wide-ranging conversation in his family's disheveled apartment, which is permeated by the rich smell of Asian spices. "I have tried to educate the people. The mayor allowed me to use city hall one time, and I invited all my people, so I could explain to them what they have to do to live in this country, to satisfy others: how to take care of our apartments, keep the streets clean, take care of our trash, and get rid of mice and cockroaches in the home."

Kim is discouraged by his lack of impact on these matters, but he is convinced that the problems stem at least in part from the difficulty of adjusting to urban American life for people who survived first in the jungle, on the run from the Khmer Rouge, and then in chaotic refugee camps in Thailand. Having narrowly escaped from Cambodia himself in the late 1970s, he notes that "the kids who grew up in the jungle or the camps had too much freedom. They come here and they watch too much TV, and then they try to follow what they see. Some of them don't listen to their parents; the only time they come home is when they want to eat something." At one point an elected leader of the Cambodian community in Revere, Kim has seen his own influence diminish; he has been accused—wrongly, he insists—of misappropriating funds from the bank accounts of the local Cambodian temple.

How did Revere—an all-American town grappling with its economic decline, among other problems—one day find itself required to absorb and assimilate so many Cambodian refugees? It is a question that many, including the mayor, have asked time and again. "I woke up one morning," Colella says with a studied grin, "and I was invited to the First Congregational Church to bring the greetings of the city, to welcome these people. I'll never forget the moment when I walked in and saw them all."

As far as anyone can determine, the Cambodian influx was truly a coincidence, a confluence of economic and social circumstances in Re-

vere and the private humanitarian and goodwill gestures of area individuals and churches. To begin with, Revere did have a large supply of
vacant, relatively affordable and spacious rental housing, which was an
attraction both to large refugee families just arriving and to others who
had already settled in more expensive and crowded quarters in Boston.
The town also had a widespread reputation, ironically, as an especially
safe and comfortable place, where people of different backgrounds had
lived together successfully for a long time.

But it was the Congregational Church and its activist pastor who
played the major role. As far back as 1975, Nick Granitsas—who was
raised in a Greek immigrant community in Marlboro, Massachusetts,
where many children did not speak English—and his wife had sponsored a Vietnamese war widow and her three children, taking them out
of a refugee camp in the United States and welcoming them into their
home. The Vietnamese family stayed for three years, and thus did a
somewhat narrow-minded New England Protestant congregation, composed primarily of blue-collar white ethnics, get to know its first Asian
family. In 1979, when the "boat people" were leaving Southeast Asia
and their tragic story was attracting world attention, a second Vietnamese family was sponsored by a young couple in the church, and then
Revere's Congregationalists declared openly that they were interested
in becoming more involved in refugee work.

At about that time, a retired Italian American Catholic man from
nearby Malden, another middle-class residential suburb, contacted
Granitsas, who recalls what happened: "We had met before through
ecumenical services. He said he'd heard that we wanted to do something with refugees, and he wanted to be part of it. This guy was a
blue-collar worker all his life. He said, 'I have a house that my wife and
I no longer need. We live in an apartment now, and I would like to
donate the house to your church.' We had him check with his adult kids,
because we didn't want to take this unless it was okay with them. We
wanted to be sure that this wasn't some impulsive thing, that he wasn't
a crazy man. In the end, he gave us this nine-room, six-bedroom house
in Malden. Between 1980 and 1985, our church sponsored more than
200 refugees, and 150 of them started their lives in America in that
house. We would put one, two, or three families there at a time, for
anywhere from three weeks to six months. It became like a halfway
house. We used it to teach them English, to acculturate them, and to get
all the early steps taken care of."

At first, the population of the Malden house was mostly Vietnamese. But by 1981, Boston, which had been selected by the Refugee

Resettlement Administration of the federal Department of Health and Human Services as a "target city," was receiving a large number of Cambodian refugees. Many of these people were helped to find homes by individual churches like the First Congregational in Revere or by regional organizations like Catholic Charities. From the house in Malden and from other temporary shelters, the Cambodians began to move into the empty apartments off Shirley Avenue. The first ones there, says Granitsas, "became the anchor, and then a good community began to form." In a typical case of "secondary migration," Cambodians who had been settled elsewhere in the country, hearing of the relatively favorable circumstances of their friends and relatives in Revere, came to join them.

It was not easy to get Revere's establishment to accept this wave of odd-looking, strange-talking newcomers. To be sure, Revere's citizens preferred that the Shirley Avenue neighborhood become home to stable families again instead of being a haven for transients. But many of them did not even know where Cambodia was, let alone why so many of its people were seeking refuge in the United States, and especially in their town. Yet the influx seemed to be accompanied by a number of positive developments. For example, when the city's school committee failed to authorize the money for special classes for Cambodians in English as a second language, claiming it had received no complaints from the refugees about the schools as they were, Granitsas filed a civil rights complaint with the Massachusetts Department of Education. He won, and that brought a mandate for change, along with state funding for compulsory bilingual education programs.

Waxman, facing an influx of Cambodian children into the Garfield Elementary School, found a refugee who had already spent some time in California and spoke decent English; together they recruited several Cambodians who had taught math and other subjects in the camps in Thailand and put them to work at Garfield. With help from the state, Waxman arranged special cultural workshops for his American teachers. "Certainly we couldn't learn the language," he says, "but we could at least try to learn about the people, who they were, why they were coming, where they were from, and so forth. We learned about certain habits of the Cambodians, their food habits, their mannerisms." He then established a "buddy system," whereby every Cambodian child was paired with "an Anglo kid who lived on the same street and was in the same grade. The first day of school was a madhouse, but it was a beautiful madhouse, with kids running around looking for their buddies."

Reflecting on the experience several years later, Waxman said "the first year we didn't expect to teach them much. Our goal was more socialization than education. They had been through hell, and we just went through a lot of hugging and kissing and making them feel welcome. The assimilation worked well. . . . The school was something more than a school. These people didn't understand the country they were in, so the school became a community center for them. They'd come to us and ask, 'How do you pay a bill? How do you call the police?' "

Meanwhile, under intense pressure, the mayor agreed to hold monthly or bimonthly meetings with various church representatives and community spokesmen to discuss the Cambodians' adjustment problems; he called in people from city departments to answer questions and hear complaints. Eventually, this led to the formal creation of Revere's own Human Rights Commission, and under the federal "gateway cities" program, Revere obtained money, albeit temporarily, to hire an official liaison to work with the Cambodian community.

Colella emerged as an unlikely hero of the whole affair. "This man has been outstanding and courageous," says Waxman. "He just stood up and said, 'I will not tolerate any racial bigotry in my city.' " Indeed, when a new, supermodern Garfield Elementary School was built in the early 1990s for an integrated population, the attached community center—complete with swimming pool—was named for the longtime mayor.

Sitting in his spacious office in city hall during his last months in office, a bust of President John F. Kennedy behind him, Colella spoke eloquently of the enduring positive qualities of Revere—especially compared to what he calls, with a slight tone of derision, "the city of Boston," home of a state government that he feels is not very sensitive to the problems of its smaller towns. "The state allowed this great migration, without much support, financial or otherwise," Colella complains. "For one year there were some state dollars to help us deal with some of the issues, and then we were cut adrift. The bureaucrats in the ivory towers in Boston can devise manuals and all that, but they escape coming to the real world. After the fact, all kinds of statements are made about how things ought to have been handled, but they're not here to give us help when we need it."

Meanwhile, with the support of various federal programs, Boston has succeeded in exporting some of its problems to places like Revere. Poor people—immigrants and others—may use so-called "mobile certificates" to obtain federal and state rent subsidies for their apartments, but then Revere is stuck dealing with most of the "special needs" they bring to its school system. Yet tax-limiting voter initiatives passed in the 1980s restrict the city council's ability to raise new funds to pay for the necessary programs. And Revere's tax base sees no particular benefit, because most of the new residents commute back to Boston or to other outlying towns to work in "service" jobs.

"You must remember that this city was built on the immigration process," says Colella, as he asserts his optimism that the Cambodian community can be successfully integrated, despite the serious difficulties thus far. "I think the key to whatever success we have had has been the educational system. I see these kids going through the school system now becoming the leaders in a few years, and I think that's when things will get even better. . . . There's been no real change in the process. People come, and they will continue to come, and that's where we're at."

As for Revere's Cambodians themselves, like generations of immigrants before them, they find their own means and methods of adaptation. These people did not come from the ranks of their country's elite (much of which was killed off by the Khmer Rouge), and they are not easily achieving the Asian "superminority" status associated with recent Chinese, Korean, and many Vietnamese immigrants to America. Some appear to be mired in poverty, while others have begun to buy their own homes.

Many of the Cambodian children have worked so hard at mastering English that they have become virtually illiterate in their native Khmer language, and this causes obvious strains in their families. Some parents, in the meantime, have become totally dependent on their children to help them with daily life; every one of the family's interactions with the system may require a child to take a day or more off from school.

Kieng Kim, worried that he and his children would be at a disadvantage in their new country, settled right from the start on a way to improve their chances: "I reduced my age by ten years, and my children's by two or three or even four years. I'm really fifty-seven but officially forty-seven. I still need more time to work; if I'm older, it would be harder to find a job. If you're eighteen and you come here, you have to start with a high grade and you don't get much education. My first daughter, I changed her age so that she could start lower, in grade nine. That's why she learned fast. She graduated from college, and now she is a social worker at the hospital in Lowell."

•

IN JULY 1992 the Revere Fire Department reported with some satisfaction that after an extensive inquiry by local, state, and federal agencies, four young men—two of them juveniles—had finally been arrested and indicted for arson in connection with the 1990 fire in the Shirley Avenue neighborhood. According to documents filed in court, they had used gasoline to start the fire in the basement of a vacant building at about 2:00 in the morning. It took more than a year to bring the suspects before a judge for arraignment, while prosecutors convinced the courts that they should all be tried as adults. Captain Fred Rappa of the fire department said he believed that the arson was at least in part racially motivated, and another law-enforcement source said that "arson against the Asian community was a kind of rite of passage for white working-class teenagers [in Revere] in the late 1980s and early 1990s." Defense lawyers failed to obtain dismissal of the case for lack of evidence. It was scheduled for trial in the summer of 1995.

Meanwhile, the Guarino murder case was still open and unsolved. Detective Gannon said there were no new or meaningful leads to explore but offered reassurance that the racial tensions in Revere growing out of the incident had "subsided." The latest tensions in Revere were said to be between rival Asian gangs.

PART TWO

HISTORY AND REALITY

THE RICH HISTORY of immigration to America has more dark moments than most of us like to admit. Over the years, this nation of immigrants, admittedly the most welcoming in the world, has nonetheless found ingenious ways to turn people away and to make distinctions among those who want to come. The zigzag policy shifts through the twentieth century reflect this ambivalence, as does the portrayal of immigrants and refugees in the popular culture—as heroes for wanting to come but often undesirable neighbors to have nearby. Many immigrants have been stunned by the hostility with which they are received and the hardships they must endure. And yet their children, as successful, well-assimilated adults, often replicate the scenario, reacting with the same hostility to subsequent new arrivals, as if experience taught no lessons after all.

In Chapter IV, I trace the evolution of American immigration policy and attitudes in the twentieth century, in an effort to understand its meaning for today. In this era, when the backlash against illegal immigrants has profoundly influenced the national political dialogue—and affected attitudes toward legal immigrants and refugees as well—it may be especially important to recognize that these issues have all been raised before. But the numbers tell only part of the story. The difference now, of course, is the greater diversity of the immigrant stream since World War II, and especially since 1960. Coping with the new reality of immigration—and turning it to the nation's fundamental advantage, as has been the case so many times before—is a test not only for the society but for individual citizens. One can only hope that calm reason will prevail.

Whereas the vast majority of voluntary immigrants and refugees once came on boats and were processed through Ellis Island, in New York Harbor, the situation today is much less orderly. The newest Americans and would-be Americans arrive most often in airplanes or buses, or on foot. They may have correct dealings with the government bureaucracy or may evade it altogether, in some cases for years. As if to symbolize the change, Ellis Island has now become a museum, restored with substantial assistance from the families of immigrants. Meanwhile, the busiest entry points for immigrants lie along the United States' 1,945-mile southern border, where extraordinary events take place every day. In Chapter V, I report on my experiences and observations along and near the Mexican border, in Texas and California. Many others have been there before me and since, chronicling with eloquence the confrontation between those who want to enter the country and those whose job it is to try to keep them out. However, no discussion of immigration today would be complete without an explanation of the new character of this old, porous frontier.

IV
COPING WITH DIVERSITY:
THE MAGNITUDE AND THE IMPACT
OF IMMIGRATION SINCE WORLD WAR II

"THE MOTIVES which cause the immigrant to come here are the foundation of the danger—he comes to better his own condition and not to improve ours. The question with him always is, 'What can I get?' not 'What shall I give?' The thought of those who come among us is to reproduce, so far as possible, the conditions of their old life, to revive the old peculiarities in the circumstances and surroundings of the new habitation. The inherent idea and the mainspring of action is a selfishness that is of itself a danger."

It was a Sunday in early February, and the Reverend Dr. Stephen H. Tyng Jr. was delivering his weekly sermon at the Church of the Holy Trinity in New York City. Having discovered that "one-tenth of our total population is foreign-born or descended from parents of foreign birth," he now worked himself into a frenzy on the subject of immigration. "The epoch of migration in which we are passing our lives," he said, "is perhaps the most impressive and important the world has ever known. Since the time of the Tower of Babel no such movement of the peoples of the earth has been known as that which is now in progress. Famine, political controversy, and social unrest are the reasons which have largely been responsible . . . The movement is now at its flood."

But there was hope, the Reverend Tyng concluded, and it lay in the "assimilative force" of American institutions. "In one generation," he declared, "these foreign additions to our population become Americans and the children of these immigrants become American citizens. The wonderful power of the English tongue has much to do with this. . . . The power of assimilation which inheres in this nation is competent to control and subordinate all foreign influences and forces. . . . The safety of our own property and of prosperity is bound up in the way in which this generation shall meet the invasion of emigration."

The year was 1881, and a report of the Reverend Tyng's peroration, clipped from Joseph Pulitzer's *New York World*, was pasted into a scrapbook by President Rutherford B. Hayes, between an analysis of the American shipbuilding industry and a commentary on the dangers of Western Union's telegraph monopoly. Hayes, having declined to run for a second term, was in the last month of his presidency, and immigration was much on his mind. Two years earlier, he had vetoed a bill that would have completely cut off Chinese immigration to the United States. This decision seemed to be motivated less by human rights considerations than by perceived treaty obligations to the Chinese emperor.

Nonetheless, according to other clippings in the presidential scrapbook, liberal orators in Boston praised Hayes for his "moral courage" in exercising his veto power. On the other hand, the California establishment—angered and seemingly threatened by the fact that 30 percent of San Francisco's population had now been born in China—was furious with the outgoing president. One report after another issued by the state legislature in Sacramento had documented "the social, moral, and political effect of Chinese immigration," and it was time to act, the Californians felt, before the character of their state was irretrievably changed. (The Chinese Exclusion Act—a measure that would surely be considered racist by today's standards—did finally become law in 1882, after Chester A. Arthur had assumed the presidency.)

In the long run, said the Reverend Tyng reassuringly, "there is no danger that this country will become a new Ireland, a new Germany or France, or a new China; it will be a republic for men, the future home for the overflow of the old countries." But the Californians, and others who felt they were bearing the brunt of "the flood" of people coming to America, were not so sure. The pace of immigration had steadily increased since colonial days, when about 4,000 people came each year; in 1880 alone, the Reverend Tyng noted, some 320,000 had arrived—or, as he put it, "75,000 more than the population of Rhode Island."[1]

Where would it stop? When would it end?

•

---

[1] *If the Reverend Tyng was referring to the calendar year 1880, he may have been right; but measured by the fiscal year, the situation at the time was even more severe. According to statistics published many years later by the Immigration and Naturalization Service, in FY 1880 there were 457,257 immigrants to the United States.*

QUAINT THOUGH the choice of words may sound today, there is something utterly familiar about the hysteria commonly expressed during America's Gilded Age, when the country was barely a hundred years old, about a "flood" or an "invasion" of immigrants, many of whom could not speak the English language very well or fully appreciate what the Reverend Tyng called "the genius of our institutions." Presidents, senators, and congressmen of recent years—and also governors—have been every bit as preoccupied as were Rutherford B. Hayes and the lawmakers of his time with questions of immigration and its impact. But the modern way is to tinker here and adjust there, expanding quotas and changing preferences, alternately granting amnesties, threatening crackdowns, and conducting visa lotteries, as the political establishment grapples with fundamental issues concerning the character of the United States and the shifting ethnic and social composition of its population.

Indeed, Leon F. Bouvier, an esteemed demographer and frequent consultant to committees and commissions studying immigration policy, named his definitive work on the subject, published in 1991, *Peaceful Invasions: Immigration and Changing America*. "Here I am, a self-proclaimed and proud Liberal advocating reduced levels of immigration!," wrote Bouvier self-consciously as he explained that he himself found his conclusions "troublesome" after years of study. "Yet, the research for this book has convinced me, more than ever, that this is the correct position for a Liberal to take."

Bouvier's argument, which has wide and perhaps growing support across the American political spectrum, is that the latest experience of immigration (or "peaceful invasion") is profoundly more difficult than the earlier ones in U.S. history. During the current, and for him more significant, invasion, Bouvier points out, about a million new immigrants have arrived each year, mostly from Latin America and Asia, and many illegally.[2] While all of the waves have been disruptive in one way or another, the previous ones—the original settlement by Europeans who overwhelmed the Native Americans and imported African slaves to work in agriculture; the mid-nineteenth-century wave that altered the religious makeup of the country; and the major influx from Europe and, to a lesser extent, Asia between 1880 and the start of World War I that led to severe, albeit temporary, restrictions on immigration—were limited in time and eventually resulted in more or less successful adaptation.

The latest wave, Bouvier contends, shows no signs of abating, and

[2] *This statistic excludes those "adjusted," or granted amnesty, under the Immigration Reform and Control Act (IRCA) of 1986.*

it is unclear whether these newcomers will be accepted and integrated as smoothly as their predecessors. Unless something is done about this soon—namely, cutting the annual influx by half or more—Bouvier and others argue, America's indigenous poor will suffer the consequences; the U.S. economy will be unable to deal effectively with foreign competition; new immigrants will fail to adapt and will be swept up in "cultural separatism"; and the population of the United States will grow too rapidly, putting unacceptable strain on the country's environment and infrastructure.

On a less lofty, intellectual level, one often hears the complaint that today's immigrants to America are entirely different from those admirable souls of generations past who arrived here penniless but struggled nobly and, by their hard work, helped build the country to its current level of greatness. It is true enough that the new arrivals are less likely than before to be white or to come from familiar cultures, making them easier to spot and, for some, more difficult to accept. Certain refugees, like the Vietnamese and other Southeast Asians, may be obvious human reminders of troubled moments in America's recent past. Others, like Mexicans and Central Americans, by taking jobs that nobody else wants, begin to seem omnipresent and are thus held responsible for the perceived decline in the quality of everyday services. Wherever they come from, immigrants are increasingly accused of pushing the indigenous underclass, mostly poor African Americans—not up, but down or out or at least aside.

This argument is based less on persuasive data than on instinct and intuitive belief. To many people whose families have been here longer, today's immigrants just *seem* to be more of a presence and a problem than ever before. The indiscriminate accusation is that many of the newer immigrants are somehow less hardworking and less worthy than those who came before, that things have been made too easy for them, that they do not share the commitment of most Americans to certain underlying values and ideals, and that they demand too much. Above all, it is said, they really do not try very hard anymore to learn English.

Indeed, in Florida, California, and other states that receive a steady influx of immigrants, there has been a strong backlash against bilingual-education programs that were originally viewed as a means to ease the strain on newcomers. Angry mainstream Americans have formed an organization called "U.S. English" to raise money and lobby for the establishment of an "official language" for the United States; their inspiration for a time was the late S. I. Hayakawa. An American of Japanese origin, Hayakawa was a scholar of psychology, linguistics, and semantics who, as a Republican senator from California, once introduced a constitutional amendment to enshrine English in that role. (Overall efforts to make English the official national language have thus far failed, but similar drives at the state or local level have succeeded in one form or another in at least nineteen states.)

The recent, widely acknowledged growth in illegal immigration has contributed to the impression that the United States government is almost powerless in the face of the latest "invasion"—that immigration policy is a mere legal nicety that has little to do with the day-to-day reality on the southern border or in the cities. In hard economic times, it becomes easy to make immigrants the scapegoats for other problems that seem to have no easy solutions. Thus the competition, sometimes lethal, between newer immigrant communities and long-disadvantaged minorities in Los Angeles; the tension between black police officers and poor Central Americans in Washington, D.C.; and the insistence by black leaders in Miami, resentful of Cuban American successes, that they no longer want to hear Spanish, let alone be expected to speak it occasionally themselves. And so it is that a bunch of drunken autoworkers in Detroit can stagger out of a bar and beat a Chinese student to death, in the mistaken belief that he is Japanese and somehow personally to blame for the continual, irrational insecurity they feel about their jobs as a result of foreign car imports.

It is possible, of course, to hold an entirely different view of today's immigration—that even in recent difficult times, when the country has been beset by economic recession and severe social problems, immigrants—legal and illegal alike—continue to make important and valuable contributions to the United States; that far from taking away the jobs of others and draining resources at every level of government, they are still adding value to the economy and promoting the nation's growth. This counterintuitive argument is not aggressively promoted on the floor of the U.S. Senate or the House of Representatives, or in state legislatures around the country. It is not particularly popular among environmentalists or others worried about resource scarcity and population growth. And it certainly has no organizational advocate that is any match for the Federation for American Immigration Reform (FAIR), the major anti-immigration lobbying group, which is funded in part by extreme right-wing interests and uses a substantial part of its $3.5 million annual budget to hire slick public relations firms to advance its case.[3]

---

[3] *FAIR, while it likes to see itself in a category with Zero Population Growth and other public-interest, environmentalist groups, has accepted at least $600,000 from the Pioneer Fund, a right-wing foundation that also supports studies on the relationship between race and intelligence.*

Contrary to popular belief and myth, immigrants are rarely a public burden after they arrive in the United States. According to an analysis of Census Bureau surveys by Julian Simon, an economist at the University of Maryland, legal immigrants draw on welfare, food stamps, and other such programs only to the same extent as—or perhaps even less than—native families. And since they generally no longer arrive in America with dependent elderly parents but produce children who make their own contributions, as families they tend to take substantially less from the Social Security program than they put in (unlike most natives). As for illegal immigrants, they may draw on such services as free medical care, unemployment insurance, and welfare less often than is generally supposed. This is largely due to their anxiety over their legal status and their fear of being caught and deported. Simon's figures indicate that practically no "illegals" receive Social Security payments, but 77 percent of them put money in, and 73 percent have federal income tax withheld from their wages. In fact, according to his analysis of the statistics, illegal immigrants, on average, pay five to ten times as much in taxes as the cost of the welfare services they use.

Immigrants who are not yet highly Americanized actually adhere more closely than most long-term citizens to what are generally regarded as desirable all-American standards and habits. According to Simon, one of the lonely advocates of increased immigration, immigrants work harder than natives, save more of what they earn, and are more inclined to start up new businesses or be self-employed. They are less likely than the general population to commit crimes or be unemployed, and, on average, they have no more children than do families that have been here longer. They not only take jobs, but also make jobs, given the goods and services they consume. And, as Simon points out, although immigrants may create short-term pressure on the labor market, in the long term this is often beneficial. Native workers with more skills may find it more possible to move up the ladder if there are immigrants to replace them lower down. If certain professionals, such as doctors, face competition from new arrivals, that could result in certain kinds of medical care and other services eventually becoming less costly to the public.

More elusive, and harder to submit to traditional economic analysis, is the fact that the United States has always depended on immigrants to invigorate its culture. It is difficult to identify very many indigenous American values not traceable to immigrant influence. Our persistent frontier ethic, rugged individualism, and aggressive materialism have been profoundly affected by the waves of new arrivals over the years. American art, music, dance, literature, drama, food, and even politics have been greatly enriched and improved by the immigrant experience. And although there have been plenty of clashes between rival groups, few would challenge the notion that the United States is a more interesting, exciting, and vibrant place, thanks to its rich mix of nationalities, ethnicities, and religions. Homogeneity, for America, would be death.

IN THE WANING YEARS of the twentieth century, hardly a day goes by that the subject of immigration does not cross the average American's consciousness. Successful immigrants are invariably in the news—sports stars, superachievers in business, young people winning music competitions, geography bees, and college scholarships. There are role models like Henry Kissinger and Zbigniew Brzezinski, the German- and Polish-born scholars, respectively, who took turns running American foreign policy in the 1970s; Manute Bol, the impossibly tall basketball player from a Dinka village in Sudan; Roberto C. Goizueta, the Cuban émigré who has taken the Coca-Cola Company to new heights of success; and Ken Hakuta, the Japanese "Dr. Fad" who made a mint importing novelty toys from East Asia. They speak with a great variety of accents and live according to many different traditions, but all have come to call themselves Americans and, in the process, helped stretch our definition of what that means.

Heroic fighters for freedom in other lands still make their way to American shores when they have trouble at home, and it is difficult not to notice them: organizers and supporters of the 1989 Tiananmen Square uprising in China, who surreptitiously slipped away from the security police; Kenyan journalists whose publications have been shut down; politicians, artists, or academics waiting to return to Chile, the Philippines, Korea, or the remnants of the former Soviet Union and other communist states in Europe. Some do go back in due course, but others return only to visit, if at all; they gradually become permanent exile-immigrants. Others, less well known and seldom remarked upon, settle more quietly and without fanfare into American life. We encounter them often—in the restaurants they run, the motels they buy or manage, the taxis they drive, or the schools their children attend. Every one of these immigrants has a story.

But for every positive image or inspiring tale of a successful or heroic or even just a satisfactory immigrant experience, it seems, there is a countervailing example, a tragic or unsavory tale. Julio González, the disturbed man who in March 1990 set fire to the Happy Land Social

Club in the Bronx, killing eighty-seven Hondurans and other Latino immigrants, had arrived from his native Cuba during the Mariel boatlift ten years earlier, when Fidel Castro emptied his prisons and mental hospitals onto small craft bound for Florida. Federal law-enforcement officials report the emergence of new organized crime syndicates in major cities (especially New York) made up of Colombian, Chinese, Vietnamese, Jamaican, Dominican, and ex-Soviet immigrants, each specializing in its own illegal enterprises and rivaling the traditional dominance of the American and Sicilian Mafia in certain neighborhoods. Many of these groups, the officials say, prey especially on fellow immigrants from their own countries and ruthlessly punish anyone who tries to interfere with them. Expert burglars who have immigrated from Albania and the former Yugoslavia have victimized supermarkets, banks, and other retail outlets along the East Coast.

Korean grocers in Los Angeles, having borrowed from relatives and friends to buy and rehabilitate businesses in neighborhoods where others fear to work, find themselves a primary target of rioters after a not-guilty verdict in a police-brutality trial that had absolutely nothing to do with them. Thousands of Salvadoran immigrants living in the Hispanic neighborhoods of Washington, D.C., wake up one day to discover that the bank where they had deposited their life savings was not a bank at all, but a scam run by a greedy fellow immigrant who had squandered all their money. Amerasian children, by now in their late teens or twenties and rejected or abandoned by their mothers at home in Vietnam or Thailand, come to the United States to embark on a desperate, and invariably futile, search for their American fathers, who, in most cases, are not even aware of their children's existence.

For these people and many more, America does not turn out to be the place they read about and dreamed of; it bears little resemblance to the country they thought they knew from Hollywood films and endlessly syndicated television series. It is, rather, a place of violence and fear and insecurity, where good fortune and bad are peculiarly and unpredictably distributed—a land of many promises but not, after all, the promised land.

THERE ARE FEW neutral "facts" about immigration that do not provoke arguments, but this much seems to be accepted: According to statistics kept by the Immigration and Naturalization Service, a total of some 60.7 million people are believed to have immigrated legally to the United States from the time the federal government began keeping records in 1820 until 1993.[4] Most U.S. immigration statistics are only marginally reliable, especially for recent years, given the increase in illegal entries; one can only presume that the earliest numbers are more trustworthy than the later ones, because there were few meaningful restrictions to circumvent at the time. About two-thirds of all the immigrants in the official statistics, or 37.3 million, are listed as having come from Europe, 14.4 million from the Americas, and 6.4 million from Asia; about 850,000 are said to have originated from other parts of the world, including Africa, Australia, and the Pacific islands.

Immigration reached its official peak—and certainly its maximum impact—during the first decade of the 1900s, when it was hardly regulated at all and nearly 9 million people arrived to seek a better life. Almost 1.3 million of them came in 1907 alone, apparently the highest year ever for new immigrants.[5] The American openness to immigration in this period was not driven exclusively by idealism and altruism. The motive, for the most part, was to obtain cheap labor for the burgeoning industries, the mines, and the sweatshops, to use hungry, sturdy Europeans in much the way that the Chinese "coolies" had been used to build the railroads during the great expansion westward. But to get those hardy European workers, the United States had to take their families and let many other people in, too, including the merchants and tradesmen who had served the workers in their countries of origin. In the process, the booming American economy enjoyed tremendous growth at the expense of Old World societies that could not feed or otherwise satisfy their own people.

The flow slowed to a trickle during the Great Depression and World War II (just at the time, not entirely accidentally, when a large

[4] *This figure also omits those granted amnesty under IRCA. There were many immigrants to the United States, or to the American colonies of Great Britain and other European powers, for more than two centuries before 1820, of course. Everyone but the Native Americans was emigrating from somewhere else, and even they are thought to have come over a land bridge from Asia into an essentially empty continent. But those who arrived early enough seem to have escaped having the "immigrant" label pinned on them by history; it is ironic, although perhaps not surprising, that the descendants of the earliest European immigrants to America have tended to be among the strongest advocates of a restrictive immigration policy.*

[5] *The highest year on record is actually FY 1991, when more than 1.8 million people were granted legal permanent residence; but all but about 700,000 of them had lived continuously in the United States since 1982 and were actually "adjusting" their status under IRCA. To benefit from IRCA's adjustment provisions, an undocumented immigrant had to prove at least four years of continuous residence in the United States beginning no later than 1982. But it has taken the INS many more years than originally anticipated to process all of the people who applied for amnesty, and thus the immigration statistics—if not the actual new arrivals—have been dramatically affected by IRCA adjustments well into the 1990s.*

number of people were trying to escape fascist tyranny in Europe and pounding especially hard on the golden door). But in the postwar era, immigration has again increased fairly steadily, with the number of people officially admitted in Fiscal Year 1988 (643,025) the highest since 1924. By 1992 that number was up to 973,977, but slipped to 880,014 in 1993 (in each case, not including adjustments under IRCA).

Interestingly, despite the recent complaints of a "flood" and the widespread impression that the number of immigrants is more significant today than ever before, officially acknowledged newcomers have fallen dramatically as a percentage of the United States population, from 1 percent in 1910 to less than a quarter of a percent in 1988. Another way to state this is that while the average number of immigrants admitted each year between 1905 and 1914 was 11.1 per thousand U.S. inhabitants, for the years from 1983 to 1992 that number was down to 3.7 immigrants per thousand. Although there were some 19.8 million foreign-born people living in the United States at the time of the 1990 census, or just under 8 percent, this figure is considerably lower than it has been at various other times in the nation's history, particularly at the beginning of the twentieth century. (Given the rate of recent immigration, however, the number of foreign-born residents, and their proportion in the overall population, have presumably increased somewhat since the 1990 census.)

What has changed dramatically, of course, is who the immigrants are and where they are coming from. Until the 1920s, the vast majority of new arrivals were from Europe (particularly Britain, Ireland, Italy, Russia, and Austria-Hungary) and Canada. But after World War I, distinctions began to be drawn among the various Europeans trying to get into the United States. Those distinctions, not always reflecting the most attractive side of the American character, took on the force of law in the "national-origins quota system" that was at the heart of the Immigration Act of 1924. The quota formula, which actually went into effect in mid-1929, sought to preserve the ethnic composition of the United States as it had stood (or was officially declared to have stood) in 1920, with a substantially white, theoretically Northern European majority. As a "eugenics consultant" told a subcommittee of the House Judiciary Committee while it was considering the 1924 bill:

> We in this country have been so imbued with the idea of democracy, or the equality of all men, that we have left out of consideration the matter of blood or natural born hereditary mental and moral differences. No man who breeds pedigreed plants and animals can afford to neglect this thing.

The introduction of this "biological basis" into immigration policy, drawing as it did on the concept of Nordic superiority, codified widely held prejudices concerning which people were to be considered more valuable and better qualified immigrants. There is considerable evidence that the quota system was intended not only to exclude non-whites, but also to cut down on the Jews, Irish, Italians, and Poles who had made up such a large percentage of the immigrant stream during the early part of the twentieth century. But there were only so many Swedes or Danes who would choose to come to America at that point. As many national quotas went unfilled and other nationalities built up years-long waiting lists, the net effect was to reduce immigration overall for at least two decades. For many politicians, policy makers, and patriotic organizations, that was a perfectly acceptable result.

The quota system was renewed in the Immigration and Nationality Act of 1952, but this time, ostensibly, less on the basis of overtly racist theories than, as a Senate report put it, as "a rational and logical method of numerically restricting immigration in such a manner as to best preserve the sociological and cultural balance in the population of the United States." The 1952 act, usually known by the names of its two principal Democratic sponsors, Senator Pat McCarran of Nevada and Representative Francis Walter of Pennsylvania, also concerned itself with excluding "subversives" from the United States. Building on the Internal Security Act of 1950, it barred aliens who were members of certain political organizations, primarily those associated with the Communist party.

The immigrant profile began to change appreciably only during the 1960s. Arrivals from certain parts of Europe had increased again temporarily at the height of the Cold War—for example, when large numbers of anticommunist veterans of the Hungarian uprising of 1956 were admitted. There were also new postwar influxes from Germany, Italy, and Britain, where the "brain drain" to America became a nationalist issue. But the most noticeable trend was the dramatic surge in the number of immigrants from Asia and the Americas. (Since relatively few immigrants now come from Canada, immigrants from the "Americas" tend to be primarily Hispanics from the South.) From 1951 to 1960, according to official statistics, there were 153,249 immigrants from Asia and 996,944 from the Americas; but from 1961 to 1970, there were 427,642 Asian immigrants and some 1.7 million from Latin America.

Some of this could be attributed to major political and military events, such as Castro's takeover in Cuba and the defeat of the United

States in the Vietnam War. But there were also important changes in immigration policy along the way. The 1952 act had introduced the practice of selecting immigrants at least in part on the basis of skills and services that were in demand in the United States. Thus, more engineers began to emigrate from Asia. Then the Immigration and Nationality Act Amendments of 1965 finally did away with the old quota system and abolished the long-standing official discrimination against prospective immigrants from the so-called Asia-Pacific triangle.

In a seeming contradiction, however, the 1965 law put an annual ceiling of 120,000 on all immigration from the Western Hemisphere. (The justification expressed at the time was that too many people might be seeking to emigrate north from Latin American countries with weak economies and rapidly expanding populations.) This provision eventually came to be seen as objectionable—by President Gerald Ford, among others—and in retrospect, its main effect may well have been to increase illegal immigration from Mexico and points south. People who ordinarily might have waited to immigrate legally may have been panicked into crossing the border as soon as possible. The Western Hemisphere quota was eventually repealed in 1978, when another law established a single worldwide ceiling of 290,000 immigrants a year, with an emphasis on family unification and the admission of professionals, people of "exceptional ability" in the sciences and arts, and skilled and unskilled workers in short supply in the United States. This worldwide ceiling was lowered to 270,00 a year in 1980, but the restriction soon became meaningless, as Congress and the executive branch repeatedly made exceptions for various special cases and as illegal immigration became a more significant factor.

Indeed, beginning in the early 1970s, the perception grew that it was more urgently necessary to control illegal immigration than to continue quarreling over who should and who should not be allowed to come into the country legally. Border controls and policy debates began to seem equally irrelevant, particularly in certain urban and agricultural areas, as thousands upon thousands of people who wanted to do so managed to enter the country, travel freely, and work at a basic wage, whether or not they had formal permission to come. Many citizens grumbled over these people's impact on the economy—and over the fact that any laws of the land could be so easily disobeyed—yet it took a decade and a half to do something about it. In November 1986, just before adjourning, Congress finally passed a law it had been fine-tuning for years: the Immigration Reform and Control Act. It instituted sanctions against employers for knowingly hiring workers who were in the country illegally or did not have legal authorization from the Department of Labor to accept employment. But at the same time, the law provided for legalization and amnesty from prosecution—or "adjustment of status"—for all undocumented aliens who could prove that they had been in the United States since before January 1, 1982. Hundreds of thousands of people have since been permitted to stay under those provisions.

The net effect of all these legal, social, and political changes was to increase dramatically the non-European component of immigration. The emphasis on admitting professionals, including engineers, opened the door to more Asians, and most of the unskilled workers came from Mexico, Central America, and the Caribbean. In the decade from 1951 to 1960, according to INS records, 72.3 percent of newly naturalized Americans came from Europe; but for the period from 1981 to 1991, Europeans were down to 14.8 percent, and Asians represented almost half (49.5 percent) of those becoming citizens. By 1992 more than half of those naturalized were Asians, and Europeans represented barely an eighth of the total. More telling still was the official INS list of the ten countries with the highest number of immigrants legally admitted into the United States in Fiscal Year 1988, not one of them in Europe: Mexico, Philippines, Haiti, Korea, China, Dominican Republic, India, Vietnam, Jamaica, and Cuba. Interestingly, after the end of the Cold War and the demise of the monolithic Soviet bloc, along with other political upheavals of the late 1980s and early 1990s, the list shifted. For Fiscal Years 1992 and 1993 combined, the top ten sending countries were Mexico, China, Philippines, Vietnam, the former Soviet Union, Dominican Republic, India, Poland, El Salvador, and the United Kingdom.[6]

By the time of the 1990 census, 32 million persons living in the United States reported speaking a language other than English at home, and more than 40 percent of them acknowledged that they did not speak English very well. In California, the numbers are particularly striking: Out of its population of almost 31 million in 1994, according to the Statistical Abstract of the United States, 22 percent (or about 6.8 million) are foreign born and 32 percent (or about 9.9 million) speak some language other than English at home. Even in Pennsylvania, which is only ninth on the list of states of intended residence for immigrants, a

[6] *The reappearance of the United Kingdom on the list probably reflects the congressionally mandated visa lotteries that legalized, or brought in, many immigrants from Northern Ireland. See Chapter XII.*

state data center reported that 108,000 residents spoke English poorly, if at all, and that more than 800,000 spoke another language at home. In other words, it was becoming far more common—and, in effect, much more feasible—to get along in America without speaking the majority's language.

The change in demographics was so striking that members of Congress representing certain ethnic constituencies whose home countries were deemed to be "adversely affected" by the various shifts in immigration policy began to press for special exceptions to the rules to help people from their ancestral lands catch up. Influential Democrats in Congress, including Senator Edward M. Kennedy of Massachusetts, successfully sponsored legislation to admit extra immigrants from Ireland, for example, and obtained for them a priority in the annual visa lotteries conducted in the late 1980s and early 1990s. Polish American congressmen from Chicago failed when they attempted the same political ploy; nonetheless, Polish immigrants benefited greatly from the lotteries. But still the Irish in Boston and the Poles in Chicago were bound to feel overwhelmed; the number of additional Irish and Polish immigrants was insignificant compared to the number of Asians and Latin Americans arriving legally and illegally every year.

Perhaps most noticed among the new immigrants (although they generally represent well under 20 percent of the total each year) are the refugees and asylum seekers, whose nationality tends to vary over time with shifts in world events and American foreign policy. In Fiscal Year 1992, for example, some 123,000 refugees were admitted, about half from the former Soviet Union, a quarter from Vietnam, and most of the rest from Laos, Cuba, Iraq, and Ethiopia. In the same year, INS received about 107,000 applications for asylum from people already in the United States, on top of a backlog of 137,000 cases already pending at the time. The agency is unable to say exactly how many of those applications were approved, but by the end of FY 1992, the backlog to be processed had grown to more than 219,000—before yet another 144,000 applied in FY 1993. A large number of the people stuck in this legal limbo (although already living more or less normal lives in the United States) were from Guatemala and El Salvador—countries where the would-be asylees' claims of political persecution ran up against Washington's correct diplomatic relationship with the regimes in power. (It was easier, for example, to justify granting asylum in 1988 to more than 3,500 people from Nicaragua, then governed by the left-wing Sandinista regime considered hostile to American interests.)

The federal Office of Refugee Resettlement generally assigns refugees from a single country to scattered sites around the United States. Theoretically, this minimizes their impact on any particular city or region, but the refugees often tend to come back together and form concentrated communities. Indeed, certain parts of the country clearly are much more affected by immigration than others. The 1990 census found, for example, that in the Midwest only 3.6 percent of the population was foreign-born, and in the South just 5.3 percent; meanwhile, in the West 14.8 percent were foreign-born. In 1993 roughly three-quarters of all newly arrived immigrants said that their destination was one of six states: California, New York, Texas, Florida, New Jersey, and Illinois. The Census Bureau discovered in 1990 that 6 percent of Hawaii's population had moved into that state from another country in the previous decade. (The comparable figure for California was 10.9 percent.)

Although there are relatively few small towns or rural areas in America that remain untouched by the immigration boom, most newcomers do tend to settle in large cities. In recent years, between 35 percent and 40 percent of all immigrants have ended up in the metropolitan areas of New York City, Los Angeles, Miami, Chicago, or Washington, D.C. Those cities—plus other key spots such as Denver, Houston, and San Francisco—are where the jobs are and where, if an immigrant is illegal, he or she can be more easily concealed.

IT IS a fundamental part of the official American mythology that everyone with something to contribute to the country is welcome, and that immigrants, once they have arrived, will be treated as equals with everyone else. Since the late nineteenth century, this ideal has been obsequiously represented by the inscription at the base of the Statue of Liberty in New York Harbor, just near Ellis Island, which was the port of entry for so many European immigrants. The words are drawn from a sonnet, "The New Colossus," by New York intellectual Emma Lazarus:

> *Give me your tired, your poor,*
> *Your huddled masses, yearning to breathe free,*
> *The wretched refuse of your teeming shore.*
> *Send these, the homeless, tempest-tost to me,*
> *I lift my lamp beside the golden door!*

Yet there are plenty of prominent American symbols that can be read the other way, to say that immigrants are not really equal. Take the song "This Is My Country," for example, with words by Don Raye, which was first presented in 1940 in the patriotic musical *Yankee Doodle Dandy,* the story of George M. Cohan. Today the chorus is often sung movingly by a choir of young people on ceremonial occasions like the inauguration of a president:

> *This is my country,*
> *Land of my birth.*
> *This is my country,*
> *The greatest on earth.*
> *I pledge thee my allegiance,*
> *America the bold,*
> *For this is my country,*
> *To have and to hold.*

And in one of the verses:

> *With hand upon my heart,*
> *I thank the Lord for this my native land,*
> *For all I love is here within her gates.*
> *My soul is rooted deeply in the soil on which I stand,*
> *For these are my own United States.*

The subtle implication is inescapable: The United States really belongs to the native-born, not to people who arrived later and became citizens by choice or chance. After a generation, a lucky family could move up to full status as real Americans—for some, if they are markedly different from the majority, it might take longer—but until then, they must sit on the sidelines.

The history of American politics and public life is full of far less subtle negative references to, and even brutal actions against, immigrants. In the early years of the twentieth century, there were few terms of opprobrium more severe than "alien." During World War I, on the strength of new amendments to the Espionage Act, the still small Bureau of Investigation in the Justice Department (later the FBI) was set loose to apprehend "enemy aliens" considered dangerous to national security. The Alien Act of 1918 led to the notorious "Palmer Raids," during which President Woodrow Wilson's politically ambitious attorney general, A. Mitchell Palmer, used the new General Intelligence Division (the GID) of the Justice Department (where the young J. Edgar Hoover worked) to round up suspected radicals in thirty-three cities. Francis P. Garvan, Palmer's confidant and head of the GID—and, incidentally, the son of an Irish immigrant—openly used terms like "alien filth" to refer to the targets of his investigations. (Such language crops up repeatedly in the history of American immigration, the implication being that newcomers invariably have lower standards of personal hygiene than the clean Americans.)

Among the 10,000 people arrested during Palmer's raids on the night of January 2, 1920, were many new immigrants who barely spoke English. Indeed, some were already American citizens or were in the process of naturalization but were nonetheless swept into squalid jail cells.[7] A few well-known anarchists were deported after Palmer's "Red raids," but most of the cases were written off as the unfortunate result of excessive zeal. During a Senate investigation of the events, Palmer insisted that his agents should be excused for any roughness in dealing with "these alien agitators whom they observed seeking to destroy their homes, their religion, and their country . . ." Indeed, he asserted that the Fourth Amendment guarantee against unreasonable searches and seizures did not apply to aliens.

Even today, the applicability of the Bill of Rights to noncitizens living in the United States is not clearly established. When Joyce Hens Green, a federal district judge in Washington, D.C., ruled in May 1992 that resident aliens are entitled to the same First Amendment guarantee of free speech as U.S. citizens, it was apparently only the second such decision in American legal history. She was dealing with the case of a Palestinian man in Houston who was fighting an attempt by the INS to deport him on the grounds that he supported a terrorist organization. In such a case, Judge Green said, the government "cannot broadly prohibit teaching or advocating unpopular tenets, or association with an organization that teaches or advocates such doctrines." The problem was particularly egregious in this man's case, she observed, because the government was attempting to deport him under the "summary exclusion" clause of the McCarran-Walter Act, which denied him access to the confidential information being used to build a case against him.

For undocumented immigrants, the situation could be much worse. Just a month after Judge Green's ruling, U.S. District Court Judge William Matthew Byrne, Jr., in Los Angeles approved a settlement of a class-action lawsuit, guaranteeing for the first time that suspected illegal immigrants get written notice of their rights, in their own language if possible, and be permitted to talk with a lawyer when they are

[7] *This phenomenon has arisen time and again in later crises of public order in the United States. Various law-enforcement agencies at the federal, state, and local levels have been accused of indiscriminately arresting American citizens of Hispanic origin, for example, during roundups of illegal immigrants from Mexico and Central America or other presumed lawbreakers. When the police set out to arrest people of a certain ethnic background, they will obviously have difficulty distinguishing citizens from noncitizens.*

arrested. Under his ruling, they would also be able to make a phone call, seek a hearing before an immigration judge, obtain release on bond, and contact a diplomatic representative of their own country.

ONE OF THE most revealing ways to track the standing of immigrants and popular attitudes toward immigration in the United States is to study the responses to questions in national public opinion polls since the late 1930s, as sociologists Rita Simon and Susan Alexander have done. The thread that runs through them all is an almost unremitting hostility toward immigrants.

In May 1938, just after the Nazis had annexed Austria, when a national sample was asked its attitude toward allowing "German, Austrian, and other political refugees" to come to the United States, 68 percent of the respondents agreed with the statement, "with conditions as they are, we should keep them out." Only 5 percent felt that the refugees should be encouraged to come, even if that meant raising immigration quotas. In a January 1939 survey, several months after Germany had taken advantage of the Munich Pact to begin gobbling up Czechoslovakia, 83 percent said that if they were members of the new Congress, they would vote against any bill "to open the doors of the United States to a larger number of European refugees than are now admitted under our immigration quota." Even in November 1947, more than two years after World War II had ended, 72 percent of those polled said that they were opposed to liberalizing immigration rules in order to accept more of the displaced persons from Europe. Not surprisingly, in most of these surveys, the opposition to a more humanitarian policy was stronger among factory workers and others at the lower end of the economic spectrum than among professionals and others with a higher education.

When President Dwight Eisenhower proposed legislation in 1953 to admit more refugees from communism and when 5,000 anticommunists from Hungary were given special status after the 1956 revolt there, the reaction of the American public was more generous, but still ambivalent. A third of the people polled in one instance thought the policy of admitting the Hungarians was too lenient. Almost a decade later, in the summer of 1965, after the immigration reform act had been passed, the same proportion said it felt immigration should be "decreased."

In the 1970s, as the Vietnam War wound down, negative attitudes toward immigration surged again; there was little public sympathy for the "boat people" who were desperately trying to escape communist rule or for other Southeast Asian refugees. In April 1975, just before the fall of Saigon, 52 percent of the people responding to one survey said that South Vietnamese evacuated from the besieged capital should not be permitted to live in the United States. Two years later, 57 percent opposed admitting more people from the temporary camps in Thailand, Malaysia, and other countries in the region. By May 1980, soon after the Mariel boatlift that brought more than 100,000 new immigrants from Cuba, 66 percent of the people participating in a Gallup poll were saying that they favored an old proposal to "halt all immigration until the national unemployment rate falls below 5 percent." As had been the case forty years earlier, people in a lower socioeconomic bracket, this time specifically including African Americans, were more likely than others to take a hard line against immigration.

In five national polls conducted during the 1980s, when people were asked whether they felt immigration should be increased, decreased, or kept at the same level, the meager number of respondents who favored increasing it wavered between only 4 percent and 9 percent. It is widely assumed that these attitudes were reinforced by the new concerns and controversies over illegal immigration. Indeed, in various polls between 1977 and 1990, from 71 percent to 79 percent said they favored banning the employment of undocumented immigrants. Similarly, when asked between 1977 and 1985 about granting amnesty to people who had been in the United States illegally for several years, from 61 percent to 65 percent said they were against it. Substantial majorities of the respondents in occasional surveys have also said they would favor the issuance of official identification cards—something long resisted by the American public—in order to help distinguish between those who are in the United States legally and those who are not.

The picture that emerges clearly from the survey data is, as Simon and Alexander put it, one of "essentially negative attitudes held by a majority of the American public toward persons wishing to come to the United States. . . . the prospect of higher immigration levels is not, and never has been, a popular issue with the American public." These attitudes are obviously a factor in initiatives such as Proposition 187, passed by California voters in November 1994 at the urging of Governor Pete Wilson, to prohibit illegal immigrants from using the state's public schools and health facilities.

Anti-immigrant feeling is often reflected in the editorial commentary and letters-to-the-editor sections of major American newspapers. Simon and Alexander found a steady drumbeat during the 1980s against immigration—and particularly undocumented aliens—from certain columnists. Writing in the *Chicago Tribune*, for example, Joan Beck complained in 1981 that "it does little good to reduce our birth rate voluntarily if immigration prevents stabilizing our population. . . . Efforts to reduce poverty are doomed to fail if, as one population expert puts it, 'the bottom of the barrel keeps filling up.' " Concerned especially about the influx of illegal Hispanic immigrants, Beck wrote later that "we are creating another big, unassimilable minority, separated not only by culture but by language and competing for jobs, political power and tax-financed entitlements with blacks to whom this nation's historic debt is still not fully settled." The op-ed pages of various newspapers frequently air the views of people like Roger Conner, the former executive director of FAIR. "The great majority of all Americans want illegal immigration abolished," he wrote in the *Los Angeles Times*. "They also want to reduce the level of legal immigration."

THERE IS SOMETHING profoundly contradictory—some would say hypocritical—about the fact that public sentiment runs so strongly and consistently against immigration in a wealthy country built by immigrants. Indeed, few of today's Americans would themselves enjoy the privileges associated with U.S. citizenship if there had not been a liberal immigration policy at some earlier stage of the country's development. And in the vast majority of cases, our ancestors came to the United States primarily to escape civil strife or in order to better themselves economically—exactly the kind of motivation that is so widely criticized, or even regarded as disqualifying, now.

But there is a history, of course, that crosses cultural, religious, and social boundaries—and becomes the stuff of novels and films—of Americans who forget, or try to deny or conceal, their personal background once they have become successful and prosperous. Every ethnic group, and many families, have their examples of people who have turned their backs on their heritage, sometimes changing their surnames in order to appear more typically and unquestionably American. In the process, they lose, or intentionally shed, the capacity to identify with the suffering of present-day refugees or the yearning of new groups of would-be immigrants for self-improvement. This is precisely what many of the new immigrants to America fear most: that their children and grandchildren, swept up by a materialist, homogenizing consumer society, will lose or reject their own identity and then fail to sympathize with others. And that is perhaps why the newer arrivals are more inclined than those who came before to reject the goal of total assimilation (a goal that would, in any event, be more difficult for some recent immigrants to achieve, for reasons of color and culture).

During the twentieth century American public life has produced some notorious examples of members of immigrant families who display a haughty contempt toward new victims of persecution aspiring to come to the United States. One was Walter Lippmann, the distinguished journalist and commentator who became an influential confidant of presidents and secretaries of state.

The son of wealthy German Jewish parents who grew up in a world of privilege in New York City, Lippmann was proud of his intellectual "disinterestedness," and he developed a studied indifference to the repression and eventual mass murder of European Jews by Hitler. He had already suggested publicly that Jews were somehow to blame for anti-Semitism, but in a number of columns in 1933 (which he pointedly left out of later collections of his work), Lippmann sounded as if he were making excuses for the Nazis. The mistreatment of the Jews, he wrote, "by satisfying the lust of the Nazis who feel that they must conquer somebody and the cupidity of those Nazis who want jobs, is a kind of lightning rod which protects Europe" from all-out war. When Hitler gave a speech that seemed to be conciliatory, Lippmann called him "the authentic voice of a genuinely civilized people"; he suggested that the Germans should no more be judged by the Nazis than the Catholic Church by the Inquisition, Protestantism by the Ku Klux Klan, or "the Jews by their parvenus." Later, as the persecution of the Jews became more vicious, he argued that the United States government should not protest loudly or officially, lest this weaken the internal German opposition. It appeared to have been lost on Lippmann that if his own grandparents had stayed in Germany rather than immigrating to the United States in the nineteenth century, his Jewish family surely would have suffered the same fate as the unfortunate millions Lippmann chose to ignore.

It is precisely because the conflict between multicultural diversity and assimilation in a complex, postindustrial society has never been satisfactorily resolved on a national level—and it realistically cannot be—that Americans seem to engage in an obsessive and endless debate over immigration. It defies and crosses traditional political and ideological lines, and recently it has become more, not less, shrill and bruising.

Yet there is a paradox about the debate. Even as lawmakers, often egged on by labor union leaders and other economic interests, speak out about the potential economic damage that high levels of immigration can visit on native-born Americans, they have nonetheless generally eased restrictions and made it simpler for people to come. The process of achieving permanent resident status, or a green card, and going on to become a citizen is far less daunting today than it once was.[8] At the same time, the enforcement of most immigration-related rules and regulations has become increasingly ineffective, sometimes even ludicrously so. Foreign students, tourists, and other visitors often overstay their visas without serious consequences, and hardly anyone seems to believe that the INS has the know-how or the resources to apprehend a significant percentage of the people who enter the country illegally. Anyone denied an extension of a visa is entitled to an appeal or two. Employer sanctions have apparently had little impact.

The result of all this is that the United States, in practice even more than in theory, has the most generous immigration policy in the world. To some other countries, which jealously guard their ethnic homogeneity, this seems absurd. Yet as we see desperate, destitute Haitians turned back at sea, and we invent new kinds of visas in order to avoid having to evaluate and compare the merits of individual cases, we are constantly forced to ask ourselves, Is our immigration policy generous enough? Does it come anywhere close to fulfilling the promise on the Statue of Liberty? Some three decades after the national-origins quota system was repealed, do the policy and the bureaucracy still discriminate unfairly? Or is this all an elaborate, self-perpetrated hoax that fools us into believing that we are regulating immigration when it is actually regulating itself?

Part of the dilemma is that the continuing high demand for entry into the United States is really a tribute to the success of the American Dream. Notwithstanding widespread international criticism of American foreign policy during the Cold War and beyond, and despite worldwide awareness of homelessness, urban violence, and other social problems here, a vast number of people persist in wanting to come and live in the United States. They are voting with their feet. Of course, underneath the constant boasting that we have developed the best political and economic system in the world lurks the basic, chauvinistic belief that if foreign peoples cannot make their countries more like ours—and most cannot, or might not care to—they *should* want to live here. If we have, in effect, oversold the American experience, that becomes our problem and complicates immigration policy.

The United States government has no reliable way of counting the

---

[8] *The Alien Registration Receipt Card, which establishes the right of a non–U.S. citizen to live and work in the United States, was originally printed on white paper. It became green, and especially valuable, after World War II, when legal permanent residents began to find the document necessary to get a job. To combat fraud, the INS introduced nineteen different designs of the card, including many changes of color, between the late 1940s and 1977, when it became machine-readable. Today Form I-551, as it is officially known, exists in various hues, including pink-and-blue, but is still usually known as a "green card."*

number of immigrants who change their minds and return to their countries of origin, or of native-born Americans who emigrate elsewhere. In this open system people depart even more freely than they arrive. Nor is it in our national nature to wonder why people leave, to conduct a sort of exit interview that might tell us how our society has failed, for some, to meet expectations. The assumption appears to be that anyone who does not want to live in the United States must be, at best, misguided or, at worst, subversive.

BUT HOW is America, this persistent object of our compulsive affection, changing? And will we still recognize her in the morning? Is it realistic to continue expecting immigrants to turn into "real" Americans? Or will immigrants, by not conforming as much as they once did, redefine what it is to be an American? The days are numbered until the European-derived white majority becomes a minority. Hardly cohesive to begin with, that white minority will presumably have a declining capacity to get away with discriminating against others who are different. By the year 2020, according to *Time* magazine, the nonwhite and Hispanic population of the United States will have more than doubled, to nearly 115 million, and the number of whites will have leveled off. Sometime in the twenty-first century—*Time* guesses that it will be in the year 2056—the "average" American will be someone whose origins are in Asia, Africa, Arabia, the Hispanic world, or the Pacific Islands.

Already great adjustments are underway. In California, where minorities make up more than 50 percent of the public school population statewide, the question of how to reform the curriculum to reflect a multicultural environment without rejecting traditional Western values and verities is a frequent topic of debate. So is the issue of whether to provide bilingual education for primary and secondary school students—and if so, in how many languages other than Spanish.

In New York City an estimated 120,000 immigrant children from 167 countries entered the public schools during a recent three-year period. To be sure, there were issues of overcrowding, illiteracy, and racial tension. One of the unique problems was finding people who could teach in Albanian, among other languages regarded here as obscure. But rather than reeling under the burden, New York school officials say they view the influx as an opportunity to rejuvenate the city's educational system and to breathe new life into individual schools that had long since been written off as failures. "Every time there's an upheaval anywhere in the world, the schools in New York are the first to absorb it," Mitchell L. Moss, director of the Urban Research Center at New York University, told the *New York Times*.

American cities no longer look the same. The variation is not just in the people, but also in the signs and shop windows. It has been commonplace for many years to see Spanish in Hispanic neighborhoods, Chinese in Chinatown, or, say, Polish in certain parts of Chicago, Detroit, or Buffalo. Today in major urban areas it is not unusual to find entire blocks with signs in Korean, Vietnamese, or Amharic. American food is no longer a category composed primarily of main courses made from ground beef and desserts created with apples. Ethnic cuisines are served at nearly every corner, and they have merged and mingled to the point where pizza bagels, gyros, and tacos sometimes coexist on the same menus. McDonald's has found it necessary to add fajitas to its repertoire. And Gerber, with an eye on the Hispanic market, has introduced guava, papaya, and mango into its baby foods.

Yet there is still cause for grave concern about the reception given to people who arrive eager to become Americans. Discrimination against immigrants, in some spheres, may be more severe than ever before. Studies reveal problems with health care, education, housing, and employment reminiscent of the conditions that fueled the civil rights movement on behalf of African Americans in the 1950s and '60s. Prejudice against certain groups runs rampant, motivated perhaps by fear but every bit as vulgar and ignorant as ever. The word on the street, as it surfaces in public opinion polls and anecdotally, is that American natives believe—as it seems they always have—that many of the new immigrants are dirty and of a low moral character. The vast majority of those who think and talk that way now, ironically, are the children or grandchildren of immigrants who were described in the same terms just a few decades ago. That people at the lower end of the economic spectrum should be so easily recruited to join in this prejudice is not especially surprising, but it is disappointing for anyone who is still idealistic about the American national character.

In a flashback to the old quota days, the "real" Americans have their distinct preferences among the newcomers. Surveys reveal that virtually all Europeans—even the nationalities once discriminated against, like the Irish, Jews, Italians, and Poles—seem to have achieved relative acceptance as equals at last. Now it is the Hispanics—and "Mexicans" in particular, a category that for many people often includes undifferentiated Central Americans—who are most disliked, with Asians (especially Koreans and Vietnamese) close behind.

Clearly, the longer a group has been in the United States, the more likely it is to win approval; therein should lie a lesson.

V

ON THE BORDER:
TEXAS AND CALIFORNIA

THE POLICY DEBATES in Washington over immigration, the forums at universities and think tanks, and the musings of editorial writers and columnists on the subject sometimes overlook the fact that for the general public, the main event takes place primarily along the 1,945-mile border between the United States and Mexico. And it is the people who live in the states along that line—Texas, New Mexico, Arizona, and California—who must routinely deal with the implications of both official policy and cold, hard reality. Of course, it matters greatly what the United States does about refugees from Bosnia, dissidents from China, the survivors of African civil wars, and people fed up with the violence in Lebanon or the political turmoil everywhere from Russia to Sri Lanka to Quebec, among all the many others who want to come to America. But the day-to-day judgments that will be rendered about how well the government is coping with and regulating immigration will inevitably relate to its success or failure in managing the southern border.

In fact, according to the INS, more than half of the illegal immigrants now in the United States overstayed their visas, rather than crossing the border illegally. But as nearly anyone who follows the news knows, America has effectively lost control of the southern border, or so it appears. And that is what counts politically and in the popular discussion of immigration.

During a period of extreme economic distress in Mexico and further south, through Central America, the obvious solution has been to push north in search of work. It has looked so easy at times that people from many other parts of the world have also come to this place to try to enter the United States, and quite a few get away with it. As we shall see below, the force that has been designated to police the frontier, the hopelessly outnumbered and haplessly outmaneuvered Border Patrol, is hardly up to the task. Adding more agents—or building a higher, tougher, longer fence—barely makes a difference. To the casual observer, it is the people flooding in who seem to call the shots, and it matters not at all what the law says. Only a minority of those who cross the border illegally are apprehended, and even they often manage to manipulate the system to their advantage—filing appeals, winning delays, doing anything to avoid deportation.

The reactions to this phenomenon in California and Texas, now the two most populous states in the union, are a study in contrasts. (In border-crossing terms, Arizona and New Mexico are still only bit players.) In California, once the Golden State that seemingly had room for an unlimited number of newcomers from around the United States and abroad, the illegal immigrants have recently run into an economic downturn, American-style, and a surge of angry nativism. The result is Proposition 187, approved by voters in a statewide ballot initiative in November 1994. If upheld by the courts, Proposition 187 will deprive anyone in California who cannot prove legal residency of access to virtually all public benefits, including nonemergency medical care and use of the public schools. Meanwhile, in the Lone Star State, also in 1994, candidates who suggested military solutions to illegal immigration were rejected, and public officials aggressively pursued business deals with Mexico rather than demonizing the undocumented workers themselves.

Although both states estimate their Hispanic population at about 25 percent of the total, there are important differences between the two, their current circumstances, and their historical relationship with Mexico. Texas declared its independence from Mexico in 1836, and its admittance to the United States in 1845 was a central cause of the outbreak of the Mexican-American War. The way the episode is understood in Mexico, Texas was lost because the U.S. military had the might to win the war, but California was grabbed as part of the spoils, along with what is now Nevada and Utah, most of New Mexico and Arizona, and parts of Colorado and Wyoming. (Including Texas, Mexico lost half its national territory overall at the time.) Some Mexicans still feel angry over what they regard as this imperialist gesture by their northern neighbors, and the dramatic contrast between California's wealth and opulence, on the one hand, and the poverty of the next-door Mexican region of Baja California, on the other, has been a lingering source of resentment.

For the past century and a half, Texans and Mexicans have gotten along reasonably well and relied upon each other in various ways. The psychological and social climate along the border in Texas (and, for that matter, in New Mexico and Arizona) is entirely different from that in California. Until 1919 it was legal to vote in Texas without being a U.S. citizen, in part because the state wanted to attract more immigrants.[1] It is not surprising, then, that while many Mexican Americans still feel like outsiders in California, they have long had a major role in Texas politics and economic affairs. The Rio Grande has always been regarded by the people who live near it on both sides as a rather artificial boundary, and there is, in any event, a large buffer zone in south Texas, New Mexico, Arizona, and northern Mexico (extending through the Mexican states of Tamaulipas, Nuevo León, Coahuila, Chihuahua, and Sonora) with an agricultural economy and its own old, blended culture. The major metropolitan areas of Dallas–Fort Worth and Houston are hundreds of miles away from the border, and their residents are not especially conscious of the illegal immigrants in their midst or moving through on their way to Denver, Chicago, or other places where they find work.

San Diego and Tijuana, however, are both relatively new cities and face each other smack against the border. There is scarcely any breathing space in between. It is as if these communities were designed to prevent people from understanding each other—with the Mexicans literally able to look northward across the frontier and envy the Californians' privileges, while the Californians look south and find all their worst fears and prejudices confirmed. Indeed, the alternative name for Proposition 187 was the "Save Our State" initiative, and those who campaigned for its approval often drew on old stereotypes of immigrants as dirty people who were urinating in the streets and defecating in the bushes of Southern California's idyllic, impeccable communities. Emblematic of the distrust that prevails along the California border is the clause of Proposition 187 that requires public employees, including policemen, public health nurses, social workers, and teachers, to report to the INS anyone, of any age, who cannot prove that he or she is in the United States legally.

Another explanation for the difference in the two states' attitudes is that California has long been more generous than Texas in the social services and public benefits it offers its residents. By their own esti-

---

[1] *The first wave of immigrants to Texas, while it was still part of Mexico, actually came from Tennessee. As James Harrington, legal director of the Texas Civil Rights Project in Austin, pointed out in the Viewpoints section of the* Dallas Morning News *on December 1, 1994, these immigrants had a different color skin (white) from the natives, spoke a foreign language (English), did not pay many taxes, and were looking for free public education for their children; but, like those who came later, they worked hard and helped develop the Texas economy.*

mates, California spends $1,600 a year on each illegal immigrant in the state, and Texas only $829. Those crossing the border at San Diego tend to see Los Angeles or other major California cities as their final destination, while many of those who arrive in Texas are only passing through. So California has more to lose from the problem and, again by the counts recorded in Sacramento and Austin, almost four times as many illegal immigrants as Texas (2 million, compared to 550,000).[2]

Not surprisingly, Texas politicians thus find less value in playing the illegal-immigrant card. Neither the last Democratic governor, Ann Richards, nor her Republican successor, George W. Bush, has expressed the slightest interest in a Proposition 187–type law for Texas. Even as several other states—most notably, Florida—jumped on the bandwagon and talked about considering similar initiatives, Texas held back.

California Governor Pete Wilson, however, made illegal immigrants the scapegoats in order to come from behind and win reelection in 1994; he blamed them for California's economic crisis and, in the process, boosted his prospects as a possible Republican presidential candidate. Luckily for him, the voters did not remember that in 1985, as a U.S. senator, Wilson had pressed for the inclusion of a "guest worker" clause in the Immigration Reform and Control Act. To keep labor costs cheap in the expensive state, he urged that workers with temporary entry permits be used when necessary to pick California's abundant crops. Nor did they seem to recall that as governor, he did little to promote the enforcement of IRCA's employer sanctions for the hiring of illegal workers. Indeed, it was revealed only in 1995 that sixteen years earlier, while he was mayor of San Diego, Wilson and his former wife had hired an undocumented Hispanic woman as a housekeeper in their condominium and failed to pay the required Social Security taxes on her salary.

While Texas politicians are often warmly received in Mexico, Wilson is a well known and widely disliked figure there. His visits to San Diego and El Paso, to complain about illegal immigration and pose for photographs with Border Patrol agents, have not gone over well in the Mexican media. At one point, Wilson sought to intervene directly with the government in Mexico City to urge that it do something to stem the flow of undocumented people across the border. The foreign ministry rebuffed him and said it conducts its official business with the government in Washington, not Sacramento. Wilson's name is prominently featured on vulgar bumper stickers and the signs at protest rallies in

[2] *The INS says that both states are exaggerating the numbers. It estimates there are 1.6 million illegal immigrants in California and 405,000 in Texas. The calculation of the costs of services for illegal immigrants is also open to question; rarely are the amounts they pay in taxes, or otherwise contribute to the state economy, figured in.*

Mexico against Proposition 187; of course, all that only improves his political standing in California.

TEXAS

AT FIRST GLANCE, the house on the road that winds through the dry brush country on Brownsville's outskirts looks like any other. In fact, it is difficult to tell when you have reached your destination after a ten- or fifteen-minute drive from the center of this grimy border town of about 100,000 people along the Rio Grande. But as you draw closer, you realize that you are in the right place: The property is surrounded by a chain-link fence occasionally interrupted with chicken wire. From tall poles at the entrance fly the flags of the United States, of Texas, and of the Vatican. Beneath them a frightened-looking Spanish-speaking guard sits in a flimsy chair just inside the creaky metal gate, waiting to check the identity and guess at the intentions of anyone who wishes to enter. A tall wooden watchtower has been constructed at the edge of the large field next to the house, but when you examine it closely, it turns out to be on the other side of the property line. The shaky-looking structure was built not so that those on the inside could post a lookout for adversaries who might be approaching, but rather to help those on the outside look in and spy on the residents of the large house and its outbuildings.

This is the notorious Casa Oscar Romero, named for the Salvadoran Catholic archbishop and human rights advocate who was assassinated by a death squad on the steps of his cathedral in San Salvador in 1980. It is a way station in the lower Rio Grande Valley for undocumented immigrants who have made it across the border safely but still have no place to go. During a period of high tension in Central America in the 1980s, Casa Romero, with the support of the local Catholic diocese, became part of a modern-day underground railroad that defied federal rules and regulations and helped refugees, political or economic, from that part of the world to settle safely in American cities without going through all of the usual red tape. Today most of its residents are people who were caught in the act of entering the United States illegally but released pending asylum or deportation hearings, or who were hospitalized after crossing the border and needed a place to rest before trying to move on. The average stay here is supposed to be only ten to fifteen days; during that time, the immigrants are fed, counseled, nursed back to health, and given new clothes. Then they are on their own.

Counting the dormitory-style rooms in the buildings behind the main house, Casa Romero has a normal capacity of 200 people. At one point, there were as many as 400 men, women, and children taking refuge here (and infuriating the suspicious neighbors, who took turns watching from the tower). At the time of my visit, on a warm, breezy Saturday in October, there are only about fifty or sixty guests. A veritable exodus has recently taken place, as a result of a highly unusual INS raid. Apparently tipped off by a local television reporter that when he dropped by to do a routine story at Casa Romero there were quite a few mysterious-looking Asians living amongst the customary population of Central Americans, federal agents had barged in and arrested a large contingent of people from India, and possibly some Iranians—no one was really sure at first where they were from—on suspicion of illegal activity. While the agents were at it, they took a number of others away, too, including several Central Americans. This has cast a pall over a place known for its defiant, almost euphoric optimism, and some of the usual clientele are thought to be staying away.

"What we try to do here is all humanitarian," says Sister Norma Pimentel, a diminutive woman in dark blue who is a member of a small Catholic religious order. She has run Casa Romero for several years and had prided herself on a good relationship with local INS officials, whom she used to invite to lunch at the house from time to time for a little consciousness-raising. Indeed, the Border Patrol never seemed to pay much attention to the comings and goings at the house. "We weren't hiding anything. We in no way want to be involved in political issues. We simply stand for something very Christian and morally right," says Pimentel. Herself the daughter of Mexican immigrants who settled in Brownsville just before she was born some fifty years ago, Pimentel is still stunned by the government tactics in the raid. Sitting on a wooden bench in the field as we talk, she recalls the experience: "It was terrifying. They had officers surrounding the house. There were vehicles and helicopters, and the officers came through the fence with guns and iron rods, ready to attack us. I felt that all of Immigration was here. One lady had to leave her one-year-old child and her husband behind."[3]

---

[3] *According to Robert E. Wooten, the agent in charge of the Border Patrol station in Brownsville, the reason for the raid was that there had been a recent influx into the area of Indians from the Punjab region, and federal authorities feared there could be a connection to religious conflict and terrorist bombings in India at the time. Several undocumented Indian immigrants had already been arrested further north. All Iranian immigrants have been considered suspect ever since the American hostage crisis in Teheran of 1979–81, and in this case they seemed to have unusual access to rental cars and other resources. As for the Central Americans who were arrested at Casa Romero, says Wooten, "Once you're there, and you look at an individual and you question them and find out they're from El Salvador or Nicaragua and here illegally, you can't just turn your back and walk away. That's not what we get paid to do."*

For Pimentel, a pool-playing, down-to-earth observer of life, the problem of illegal immigration is simple. "I don't think it's good for them or good for us that these people migrate into this country," she concedes. "But their own countries are in such a bad situation, and our foreign policy must have something to do with it. They're here, and you have to deal with it. Treating them like criminals is not an answer, and that's what I feel [INS] does to them. These are human beings, and I would say that the only crime they have committed is to decide to leave their country and try to have a chance at a better life. It's hard to say what is the best solution. But there needs to be a change in immigration law, to make it more humanitarian toward people who are not a threat to our country. . . . Many of them will go back eventually. They will find that the American Dream is not here anymore. But first they need to come and make some money to help their family."

It is not difficult to find people at Casa Romero whose stories tug at the heartstrings. Take Miguel Serrano, for example. A plumber in his twenties, he had set out from his village in Honduras four months earlier with the goal of reaching Houston, where he has heard that there is plenty of work available for the fabulous sum of five dollars an hour. He had various setbacks along the way but finally found someone to give him a ride to the Mexican border town of Matamoros, just across the river from Brownsville. Twice he crossed the Rio Grande, only to be caught by the Border Patrol and shipped back to the Mexican side. On one of those occasions, he had paid a coyote $250 to take him in a pickup truck past the daunting Border Patrol checkpoint at Kingsville, 119 miles north, but he was easily detected lying under a blanket in the back of the truck. Now, after three days without sleep or food, Serrano has made it safely across the river again; just two days before my visit, he had staggered into Casa Romero on the verge of collapse. As soon as he gets his strength back, he tells me earnestly, he will find a way to earn $30—the more reasonable price demanded this time by someone he met at the house who claims to have a foolproof method of evading the checkpoint.

"It's been four months, and I haven't been able to find work," says Serrano during an interview in the nurse's office at Casa Romero. "My mother, my wife, and my child really need things, and I want to help them. Sometimes I want to cry because of all of the bad luck I have had." Should he be arrested again by the Border Patrol and request asylum in the United States, Serrano realizes, he has virtually no chance of prevailing, because his desire to immigrate is based purely on economic need. Given that there is little work available in the Rio Grande

Valley and that it could be difficult to get all the way to Houston (350 miles north) without a well-placed network of friends, some people at Casa Romero have suggested he might be better off cutting his losses and returning home before Christmas. "I have a lot of fear of returning," he says, "just because of the suffering, going through so many days of hunger and not sleeping. And I would hate to have to return home with my arms empty." But "wouldn't your family be happy to have you back, no matter what?" asks Caroline Raymond, a former Spanish teacher from New Jersey who works at Casa Romero on behalf of the Mennonite Board of Missions. She is sitting in on our conversation, helping to translate. "That's true," Serrano replies. "They love me and everything, but they're only eating once a day, and it would be nice to be able to return with something."

This is a common theme, says Raymond in an aside. "The worst thing of all for [the more desperate people at Casa Romero] would be if they had to return home with nothing to show for their hardship. They would be so ashamed, because their families are just waiting. Another person said the same thing to me the other day: 'I'm not afraid of the police, I'm not afraid of anything, I'm just afraid they'll send me back with nothing.' "

Then there is the case of Edgar Quintanilla, a more educated man who had left his pregnant twenty-three-year-old wife and young daughter in Guatemala City two months earlier; he has since learned that his son has been born. He claims to have a strong case for political asylum: He had worked first in private business and then in the army, where he was eventually put in charge of investigating the theft of a large quantity of food, clothing, and other supplies. When he began to take this assignment seriously and discovered that the ringleader of the corruption was actually his own boss, he says, he in turn became the target of a vindictive investigation. "To get information out of me, they tortured me," Quintanilla says. "They started to make anonymous calls to my house, saying that I better leave my job or I would be a dead man. When I turned in my information [on the theft ring], they sent me out on another investigation that was a trap. There were grenades and a lot of shooting. Two of my friends died, and three were hospitalized. For some people in the army, I don't exist. They think I'm dead."

Although he tried to go underground and use a different name, Quintanilla says, the anonymous threats resumed. Now feeling that he was in danger from both the Guatemalan military and the leftist guerrillas fighting against it, he decided to try to escape to the United

States.[4] "I left immediately, with just the clothes on my back and the little bit of money that I had," he recalls. "I told my wife I was leaving for my own safety, but I didn't tell her or my parents [who lived next door] where I was going. I didn't want them to know, so that no one could force the information out of them."

Traveling by bus into southern Mexico, Quintanilla says, he was repeatedly harassed, often by the police themselves; just after passing through one checkpoint, he was robbed of all his money by thieves with guns and knives. That was when he took to the rails to continue his journey north, riding freight trains and getting off occasionally in small villages, where he survived on the plates of beans that sympathetic peasants offered him. Finally, after hiding from the Border Patrol, he swam across the river and, following a tip he had received in Matamoros, made his way to Casa Romero. Quintanilla has been allowed to stay there longer than usual, as he awaits the arrival of a Canadian diplomat based in Dallas who will interview him to determine his eligibility for a Canadian asylum program. "I would like to apply here in the U.S.," he says, "but to do that, I would have to turn myself in to Immigration, and it's almost certain they'd put me in the detention facility. I don't have anybody who could get me out."

THE "DETENTION FACILITY," in this case, is the Port Isabel Service Processing Center in Bayview, about thirteen miles from Brownsville, a vast (164-acre), rather informal INS prison camp on the grounds of a former naval air station that closed in 1960. When stretched to its limit, it can hold as many as 1,600 people, but at the time of my visit, it has a population of 668, with about four men interned for every woman. Most have been arrested trying to enter the United States illegally and are awaiting "processing" of one form or another—deportation hearings, resolution of asylum claims, examination of documents, consideration of requests for release on bond, and the like. Others may

---

[4] *It is often difficult, of course, to draw as clear a line as U.S. policy dictates between political and economic motives for immigrating. But many undocumented immigrants from Central America cannily try to describe, or even invent, a plausible threat to their safety from the left, because they know this will improve their prospects for being granted political asylum in the United States. It is an established fact that INS decisions on asylum are based more on the relationship of particular governments with Washington than on the merits of each individual's case. Thus, while the Sandinistas were in power in Nicaragua, it was easier to win asylum by claiming political persecution by that left wing regime, which was hostile to the United States, than by being an opponent or a victim of the American-supported anticommunist regime in El Salvador. In Guatemala, Quintanilla's home, Washington has generally supported the military-backed governments against a left-wing insurgency.*

have had legal status in the United States but violated the terms of their visas or work permits and got caught. There is a surprising variety of humankind here, including people from China, Pakistan, and assorted countries in Central and Eastern Europe, in addition to the Central Americans.[5] Port Isabel is the United Nations of INS detention camps, and so there can be language problems that delay the resolution of some cases. But superficially, all the detainees look the same. Men and women alike, they are dressed in identical bright orange two-piece outfits; the reason for the color choice, I am told, is that it makes it much easier to spot them if they should try to escape.

This is the largest such INS processing center in the United States, and it is like a world unto itself. It has its own water and sewer plants, mechanical facilities, a large kitchen, separate men's and women's dormitories and libraries, and several playing fields. As Jesús ("Jesse") Rosales, a member of the staff, points out during an extensive tour that he proudly gives me, "We're responsible for these people twenty-four hours a day. Everyone is treated equally and fairly. We see to everyone's needs, and everyone is intermingled. We don't separate nationalities."

Among the amenities provided are washing machines, which the detainees are encouraged to use, free of charge, to launder the clothes they were wearing when they arrived at the processing center. ("They may have been wearing the same clothing for quite a while," says Rosales with a chuckle, "and therefore it's advantageous to us as well as to them" that they wash it.) In addition, there are color television sets, videocassette players (with Spanish- and English-language movie rentals provided on contract by a nearby video store), stereo systems, sewing machines, typewriters, Ping-Pong tables, and pay telephones. Weightlifting equipment is available for the men's use, and a nun visits twice weekly to offer aerobic exercise classes for the women. Uniforms can be borrowed for soccer, basketball, and volleyball. When someone can be found to teach voluntarily, English classes are also offered.

Regular religious services are provided, and also a health clinic. Everyone is given a general medical checkup and a skin test for tuberculosis on arrival. There are isolation wards for those with chicken pox, measles, and other communicable diseases, and emergency medical technicians, dentists, and psychiatrists are on call. If hospitalization is necessary in a nearby community, the INS picks up the tab. With the

[5] *Mexicans are generally not held at Port Isabel. Once apprehended, unless they are suspected of serious crimes (in which case they are charged and sent to a real prison, pending court proceedings), they are usually just taken back across the border.*

certification of the medical department, a vegetarian or non-pork diet can be arranged. Detainees are encouraged to put their jewelry, airplane tickets, any currency worth more than $30, and other valuables in the vault on arrival, but personal checks they may have received or written can be cashed before departure.

Despite this friendly aura, there is round-the-clock camera surveillance of the entire facility, inside and outside, except for the private double bedrooms in the women's dormitory. Outside security guards are also on hand to help maintain order, and they are the subject of some controversy. There are persistent reports that many immigrants—sometimes Salvadorans, at other times Haitians, or whoever else is most unpopular or restive at any given moment—have been subjected to verbal abuse and even nighttime beatings at Port Isabel. The authorities have steadfastly denied this. A few victims have gone to court charging brutality and won their cases. At the very least, says Lisa Palumbo, an attorney from Philadelphia working with Proyecto Libertad, an immigrant-rights group based in nearby Harlingen, there is substantial evidence of "psychological abuse." That usually takes the form of guards trying to bully the detainees, telling them that their efforts to stay in the United States are hopeless and that they should accept deportation.

Most people in the camp get a fresh orange uniform twice a week, but "volunteer workers" get one every day. Beyond that, the reward for taking on one of the dozens of available assignments—cutting the grass, landscaping, cleaning, painting, or working in the garage or the kitchen —is only a dollar a day. "We used to give them a pack of cigarettes each day," says Rosales, "but then the Surgeon General said that smoking causes cancer, so Congress changed it. Whether you work eight hours, four hours, or two hours, you get paid a dollar a day. A dollar is not much, but it's better than no dollar at all. We have a contract with a vending company; they can use the money to buy candy and soda pop."

A major part of the daily business at Port Isabel consists of legal procedures. Facilities are provided for lawyers (usually public defenders and members of legal-aid organizations) and paralegals to meet privately with their clients. Frequently repeated videotapes and prominently displayed forms and charts explain to the detainees the ins and outs of immigration and deportation procedures. The challenge is for each detainee to obtain representation by turning up on a volunteer lawyer's or paralegal's daily "visitation list." Under strict rules set in federal court decisions, the authorities must produce everyone on that list for an interview within fifteen minutes of the legal representative's arrival at the detention center.

This was not always the case, according to Linda Yanez, a nationally recognized immigration lawyer from Brownsville. In the early 1980s, she says, "the INS had all these Salvadorans and they were shipping them out every week, but nobody knew, because we didn't have any contact with this place. They would take them en masse before judges and ask them questions as a group: 'If you're from El Salvador, raise your hand. If you came in illegally, raise your hand. Okay, you all waive your right to appeal? Yes? Then here are your deportation orders, and you're gone.' That's what would happen. No lawyers, nothing." As a result of lawsuits brought by Yanez and others, each person's case must now be handled individually.

Still, there are long lines of people with anxious expressions on their faces outside the cubicles and offices where the daily legal consultations are being held. In most cases, the lawyers and paralegals are strangers to their clients. The immigrants know that unless they have an unusually compelling political case, they will probably be deported within thirty days of their arrival at Port Isabel. If the prospects look bad and they can arrange for "voluntary departure" before any judgment is entered against them, there is always the hope of getting in legally—or having better luck on the illegal route—in the future.

Many of the hearings are actually held on the grounds of the Processing Center itself, in a separate building housing small courtrooms presided over by "immigration judges" sent out for a year or two at a time by the Executive Office of Immigration Review in Washington. They have generally been recruited out of private practice, and they are, it is said here, "the lowest form of federal judge"—endowed with the title and trappings of judicial authority but given jurisdiction over only one basic type of not-very-interesting case. For the most part, they do not look and act as if they are enjoying their assignment to South Texas. In one courtroom that I visit on a Friday morning, an impatient judge, who is originally from New York and speaks no Spanish, dispenses with the asylum claims of the frightened-looking Central Americans who come before him in about ten or fifteen minutes each. There is a semblance of due process to the hearings, and a beleaguered interpreter seems to be making a sincere effort to explain what is happening to each defendant. But the judge, prodded by an equally beleaguered, prosecuting attorney who works for the INS and handles hundreds of similar cases every week, chides the undocumented immigrants and their lawyers not to expect him to believe their elaborate stories of probable persecution should they have to return home.

Asked during a break whether he would be willing to talk anonymously about the frustrations of doing this work on the frontier, the judge declines brusquely and refers me to a spokesman at Immigration Review headquarters in Falls Church, Virginia. He is skeptical of "the media" and does not even want me to know his name (which is, of course, a matter of public record).

A few of the defendants here win delays. Others may go free on bond, obtain permission to travel to another city in the United States, and then file for a change of venue for their asylum or deportation hearings. That is the preferred strategy of the public-interest lawyers here—to get their Central American clients out of the Rio Grande Valley as soon as possible and win them time to build a careful case on the merits that can be heard someplace where the judges may be more open-minded. But the best that some can hope will happen is for their file to go astray in the system, a not uncommon occurrence. Those who lose their cases immediately, unless they have some plausible grounds for appeal, are returned to the dormitories, perhaps for a few days, until transportation can be arranged for them to their countries of origin. "We're not in the business of separating families," says Rosales reassuringly. "If we have a husband and wife, or other family members, then when it's time for them to be removed and we have to send them back to their country, we make every effort to see that they go home together."

Rosales, who estimates that his own family has been in the lower Rio Grande Valley for four or five generations, living on one side of the border or the other, has no trouble defending his work, and he is, indeed, one of the most enthusiastic spokesmen the INS could ever find. He is a small man, with an unfailingly positive demeanor. Born and raised in Harlingen, he traveled with the military as far as Alaska but eventually came back, obtained a college degree in law enforcement, and worked his way into the job of his dreams. "This is the best thing that's happened in my life—other than my family, of course. I'm a proud American, and I feel we're doing something good here. We're looking out for people. It's humanitarian and compassionate," he tells me during our tour of Port Isabel. "As long as there's poverty in Third World countries, you can't blame a human being for trying to make a better life for himself and his family. A lot of these people are coming here for economic reasons. If I were in their shoes, I'd probably do the same thing. We're not asking them not to come, we're just asking them to try to do it legally. The law's the law."

A few miles away, in Los Fresnos, I visit a detention center of an entirely different sort—a converted hacienda where "unaccompanied minors" who have been picked up on their way into the United States await some determination of their fate. Here, along another country road, Homer Tamez, a former Texas probation officer, runs what is, in effect, a group home for about sixteen young men and women who have become separated from their families and have no place to go. It is owned and organized by a private organization, International Educational Services ("Or is it International Emergency Shelters?" wonders Tamez), under contract with the INS. In recent years, the residents have ranged in age from a year old to eighteen; most were from Central America, but some landed here from as far away as Taiwan or Hungary. At this moment, they are all teenagers who speak Spanish, if they speak at all.

The official goal of this program is "family reunification," either in the United States or back at home. In one incident that received a great deal of attention, a four-year-old Central American girl managed to stroll across the bridge between Matamoros and Brownsville by herself; she had memorized all the vital information about her family, and they were found within a few days. But sometimes it may take six months or more to bring about such a result. In the meantime, in a large modern rambler of a house where the gates and the doors are never locked, the mostly teenaged immigrants play Ping-Pong, listen to blaring rock music, and appear to enjoy a certain camaraderie. If they are difficult, they undergo various "behavior modification" schemes. Everything takes place in Spanish, and on the surface it is a low-key operation. Although officially in custody, the residents appear free to wander off but rarely do. By their general cooperation and their participation in education programs (including English classes) and household chores, they can earn points toward a weekly allowance of five or six dollars; efforts are made to teach them how to manage that money wisely. When they misbehave, they are denied access to television or the swimming pool.

In about 70 percent of the cases that arrive at Los Fresnos from Central America, Tamez says, parents have actually sent their children out, planning to join them later and hoping they will, in the meantime, connect with relatives in the United States.[6] "The first two or three nights the kids are here, they are so scared that you find many of them sleeping under their beds," Tamez says. A few, having suffered from malnutrition in the past or on their journey, overeat and soon become sick from the rich or greasy food. Some of the young women in his care,

---

[6] *There is a separate detention facility, or shelter, nearby for entire families that have been arrested crossing the border together.*

Tamez discovered, had been raped on their way through Mexico and, as a result, have now been rejected by their families. In one case, he recalls, a teenage girl was told by her father, "You are no longer a virgin. You could have prevented the rape. But you are not a lady anymore, so I don't want you." They, and others whose American relatives refuse to take them in, become very difficult to place—the district director of INS only occasionally approves sponsorship of an undocumented child immigrant by people who are not related to him or her—and their palpable sadness hangs heavily over the house. Some lie silently in their bunk beds, while others seem almost glued to couches, staring at a television set or into space. For everyone, there is the looming dread of deportation back to an unhappy, deprived existence, unless something else can be worked out.

One seventeen-year-old boy from a provincial city in Nicaragua, who says he left home to avoid military service, tells of being sexually molested by a man in Mexico who identified himself as a priest and gave him shelter. Once he escaped from that tormentor, he says, he was beaten up by bandits and twice had money stolen from him by Mexican immigration officers. Each time, he found work again and earned money to try to get across the border. Once he did cross, he had almost made it to Houston when the Border Patrol finally arrested him and sent him to Los Fresnos. A former athlete, he arrived at Tamez's facility hungry and looking like a skeleton. After he regained his strength and rebuilt his body, he acted out his anger and became a behavior problem at the house, punching holes in the walls and otherwise resisting the rules. Now calmer, he is nonetheless defiant. "He's made it very clear to me," says Tamez, "that if he's told he's going to be deported, he does not intend to go. Or that if he does go, he'll be back."

Indeed, many of these teenagers are street-savvy, better at beating the system than the system is at handling them. One sixteen-year-old boy from Honduras, "Tony," abandoned by his mother and left to care for his younger sisters when he was only eleven years old, reveals that he has had several previous sojourns on his own in the United States. He speaks knowledgeably about El Paso, Austin, and San Antonio and boasts about excursions he says he has made to Arizona, Florida, and California. Although he is illiterate, Tony has managed remarkably well, finding menial jobs and relying on the kindness of strangers. Each time, "when he's tired of working and cooking for himself, he just turns himself in," Tamez explains. While he waits for the wheels of the deportation process to turn slowly, this time he finds food and shelter, and some indulgence, at Los Fresnos. Tony's goal in life, he tells me, is to see

New York City, and Tamez is convinced that he may take off at any moment to realize that or some other ambition.

Tamez, who seems to become very close to some of the youngsters in his care, has an ambiguous role. He grew up in this corner of Mexamerica with many of the people who are in charge of policing the border or punishing those who are caught crossing it illegally; the deputy director of the local INS office, for example, was a school chum. Yet Tamez does not see himself as part of law enforcement, and he feels that one of the strengths of the home he runs at Los Fresnos is its bureaucratic distance from the formal INS and Justice Department structure. He takes bittersweet pride from the fact that many of the young people who leave after a long stay are on the phone within forty-eight hours, asking his advice or pleading to come back. But he recoils from the notion that his facility could be seen to be performing a sanctuary role like that of Casa Romero. "I believe in rules, I believe in regulations, and I believe in standards," he says, insisting that he would never tacitly encourage violating immigration law.

Mostly, though, Tamez worries that for every immigrant teenager who comes through Los Fresnos, there are dozens, if not hundreds, more out there on their own in America, dispersed across a vast country without anyone who feels responsible for them. There is no count. No one knows who they are, where they are, or what will become of them.

THE 868-MILE Texas border with Mexico is, by any standard, easily penetrable, and the law-enforcement net stretched across it by the INS is very loose indeed; some would say hardly more than symbolic. For anyone who is truly determined to get into the United States, it is not difficult to slip through. There are, to be sure, occasional upgrades in the enforcement effort, with impressive results. For example, in the Brownsville area, which is part of the Border Patrol's McAllen Sector, there was Operation Hold-the-Line in 1989, the stuff of local legends, when that segment of the border zone was flooded with extra agents and the Port Isabel processing center suddenly found itself with some 2,000 new arrivals (requiring major reinforcements of personnel and equipment). Many of them had to be detained outdoors in tents. The next year, when additional agents were brought to Brownsville temporarily from other parts of Texas, Operation Summer Heat produced about 4,000 arrests in a thirty-day period.

In the fall of 1993, all the way at the other end of Texas, an angry regional Border Patrol chief in El Paso, Silvestre Reyes, pressured Washington to give him a special allocation of $300,000 to pay overtime for a round-the-clock Operation Blockade. (He is the same man who, as the sector chief in McAllen, had ordered the controversial raid on Casa Romero a few years earlier.) Deploying 400 officers as a "human fence" along a twenty-mile stretch of the frontier between El Paso and its Mexican twin city of Ciudad Juárez, Reyes received national publicity for dramatically reducing the flow of undocumented immigrants across the border. The net was suddenly so tight in this one spot that for a time (at least until new routes could be found), the number of people picked up for crossing illegally declined by 80 percent; they were simply unable to get through. Meanwhile, the El Paso police said the blockade had significantly lowered the incidence of burglaries and other petty crimes in the downtown business district. There was a substantial cost to be paid, however, as El Paso retailers saw their trade fall by 10 percent to 15 percent and many housekeepers and other undocumented Mexican workers were unable to make their daily trip to low-wage jobs in Texas. Catholic bishops on both sides of the border criticized the operation for putting high-profile, short-term police accomplishments ahead of the larger economic interests of the region and its many poor families.

More typical, though, is the staffing available to the Border Patrol in the Brownsville area at the time of my visit—approximately forty officers to cover all shifts over a seventy-eight-mile stretch of the Rio Grande, heading inland from its mouth on the Gulf of Mexico. This is a particularly popular transit point because it lies at the end of the most direct route from Mexico City and the Mexican interior to the United States. Many potential immigrants have learned that unless they have family or other support waiting for them in California, they are probably better off trying to cross the border here. Transportation is relatively good through Mexico to Matamoros and then onward into Texas from the lower Rio Grande Valley, but there is little of the confusion and danger associated with the Southern California freeways. Because Texas politicians have put far less pressure on the INS than their California counterparts, the chances of being caught may be lower here. Local observers estimate that the average daily capture rate lies somewhere between 10 percent and 30 percent of those crossing illegally, but no one really knows.

"To be honest," says Robert E. Wooten, chief of the Border Patrol station in Brownsville, "we can effectively cover only about six or seven miles of the river," even then concentrating primarily on the urban area between and around the two local bridges over the Rio Grande, which accounts for a stretch of but three or four miles. "There's so much left undone. This station needs about 120 agents in the field, not counting clerical support. We're putting a dent in illegal immigration here, but we're not a big stumbling block,'' Wooten admits.

Even a dent would seem to be an exaggeration, on the basis of the long Friday night duty I spend in the company of Border Patrol agent Rory Craft. A large, thirty-four-year-old black man from a ghetto neighborhood in Cleveland, Craft took up law-enforcement work after obtaining an agricultural degree from Ohio State. He is a thoughtful, introspective loner who has already begun studying toward a master's degree and plans one day to earn a doctorate. In the meantime, he enjoys the quiet life in the Rio Grande Valley, where he believes he is serving his country on the front lines. He eschews the vulgar, anti-immigrant patter that I hear from some of his more macho colleagues, in favor of philosophical musings about what draws people to America. Still he must endure constant frustration in trying to police the frontier.

There is no fence here. And at Brownsville, the Rio Grande, despite its name, is a small river that twists and turns unpredictably and often looks like little more than a minor stream or a brook. As its path has shifted over the years, so has the border; there are places now where the river bed is so narrow and in dry periods the water level so low that it is literally possible to walk across, hopping from rock to rock. Indeed, the easiest spots to cross the line in the dead of night are those where Brownsville and Matamoros come so close together that they are indistinguishable from even a short distance away. The grass on the river-banks is tall and thick, providing excellent hiding places, and the roads nearby on the U.S. side are sometimes only narrow dirt tracks. There are no streetlights. Certainly the people who live in the neighborhoods that lie just beyond the sorghum fields or citrus groves or garbage heaps on either side of the border look no different from each other, and they are, at best, indifferent to the effort to keep undocumented immigrants out of the United States. There is plenty of help available for those who have gotten through. The many safe houses where they can find temporary refuge are well concealed, but everyone knows where specialized taxis are lined up near the border, waiting to whisk new arrivals out of heavily patrolled downtown Brownsville cheaply and quickly.

To be thrust into this environment as a border guard, driving a large, lumbering light-green van that can be heard from hundreds of yards away, is not an enviable situation. At times the tactical advantage seems to lie clearly with the immigrants, and it is difficult to say who are the hunters and who the prey. Often the Border Patrol officers are pelted with stones, and there are places under Brownsville's two bridges where, if they are on foot, they are literally spat upon by bandits and teenaged border-crossers who know all the tricks and easily evade capture. There has been a significant amount of drug traffic in this area over the years, and in the season after Mexico's marijuana crop has been harvested, the agents feel especially vulnerable.

During our nocturnal prowl together, Craft follows what he tells me is a familiar ritual. He seems resigned but slightly apprehensive. One of our first stops is the eerily dark and silent railroad yard on the edge of Brownsville, a dangerous place, he says, because the switching of the freight cars occurs very quietly and many of them contain toxic chemicals. After we have pulled in and sat talking for a few minutes, Craft gets out, looks underneath and between some of the trains, and then climbs up and shines his high-powered flashlight into the boxcars but finds no one. Later in the evening, he learns on his two-way radio, to his dismay, that several people were actually found stowed away on the same boxcars when they arrived at the freight yards in Harlingen, twenty miles north. He rationalizes (as do I, for that matter) that they must have hidden in the bushes and hopped on board only as the train left the Brownsville yard; certainly we could not see them. Next, we patrol along the river, and Craft, one hand always poised to draw his revolver, searches in the bushes and shines his light into parked cars, looking for other "aliens" who might be hiding. He turns up only startled lovers or derisive young people drinking beer.

There was a time, Craft says, when the Border Patrol could just look for people whose clothes were wet from crossing the river and know they were "illegal" (thus evolved the pejorative term "wet" or "wetback," used here by some to describe a Mexican, or even any Hispanic). Now many bring along a change of clothes in a plastic bag or have coyotes who steer them to the drier areas. Still, Craft explains as we cruise the city streets near the border, he believes there are reliable ways to pick out "an illegal alien" in a crowd. "They just look like they don't belong. You could see an illegal Mexican who is around a bunch of Americans, and you can still tell. Just like you can pick out anybody who's a foreigner, no matter if they're white or black. It's body language." This was especially true, he says, when he had the duty of patrolling the local airport. The undocumented immigrants with enough money to fly were dead giveaways; they acted nervous and looked as if they were worried about being caught.

The two-way radio describes a fair amount of action on this Friday night: ground sensors going off in the western part of the McAllen Sector, suspected drug runs, a futile chase, and the like. Craft has had his share of excitement in the past, too, and he has plenty of war stories to tell. For example, there was the time when, as a trainee, he was confronted by a youngster wielding an ice pick in an abandoned hotel in a notoriously tough border area near Brownsville called "the cut." (His supervisor let him keep the ice pick as a memento.) And he still remembers with amazement the discovery that a quiet, intelligent young Mexican boy who had befriended him turned out to be a sixteen-year-old cold-blooded murderer.

Perhaps it is because he is being restrained and avoiding the real hot spots while a visitor is along, but Craft's only action on this shift involves taking custody of three young Mexican boys from the Brownsville Police Department at a corner gas station. They had been picked up for loitering after crossing the border illegally. Two of them are only eight years old; the police say that the third one, taller and more brazen, is sixteen, but he tells Craft he is fourteen and confides to me that he is really only twelve. He definitely seems to be in a state of altered consciousness, whether from drinking alcohol, taking drugs, or (a favorite around here) sniffing paint or chemicals. The three boys are herded onto benches in the locked area in the rear of the van and driven back to the border. They sit and laugh as they watch the ungainly Craft struggle to help two even younger children lift a large bag of onions over the barbed wire barrier near the INS and Customs station. At about 11:00 P.M., after making a record of the names they gave him and completing elaborate paperwork about their apprehension, Craft lets the boys out of the van and sends them walking across the bridge to Matamoros. He figures they will be back in the morning.

Craft says he can put up with unproductive stints like this, but not with the negative public image of the Border Patrol. "We're out here running a risk," he says, "but we get portrayed as mindless Neanderthals. It's like a type of zealotry that exists with certain alien-rights groups. No matter what, we're going to be portrayed as the evil side. There's no gray areas. But the Border Patrol ends up doing a lot of humanitarian things."

He offers examples: "The year before last, it was unusually cold weather down here. We had about thirty or forty Nicaraguans cross the river one day, when it was about thirty degrees. They undressed, crossed nude or seminude, and some of these people came close to freezing to death. And we were the ones out there, taking off our coats and jackets, trying to get them warm. Last year, some of our agents encountered a group of women and children [crossing the border]. It was real cold outside, and they took them right to the Red Cross shelter, where they were able to get proper medical attention. They weren't thinking about apprehensions; they were more concerned about getting these people to a warm place and having them looked after. We do a lot of things like that, but it never seems to get mentioned. It's ignored. That's one of the things that really get at me, when some of these groups are criticizing us. They're not the ones on the river risking their lives. Sure, we're apprehending illegal aliens—that's our job—but a lot of the agents here do have a degree of sensitivity. We aren't mindless Neanderthals.''

NOT ALL MEXICAN immigration or visitation to the United States is illegal, unauthorized, or illicit. Far from it. During the three-year period following passage of the 1990 immigration bill—which, among other things, made it possible for people who received amnesty under the Immigration Reform and Control Act of 1986 to bring in their immediate relatives on an expedited basis—Mexico was estimated to be sending north at least 100,000 permanent legal immigrants a year, vastly more than any other individual country. Indeed, American consular officers stationed in various Mexican cities deal daily with an avalanche of requests to cross the border legally and for varying periods of time. In the northern industrial city of Monterrey alone, the busiest U.S. consular post in the world for visas, more than 160,000 nonimmigrant, or visitor's, visas (valid for periods ranging from one month to ten years) were issued in 1991. Some percentage of these, it can safely be assumed, will have gone to people who were planning an extended, perhaps even lifelong, visit.

The processing of requests for the assorted types of visas requires a great deal of patience but also generates a considerable measure of cynicism on both sides. "If you interview fifty people [who are applying for immigrant visas] here on a given day, you can be reasonably sure that at least ten of them are lying to you," said one foreign service officer who spoke with me at his post in Mexico but asked not to be identified by name. "You can also be reasonably sure that two or three of them are concealing some serious ineligibility and know that they are. I know I'm not going to succeed absolutely [in identifying those people], but I'll do my damnedest." Still, it is a given that a certain number of applicants are getting away with using phony birth certificates, which are easy to obtain in Mexico, or claiming marriages and other relationships that are fraudulent. Such cheating is encouraged, in the view of this veteran of visa lines around the world, by the U.S. immigration laws' heavy emphasis on "family unification." Some people who lack the parents, spouse, or children to qualify them for a priority visa simply create them for the occasion.

Those who do not qualify for expedited processing but instead fall into traditionally lower categories of visa preference (siblings of U.S. citizens or legal residents, for example), may have to wait a very long time for official approval to immigrate. Because of numerical restrictions on the number of people in each category of preference who can be legally admitted each year from particular countries, Mexicans being sponsored by their American siblings in the early 1990s went onto a twelve-year waiting list. And that was considered a material improvement over the fifteen-year backlog that had prevailed during the late 1980s. But reality can be quite different from the official version of events. "Oftentimes, by the time these people get around to being processed," admits the same consular officer, "they've already been in the States for quite a while." Some have had student or work visas; others have been skirting the law as long-term visitors or taking the chance of staying without a visa. When finally called in for an appointment, they simply return from their American homes to the appropriate consulate in Mexico—for immigrant visas, it is usually Juárez or Tijuana—to pick up their formal stamp of approval. For those living in the southwestern United States, it can all be done by car, and the whole round trip takes only a day or two.

Do the American diplomats feel as if they are participating in a charade, helping trick their own country into letting more Mexicans immigrate? They apparently try not to think about it. "In all seriousness," said the consular officer, "when we talk about immigration at this level, we are mostly concerned with the absolute logistics of getting things accomplished. We have had to adopt measures to accommodate the enormous pressures. Despite all the problems and the pitfalls, we have managed to process increased numbers of people."

In places like Monterrey, the approval rate for nonimmigrant visas is up around 85 percent, and, as one American diplomat there put it, "we're more inclined to give a maximum visa [for a longer stay] than a minimum one, mainly because we're dealing with such huge numbers that we don't want to have to see the same people again." There is, in any event, a certain assumption of futility in denying a visitor's visa to Mexicans who apply. It costs only about six dollars for a one-way bus ticket from Monterrey to Nuevo Laredo (the old twin border city of Laredo, Texas), a three-hour trip that is easy to make with or without permission. It is similarly easy to reach Reynosa, the newer community that has sprung up across the river from McAllen. Billboards along the roads in the Monterrey region advertise the outlet malls and other bargain stores in Laredo and McAllen (which are closer, smaller, and more welcoming places than Brownsville) and give very specific instructions in Spanish on how to find them. Everyone on both sides of the border knows that the economy of these Texas border towns is highly dependent on free-spending shoppers from Mexico. A story much told at the American consulate in Monterrey has it that an official there who one morning denied a visitor's visa to a Mexican found himself standing in line behind the same person at McDonald's in Laredo just a few hours later.

For the Mexicans, this cross-border traffic is all part of their obsessional love-hate relationship with the United States. There is a sense of shame that in one region of Oaxaca state, some of the poorest villages are now inhabited primarily by women and children, because most of the able-bodied men have found it necessary to go north, legally or illegally, to make money they can send home. Yet, at the same time, there is a sense of pride that the men have the strength and the courage to do something about their families' plight. Whether talking with businessmen in Monterrey, government officials in Mexico City, or people who are actually crossing the border at Matamoros, one hears the argument that the migration is a temporary phenomenon that will go away as soon as Mexico's economy is stronger. Mexicans greatly admire the United States, its culture, and the opportunities it offers, it is said, but would really much prefer to stay in Mexico if they could.

"You should see how many legal Mexican residents of the U.S. come back at Christmastime to visit their relatives and spend the holidays here. There are caravans of cars crossing the border," says Mauricio Posas Garsa, who runs a factory outside of Monterrey. "Many people from other countries, they don't want to know anything more about their country after they leave and start a new life. But Mexicans still love their country and want to come back." In fact, many Mexican immigrants postpone becoming U.S. citizens; some live for years, even decades, content with the green cards that give them legal status while they wait for the perfect moment to return home. Once the North American Free Trade Agreement (NAFTA) takes full effect, Posas Garsa argues, there will be a significant change in the immigration pattern. "In the long run," he says, "if the business and economic situation in Mexico improves, if people have decent jobs and a chance of earning more here, they will not be so tempted to go to the U.S."

But it could be thirty years or more before there is any meaningful or widespread economic improvement in Mexico and Central America. And in the meantime, another sordid and ugly business has grown up within Mexico as a side effect of the immigrant traffic; it involves the

systematic exploitation and brutal treatment of those who are trying to
leave and those who are passing through from Central America. In
some instances, the bandits and the policemen have become virtually
indistinguishable from one another in their vicious treatment of the
strangers who arrive in their towns. As a result, new watchdog units—
most notably, near the border, "Grupo Beta"—have been created, theoretically to protect the immigrants; the members of these units, in turn,
have been accused of committing their own abuses.

Andrés Cuellar, a human-rights activist in Matamoros, across from
Brownsville, estimates that in a typical week, as many as twenty Central
Americans may be arrested by the local police there. A few are charged
with legitimate violations, but many, he says, are tortured, denied food,
and held incommunicado. Occasionally the pretext is given of an investigation into the smuggling of aliens or drugs through Mexico, but
the immigrants are usually held or released entirely at the whim of local
commanders. Once they have been robbed of any money or possessions
they may have brought along, the Central Americans are generally
deported across Mexico's border with Guatemala, to make their way
home or to try again.[7]

Dealing with these problems is a principal duty of Mexico's National Human Rights Commission, which is based in the capital and
reports directly to the president. Its goal, says Miguel Iguiñiz, a member of the commission, is to "tear down the wall of impunity" that
Mexican law-enforcement officials have used to persecute immigrants.
"We have not done all that I would like to, but things have started to
change," according to Iguiñiz. He cites a few instances around the
country where "local authorities are punishing their own people [who
have been caught mistreating immigrants]. That's a hard thing to do."
Others, however, suggest that the commission is toothless, that it does
not really have enough clout to make a difference in Mexico's authoritarian political culture.

[7] *Mexico, which used to have a rather nonchalant attitude toward the traffic across its own
southern border, instituted much tougher enforcement measures during the presidency of Carlos
Salinas de Gortari. According to figures provided to the U.S. Embassy in Mexico City by the
Mexican government, only 15,000 people were deported altogether during the six-year period before
Salinas took office. In 1988, his first year in office, 13,000 illegal immigrants (almost all of them,
presumably, from Central America) were arrested and deported; by 1991, that number had
increased to more than 133,000. As one official at the American embassy put it, "They are finally
looking at their own back door." The tougher Mexican attitude is generally welcomed by the INS,
since it tends ultimately to reduce the flow of Central Americans into the United States; but some
American policymakers accuse the Mexicans of hypocrisy for, at the same time, advocating weaker
enforcement along their northern frontier.*

Ultimately, Iguiñiz says, the solution to the many problems of immigration across the U.S.–Mexican border will be neither to encourage it nor to restrict it, but to "respect it" as an inevitable phenomenon. "We should let them go, and you should let them come," he says. "There should be a joint agreement on immigration, with legal migrant workers allowed to cross and return. Mexico should have a quota, perhaps 200,000 a year. The border cannot be rigid. These people have a basic right to live, and crossing the border is responding to that right. They have to go. It is a human need. And there is not much the authorities can do at the border to stop that immigration."

As for the resistance to such numbers by African Americans and others who feel economically threatened by immigration, "I can understand their feelings," Iguiñiz concedes. "But I think that your society as a whole should make more of an effort to educate people about human rights, tolerance, interdependence, and the benefits the U.S. has received in some periods of history from being close to Mexico. They must understand that you cannot have a tightly sealed border when you are dealing with people."

NO ONE is about to say so publicly, but Iguiñiz's proposals have implicitly taken effect already in the lower Rio Grande Valley. The Border Patrol has essentially written off the area as a transitional zone, where at any given time a certain number of undocumented Mexican immigrants are bound to live and work, and many others to pass through unchallenged. (The attitude toward Central Americans is not nearly so permissive, which is why their lawyers try to move them out quickly.) Especially toward the end of some months, when the Brownsville Border Patrol station has used up its overtime allowance, there are nights when the border is hardly policed at all; that fact is well known on both sides of the river. A far more credible effort is made to intercept people at places like the Kingsville checkpoint along Interstate 77—situated, Temecula-like, in one of those mountain passes that anyone traveling by land must go through en route to Corpus Christi, San Antonio, Houston, or beyond. Mexicans who can find something to do further south are likely to be undisturbed.

As a result of a constant infusion of Mexicans and a lack of major industrial development, "the valley" has changed relatively little over the years, retaining its agricultural economy and its unique Mexican-American character. "It's a very distinct culture," surprisingly isolated from trends even in other parts of Texas, says Lisa Palumbo, the attorney from Proyecto Libertad. "There is a certain calmness here that is nice, but on the other hand, it feels oppressive at times. There's a lot of pressure in life here. People are struggling, and you see it every day." The Brownsville-Harlingen metropolitan statistical area is wealthier by far than Matamoros, where about half a million people live on the other side of the river mostly in poverty, but it still has a cost of living and an average per capita annual income that are among the very lowest in the United States. It has a fairly steady unemployment rate of about 10 percent (in some counties, even higher). Harlingen, in particular, despite modest population growth, a modern airport, and excellent interstate highway connections, remains a sleepy Western town with a quiet main street that features small old-fashioned shops and a family-owned all-night café. It is about half the size of Brownsville and is just far enough away from the border not to share Brownsville's high crime rate, red-light district, and civic cynicism.[8]

On the edge of the valley's cities and small towns are squalid *colonias,* housing developments where large impoverished immigrant families, documented and undocumented alike, still live in conditions not much different from those they left behind in rural Mexico. While they may write home that they have their own houses, just like the typical *norteamericanos* everyone has seen on television, they confront daily life without running water, indoor plumbing, sewage lines, paved streets, or, in some cases, even electricity. They have to wonder what they really accomplished by crossing the border. (Some of the *colonias* were built by unscrupulous real estate developers who sold tiny shacks to naive immigrants for a dollar down and ninety-nine dollars a month for fifty years.) These are the unskilled workers who did not have family or friends waiting for them in Houston, Denver, or Chicago and must eke out an existence here on the fringe and hope that their children will one day do better.

Even in a substantially Hispanic environment, these people are outcasts—worse, scapegoats for the local well-to-do Mexican Americans who have turned very conservative. As they accumulate more and more material possessions, some of the established *mexicanos* in America complain loudly about the welfare burden the new immigrants represent. "There's a real heavy emphasis on assimilation here," says Linda Yanez, the immigration lawyer, who likes to point out that her own ancestors were in the region well before the *Mayflower* sailed. But when

---

[8] *Harlingen earned fleeting and dubious celebrity during the 1980s, when President Ronald Reagan, justifying his administration's support for the* contra *rebels in Nicaragua, cited it as the first American city that might be threatened by the Sandinistas if they were to march, or even just spread their allegedly procommunist philosophy, northward through Mexico.*

does a Mexican become a Mexican American, and when just a plain old, garden-variety American? "People whose parents or grandparents came illegally will say, 'I made it, I'm anglicized, I'm not going to teach my kids Spanish,' " explains Yanez. "They want to be as white as possible."

It is a scenario that many of the pillars of today's community lived through in their own youth. Some are still bitter. Igno Peña, for example, runs the South Texas Immigration Council, which tries to help poor Mexicans in the valley avoid deportation and move toward becoming naturalized citizens. As we sat talking in his modest storefront office on a Harlingen side street one Saturday morning, he told of being born in an American hospital in 1949, shortly after his parents had made the journey from central Mexico and crossed the border illegally. He has a vivid memory of the moment, a few years later, when federal agents raided his family's little house, put them all on a bus to a detention center, and then shipped them back to Mexico. This was during the INS crusade of that moment, Operation Wetback.

The Peña family got back across the river into America fairly quickly. His parents obtained legal status in the 1950s, and Igno and his younger brother soon managed to enroll in the local public schools. Elementary school, where the population was uniformly Mexican, went smoothly for them, but Peña recalls that "it was in seventh grade where we first mixed with Anglos," and that was when the problems began. When they and the other immigrant children spoke English, they sounded funny, even to the people from more established families with Hispanic surnames, yet when they spoke Spanish amongst themselves, they got into trouble. "This was in the early sixties. They would give you a warning: 'No more Spanish, or you go to the office.' There would be no questions asked. If you disobeyed the order not to speak Spanish, you'd be sent to the principal for punishment. You'd bend over, and he'd give you one or two strokes with the paddle."

Although things have never gone quite as far as in California, there has been a history of tension in Texas over access to the public schools for illegal immigrants. In 1975 the Texas state legislature enacted a law withholding state funds from local school districts for the education of children not "legally admitted" to the United States and authorizing the school districts to prevent them from enrolling. In a landmark decision in 1982, the U.S. Supreme Court declared that law to be in violation of the Equal Protection Clause of the Constitution. Justice William Brennan, writing for the 5–4 majority, said that a state could not "deny a discrete group of innocent children the free public education that it offers to other children residing within its borders."[9]

While that test of the Texas law was still pending in the federal courts, the Texas Education Agency tried an end run, using the Brownsville School District—the school system with the highest population of illegal immigrant children in the state—as a worst-case scenario. The agency argued that the illegal immigrants' presence affected the economic interests of the state and compromised the Brownsville schools' ability to educate the students who were legally in the country; this objection was swept aside. Public officials in Brownsville insist that its school district now spends some $20 million a year to educate children who live there illegally or do not actually live there at all, but commute daily across the border from Mexico.

Although he has four thoroughly Americanized children, Peña says he is still stopped occasionally by the Border Patrol and quizzed about his immigration status. He speculates that this is because he "looks Mexican" and drives a pickup truck. "They think I'm one of these undocumented people that has some sort of schooling"—a category often singled out for particular harassment. Indeed, he says, "down here Hispanics always do have to carry identification cards. At one point, INS was issuing immigration documents to citizens that didn't speak English. It was helpful. There are a lot of them, and there's very little difference [in appearance] between them and the people coming in. If you're there with your documents, you can avoid harassment." Whenever there is a furor over the possibility of instituting a national photo identification card as a means of dealing with illegal immigration, Peña adds, Hispanics in south Texas laugh. "We're used to carrying IDs," he says.

Hernan González, who was also born in the valley in the late 1940s to undocumented immigrant parents, went off to the air force for four years after high school. He eventually came back to earn undergraduate and master's degrees and to have a career as a social worker in the Hispanic community. He was one of the guiding lights behind the creation of Casa Oscar Romero. "I don't go as far as some of my colleagues, who claim that the border doesn't really exist," says González.

[9] *The Supreme Court decision came in a case known as* Plyler v. Doe, *arising out of the attempt by the schools in Tyler, Texas, to enforce the 1975 law. In a concurring opinion that foreshadowed the controversy over California's Proposition 187 (enacted in late 1994), Justice Lewis Powell argued that the illegal immigrant "children should not be left on the streets uneducated." Civil rights groups that later sued to prevent the enforcement of Proposition 187 would cite* Plyler *as a relevant precedent.*

"I think it does exist. There is a real division of economic, social, and political systems" between the United States and the countries to the south. But, he adds, "there is a flow of people and family relationships" that transcends the official frontier and renders it irrelevant in many people's lives. They cross back and forth all the time, he says, treating it more as an inconvenience than a meaningful barrier.

González tells the story of his son, at age seven, asking, "Dad, do you know any illegal aliens?" "Yeah," the father answered, "your grandpa and grandma!" His consciousness raised, the boy said, "Oh!" and dropped the subject.

The only real strangers in the valley, according to González, are "the snowbirds," the 100,000 or so people who come to winter there every year from the upper Midwest and Canada. They stay in trailer parks and mobile homes but venture out in the mild weather to sample life along the border and the Gulf, which they find exotic. As González describes them, "They are usually over fifty-five, and they have already raised their kids. They have culture shock here. They say, 'Hey, you're educating Mexicans.' We say, 'No, these are American kids,' and they are amazed. You can see all the mainline American views personified in these winter visitors."

For González, with all the Mexicans and the others who come through, the Rio Grande Valley has become, in effect, a new Ellis Island, a place where American principles of diversity and tolerance have been put to another impromptu test. "People accepted cultural diversity when it meant primarily white folk who were diverse from other white folk," he says with a laugh. "But now we find that people come in all different colors and shapes. We are asking what flavor America we really want. If we want to be true to a value system that is very inclusive, we should have a Statue of Liberty right here on the river."

In the balmy autumn twilight, I take up Sister Norma Pimentel's invitation to return to Casa Romero for Saturday night Mass. It is held outdoors, under the still-green trees, and about forty people from the odd assortment of Central Americans now staying at the house sit intermingled with staff members and visitors on folding chairs or long wooden benches that are splintering and badly need a paint job. It is an avant-garde affair, and rather than hymns from a hymnal, they sing upbeat Spanish songs of protest and hope from a homemade song sheet. Accompanied by a guitar, they clap heartily to the beat, with a staccato triple clap between verses and choruses; the children, whose faces look otherwise somber, seem particularly to enjoy this.

The actual service is conducted by a missionary priest who comes originally from Chicago but has worked in the Rio Grande Valley for several years. Riding his weekly circuit, he arrives in a car, steps out, and looks around; after a few minutes of chatting with individuals and learning that they are mostly from Guatemala or Honduras, he takes his place at the makeshift, portable altar atop a card table. He sings and claps, too, with great gusto. "You must forgive the *norteamericanos,*" the priest tells the worshipers during a brief sermon in Spanish. "They are the children of immigrants themselves. They understand what you want, and they know what is right. You must have faith. Someday soon they will welcome you." Then he gets back in his car and drives on to his next stop.

CALIFORNIA

It is a clear, beautiful July evening in Tijuana. The air is crisp in Colonia Libertad, a community that was originally established in the 1920s as a squatter colony for Mexicans who had failed in their effort to settle in California but did not want to return to their home villages. Located right on the U.S. frontier, it is still one of this seething border city's most dilapidated, ungovernable neighborhoods.

At dusk on this Monday, Colonia Libertad is settling down to its standard nightly business of shipping people off to the United States. A heavy quiet descends as the sun reaches the horizon, but there are still a few wisps of radio music in the air, along with the fading shouts of children playing. Electric lights (usually bare bulbs) shine from many windows, most of which have bars on them. In some of the little houses stacked up along the hillside one can see a family gathered in front of a television set, seemingly unaware of (or at least indifferent to) the ritual that is unfolding outside. They are watching old American movies or a Mexican news anchor who is droning on about the prospects for a North American free trade agreement, which is in the final stages of negotiation.

In the distance, a half mile or so inside Mexico, a Ferris Wheel turns slowly. Overhead, about every ten minutes, a plane banks steeply after taking off from the Tijuana airport, whose runways abut the border; if you sit on the right side of the plane during takeoff, it is said, you can have a brief good view of the border-crossing action below.

A sturdy, new, twelve-foot, black corrugated-metal border fence—apparently fashioned out of high-tech materials left over from the Persian Gulf War—was extended into this neighborhood just about a month ago by the U.S. Army Corps of Engineers, with the help of the National Guard. It replaced a rickety, old mostly chain-link barrier that heavy rains had washed away in places. About every twenty feet, where the new opaque fence sections are joined, one can look through small, oddly shaped holes to see the famous "soccer field," or *cañón zapata*, on the American side. This is one of the spots where equally skittish would-be immigrants and U.S. Border Patrol officers have been acting out a cat-and-mouse game for decades. Its name comes from the fact that for years brazen young men from Mexico and beyond actually passed their time and used up their nervous energy playing soccer here, just along the border, until they felt ready to make a dash for it deeper into the United States (or were chased back into Mexico). There were even lines on the field and metal goals with nets until the Border Patrol took them away. In those days, sympathetic Mexican priests would sometimes come across and say an impromptu Mass for the hundreds of people who would gather at a time, as the Border Patrol watched helplessly from a distance. Now the field is hilly and barren, unusable for religious rituals or soccer or any other sport—made that way on purpose, churned up by earth-moving equipment, as an angry American tactic in the unwinnable immigration war. Viewed through the fence at this hour from the last centimeter of Mexican territory, it is dark and forbidding.

But if there is a no-man's-land just north of this section of the border, the city of Tijuana rubs provocatively up against it on the south. In this neighborhood, Colonia Libertad, there is a virtual river of trash in the dusty, unpaved street that runs steeply downhill on the Mexican side of the fence, past a quaint old granite marker that once indicated a quiet, barely tended international boundary. The fence has been neatly trimmed around the marker, but you can still fit a hand through to wave or make an obscene gesture into the void beyond. The marker has been autographed by hundreds, if not thousands, of people over the years, and their names wear off slowly, one group at a time. Now, despite its inconveniently rough surface, the fence is also attracting elaborate bilingual, vulgar graffiti, which usually consists of insults aimed at the Border Patrol (or *la Migra*, as it is unflatteringly known around here).

Occasionally, someone walking—or staggering—down the street picks up a piece of crushed plastic, drywall, or broken glass and tosses it with a laugh and a curse over the fence, unceremoniously exporting it to the United States. But mostly, little piles of garbage are being burned in the dust and the remains kicked around; the acrid black smoke produced by smoldering plastic curls up to fill the nostrils and burn the eyes. Stray dogs, thin and slow, sprawl listlessly in the street or pick through the leftovers from the trash. Their somewhat more energetic puppies, nipping at one another and at the ankles of passersby, are so numerous that it requires a considerable effort and a very good sense of balance to avoid stepping on them.

At the bottom of the hill, on a large concrete slab with jagged edges, not a hundred feet inside Mexico from this most-crossed frontier in the world, a hectic little open market is operating at full tilt. At its center, under a bright blue plastic awning that can be seen easily from a distant ridge on the U.S. side, stands Don Chava, about fifty years old and six feet tall, a hefty, flamboyant presence with a Mexican cowboy hat and a loud, hearty laugh. He is so strong that his handshake or his arm around the shoulder is enough to make mere mortals shrivel. By all accounts, Don Chava is considered the man to see before setting out across the border from Colonia Libertad, because he is full of relevant experience and practical advice. He is also alleged to be the only person who can more or less guarantee the security of journalists and other visitors to these precincts with no real business to transact. "Once everyone sees that we know Don Chava," my guide, an artist friend from San Diego, reassures me, "we will be safe" from the border bandits (the *cholos*) and the other unsavory characters who prowl the area on both sides and exploit—sometimes even kill—the vulnerable people waiting to cross.

Accompanied by a young Mexican filmmaker who has spent a lot of time here before, we have parked my friend's California-registered car at the top of the hill, across the street from the fence, and walked down to the market. It is such a busy spot that Don Chava, who keeps a radio blaring during the day, has plans to construct an area for dancing. He greets us with an earthy smile and a friendly grunt. Like any border entrepreneur, he seems proud of his commercial operation, and our small talk does not really distract him from business. He sells cigarettes and chewing gum and other products useful to the traveler, but he keeps one hand on a long wooden stick that he uses to stir a huge cauldron full of pork fat over a wood fire. The stick doubles as a club to help maintain order; the pork fat, purchased by the chunk and then chopped into small pieces with Don Chava's impressively long butcher knife, is apparently favored as a predeparture snack; it is supposed to bring good luck for the daunting journey. Its heavy, greasy smell permeates everything under and around Don Chava's awning.

"You can buy anything there," one local expert had told me in describing the market near the soccer field. "Information, maps, San Diego bus schedules, clothes, drugs, sex, or someone who will promise to guide you past the Border Patrol" (but may or may not be able to deliver on that promise). Some people are walking around, as if at a sports event, hawking hot tacos and fajitas; they are using portable metal warmers that look as if they have been recycled from American baseball parks. The most ubiquitous vendors, however, are those peddling nothing more exotic than soft drinks and beer from all-American "Playmate by Igloo" picnic coolers. These hawkers are, in equal parts, jovial and aggressive.

One sturdy Mexican woman seems to have a special franchise on a strategic location just a few feet inside the United States, above a gulley where there is an inexplicable break in the fence. Down below, what appears to be raw sewage flows unimpeded onto the American side. It takes some fancy footwork and a hop around a corner of the fence to reach this woman, but it is virtually impossible to cross the border here without passing her. She tells us she is from Oaxaca, in the south of Mexico, more than twenty-one hundred miles and several ancient civilizations away. "I've been doing this every night for eight years," she says with a chuckle, pleased by the attention we are paying her. "They should have given me a green card by now." As her two young children cavort nearby in costumes and masks and then settle down to throwing stones at the broken pipes below, she sells cans of Coke, Diet Coke, Pepsi, and orange drink from her cooler for fifty cents apiece. Also, from several overstuffed plastic bags, she markets secondhand woolen sweaters and cotton sweatshirts. "It can get cold out there," she warns her frightened customers with an ominous wave toward the soccer field.

Mid- to late-summer is the busiest season on this stretch of the border, as word spreads deep into central and southern Mexico about the plentiful work that is available picking crops in the rich fields of Southern California. Monday has been measured to be the quietest night of the week; the traffic builds to a crescendo on Friday and Saturday nights, as many people who do have menial jobs near the border zone in Mexico try to cross just after they have been paid for the week. If they get caught by *la Migra* and deported, they may be extremely cooperative with the U.S. authorities, in the hope that they will be processed in time to be able to report back for work in Mexico the next Monday morning. Then at least they will have failed efficiently, and they can try again another day soon.

But on this nearly cloudless Monday night, illuminated by a full moon, there is plenty of human traffic. Every five or ten minutes, a group of seven or eight people—men and women of all ages, sometimes accompanied by several children—suddenly and somewhat mysteriously emerges from the depths of Colonia Libertad, almost like pop-up figures in a carnival game. Their clothing and demeanor make it easy to tell whether they are worldly wise city slickers who come from Mexico City or Guadalajara or live near the border, or bumpkins who have traveled for days from the countryside to take their chances; somewhat more than half seem to fall into the latter category. First the groups sit and wait, some more quietly than others. Then, on some instinct or signal that is not obvious, they stride or stumble forward together and make their way to the opening in the fence. Each person carries nothing more than the clothes he or she is wearing, plus a tote bag or a plastic sack. A few women have their babies strapped to their backs or rock them in their arms to keep them quiet. There is something incredibly humdrum and unexceptional-looking about the process, and yet for each person—some trying for the third or fourth time, or more, to enter the United States—the stakes are very high. This is reflected in the hush that surrounds every new batch of people as it approaches the break in the fence.

The young man in dark clothes at the front of each contingent is usually its guide—the name *pollero* (the leader of a group of *pollos,* or chickens) is used interchangeably with coyote—who has collected an advance fee per head. The rate currently being quoted for passage from Tijuana all the way to Los Angeles ranges from $200 to $400 each in cash, depending on the experience and reputation of the guide, the size of the group, and various other market forces. Some of the voyagers may have paid a larger amount to cover a longer trip up from the south. No pesos are accepted, and there is, of course, no money-back guarantee of success.

The *polleros* are cynical, often cruel, characters, experts at spreading risk around and protecting themselves in a crisis. Some desert their *pollos* at the first sign of trouble, or even turn on them and rob them. It seems to be up to each *pollero* to decide whether or not his charges have enough time to pause at Don Chava's market. Some groups appear to be in a great hurry, while others act more casual and confident; a few actually pick up extra recruits at the market. Occasionally, men who appear to be in their late teens or early twenties set out boldly on their own or in pairs. No one really knows which way is most likely to bring success: alone, in a large group, or in a small one. It is assumed that although a large contingent is more likely to be noticed, there is some safety in numbers—that when a big group is spotted and chased, at least one or two of its members are bound to get away. The standard instruction is, "If you see *la Migra*, run"—somewhere, anywhere.

In stark contrast to the *barrio* environment of Colonia Libertad, it is eerily dark and silent on the American side of the border. The first impression is of a moonscape with little light but many ominous shadows. When I first cross onto U.S. territory, there is a faint tinge still of the deep-red sunset, and a few stars are out, but they do not help me see. The ground has been churned up again recently by heavy equipment, and in places the loosely packed dirt furrows created by large tire treads still crunch underfoot; now and then I can hear people cursing under their breath in Spanish as they lose their balance. The only other consistent sound is of men urinating against or near the fence before they set out. Most people pause a few minutes to let their eyes adjust to the darkness, make the sign of the cross on their chests, and then begin an almost allegorical ascent. Viewed from near the break in the fence, they seem to crouch down and inch slowly upward; soon they are mere silhouettes that blend into the furrows and are obscured by what little brush remains on this much-traversed land. Blink quickly, and they have disappeared.

There is a temptation to compare this stretch of territory to a demilitarized zone between two warring countries, but it actually seems plenty militarized. In the distance and up a steep hill, no more than half a mile away, there are the faint headlights and the dull buzz of Border Patrol vehicles—cars, vans, motorcycles, and dune buggies. Their drivers are crisscrossing the landscape, as they try to figure out how to improve their nightly percentages by intercepting large groups of "aliens" rather than just the odd stray. Sometimes a helicopter flies over a nearby patch of land, its searchlights sweeping back and forth across the terrain. For me, if not for the immigrants around me, there is a chilling awareness that even though it looks pitch dark and feels totally isolated here, one can be spotted easily enough by an experienced eye through the officers' high-power infrared binoculars. And there is a strong possibility that any movements or body heat will be picked up by the Border Patrol's electronic sensors. Randomly hidden in the ground, they set off alarms and flashes on the computer screen at San Diego Sector headquarters several miles away. In any case, one is liable to have a vehicle from *la Migra* careening in one's direction within minutes.

AT MYRIAD other points in the porous fourteen-mile-long border zone east and west of the soccer field, between the Pacific Ocean and the Otay Mountains, an equally dramatic game is played out daily; but each spot has its own unique rituals and procedures.

At *las playas* (the beach), for example, where a chain-link fence tapers off into the Pacific, the action tends to occur early in the morning, when there may be heavy fog and the Border Patrol generally has fewer people on duty. The more physically fit immigrants may actually swim across the water frontier and, after getting through a nasty sluice that carries the heavily polluted Tijuana River out to sea, make their way to a predesignated spot in the hippie community of Imperial Beach, where someone has left them a change of clothes. Another ploy, particularly for young men immigrating alone, is to buy jogging gear and slip across in the guise of Mexican Americans out for a morning fitness run along the beach. Once they have made it into a busy section of San Diego, they can attempt an unobtrusive journey on to Los Angeles by train or bus. Other people crowd into small boats and try to travel up the coast beyond the Border Patrol's highway checkpoints but are often picked up soon after, or even before, coming ashore.

Some spots along the border have exotic names, such as Smuggler's Gulch, and notoriously violent reputations to match. Then there is "the levee," in a much more urban area of Tijuana. Just across the street from a neighborhood of restaurants, shops, and other commercial establishments on the Mexican side, one can climb a short embankment and look over to the United States. In between lies a broad concrete viaduct with sloping walls, perhaps fifty meters across, which in the rainy season becomes a kind of canal carrying water that has overflowed from the Tijuana River. The U.S. government has seen to it that the levee is never engulfed in darkness like the soccer field. On the contrary, in recent years the levee has been brightly floodlit throughout the night from the American side, in order to make it easier for the Border Patrol to observe what is happening and, theoretically, to cut down on illegal entries.[10] And so when it is dry, as it is most of the year, the viaduct becomes almost a sunken sports arena for a public contest between those trying to immigrate and those trying to stop them, complete with spectators. But because this is another place where a high, opaque fence runs along part of the American side—in this case, set back from the border and positioned instead at the top of the other bank of the viaduct—the spectacle can be fully appreciated only if viewed from Mexico.

Couples from Tijuana often use the five-foot-wide path on top of the levee for walks or bicycle rides, but many people also take advantage of it as (literally) a jumping-off point for getting into America. Here the

---

[10] *The impetus for this tactic came originally from a conservative group called Light Up the Border, whose premise was that fewer undocumented immigrants would get through if they were deprived of darkness as a cover. Periodically, members have driven their cars to the border at night and shined their high-beam headlights across for hours at a time.*

high-risk action generally begins in the late afternoon. Young men, in particular, sit at the edge of the levee in clusters, many of them drinking beer or sniffing glue. As it gets later and as they become more intoxicated, they venture forth, almost as a human wave, and begin to taunt the uniformed men and women from *la Migra*, who are scattered around in plain view. Some of the more daring characters actually take tables and chairs to the bottom of the viaduct, which is officially inside the United States, and have open-air parties. They sit there drinking, laughing, playing card games, and gambling, in effect daring their adversaries to come after them.

When the Border Patrol finally responds to the provocation and zooms through on their dune buggies or motorcycles, most of the border crossers scrape up their possessions and scramble back up the Mexican side and over the top of the levee to safety. But the trick is to engage the Americans in enough of a distracting pursuit to let some of the immigrants run the other way and get as far as the fence on the U.S. side. The Border Patrol is on to this tactic, of course, but some officers find it hard to resist the engagement. As soon as a substantial quantity of immigrants have made it to the fence, they hoist or pull one another to the top and once more tease *la Migra*. Far superior in numbers, they again hope to create a distraction that will give some of them an opportunity to slip through the next phase of the net—to jump to the ground and disappear quickly into the California darkness.

There is a tremendous amount of litter in the vicinity of the levee, and one of the first things a passerby notices is the large number of plastic garbage bags scattered everywhere. That is because when there is water in the viaduct, it is so polluted that the immigrants who plan to wade through it pull plastic bags up over their feet and legs to protect their shoes, their clothes, and their skin. They shed the bags as soon as they reach the American side, so as not to be easily identifiable. But no one ever seems to bother cleaning up the bags.

The chase at the levee makes for a dangerous game, yet it is played out by the would-be immigrants with a mixture of humor and fatalism. On a busy night in peak season, as many as 800 or 1,000 people may have spent some time at the levee before the sun rises again, and perhaps several dozen, or even a hundred, get through undetected on any given night. These are uneducated but shrewd young men, clever at aggravating and often outsmarting the hapless Border Patrol officers, who are an integral part of their complicated love-hate relationship with the United States. Shouting through the fence or from on top of it, they insult the America they long to be a part of, using whatever few English words they know. They joke and laugh among themselves, but if they spot any Americans passing nearby, switch at once to begging for hand-outs and crying for help. They spin out long tales of hardship and hope, many undoubtedly true. There are floods and earthquakes at home, wives or girlfriends who have disappeared up north, jobs that have been promised in Los Angeles. They will take any chance and risk any harm to reach the life that looms so tantalizingly just a few feet away.

Appropriately enough, the first goal of those who do make it across the border from the levee is to reach a great symbolic American insti-tution, the big Kmart in San Ysidro, a working-class, primarily His-panic town that is wedged in just south of San Diego. Kmart's tall illuminated red letters and its other lights can be spotted from afar, and if you come across the levee at the right place, it requires a sprint of only a few hundred yards to get there. Crouched figures often can be seen darting between cars in its parking lot. Once inside, mimicking television commercials they have seen and plying the long aisles with shopping carts, the immigrants hope to be indistinguishable from the largely Hispanic clientele, most of whom are either American citizens or middle-class Mexicans who have crossed legally to go shopping. Even if the Border Patrol does raid Kmart, it is unlikely to manage to ask everyone there for identification.

McDonald's and Burger King are nearby, too, but although their food is popular in Mexico, it is generally considered risky to linger there. If they arrive during business hours, however, they may pause at the nearby outlet mall to buy some new, inexpensive clothes, camouflage for their onward journey.

There are other impromptu crossing points near Tijuana, in places where the fence is weak or disassembled or, sometimes, where deter-mined and well-equipped people can dig a hole and crawl underneath without ever being detected. Elsewhere it is easy to jump down into seemingly deserted American territory from a retaining wall along a Mexican highway that hugs the border. At just such a spot, as I tour the U.S. side one afternoon with representatives of Border Watch, a Quaker group, we stumble across a family of five—a husband and wife, their teenage son, a daughter who is about ten, and a year-old baby girl—perched openly and impassively on a row of large rocks about twenty-five feet inside the United States, just waiting to make a run for it. They tell us that they have traveled in a truck from Michoacán, a state some eighteen hundred miles to the south, over a period of three days and two nights. They look pale, exhausted, and hungry. They have a small, clumsy suitcase and several bulging plastic bags for their clothes and the other few belongings they have brought along; some other items have already been traded for food.

Just behind and around the rocks where they are sitting, sewage is trickling from Mexico into the United States and then running off into little rivulets. It gives off a horrible stench, but the family waits stolidly and silently, as if this is the most minor of their problems. With desperate, single-minded concentration, the father stares at a distant ridge, where two green Border Patrol vans are parked and several officers are conferring; if *la Migra* could only be distracted, or called away to some other hot spot, the family might have an opportunity to move ahead quickly. The father, obviously uncertain about whether we can be trusted, talks to us guardedly. Someone will be waiting for them in San Ysidro, he says, the first step in a chain of contacts that is supposed to get them safely all the way to San Jose, 483 miles north, within a few days. There they will have family, a place to stay, plenty of food to eat, possibly even a job or two. His greatest fear, he says, is that they might panic and become separated as they cross—that he and/or his wife and the baby would get through without the two older children, or that the children would find themselves alone in America without their parents.

The most serious danger for this family, and for any other people crossing the border furtively in this region, actually lies along the same route that could eventually take them north to safety—the busy freeway. On several interstate highways in the San Diego area, large yellow warning signs have been put up depicting a family holding hands and running across the road. They reflect the fact that the Mexicans and others who come through Tijuana and have no transportation arrangements on the U.S. side cannot get far before they encounter Southern California's intricate network of expressways, assuredly bigger and more crowded than any road they have ever seen before. Typically, the undocumented immigrants will wander through neighborhoods for hours at night, or walk for miles on one side of a freeway or along its median strip, trying to calculate the best way to find a ride or otherwise get up to Los Angeles. Eventually, however, they come to a blockage, or for some other reason find it necessary or desirable to try to cross the expressway.[11]

"What happens," explains one local activist sympathetic to the immigrants' plight, "is that the man stands at the edge of the freeway

---

[11] *Groups of undocumented immigrants can sometimes be seen walking on the median strips of the freeways in Southern California; they are presumably aware of the informal agreement that the Border Patrol will not attempt to pursue or arrest them there, but will defer to the California Highway Patrol (which tends to ignore them). Some people, however, claim to have seen coordinated chases in recent years, in which the Highway Patrol and Border Patrol herd immigrants onto private property and handcuff them, or close the exits and entrances on a stretch of freeway for a period of time in order to sweep in and trap large numbers at once.*

with his wife and children behind him. They are all holding hands and form a line. When he thinks the way is clear, he starts running and pulls the others along behind him. But if you're from Zacatecas [another southern Mexican state] and you've never experienced a three- or four-lane highway with people going seventy miles an hour, and if there's a curve in the road, it's easy to miscalculate. Your perception of the distance is distorted, especially in the dark or at dawn. Besides, these people aren't Olympic track stars to begin with, and they may have been traveling for four or five days already. They're hungry, they're weak. Often the man makes it, but the woman or a child behind him gets killed." Others who may be killed include "bailouts," undocumented immigrants who panic and jump out of the vehicles in which they are riding as they approach a Border Patrol highway checkpoint. Those who do get across the freeway safely usually do not feel they can take the risk of stopping to tend to those who have been hit, but leave the body (or bodies) behind and continue their journey.

No one has discovered an easy method of preventing or dissuading the frightened illegal immigrants from crossing the freeways in this manner, and the warning signs have had little effect on driving habits. Nor does anyone know exactly how many such accidents occur in a typical year—some say hundreds—because there appears to be no systematic attempt to keep records. For many, it would be an uncomfortable bit of data to have. But it is easy to find people in the San Diego area who have seen this happen or have friends who have had the experience of hitting some mysterious creature or object on the road at night. For the immigrants and for local Hispanics, one freeway where the problem is especially bad has taken on the nickname, *el camino de la muerte* ("the highway of death").

"My first experience with this was on I-805," recalls one Border Patrol agent, who asked not to be identified by name. "My partner and I had stopped to get a soda at 7-Eleven. A civilian pulls up and says, 'I think there's a body on 805.' So we said, 'Okay, we'll go check it out.' Sure enough, we were driving south, looking into the northbound lane, and you could see there was something out in the road. My partner called to get help, and I was trying to get out there to see if I could render assistance to what appeared to be a person on the road. But there was so much traffic. It was a Saturday night, at about eleven o'clock, and that's when everybody's coming back from Tijuana and they've been drinking; there was no way I could have even made it out there to try to give that person help. But as I was trying to slow traffic down with my flashlight, I saw the body just get hit several more times. By the time we were able to get traffic stopped, the guy had been hit maybe ten times already. Who knows how many times he'd been hit before that. All he looked like was an animal out in the middle of the road. He was probably no more than three feet long after they got through with him.''

The standard practice in such cases is for the California Highway Patrol simply to put the anonymous corpses, or what is left of them, into body bags and ship them immediately to the morgue in Tijuana. Sometimes a body may be identified by a name that was found on a piece of paper in his pocket—perhaps of a cousin somewhere in California whom he had hoped to reach. If there was a phone number on the paper, the relative may get a call and learn why his Mexican family never arrived as expected.

ON ANOTHER NIGHT, I have an entirely different tour of this border zone from the American side. My guide is Carmen Mendoza (not her real name), a woman in her early thirties who has been a Border Patrol officer for eight years and whose husband also works for the agency.[12] She is from the small town of El Centro, in the California desert, about fifteen miles from Mexicali, the capital of the Mexican state of Baja California and a border town with a name that portrays its location and its role more graphically than most. Like many of the other Border Patrol officers assigned to the San Diego sector, Mendoza is herself Mexican American, and she is not unaware of the inherent contradiction between her own background and her work.

"I do have some relatives who feel that what I'm doing is not right," Mendoza says. "My parents just see this as a law-enforcement job, but my other relatives who live in L.A., they think of it more as, 'Oh, you're the big bad *Migra* down there, catching all those poor undocumented aliens.' Even my family down south in Mexico [in Tijuana and in Sonora state] have nothing against what I do. I think I get more bad press from my relatives in L.A. than I do from my relatives in Mexico." As for her own reflections about her role, "To me, the U.S. is my country and I'm out here doing the best that I can. My views are probably very different from other [Mexican Americans], but you know, you see all these undocumented migrants getting all these free handouts in just about anything and everything, from welfare to unemployment to jobs that I see my children in the future might not have. I have

---

[12] *Most Border Patrol officials whom I interviewed during the research for this book were willing to be identified by name, but this person, assigned by her supervisors on short notice to accompany me, without any real opportunity to decline the assignment, was assured that she could remain anonymous.*

nothing against the people, but I think that something should be done. You think about opening the borders completely, it would cause chaos."

With Mendoza at the wheel, we cruise over dirt roads through a hardscrabble area just near the border where there are scattered "ranchitos"—little shacks that look as if a strong wind could blow them over at any moment—many of them occupied by squatters who are believed to be American citizens or holders of green cards, but who often harbor people who are in the country illegally. There are signs posted on trees, issuing a general invitation to a wide-open party that was held along the border a few nights earlier. This is an odd little dark corner of America, just inside the line, a place with lots of junk piles but no electric or sewer service. Some of the ranchitos, however, have septic tanks and are illuminated by generators.

The view from Mendoza's pale-green Border Patrol van on this night is a bleak one, full of high-tech efforts with frustrating, minimal results. The fence is weak and unreliable here, in some places the result of immigrants having simply driven through it in vans or pickup trucks. (This is thought to be a favored technique of those who are smuggling drugs across and want to make a very quick getaway.) At one spot, a narrow patch of ground has been hollowed out under the fence and a huge battered piece of corrugated cardboard, perhaps from an old refrigerator carton, sits nearby. It has obviously been used to give many small people a ride under the fence and across the border through a little mud canal.

Not far away is a stretch, perhaps thirty meters wide, near the runways of the Tijuana airport, where there is actually no fence at all; it is affectionately called the "Corn hole," because the land just along the boundary line there is said to be owned by one Mr. Corn, who has thus far prevented the federal government from constructing anything on his property. Even as we drive by, small groups of people are walking back and forth along the border, obviously trying to calculate the best moment to make a run for it. It is very dark here, but the Border Patrol's infrared-scope truck, a kind of giant binoculars on wheels, is known to be somewhere in the vicinity. As we move into a better-lit area where the National Guard has parked its heavy equipment and machinery, we can see the shadows of people who are running furtively between and underneath the vehicles, not exactly intimidated by the close presence of *la Migra*. But the immigrants may be on the lookout for what are known in the trade as "lay-ins" by Border Patrol agents, who hide individually or in pairs and wait to have their next movements determined by radio communications from the scope truck.

"I don't think it really keeps them out," says Mendoza of the fence, in a moment of naughty candor. Indeed, she confides that sometimes an opaque fence is more a liability than an asset, because it prevents her and her colleagues from seeing what is happening just a few feet away on the Mexican side. "The reason that a lot of times we don't have the agents right up against the fence is that we've had some bad incidents," she says. "What the aliens do is they park cars up close on the other side. Then they get up on top of the cars, and when they see or hear you coming [in a Border Patrol vehicle], they throw rocks and stuff over and try to hit your windshield." In what is essentially a guerrilla war, a broken windshield counts as a victory in a minor skirmish for the immigrants. Any vehicle disabled in this manner, even temporarily, is one less that is available to help monitor and apprehend illegal entries.

Understandably perhaps, Mendoza's conversational description of her work is marked by the numbing depersonalization common to the patter of any law-enforcement personnel who are on the firing line day after day. When individuals are arrested from the "alien traffic," they are "stockpiled" in the rather dank, grim-looking men's and women's detention cells at the Border Patrol's Brownfield substation. Their names—or the names they choose to give—are noted in the records. Except for those suspected of the more serious crimes of smuggling undocumented workers across the border in large numbers or trafficking in drugs (who are booked and taken to a more secure facility), as soon as there are enough customers to make it worth the trip, they are usually trucked back across the border to Tijuana and set free. Logistically, it would be impossible to hold on to them all. "At the end of the shift," Mendoza says, gesturing toward some very scared-looking people in the female cell, "we just get rid of everything."

But for intelligence and predictive purposes, a particular effort is made at least to count and keep track of the "OTMs" (the "other than Mexicans," usually from Central and South America but sometimes from as far away as China). On a typical night, in Mendoza's estimation, these people from further away represent about 5 percent of the catch, and some may have paid a coyote thousands, rather than hundreds, of dollars for their supposedly safe transit across the border. They tend to be friendless, vulnerable, and somewhat easier to stop.

Back at the spit-polished San Diego Sector headquarters, where Mendoza delivers me at the end of our excursion, one could easily develop a more upbeat, even glamorous view of those who police the border and how they do it. Here there are elaborate, detailed maps of the border area on the walls, alongside various plaques and photographs of INS and Justice Department officials. Seated at bright, flashing consoles and wearing headsets, supervisors glide back and forth on wheeled chairs in front of their control panels and bark orders over the radio to their people in the field, dispatching agents carried by everything from horses to all-terrain vehicles to helicopters to investigate the latest trouble spot. The only problem, whispers one of them to me in an aside, is that the computers are often down and many of the alarms are false; the underground sensors are just as often set off by rabbits or Border Patrol vehicles as by humans on foot, he says.

Indeed, explains Mendoza, even on the very best night under the most optimal circumstances, in her estimation the apprehension rate in her territory never exceeds 25 percent of those crossing the border illegally. But, she adds, "I enjoy my work. Daytime is rather slow, not much going on. Nighttime is the busiest; I like working the night. And if you like the outdoors and you don't mind eating a little bit of dirt, this is a good career. I tell you, working for the Border Patrol, you get to see some of the most beautiful sunrises and some of the most beautiful sunsets."

TIJUANA HAS a terrible reputation. Americans usually think of it as the destination of hardened criminals on the run, where prostitutes and every manner of sexual deviant sell their services and where the desperately ill flock for unconventional, often worthless, treatment. Over time, the city came to symbolize sleaze, and was the butt of cheap jokes. Tijuana was the seamy, dirty mirror image of pristine San Diego. Here, after all, is where the ruling party's candidate for the presidency of Mexico was assassinated in 1994. The Tijuana bullring, just near the border and easily visible from the American side, made it seem genuinely Latin, even exotic, but hardly worthy of being in the same category with favored destinations like Mexico City, Acapulco, or the Yucatán. Californians going south on vacation nearly always passed by Tijuana quickly, in favor of Ensenada and other destinations deeper into Baja.

There is, of course, another Tijuana: a sophisticated commercial center and a social and intellectual hub of northern Mexico, an urban area experiencing such a boom that some demographers predict it will be home to the largest concentration of people on the west coast of the Americas soon after the turn of the century. Its official population is already around two million, but perhaps another million are estimated to make up an additional "floating population," living in the streets or in other places where they are not easily counted.

Beginning in the 1970s, Tijuana became one of several centers of the *maquiladora,* or border industry, movement. Intended to reduce labor costs for U.S. industries while also creating large numbers of jobs for unskilled or semiskilled Mexican workers, the *maquiladoras* were authorized to import U.S.-made components and other materials into Mexico duty free. When they shipped their finished products back to the United States, duty had to be paid only on the value that had been added to the materials. An estimated two thousand *maquila* factories or assembly plants have been created along the U.S.–Mexican border over the years, with about a third of them located in the Tijuana–San Diego basin. This has triggered an enormous influx of people from impoverished areas in the Mexican interior, with all the obvious consequences for Tijuana and its beleaguered infrastructure. Decent housing is hard to find, the roads are inadequate for the traffic they must handle, and the fresh water supply is uncertain. Law enforcement, needless to say, is unreliable at best.

Even if, as some believe, the *maquilas* cut back temporarily on the pressures for cross-border migration in search of work, they have created other horrendous problems in the border region. Some of the *maquilas* are held responsible for horrible pollution, which is beyond the reach of the U.S. Environmental Protection Agency and overlooked by its admittedly feeble Mexican counterpart. In certain instances, toxic effluent from hastily constructed heavy industries near the border has been blamed for dramatic increases in severe birth defects and serious illnesses on both sides. Drums that once held toxic chemicals and were thrown out by the factories have been reused for drinking water by people who cannot read the English-language warnings on them. Workers are often consigned to live in squatter camps just south of the border, collections of metal or cardboard shacks built from materials discarded by the factories; they have dirt floors and no plumbing, and the families who live there must often burn old tires to keep warm in the cold weather.

More typical of the *maquila* phenomenon, though, are the low-key, almost invisible electronics assembly plants that are tucked away in the side streets and alleyways of Tijuana. According to its director of engineering, César López Ramos, one *maquila* that I visit on a summer afternoon employs 473 people producing telephone headsets for a company based in Santa Cruz, California. Its premises are clean, quiet, and air-conditioned, and there seems to be no obvious safety hazard from the soldering and other detail work being done. But the wage profile is enough to fulfill the worst nightmares of American labor unions that warn about the loss of jobs to Mexico. By putting in more than nine hours a day five days a week (fulfilling precisely the Mexican work week of forty-eight hours without spilling over onto Saturdays), the employees here are turning out almost five thousand headsets every day. In exchange, López Ramos says, beginning employees are paid $4 a day, the Mexican minimum wage; on the non-supervisory level, with a good work record they can eventually progress to earn double that amount. Anticipating an American's reaction, López Ramos points out that the employees are also entitled to eat a hearty breakfast and lunch at the plant every working day for a grand total of only twenty cents a week, and that they enjoy excellent health benefits. Besides, he adds, most of the workers are illiterate peasants who came from villages where such wages would be regarded as a veritable fortune.

The unspoken subtext of the conversation is that only through such arrangements can American electronics companies hope to compete even minimally with their Asian counterparts. Without the *maquilas,* López Ramos implies, U.S. companies and their workers might not have any market at all for the components and other materials they are still producing.[13] But the unknown factor is how many of the Mexican workers—especially those who have brought their families north and enjoyed a first taste of urban life but may still be consigned to live in squalor—will decide to attempt another leap forward by crossing to the promised land across the border.

This is among the issues studied by Jorge Bustamante and his colleagues at the Colegio de la Frontera Norte. Located about ten miles from downtown Tijuana, on a promontory with a spectacular view of the Pacific Ocean, the colegio conducts surveys and seminars and publishes journals that treat the economic and social aspects of a relationship that is viewed north of the border almost exclusively in political and law-enforcement terms. It also produces headcounts and other numbers that may be the only reliable alternative to the statistics on illegal immigration across the U.S.-Mexican border that are turned out by the American government. Bustamante himself, a large, blustery man who talks about the border the way most people talk about their neighborhood, insists that the INS "consciously exaggerates the phenomenon" for its own bureaucratic purposes. "To the public and the press, they just say, 'Last month, we apprehended ten thousand illegal

---

[13] *With the implementation of the North American Free Trade Agreement, the* maquiladoras *may lose their special edge.*

aliens.' They don't tell you that they made ten thousand apprehensions [many of them of the same people, arrested two or more times each]. If Americans would understand that difference, it would mean a totally different picture."[14]

Through a variety of techniques, including analyzing aerial photographs and conducting random interviews at the border, the colegio has calculated that the maximum number of people attempting to cross the border in or near Tijuana in a peak twenty-four-hour period in August is around 2,350; in July the highest figure tends to be about 1,700, and the number drops off considerably during the winter months. But Bustamante believes that the Border Patrol succeeds in preventing the immigration of more people than it admits or others recognize— perhaps a third, on average, of those who try—and he suggests that the agency's percentages may actually be increasing as a result of stricter measures. However, he does not seek to minimize the issue: In the summer of 1991, according to Bustamante's studies, there were approximately 1.75 million undocumented immigrants from Mexico living in the United States, 60 percent of them in California and of that 60 percent, 70 percent, or some 735,000, of them in the Los Angeles metropolitan area. Furthermore, he believes that more than 50 percent of all the Mexicans working illegally in the United States at some point crossed the frontier in or near Tijuana. He recognizes that this "concentration" causes a major problem.

Where Bustamante differs with the conventional wisdom is on whether this is a new problem and whether the American government shares any of the responsibility for it. For example, he rejects the notion that large-scale Mexican immigration to the United States has emerged only in recent years. "Mexico, as a country of origin, has been a constant throughout the century," he insists, pointing to studies he has done that cover the period back to 1907. "But sometimes people notice Mexico, and sometimes they don't. It has to do with the health of the U.S. economy. In periods of economic recession, the visibility of Mexicans is more widely recognized. And in periods of economic expansion in the U.S., that negative visibility tends to fade away and is sometimes replaced by a positive one. When the economy is good, people start saying Mexican workers are very reliable. During

---

[14] *According to official INS statistics, about half a million people are apprehended annually in the San Diego Sector, out of a total of 1.2 million who are arrested along the U.S.-Mexican border. These statistics do not distinguish between single or multiple apprehensions of the same people.*

a recession, Mexican immigrants become scapegoats of social and economic calamities."[15]

Today, Bustamante says, because no other easy answers can be found, Mexicans are blamed for other calamities, such as the intractable illegal drug traffic into the United States. "Anyone who knows a little bit about drug traffic," he insists, "realizes that the drug traffic that counts doesn't go on foot in the same place where undocumented immigrants go across. It goes in automobiles, freighters, planes, and boats; it is more than a human being can carry, and it doesn't go by this route. But a lot of Southern Californians believe that behind every undocumented immigrant there is a drug trafficker." Thus, they are vulnerable to emotional demands to increase patrols, erect new and tougher fences at the border, and cut benefits.

"The fence is politics," continues Bustamante—a mere sop to California congressmen under pressure to demonstrate progress on multiple problems at the same time. "It's for the consumption of American constituencies; it doesn't have anything to do with the reality. They put up the new fence, and of course, the drug traffic goes on, business as usual. And undocumented immigrants have a little bit of a problem, but soon they again go about their business as usual, too. So everybody's happy. The people who believe that drug traffickers are the same as illegal aliens applaud the measure, because it's stopping both drug traffic and illegal aliens, according to them. The drug traffickers are very happy, because they think it is a joke. If you have a twenty-mile fence in two thousand miles of border, it takes some magic thinking to believe that it's going to stop drug traffic!"

Politics, Bustamante believes, is also what prevents the U.S. government from taking steps that would be more effective, such as including labor migration in the terms of any free-trade agreements that are negotiated between the two countries. "The Mexican government is saying, 'This is not a crime-related phenomenon. This is economic, labor-related, a very natural phenomenon that should be negotiated

---

[15] *During the Great Depression, Mexican workers—both legal and illegal—were frequent targets of demonstrations and deportation drives. By the early 1930s, the Mexican American population of the United States was about 1.5 million, spread across the agricultural areas of California, Texas, Arizona, and Colorado, and the industrial centers of the Midwest. But in Detroit and Gary, Indiana, racist propaganda and physical threats soon convinced many people to return to Mexico. Los Angeles County gave thousands a free one-way train ride across the border, in an effort to cut the city's welfare costs. The "repatriation" effort was a short-lived cure for American economic woes, however; most of the so-called Chicanos returned as soon as the hysteria against them began to subside. The episode, writes historian T. H. Watkins, combined "racism with selfishness and desperation."*

bilaterally.' The U.S. doesn't accept that," he complains. Indeed, Bustamante points out, there is a paradox inherent in the status of undocumented workers once they arrive in the United States. On the one hand, "they become labeled as criminals and society looks at them as the enemy"; on the other hand, "U.S. employers take advantage of the reduced cost of labor, and the economy gets wages down because of the workers' presence in the United States." The employer sanctions contained in recent immigration laws are only halfheartedly enforced. The same people in Southern California who clamor for the exclusion of undocumented workers employ them at rock-bottom wages (which are, admittedly, a great improvement over what they could currently earn in Mexico).

"This is a situation that is well understood by many economists in the United States," adds Bustamante. "They have said publicly to the president, to many presidents, 'Immigration from Mexico is good for the U.S. economy.' So, there is not an absence of information, but this is something that it would be costly for the U.S. to change. You have to ask yourselves, 'Do we need this labor?' If the answer is 'yes,' then you should be able to pay for it, which you're not doing right now. The U.S. finds it perfectly all right to maintain this situation and take advantage of these conditions. And these conditions were not established yesterday. . . . But who's going to take the position, 'yes, yes, negotiate bilaterally with Mexico,' knowing that it represents a higher cost, just in the name of justice? That doesn't sell very well in the United States."

Meanwhile, according to Bustamante, although Mexico has no explicit policy of attempting to export labor to the United States, the immigrants are regarded by Mexicans more as heroes than as criminals. This is a classic syndrome in countries that have sent many generations of people to the United States in the course of its growth and development. It is accepted that people will do what they must, including breaking the law, in order to get to America and make a living. "Families feel proud about having a relative, whether it is a man or a woman, who goes to the U.S. in search of a job. In Mexico, the undocumented immigrants who go north have the reputation of being hardworking and some of the best people that we have. Those who take the risk of the journey are the most determined and strong-willed," Bustamante says. Besides, they invariably send or bring money home to those who have been left behind. Whether laws like California's Proposition 187 will deter the illegal immigrants from coming is utterly unknown.

•

WHAT THE IMMIGRANTS may find on the American side of the border is another matter entirely. For those who do not have family waiting to help them, or who never journey far beyond the border, daily existence in the promised land can be very grim indeed. This is certainly the case in the so-called encampments in the northern part of San Diego County, where an estimated 20,000 people from Mexico and Central America, documented and undocumented alike, live in deplorable conditions without any modern facilities or public services, but often within shouting distance of plush, expensive housing developments. They have migrated perhaps twenty or thirty miles inside the United States, but, in most cases, are doing back-breaking work at very low pay. Their lives have hardly changed at all.

On a Friday afternoon in September, accompanied by the Reverend Rafael Martínez, a Protestant chaplain who is an advocate for these immigrants in "north county," I visited Los Diablos camp, a grisly, dusty squatter colony of several hundred people tucked away behind a stand of trees on the floor of a canyon near the wealthy bedroom community of Encinitas. The scene is like something out of a heartrending public television documentary about an impoverished Third World nation. The tiny shacks that serve as homes for as many as five or six people have been constructed from scraps of plywood, thin metal, and sheets of plastic. Most of these materials were scrounged from the trash heaps of the vast nurseries nearby, which grow plants and shrubs to feed the insatiable appetites of the housing developments that are transforming the dry mountainsides in the area. Some of the residents of Los Diablos work in the fields of the nurseries, and the large containers they have brought home to carry water or use as furniture still bear the poison warnings from the pesticides they once held.

Within Los Diablos, we are told by one man, there are three distinct neighborhoods, one for people from Oaxaca, one for those from the Mexican state of Guerrero, and another for Guatemalans. Many of the people are single, but there are at least twenty families living here, too. The shacks seem surprisingly secure, and a number have locks on their doors; most have addresses painted in large numbers and letters on the walls or doors. Old bicycles are parked outside of some places, and clothes and towels are hanging on scrawny bushes to dry. Next to one dwelling is a grave. Its marker has a holy picture at the top and reveals that the person buried there was killed, apparently in a fight, on December 23, 1990. All around the grave are old beer bottles covered with melted wax, the remains of impromptu candles to the Virgin of Guadalupe, the patron saint of all Mexicans. Nearby there is a small rosebush, and then a tiny memorial to someone else; defined by stones but now somewhat overgrown by weeds, it consists of a cross, a plastic Santa Claus, and a plaque with an illegible inscription. A neighbor is digging out a ditch, to create a channel for waste water that otherwise might soon overrun the grave and the shrine.

The entrance to Los Diablos is marked by a tall wooden arch built from scrap lumber, a whimsical echo of the ones in Western movies and at touristy dude ranches. Underneath, in what could be called the town square, young boys kick a soccer ball into the air; the dust in the unpaved street is much too thick to permit any real game on the ground. Scattered around the camp are several blue plastic awnings stretched between sticks, where people can sit in the shade, and there are even a few large umbrellas with rusted metal tables underneath—makeshift outdoor cafés amidst the squalor. Huge electrical lines pass tantalizingly overhead, on their way to the nearby developments and eventually to San Diego, but their power is untapped here. Old generators that put out thick exhaust provide the juice for the few lights and television sets that operate in the camp every night. At the periphery, there are several large dumpsters and blue portable toilets, provided through an informal agreement between some of the nursery owners and Martínez's North County Chaplaincy. There is even a small parking lot, for the more prosperous residents who have cars and drive to work. (Some people, Martínez points out, have lived here for many years and, since they pay no rent, have actually managed to accumulate significant material possessions.)

On this Friday evening there is a lot of action at Los Diablos. For most people it is payday, and a number of vans and cars have arrived at the edge of the camp. Some belong to food vendors, who have a captive audience for the underground grocery business they do off the books and the tax rolls (and many of whom, according to Martínez, have become millionaires in the process). Another van yields tables that are soon piled high with used clothing that is for sale; the residents converge quickly to pick it over and make their deals. As it gets darker, the mariachi music emanating from radios and boomboxes grows louder, and it becomes clear that a lot of people are drinking heavily. Suddenly, as if from nowhere, a number of overdressed women emerge and begin making their way among the vendors and through the camp. Viewed from closer range, it is obvious that some of them are actually men dressed as women, transvestite prostitutes who know how to take advantage of the weekly influx of cash. Many of these visitors apparently cross every Friday from Tijuana, which is said to be the only major city in Mexico that does not have a serious public health campaign targeted at AIDS.

The encampments have existed for years, usually on private land, and they originally housed primarily undocumented immigrants who wanted to stay out of the sight of the Border Patrol and other law-enforcement personnel. "They were doing agricultural work, but they could not take the risk of coming into the cities or being very visible," says Martínez. "So they built these little boxes in the bottom of the canyons, under bushes. You could sometimes stand literally no more than ten or fifteen feet from a large camp and not see it or know it was there. The people would crawl out, go to work, and then crawl back in. It was a really invisible population."

According to Martínez, some 85 percent of the people living in the camps today are fully legalized, as a result of the amnesty provisions of the Immigration Reform and Control Act of 1986. They can take the chance of being more visible. The camps are somewhat less concealed, and their residents often do venture out into urban areas, but they still must survive in an extraordinarily hostile environment. "The people of Encinitas [and other similar communities] don't want to allow any low-income housing, and so this is the alternative," Martínez says. Of course, whenever they discover (or rediscover) camps nearby, the wealthy citizens who have just moved into million-dollar homes begin to worry about their property values. Typically, they panic and call the state health department, which investigates, finds unsanitary conditions, and evacuates the area being complained about, at least temporarily.

In one case during the late 1980s, recalls Martínez, "we tried to convince them that to close down the camp would create a situation where about four hundred people would be thrown out on the street. But that's exactly what they did. So these people were thrown out, and their homes were destroyed. They simply crossed the road, went over a hill, and came to an empty area, an old county dump that was closed. They just started building again. This really produced very strong negative reactions from the people of Encinitas. It was the beginning of the animosity and the persecution of these people and of agencies like ours, which try to help them." Eventually, by employing security guards, Encinitas won its fight against that particular camp and drove its residents away. But this was just one battle in an epic struggle. As Martínez explains, "Sure, you can come and tell two hundred people, 'No, you cannot be here,' and make their lives so miserable that they leave. But five or six months later, there's going to be another hundred people arriving who are different. Unless you do it over and over again, they're going to establish themselves in these places that have been abandoned by the others. So some go, and others come."

Eventually the community's anger came to be focused on Martínez himself and his social service agency. "They insist that we are working only with illegals, and that is not true," says Martínez, sitting in his modest office in an old converted house just near the freeway. "But we don't ask for passports when people come here, any more than a church asks, or the grocery store, or the hospital or the schools. I'm not working for the INS. They say that I encourage [the undocumented immigrants] by providing assistance and services. That is absurd. The people come here because we give them a loaf of bread, or a jacket on a cold night, or a blanket. They come here because they need jobs to feed their family." Repeatedly the city of Encinitas denied the North County Chaplaincy access to any public funds, and finally the city government moved to evict Martínez's project from its offices. Although the house had served as an office for one of the major landscaping companies for several years, and is in a neighborhood with a gas station, a fast-food restaurant, and a warehouse, the city declared that it could now be used only as a family residence.

"There's nothing like San Diego County in terms of the vitriol," says Claudia Smith, who runs the Oceanside office of California Rural Legal Assistance, an organized defender of the poor and downtrodden that has clashed with the authorities ever since it was founded in the late 1960s. "I have never experienced the level of anti-immigration feeling that exists here," she says. "Immigrants—largely undocumented immigrants—actually subsidize what is a relatively comfortable lifestyle here. You can go to a city council meeting, and you will have senior citizens who live in some condominium project just railing against immigrants. And the next day you will get a wage claimant who has worked on their lawn who's not even getting paid the minimum wage. These people make no connection to the fact that the condominium fees are kept low largely because all the service-type work in this county is done by immigrants, both documented and undocumented."

Originally from Guatemala herself, Smith believes that many Southern Californians had unrealistic expectations of the 1986 immigration reform law: "They thought you weren't going to see little brown men walking around anymore." But attaining legal status set the immigrants free to walk around more, and the law really did nothing to stem the steady flow across the border. "What people don't seem to realize," says Smith, "is that there's a new wave of immigrants coming up, beyond the usual ones. You're getting a lot of urban people now, from around Mexico City. But even more important, you're getting indigenous people, from both Mexico and Guatemala, and that really is a new trend. You're getting people from deep in the interior, from areas that hadn't sent fathers and sons north before—people who are not necessarily fluent in Spanish. They have their own languages. And they face particular prejudice here, because their skin is browner. On the job, their Mexican supervisors call them *'indios.'* "

Echoing the thoughts of Bustamante on the other side of the border about federal policy, Smith complains of hypocrisy in the attitudes of local governments in Southern California toward the immigrants. Despite the dependence of the growers on cheap day labor, for example, some communities have attempted to enact bans on public solicitation of work and curbside hiring. Similarly, despite a concern about criminality among young migrants on the street, laws like Proposition 187 seek to get the children of undocumented immigrants out of the public schools..It is a misconception, Smith points out, to believe that the people affected by such measures will simply become discouraged and go home. On the contrary, they will find other—sometimes illegal— ways to support themselves and their families. Teenagers who are refused an education and have too much time on their hands, she asserts, are more likely to turn to crime.

Meanwhile, according to Smith, Mexican and other Hispanic immigrants are falsely accused of committing felonies that are really the work of "rob-and-return" gangs from Tijuana, who know how to evade the Border Patrol and cross back and forth routinely. "If you really push any law-enforcement person here," Smith says, "they'll agree that the long-distance immigrants are responsible only for survival crimes, petty thefts like a blanket from a clothesline. Yes, we do have clients that shoplift aspirin and drops for their eyes during flu season, but that's the extent of their crime. But the Border Patrol, which has become very adept at the PR battle, just lumps them all together. It scares everybody." Indeed, most of the studies, often sponsored by state legislators, that portray the horrendous burden that undocumented immigrants pose for California, Smith asserts, are based on faulty data, including inflated numbers, and flawed methodology. But the result, she complains, is to "give people a rational veneer for their irrational arguments against immigration. Alien bashing is now politically correct in all sorts of different strata."

The studies inflame the passions of, among others, former mayors and congressmen from the region, who are particularly active in local anti-immigrant organizations that have emerged in recent years, such as Light Up the Border, Wake Up Washington, and American Spring. Frustrated by what they interpret as federal indifference to the impact of illegal immigration on Southern California, these groups have not stopped at supporting initiatives like Proposition 187. They have urged citizens to take matters into their own hands and have come very close to endorsing vigilante actions to reduce immigration. Sometimes their rhetoric is reminiscent of the language used by the Ku Klux Klan during the 1960s' crusades of the civil rights movement in the South. (Indeed, the Klan, in its heyday, opposed immigration and complained about its impact in northern cities.)

Few people pay attention to the crimes committed against the immigrants. It has been difficult, for example, to get local police or the Border Patrol to investigate seriously the gangs of white teenagers from San Diego County who make a sport of getting drunk and going out at night to shoot at people trying to sneak across the border in isolated locations.

Much of her legal work, Smith says, consists of representing people who have been denied even the minimal pay they were promised for doing menial work. "I have probably yet to see more than half a dozen of my clients who haven't been stiffed at some time, and badly. A man will hire someone to dig a hole for a pool and say, 'It's ten days of work, and I'll pay you at the end.' He picks you up every morning, and you dig for eight days. Then on the ninth day, he stops coming. The worker has no idea who it was, where he was working, he doesn't even know the person's name. Or there will be a matron in Rancho Santa Fe who has a Jaguar sitting in her driveway, but refuses to pay the twenty dollars she owes somebody. It's horrible, but it's absolutely endemic here. It's mind-blowing."

Most disappointing to Smith is that the Mexican American establishment in Southern California has done so little to defend the embattled immigrants. "They are concentrating their energies on trying to get some type of political power, to get on school boards and things like that. Maybe these immigrants are just one step too close to their own immigrant background," she says.

In Smith's view, this just adds to "the incredibly lonely experience" of many who cross the border, even those who have become fully documented. "What you have is unaccompanied men who are away from their families for months, sometimes years on end. You walk into these encampments, and the loneliness is sometimes palpable. It's sad, especially around Christmastime. That's something people don't really think about. It's not just the cheap wages and the horrible housing, but how lonely it is. And they're rebuffed day in and day out. You don't know what guts it takes to get up and go stand on Camino Real and have people look at you like you're dirt. You run up to their car and ask for a job, and you get rejected. You walk into a store and you smell, and somebody looks at you. These people are so resilient. I cannot fathom being able to cope with so much rejection."

PART THREE

FROM MELTING POT TO MOSAIC

A s IMMIGRANTS arrived in America from overseas during the past century, they invariably tried to re-create the sense of community they had experienced in the old country. That usually meant trying to live near, and otherwise associate with, people with a similar background. The official ideology was somewhat distant from reality; the melting pot, it seemed, would take a generation or two to warm up. In some places, the preoccupation with separateness could reach absurd extremes, with different ethnic groups living in enclaves just a few blocks or miles apart but having little to do with each other.

This was just as true in small towns and in the countryside as in the big city. In a narrow strip of land incorporating the sand dunes at the southeastern tip of Lake Michigan, for example, immigrants establishing first or second homes in the early 1900s—many of them having first lived in Chicago or other cities—settled in distinct small-town clusters: The Lithuanians came together in Beverly Shores, Indiana, while the Irish crossed the state line and established a dominant position in Grand Beach, Michigan. The Czechs chose nearby New Buffalo, but the Greeks and the Italians moved into Stevensville. Meanwhile, the Germans went to Bridgeman, Jewish families to Union Pier, and the Swedes to Harbert. Precisely how and why this happened, no one seems to know, but there are remnants of these ethnic dividing lines even today.

Dealing with a somewhat broader canvas, in this section of the book I tell the stories of six distinct ethnic communities that have migrated to particular American cities in recent years: the Hmong (from Laos) in the twin cities of Minneapolis and Saint Paul, the Cubans in

Miami, the Poles in Chicago, the Ethiopians in Washington, the Koreans in Los Angeles, and the Mashadi (from Iran) in Queens and Long Island, New York. With the exception of the Cubans, who wanted to stay nearby in order to reconquer their island upon the demise of Fidel Castro, and the Poles, who were joining up with an earlier generation of immigrants from their country, there is no truly reliable explanation of how these groups chose where to congregate. But finding strength in numbers, they have all made their mark as distinct communities.

Like the individuals from various parts of the world who have been introduced in earlier chapters, these six immigrant groups have little or nothing to do with each other. What they do have in common is that all came to the United States to escape economic, political, or social crises at home, often growing out of some element of a failed American foreign policy (such as involvement in the Vietnam War or support for dictators like the Shah of Iran and the emperor of Ethiopia). And to a remarkable extent, they have each managed to remain separate from everyone else, clinging to language, culture, and folklore in what seems, at least so far, to be a more lasting way than earlier generations of immigrants. For some, the choice may be more voluntary than for others, who are racially distinct; yet a mutual reinforcement has emerged. In an America that tends to ignore its own social history and prefers its people true-blue and homogenized, that has sometimes seemed like a threatening phenomenon, almost a rejection of the national ethic. But that is precisely what has changed about immigration: A group that reaches critical mass today can dare not to aspire to total assimilation, but rather choose to stand apart. Under the new ground rules, it turns out, in order to get ahead, it may be necessary to stick together.

In the process, the myth of the melting pot has all but vanished. Of course there are linkages of every kind across the boundary lines—marriages and business deals and strategic political alliances—but there is a new legitimacy to being different. It is all-American.

VI
MANIPULATED BY HISTORY:
THE HMONG

SAINT PAUL, MINNESOTA

PADEE YANG has always been an outsider. She was born in a Lao village, the fifth of eleven children of an itinerant Hmong folk doctor and his wife. "We lived there until I was eight. I thought I was Lao. We spoke only Lao. And we made fun of the Hmong people," she recalls with considerable embarrassment as we talk over lunch at a tiny shopping-center Chinese restaurant in an industrial neighborhood of Saint Paul. When I meet her, she is in her mid-twenties, a weary but studious-looking young woman who has already endured a lifetime worth of trouble.

Soon enough the eight-year-old Padee Yang had learned the truth. Her father was sent to work in a Hmong village in the hill country of Laos, and there she came to realize that she was actually a member of this controversial minority group that she and her friends had mocked. The Hmong were not merely alienated from the majority Lao people, but at the time a vast number of them were actually participating in a covert war, organized by the U.S. Central Intelligence Agency, against the Pathet Lao (the Laotian communists) and the Vietnamese communists whose supply lines ran through Laos.

There was barely time for Padee Yang to get adjusted to this new home among her own people; indeed, today she does not even know where to find the village on the map. Within two years, before she was ten years old, her family had to move again, this time more quickly and with all their neighbors coming along. The war was not going well, and there was a fear that when the communists came to power in Laos, they would take brutal reprisals against the Hmong, and especially anyone who had anything to do with the CIA's "Secret Army." So the entire village packed up what they could carry and left together, to walk out of the country. Padee Yang has no idea how many people there were in all; etched in her memory is a line that extended as far as the eye could see. "There were so many small children," she remembers. "We were walking up and down the hills in the rainy season, so the road was very difficult." Many of the frantic Hmong refugees had it far worse, of course: On their journeys out of Laos, they encountered land mines in the jungle, were massacred in ambushes, died of starvation, or drowned as they tried to swim across the Mekong River. The people of Padee Yang's village trudged on steadily—and more or less uneventfully—for three, or perhaps four, weeks before reaching Thailand.

The original plan was for the family to go to France. Padee Yang's father had worked with many French people in Laos and he spoke French, so it seemed like the natural thing to do; the word was that France offered a warm welcome to political immigrants from Southeast Asia. But in a refugee camp in Thailand, where he was assigned to run the medical unit, Padee Yang's father came into conflict with other Hmong. As she recounts it, some of the people working under him tried to exploit the refugees by charging them for medications that were supposed to be distributed free. Her father found out about this racket and put an end to it. Shortly thereafter, at a party given in his honor by French and American aid workers, some Hmong presented Padee Yang's father with a bottle of wine as a gift. When he drank from it he became violently ill, and he soon died; the Thai doctor who treated him told the family that he had been poisoned.

Alone in a crowded refugee camp with eleven children ranging in age from eighteen to two, speaking no language other than Hmong, Padee Yang's mother decided not to go to France after all. Instead she accepted an invitation at the end of 1976 for her family to join a cousin who had previously immigrated to America. They took their first bus ever to Bangkok, and then their first airplane to the United States, on their way to settle in a place they had never heard of—Providence, Rhode Island.

"We thought of America as a rich country, the best country ever, where you could get anything and everything was available. They never mentioned that you have to work," says Padee Yang, remembering the first days after her arrival. "We expected to see all white beautiful people. But when we came to Rhode Island, they put us in a neighborhood with all poor people, and we didn't see white people at all. And we thought, 'This is not America, because we walk outside and all we see is black people, and we hear Spanish and Portuguese.' . . . When we were in the camp, we saw pictures from Hmong people who had been here before—beautiful pictures. But we were in this rotten neighborhood, and it was nothing like that. . . . We had a lot of disappointments. Even the weather. At first, when it snowed, we thought it was so white and beautiful, America is so clean. But then a couple days later, it got dirty and yucky."

Because Padee Yang's family had been invited to Providence by relatives, they were not assigned another sponsoring family, like most refugees. But their cousin, not so settled herself, was busy working and did not have much time to pay attention to this enormous contingent that arrived on her doorstep. For the first few weeks, they actually had no home at all and stayed in the basement of a church. "It was dark and big. The refrigerator made a funny noise, and we were all scared," Padee Yang recalls. "My mother was worried that something bad might happen, so she would make us all go outside. But then we were too cold."

Finally they moved into a rundown two-bedroom apartment with unreliable heat. "It was really cold, but we didn't know what to do or who to call. We didn't know how to talk, and people made fun of us when we tried. We could tell from the expression on their faces that we were not welcome there. So we started staying inside. We would lock our door and not go out. I remember how angry I was at my mom for bringing us to this country. And she was very upset, too. She wanted to go back. . . . We went through all these difficulties, compared to refugees who come here these days and have a lot of social service agencies that help them. But one of the advantages was [that] it forced us to learn faster."

Learn they did. Padee Yang's mother soon went to work in a factory, assembling small pieces of jewelry; her workplace seemed far away, the hours were long, and the pay was bad. The two oldest sons got jobs, too, to help support the family. The middle children went off to school, all but one—a fifteen-year-old daughter who had to stay home and care for the three youngest children. She in turn rebelled and insisted on getting her own education, but she stayed in high school for only two years before following the traditional Hmong route: early marriage. Her husband was from a Hmong family that had settled in Wisconsin, where he was attending college, and before long Padee Yang's entire family followed the newly married daughter to Oshkosh. "Believe me," says Padee Yang, "when we moved there, nobody knew us. They were all surprised, and they looked at us in a funny way. But they were not as bad [as the people in Rhode Island], and soon they welcomed us. My mom made friends, she went to school, she passed her citizenship, and she got her driver's license."

As for Padee Yang herself, at a Hmong New Year's party she met a young man whose family, along with seven others, had been sponsored to migrate from the refugee camps in Thailand to South Dakota. At sixteen, she got married, too, and moved to Sioux Falls. She was following tradition, but she was also escaping—removing one more burden from her mother and at the same time liberating herself, albeit temporarily, from some of her responsibility for her mother and her siblings.

Padee Yang's in-laws were very different from her own family. They had never been converted to Christianity, but followed ancient, animist religious customs. Her father-in-law had been a city official under the French colonialists and the independent royal Laotian government. His first job in South Dakota was shoveling snow, and this change in status had caused a major blow to his self-esteem and taken a severe psychological toll.

After two years in South Dakota, Padee Yang and her husband moved to the Twin Cities because, she says candidly, "there was no welfare program [in South Dakota] for people like us. My husband was very young, and he was working in a big meatpacking plant. I saw that he couldn't do that for the rest of his life, but he couldn't go to school because he didn't have the money. So I thought we should move to Minnesota and take advantage of the system here. We did, and he finished school and got a good job as a computer-programming technician."

In fact, Padee Yang and her husband were on public assistance for a relatively short time. While he was studying, she worked as a waitress and a hostess in a restaurant and eventually, as her English improved, as an interpreter for other Hmong in their dealings with public agencies. Once her husband went back to work, she returned to school and found a job at the American Refugee Committee in Minneapolis; later she helped launch a new self-help organization, the Hmong-American Partnership.

Padee Yang and her husband moved out of public housing and bought their own home in a quiet middle-class neighborhood. Their three children go to parochial schools and now speak more English than Hmong. What was left of her family in Oshkosh—one brother is the pastor at a Hmong church in California—eventually moved to the Twin Cities. She helped pay for three of her younger brothers to attend a parochial high school, and they have all gone on to college. Padee Yang also helps her mother, who has lost much of the English she once learned and is back on public assistance, and her oldest brother, who has suffered from an illness that his family has been told grows out of his difficulty adjusting to life in the United States.

THE HMONG are believed to be among the most ancient people in Asia, with a long and painful history of statelessness and migration. Their lifestyle was traditionally pastoral, and they survived thousands of years without a written language, depending on an oral tradition of folktales to preserve their culture. It has long been said that they originally inhabited the plains of southern China, but newer research indicates that they probably arrived there from southern Russia or the Iranian plateau by way of central Siberia. As they migrated southward through China, they first occupied rich farmland, where they grew rice and raised livestock, and later the mountains, where they learned to cultivate opium poppies. The Hmong were invaded and conquered over a number of centuries by Han Chinese from the north, who regarded them as rivals and enemies and named them "Miao" or "Meo," which was originally translated as "barbarians." As a conspicuous minority, sometimes suspected of having more in common with Western people than with their neighbors—many were, at one stage, blond-haired and blue-eyed—the Hmong were subjected to great humiliation and, in certain periods, even genocide.

Many Hmong, perhaps as many as five million, still live in China today, but beginning in the early decades of the nineteenth century, thousands of families trekked south, in almost Biblical fashion, crossing mountains and forests in search of a new place to live. Others followed later. They settled in Vietnam, Burma, Thailand, and especially Laos, where—at least 300,000 strong—they came to represent about a tenth of the population by the middle of the twentieth century. Like the Chinese, the Lao majority treated the Hmong with suspicion and often tried to keep them apart from the rest of the nation. For their part, the Hmong resisted assimilation, as they had done elsewhere. Indeed, few Hmong in Laos received any significant amount of education. (The Hmong language is about as distinct from Laotian as it is from English, according to people who know both.)

During the fighting in Indochina toward the end of World War II, the Hmong openly opposed the Japanese and gave refuge in mountains and caves to the Free French survivors of some bloody battles. This endeared them to the postwar French colonial administration, but at the same time made the Hmong an obvious target for the Pathet Lao and Viet Minh, who now escalated their nationalist war against the French. When the United States, in turn, assumed responsibility for what was portrayed as the defense of Western political interests in Southeast Asia, following the French defeat and departure in 1954, the Hmong inherited new allies and protectors—the Americans.

Beginning in the early 1960s, under the CIA's supervision, the Hmong in effect manned the Laotian front of the Vietnam War. They were renowned for their ability to operate in rugged terrain. They often managed to hold off the North Vietnamese troops who poured down the Ho Chi Minh trail, and they courageously helped rescue American pilots shot down during bombing raids on communist positions. Thus, the Hmong came to be regarded, at home and abroad, as American mercenaries. They ignored the various peace agreements that were reached as the war in Southeast Asia wound down (including the North Vietnamese–American accords signed in Paris in 1973), and fought on. About 30,000 Hmong warriors are estimated to have died for the cause between 1965 and 1975, and at least a hundred thousand others were displaced from their homes.

The Hmong may be the last true believers in the futile Southeast Asian war against communism. They still talk proudly of their exploits, and having fought with the CIA in the Secret Army is a badge of honor in the Hmong immigrant community. When I sought out war veteran Vu Yang in his yellow-and-brown ranch home in the suburbs of Saint Paul, for example, he was more than happy to describe his exploits as an airborne communications technician during the war. Sitting in his knotty-pine-paneled basement recreation room in front of a military tapestry and a photograph of himself in uniform, while a stolid brother-in-law looked on silently and a large number of children ran around upstairs, Vu Yang told of his recruitment and subsequent commando training at a secret base in Thailand in the late 1960s. According to the dictates of General Vang Pao, the commander of the CIA-supported force, "every [Hmong] family had to have at least one person in the war," says Vu Yang. "If you didn't have a son, then maybe the father would have to go." In his case, he says, many family members served, including two older brothers and an uncle.

For four years beginning in 1970, Vu Yang recalls with pride, he lived on an American base in U Dorn, Thailand. "Every day, at six o'clock in the morning, I got on a C-47 or another plane and flew over my country. I was always on the first plane going in, and every night on the last plane coming back. We were listening to the communists and also communicating with our ground fighters. We had a big radio in the plane with many frequencies. We only landed to eat or to get more gas. . . . We were shot down many times, but I'm glad to say the bullets never hit my body."

In May 1975, the month after Phnom Penh, the capital of Cambodia, fell to the Khmer Rouge and Saigon, the capital of South Vietnam, to the North Vietnamese and Vietcong, the Pathet Lao moved to take over the Laotian capital of Vientiane. Vang Pao decided to give in and evacuate his Secret Army base at Long Cheng. Soldiers like Vu Yang, who were thought to be in immediate danger of retribution by the communists, were given priority for evacuation to Thailand and resettlement in the United States; the CIA arranged to fly them out quickly. But in fact, most of the Hmong who, by the broadest definition, had anything to do with the clandestine American presence in Laos felt that the United States had an obligation to take them in. There was widespread talk of an explicit, solemn "promise" that U.S. officials had made years earlier to the Hmong—"If the Americans lose this war, they will not forget what the Hmong people have done to help them," according to one version. Very few Hmong felt that their lives had not been disrupted by this brutal war, and so once the prospect of danger was raised, more and more people, like the residents of Padee Yang's village, became convinced that Uncle Sam should and would take care of them. Estimates vary of the number of Hmong who attempted to leave Laos in 1975–76, but there may have been as many as 120,000; it is generally believed that no more than half of them succeeded in reaching Thailand on the first try. Some turned back and resumed their resistance activities. Others ended up in communist "reeducation" camps. Many died.

As long as they remained in refugee camps in Thailand, most of the Hmong escapees were not convinced that they were safe. Although they felt that moving to America was in their case an entitlement, they were desperate enough to do anything to be admitted. If it seemed necessary, they fabricated family relationships to other refugees, and they accepted sponsorship to go anywhere in America under almost any circumstances. Like generations of refugees and immigrants before them, they often agreed to misspelled, or plainly wrong, names on arrival in the United States, rather than risk alienating an immigration officer or slowing down the process.

There was another wrinkle, too: In Hmong culture, birthdates and ages do not have great significance. When asked for that information on arrival, some Hmong panicked and simply made up a date, perhaps saying that they were arriving on their birthday. For many, after all, this represented a new beginning, a kind of rebirth. Often, by accident or design, every member of a large family would choose the same birthdate; if they were interviewed by different immigration officers, no one noticed. Padee Yang tells of a family where all five children have the same official birthday, but in different years, and of another in which, because of confusion on arrival, a son was declared to be ten years older than his mother.

No ONE seems to be sure just how, when, or why the Hmong selected the Twin Cities as a favored place to congregate. Many people claim to have been among the first to arrive there, including Leng Wong, a onetime official of Neo Hom, or the United Lao National Liberation Front. The Front raises money among Hmong refugees and immigrants for the anticommunist resistance forces, led by Vang Pao, that allegedly still plan to invade and reconquer communist-ruled Laos. (Vang Pao now divides his time between Thailand and California.) Leng Wong came to Minnesota in 1976, and through a combination of his political activities and his work in the state's refugee program service, and later the Minnesota Department of Human Services, he may actually have helped provoke a "secondary migration" of Hmong to the Twin Cities from other parts of the United States where they had been settled.

The official U.S. government policy is to attempt to disperse each wave of refugees around the country, in order to minimize any temporary negative impact on local economies and to make it easier for them to become settled and accepted. But this tactic rarely succeeds. Historically, each immigrant group has tended to collect in a few places—selected logically or serendipitously—where its large numbers make the newcomers feel more comfortable and permit them to build their own social support structures. Freedom of internal movement being a fundamental part of the American way of life, of course, federal, state, and local officials are powerless to prevent this from happening. New arrivals, like everyone else, vote with their feet.

There are now an estimated 17,000 Hmong living in the Twin Cities, out of a total of some 125,000 in the United States.[1] More Hmong live in California, particularly in agricultural regions like the Central Valley near Fresno, but probably not as many in any single urban area

---

[1] *These figures are rough estimates, based on the 1990 census. The Minnesota Department of Human Services believes that, given their early marriages and high birth rate, along with secondary migration, the Hmong in the Twin Cities may now number as many as 30,000.*

as in Minneapolis and Saint Paul. Several parts of Wisconsin also have large concentrations. Unlike other recent Asian immigrant groups, such as Koreans, Vietnamese, and Cambodians, the Hmong have tended not to attract a great deal of attention or publicity in the places where they settle. One exception was during the late 1970s and early 1980s, when there was an outbreak in several states of sudden unexplained deaths of Hmong men in their sleep—a phenomenon that still has not been adequately understood but is more prevalent in the refugee camps in Thailand and may be related to a thiamine deficiency among Southeast Asians.

It is in the Twin Cities that the Hmong probably stand out more than anywhere else. Being with others who fought in the war—and who might like to fight in another—was evidently a motive for some of the Hmong who came to Minneapolis and Saint Paul. For others, family and church ties were a factor. A few who lived in the colder, higher elevations in Laos also insist that they find the harsh Minnesota climate congenial. But one member of the Secret Army, Vu Yang, was among the many Hmong who freely acknowledged to me that the liberal welfare system in Minnesota generally, but especially in the Twin Cities, was a key attraction. So was the warm welcome extended to newcomers. "I visited many states, and I think I like Minnesota the best," said Vu Yang. "The people here are nice, the leaders listen to us more carefully, and mostly they work on what you ask for."

"This was a big chance for Minnesotans to show how nice they are," says Ruth Hammond, a journalist and teacher who has extensively studied the Hmong in the Twin Cities, with a trace of cynicism in her voice. Indeed, social activists from Minnesota actually visited some of the resettlement camps in Thailand and recruited Hmong to settle in their state. "The Hmong have made people here feel less provincial," Hammond continues. "Minnesotans appreciate their embroidery work and their food; they respond positively to some of the most visible Hmong characteristics. In terms of gratification, I think a lot of people in the Twin Cities have gotten a kick out of helping the Hmong—more than, say, helping black people. You can identify with the Hmong as needy people who have not created their own situation."

Certainly Minnesota made more sense as a place for the Hmong to gather than some of the communities to which they were originally sent. Take the case of Christopher Thao, for example, the son of illiterate parents and one of eleven children, who dreamed of coming to the United States to get an education. He is now one of the great Hmong success stories, but getting to that point required a considerable odyssey.

As an eighteen-year-old refugee arriving on his own, Thao was assigned to a sponsoring family near Jasper, Arkansas, a town in the Ozarks where he found that he was the only Asian person within thirty miles. After six months living with an elderly childless couple in a mobile home in the countryside, Thao says, he yearned to be reunited with some cousins who had settled in Philadelphia. "So I called up my voluntary agency, my caseworker in New York, and said, 'Look, I'm very lonely here. My sponsors like me, they take good care of me, but I just can't survive this way.' I asked him to send money for the bus fare to Pennsylvania."

The bus fare arrived. But his sponsors were surprised and offended that he wanted to leave, Thao remembers, and only reluctantly did they take him to the bus station in a nearby town. At that point he did not have a cent to his name, and they were not about to give him money. From a payphone at the station, he made a collect call to an American missionary he had once met in Laos, who quickly found someone in Jasper to bring him ten dollars for spending money on the twenty-five-hour journey to Philadelphia. But on Thao's arrival there, the church that had sponsored his relatives refused to help someone who had abandoned his original placement. Once again he contacted the caseworker in New York, who then paid his bus fare onward to a resort in the Pocono Mountains, north of Philadelphia.

There Thao became a janitor. Nearby, he discovered East Stroudsburg State College and talked an official into admitting him as a temporary, nondegree student. Relying on special refugee programs, including student loans, Thao was advanced to regular student status after a year and stayed on for a second year. By then, his parents and all of his unmarried siblings had arrived in the Philadelphia area, and he transferred to West Chester State College, which was much closer. He took a year off there to serve as a refugee caseworker himself, in order to help support his family, but then resumed studying. Late in 1980, however, Thao's parents suddenly decided they wanted to move to Minnesota, to be near other friends and relatives, and he dutifully followed, moving them in his car at Christmastime. Another stint of work followed—writing lesson plans for teachers in the Minneapolis public schools who had Hmong students—and finally he finished his undergraduate degree in a year and a half at Hamline University in Saint Paul.

Thao's life was then radically transformed by the fact that his father, who hoped to see his son become a lawyer, was critically ill with heart and kidney disease. He enrolled at William Mitchell College of

Law in Minneapolis and, making up for much lost time, rushed through in two and a half years. A month after his graduation, his father died.

As the third son in his family, Christopher Thao had already taken another major step to please his father: "In 1981 he said to me, 'Son, you are not young anymore, you are twenty-four, and I'm very old and sick. I don't know when I'm going to die, but I beg you to get married, so I can be relieved of this anxiety of you being a bachelor.' . . . So I called up my cousin and a few of my friends, and I asked, 'Do you know any beautiful girl who would be good to marry?' I did very odd things. My cousin said, 'Well, in the duplex where we live, there are three [Hmong] girls upstairs. Why don't you come over and take a look?' So I went and met them, talked with them, and I saw one I thought looked especially good. I talked to her, and wrote her and called her a few times. We got to know each other for a month, and then we got married. . . . I believe it was a good decision, but it was not based on romance; it was based on my commitment to make good on the promise I made to my father. . . . And we had to have children right away, so that my father could watch them grow."

Before long, Thao became the first Hmong licensed attorney in the United States, and he joined a major law firm in downtown Saint Paul. But the conflict between traditional and modern, Hmong and American, continues to play itself out in his life every day. A short, intense man with a quick step, Thao looks every bit the establishment lawyer in his white shirts and ties, and he has a spiffy office in a modern building. Only the pictures on his office walls imply any link with Southeast Asia. But the bulk of his caseload revolves around personal injury, liability, and malpractice cases for the refugee and immigrant community—not only Hmong, but also Lao, Vietnamese, Cambodians, Hispanics, and Ethiopians and other Africans. This is no doubt profitable for his firm, but consigns him to the special category of immigrant lawyer. And then there is the volunteer work, which Thao estimates takes up about half of his time: "It's very difficult to serve and at the same time make a living, because the demand is so great. People call me up saying, 'I'm applying for Social Security disability, do you know what the rules are? Where can I get help?' or 'Welfare cut me off, what am I going to do?' I cannot respond to them all. Sometimes I have to say, 'No, that is not an area of my practice, and I cannot help you.' I have to refer them to some other people."

At the time we met, Thao had five children under the age of eight, and his wife, who had previously worked as a seamstress and an electronic-board assembler, was now staying home to care for them.

They live in an upper-middle-class suburb, where they were among a very few nonwhite families when they first arrived. Their oldest daughter, who barely spoke English when she entered kindergarten, is now, by Thao's account, a star in school—"number one in spelling"—a classic young Asian immigrant high achiever. But at home, the parents and children still try to speak Hmong to each other and otherwise live according to Hmong traditions.

That is Christopher Thao's dream: that it is possible to have "a strong sense of being a Hmong and maintaining your values as a Hmong, but also to become like other members of the community. What we will see in the future is that as Hmong enter their own homes, they become Hmong, and as they walk out the door, they will become more like Americans."

THIS DREAM is far from being realized by most of the Hmong in the Twin Cities, who do not even know anyone they would classify as "an American." The majority of adult Hmong are either unemployed (at least 30 percent) or severely underemployed with low wages. Indeed, many Hmong immigrants are not really doing anything in their new home country, but merely subsist, exploit the system, and wait for they know not what. The older men, in particular, tend to feel hopelessly displaced and, as a result, suffer from bouts of depression. They have lost the special status they had in Laos but have failed to pick up new survival skills here. Few have made a serious attempt to learn English, in part because they have no significant educational background for it and because they feel embarrassed to be in a class with women or much younger students, as would usually be the case in English-as-a-second-language courses. Most were country people who, for political or security reasons, may have been temporarily grouped into Laotian cities by the CIA but never adapted to urban life.

According to Ly Vang, director of the Association for the Advancement of Hmong Women of Minnesota, this has caused great problems and often violence between husbands and wives in many Hmong immigrant families. "With a lack of education and job skills, ninety percent of the women were isolated and homebound" after they arrived, she says. The men were at home, too, with nothing to do. Initially reluctant to rock the boat by doing anything more radical, organizations like hers found that they had to start by teaching skills as basic as housecleaning and child care to women who were adapting to a totally new environment, where there was no longer a dirt floor or, for that matter, a relative next door who could be counted upon to baby-sit.

Once the women had gained confidence in those areas, it became possible for the self-help groups to do more. Gradually, Ly Vang says, some Hmong women came to see working outside the home as a way to improve their plight, and their husbands grudgingly accepted the idea. She estimates that as many as 40 percent of the Hmong immigrant women in the Twin Cities now have outside jobs. Indeed, she has evidence on the premises: As we spoke in Ly Vang's storefront office in a rundown neighborhood of Minneapolis, about a dozen preschool children played and sang in a day-care program in a back room. On the walls were drawings teaching the English alphabet, a chart listing American holidays, and a poster explaining the virtues of "studying hard."

There are many other aspects of the adjustment that have been difficult. If they or their children become ill, Hmong immigrants often consult traditional healers, who employ herbal cures and shamans, and this clashes with local custom, not to mention the rules for reimbursement under Medicare and Medicaid. Oblivious to the civil and criminal court system, Hmong tend to use their own method of resolving personal disputes, judging people according to their unique community standards and assessing their own penalties. (A husband might have to pay a fine, for example, if his wife commits suicide.) It can be awkward, to say the least, when the Hmong engage in their traditional rituals for weddings, funerals, and other special occasions. To celebrate these events properly—or to expel the evil spirits from a sick person or call the soul into a newborn baby—may require the slaughter of a live cow, pig, or chicken on the spot. While this has spawned some new animal-raising business ventures on the outskirts of the Twin Cities, it has also caused quite a few tensions with unsuspecting neighbors, especially in public-housing projects.

On arrival in America, most Hmong, like Padee Yang, lived in conditions that greatly surprised and upset them—perhaps as many as six or seven to a room. The desire to escape such conditions exacerbated the tendency for Hmong girls to marry when they are very young, but so did the welfare system; each time a new family unit was established, it could hope to get on the welfare rolls in its own right. Typically, seventeen-year-old girls begin to feel intense pressure from their parents to marry and then to demonstrate their fertility within the first two years. It is rare for Hmong girls in the United States to remain single until they have reached twelfth grade, or childless until they are nineteen. Because the bride price, or "nurturing charge," collected by parents from their daughter's prospective husband is generally lower here than it was in Laos, the average age of Hmong immigrant girls at marriage may actually have declined in America. Some have been known to get away with marrying as young as thirteen, and Minnesota law permits the marriage of first cousins if this is considered acceptable in one's traditional culture. Under the circumstances, the question has been raised by social service agencies whether young Hmong girls are really enjoying the equal protection of the laws promised by the U.S. Constitution.

Indeed, some young men follow the traditional custom of going with a group of friends to kidnap their bride from her parents' home. In one celebrated case in July 1991, a Hmong man from Lafayette, Colorado, was charged with sexual assault, and he and his parents accused of kidnapping, after they brought a fifteen-year-old girl from Fresno, California, to be his bride. Insisting that they had paid more than eight thousand dollars to the girl's parents, who eagerly participated in the transaction, the man's family complained that it was being persecuted by the civil authorities for adhering to its traditional cultural practices.

Not surprisingly, given better health care and lower infant mortality than in Laos, the average size of Hmong families in the United States has not shrunk significantly and, in some circles, may even have grown. Since fewer Hmong mothers breastfeed their children here, they may ignore traditional guidelines regarding the spacing of their pregnancies. Ironically, many Hmong couples in the Twin Cities, having married young to benefit from public assistance, later find it easier to support their large families if they get what is commonly known as a "welfare divorce"; then the wife who stays home with her children can continue to collect welfare, while the husband goes to work. In order to avoid getting caught surpassing legal limits on their income, Hmong families on welfare also tend to keep all their resources in cash or material possessions, but that in turn makes them more vulnerable to holdups, especially by young, alienated members of their own ethnic community.

Long-term dependence on welfare and other forms of public assistance among the Hmong in the Twin Cities is estimated to be as high as 50 percent or 60 percent. And because of their large families, the Hmong are the only ones who can easily qualify these days for some of the most spacious four- or five-bedroom public housing units in Minneapolis and Saint Paul. Indeed, in the estimation of Saint Paul's former mayor, Jim Scheibel, 85 percent of the public-housing units in his city are filled with Southeast Asians, primarily Hmong.

Meanwhile, the Hmong have come to be regarded as relatively reliable and desirable public housing tenants who pay the rent on time. This gives other minorities—particularly African Americans—the impression that the Hmong are benefiting from favoritism in the distribution of public resources. Many Hmong are quick to claim that they improve any neighborhood where they settle, and to express contemptuous, if not racist, attitudes toward black families. Where blacks and Hmong do live side by side, they tend not to get along well at first. And as blacks find themselves bumped out of their old neighborhoods into seemingly more rundown, and yet more expensive, areas, they tend to harbor resentment against those who appear to have replaced them—in this case, the Hmong.

More than 50 percent of the Hmong in the Twin Cities are under the age of eighteen, and that percentage is obviously growing. As the stories of Padee Yang and Christopher Thao demonstrate, Hmong culture, like many others in Asia, requires a high degree of filial piety. Adults take care of their parents and expect that their children will, in turn, eventually do the same for them. But there is serious question whether this tradition will be able to survive transplantation to the United States. Already grandparents and grandchildren can barely communicate with each other, linguistically or otherwise.

Moreover, Hmong teenagers appear to be suffering from an identity crisis. They want to be, and may feel that they are, just like their peers in mainstream American society, while their mothers and fathers, particularly at the lower end of the income scale, have no choice but to preserve a distinct Hmong identity. The children, and especially the boys, develop American habits and tastes without the means to pay for them; they become highly Americanized without being socially integrated. No matter what they do to conform, they will still look different. As some of the youngsters exhibit their alienation—wearing punk hairdos, skipping school, and joining gangs—and others their ambition to succeed, both groups tend to reject their parents as irrelevant and treat them with disrespect. "They spend very little time with their parents, and they have no other role models," complains Christopher Thao. "The ones who misbehave are considered bad apples" and get written off early. Some turn to lives of crime, preying on trusting, older Hmong who are willing to open their apartment doors for them.

"These kids are in a tough situation," observes Ruth Hammond. "They haven't gotten the guidance they need from their families, and they don't get the support they need from the American culture either. If they follow the traditional Hmong route of early marriage and all that, they're going to fail in American terms. But usually no one from the American culture has embraced them, so why should they try an American life? . . . In some ways, the kids have the worst of it. They have been the victims of hostility more than their parents have. In school, they are the target of racial insults and discrimination. So they're mad at both worlds."

One side effect is psychologically battered parents, who have to deal with this crisis in their own household along with other serious problems. "Here the children are not taught to obey their parents," complains Lao Her, who, along with her husband, Neng Thao, repairs stained-glass windows. "Here the schools teach freedom, so children think they can do anything. But it isn't true. It's confusing for the parents and the children." Lao Her and Neng Thao cannot afford to pay for child care or summer activities, so when I visit their workshop on a hot August morning, the younger two of their three daughters are sitting quietly off on the side, one reading *Charlotte's Web* and the other a more advanced paperback novel. The couple prefers to have their children nearby, in order to keep tabs on them; they worry about the bad influence their American peers might have on them. The ten- and fifteen-year-old girls seem passively content, but their parents are in a state of agitation as they discuss their lives with me. The children "don't really know where they are. They don't know anything about our country [Laos] and how beautiful it looks," says Lao Her plaintively.

Neng Thao and Lao Her had been part of an idealistic experiment, the Restoration Guild, which taught them and several other Hmong immigrants a completely new skill—the rehabilitation of stained-glass windows from small-town and rural Minnesota churches. This created jobs while fulfilling a need, but economic hardship has reduced the customer base. Now they are the only two members of the group left doing the work, and it is somehow pathetic to see them struggling away in a corner of the guild's cavernous workshop on the third floor of a converted warehouse in Saint Paul.

"So far, we are surviving," says Neng Thao, who was a soldier in the Secret Army and a sometime businessman in Laos. But he makes no secret of the fact that he is not happy in the United States: "Since we got here, things have become harder. We don't know how to communicate or write. We have not had much chance to go to school or have good jobs. But we don't have a choice. There's no place else to go." Given a chance, Neng Thao says, he would prefer to return to Laos. The youngest daughter in the family, Sia, looks up quizzically as she hears her father say this; asked if she agrees, she replies, "No."

Vang Thao, who was also a soldier under the CIA's command from the age of sixteen until "we lost our country," now works on an assembly line making plastic plates. For him, there are no illusions about returning to Laos, but his frustrations with family life are profound. "My children live the new way," he says as a cousin translates for him, "and there is no way to teach them, no way to discipline them. At home [in Laos], it was okay to spank them. Here it's against the law. And here, if your wife has an affair, you don't have the right to do anything about it. There is too much freedom." While we are speaking in his living room, a son, one of his six children, walks in, as if on cue, puts on his high-top sneakers, and says he plans to go out. Vang Thao asks him to stay and look after his younger sister. They quarrel in Hmong, and soon the son goes out anyway. "Ten or twenty years from now, our children and our grandchildren will still carry Hmong names, but they will have nothing else left of their culture," says Vang Thao, shaking his head. His cousin, our interpreter, has just one disagreement: He is not so sure they will bother keeping their Hmong names.

ON A SUNNY, breezy Saturday afternoon, I go to a widely publicized "intercultural festival event" sponsored by the crime prevention program of an organization called the Southeast Asian Community. It turns out to be a mostly Hmong affair—there are few other Southeast Asians on hand, let alone people from mainstream "American" groups—in a large open park surrounded by public-housing projects. The modern skyline of Minneapolis looms in the distance, almost like a mirage. A large contingent of police officers is distributing fliers in Hmong, Lao, and Vietnamese, that explain how to call 911 in an emergency. Other brochures are available, in those languages as well as Khmer (Cambodian), telling battered women how to recognize their plight and seek help.

Young boys play soccer and other games, but most of the action takes place under makeshift blue and green canopies, where Hmong women do a brisk business in food and handicrafts. The most popular items, as usual, are embroidery wall hangings that purport to tell the story, past and future, of the Hmong people. The most prominent, identifiable features in some of the embroidery panels are large white airplanes and people walking. The planes are pointing both east and west, and it is clear that at the end of the story, they are triumphantly taking the Hmong home to Laos.

This is no surprise, since Hmong life in the United States is infused with an ethic of return. Schoolchildren often draw themselves as soldiers going back to fight the Vietnamese communists, and some of the youngest, even though they were born in the United States, have been known to spin elaborate tales of the hardships they endured coming to America.

This impulse to return is easily exploited by Neo Hom and other followers of General Vang Pao, who conduct frequent fund-raising campaigns in the Hmong community to underwrite their allegedly imminent, CIA-supported reconquest of Laos. The more worldly members of the Hmong community suspect that much of the money collected is actually used to finance the decadent lifestyle of Neo Hom leaders in California, and they accuse Vang Pao of taking advantage of the patriotic emotions of impoverished Hmong. Perhaps worse, Vang Pao is thought to have infiltrated a number of former Secret Army fighters back into Laos from the camps in Thailand, with the mission of convincing other Hmong, who may still have been trying to leave, that they now must stay behind and await the U.S.-organized invasion. Some villagers are known to have been caught planning for that great event and then punished by the Laotian communist regime.

Intrigue is a central ingredient of Hmong politics in the United States, and reformists charge that Vang Pao and his sometimes surreptitious associates have rigged the outcome of elections in various Hmong community organizations to make certain that people who support his policies win. Journalists who write about these matters, including Ruth Hammond, have occasionally received death threats. Despite the absence of any concrete signs of a renewed conflict in Laos, Vang Pao does seem to retain considerable influence over his brethren. When he let it be known in the early 1980s that he wanted more of the Hmong to gather in California so that they, like the Cubans in Miami of two decades earlier, would be prepared for training to retake their homeland, there was a significant exodus from the Twin Cities to Fresno. But the migrants soon discovered that they could not all have their own farms in California, as some believed they had been promised, and most returned to Minneapolis and Saint Paul. Still, after Vang Pao announced that he was opposed to any further resettlement of Hmong refugees in America, the flow from the camps in Thailand slowed to a trickle.

Inevitably, the question is raised whether the majority of Hmong immigrants accept the idea of making the United States their permanent home, whether America will effectively be the last stop for this migratory people. Those who arrived more recently are apparently far more realistic about what would await them if they attempted to go back to Laos. A steady decline in Hmong dependence on welfare—for example, in the small towns where they live in Wisconsin—may be a sign of willingness to accept responsibility for their own fate in the United States. This would appear to be a necessary transition, eagerly awaited in the Twin Cities. "The taxpayers were beginning to grow impatient," says former Saint Paul mayor Scheibel, discussing the slowness of the Hmong to become more self-sufficient. "People don't give [newcomers] very long. They ask, 'Why aren't they earning money? Why are we continuing to support them? Why are they filling so much of our public housing?' "

The Hmong may take more generations than most to fulfill the stereotype of the upwardly mobile immigrant group that beats all odds and succeeds on traditional American terms, making its own unique contributions to the general welfare. But Christopher Thao points proudly to the fact that more Hmong are graduating from high school and going on to college. Indeed, there are now more than a thousand Hmong college students in the Twin Cities at any given time, he says. Home ownership is also increasing among the better-educated, more ambitious Hmong. About 13 percent of Hmong homes in the Twin Cities are owned by their occupants, according to the Hmong American Partnership, and a few successful Hmong have bought several houses and become landlords.

In 1991 a major breakthrough occurred when Choua Lee won an at-large seat on the Saint Paul school board and became the first Hmong elected to public office in the United States. The twenty-three-year-old woman, who campaigned on the theme of "a fair shake for Hmong" in the city schools, polled more votes than any other candidate in the race—a sign of acceptance by the larger community that once could not have been imagined.

Still, most of the Hmong in the Twin Cities spend their lives in a closed, albeit good-humored, circle. They are persistently "isolated," says Scheibel, notwithstanding the best-intentioned efforts to integrate them into schools and other community institutions. They often attend ceremonies, celebrations, and parties of their own at an exhausting pace, consuming as many as twenty hours a week. Rarely are they drawn outside this world, because many of their jobs involve dealing almost exclusively with other Hmong. One positive consequence is that there appear to be no Hmong among the homeless on the streets of the Twin Cities. "There's always room for somebody else in their homes," notes Scheibel. "They have reminded the community of the importance of family and sharing."

As Ruth Hammond sees it, "The Hmong will be different from most other immigrants. I don't think they came here to take advantage, but they do. They were manipulated by history. . . . I get no sense of them throwing in their lot with the future of America."

"I'm going to be here forever," insists former warrior Vu Yang, who works as a "bilingual paraprofessional" for the Minneapolis public schools but puts much of his energy into an antidrug program, trying to convince villagers in Thailand not to grow opium and Hmong-Americans not to use drugs. But he too is having trouble adapting. There is a difference, Vu Yang notes, between "the big freedoms," which flourish in the United States, and "the little freedoms," which he feels were greater in Laos. "There you don't have to buy land for farming. You don't need permission to cut down a tree in the jungle. Here life is too organized, too formal, too under control," he says.

Even Padee Yang, who could be regarded as a Hmong who has made one of the more comfortable transitions to a new life in America, says, "I still feel that I have something over there. . . . I didn't have a chance to say goodbye."

VII
A LONG VACATION:
THE CUBANS

MIAMI

IN THE SUMMER of 1962, when Adis Vila was an eight-year-old girl in a small town thirty miles outside Havana, her mother told her she was going to reward her for her good grades in school with a vacation in Florida. There had been quite a bit of turmoil in Cuba during the child's young life, as Fidel Castro seized power from the old, corrupt dictatorial regime, but nothing seemed out of the ordinary about this adventure. After all, there were relatives to visit, and America was supposed to be an exciting place. They boarded a KLM flight and, after half an hour or so in the air, landed in Miami.

"Shortly after we arrived," says Vila, her voice as grim as the recollection, "my mother told me that we were staying, that this was not a vacation after all, and that my father would probably not be able to join us for a long time. We went to live with my father's sister, who turned out not to be very nice. . . . Thirteen days later, she told my mother that in Miami everybody had to find a place for themselves." For the next four years, the mother and daughter lived in a garage apartment behind another Cuban family's house in northwest Miami, where the rent was $45 a week. In anticipation of the arrival of Vila's father, they moved for a time to a $65-a-week place. He did turn up, shortly before her thirteenth birthday—as one in a group of refugees exchanged by Castro, in a bizarre Cold War deal, for some American agricultural equipment—but things were not the same. Vila's parents soon divorced, and she and her mother had to downgrade their accommodations once again.

It is a classic immigrant's tale, the epic struggle of a mother and daughter, surviving against the odds: A woman who had never worked in Cuba, taking three buses to get to a clothing factory, where she was a "finisher," with low wages, terrible working conditions, and no benefits. A teenager who "grew up very quickly and learned the value of money and of an education, and sought to become very independent and to do everything I could." Together they went to work nights at the Orange Bowl, wrapping hot dogs and dispensing soft drinks. The daughter, perfectly bilingual and soon a star French student as well, got promoted to be a cashier and then a souvenir stand manager, while the mother, unable to master English, remained a food stand helper. Together, after a late game, they would make their way home at eleven or twelve o'clock and figure out how close they were to having the money they needed for the rent or, in a good month, new clothes.

Today Adis Vila is a lawyer. She has been a member of the cabinet of a Republican governor of Florida in Tallahassee and an assistant secretary of agriculture in Washington during the Bush administration. Along the way, she was a champion high school athlete (the only white girl on the softball team) and a standout student at a preppy southern women's college (the only Cuban in her class). She graduated from the University of Florida Law School with honors, had a Rotary Foundation fellowship in Switzerland, was a White House Fellow, and then served a stint in the European bureau of the State Department and another at the Commerce Department. She is a member of the Council on Foreign Relations. And for a time, she was the only woman professional in a spiffy Miami law firm. She is tough and hard-charging and, by the way, has still not forgiven President John F. Kennedy for his "treacherous dealings" at the time of the Bay of Pigs invasion, which occurred when she was seven years old.

TWENTY PERCENT of all Cubans—at least 1.2 million of them—live outside their country. Of them, more than half, perhaps even three-quarters of a million, are in or near Miami. The Cuban migration to the United States in the early 1960s was unique, not only because of its size and suddenness, but also because it was essentially invited and stimulated by the American government. Frustrated by Castro's turn toward communism soon after taking power in 1959 and by his growing, virulent hostility to U.S. interests, officials in Washington responded by opening the door to Cuban refugees. Their hope at the time, of course, was that the cream of Cuban society would take a prolonged vacation in Florida, of the type that Adis Vila's mother promised her, and then, from a perch barely a hundred miles away and with a little help from their friends in the CIA, figure out how to go home and get rid of Castro.

But the Cuban refugees soon turned into long-term immigrants. They failed to retake Havana (not for lack of trying), but they quite methodically conquered Miami. As the Cuban-born sometime mayor of Miami, Xavier Suarez, is fond of saying, "The Irish needed fifty or sixty years to get control of Boston, but we took over this city in less than thirty years." By all accounts, it was not especially difficult. In the words of George Volsky, who had been a Polish refugee in Cuba after World War II and then fled to Miami in 1960, "This is a place that is devoid of any permanent establishment." Charles Zwick, a banker who himself arrived from Washington in 1969 after serving in the Johnson administration, adds that when the Cubans first got to Miami, "this was a small southern town, with no roots and no power structure. Everything was up for grabs." In this sleepy city on Biscayne Bay, there was hardly any big-league business activity to speak of—fewer corporate headquarters than in Atlanta or even Jacksonville. It was easy to become a big shot quickly.

But the way Cuban Americans remember it, there was plenty of hardship, discrimination, and exploitation during their early days in Miami. Doctors had jobs washing dishes in restaurants, and society ladies from Havana found themselves cleaning other people's houses. In the public schools, Cuban children were a group apart. There were few teachers who could understand, let alone speak, Spanish. One woman (like Vila, now a lawyer) recalls that the only way she was able to afford lunch in her school cafeteria as a young child was to spend half the lunch hour in the kitchen, drying trays.

Soon, however, the seething American hatred of Castro translated into sympathy and special consideration for the Cubans. A federal law was passed, waiving the usual waiting period and allowing them to apply for permanent-resident status (a green card) after only a year, faster than anyone else. The term "affirmative action" was not yet widely used, but an early form of precisely that concept benefited the Cubans in both the public and private sectors, giving them a chance to catch up with native-born Americans. There were special scholarships and other opportunities for the brightest Cuban students, and good jobs in the service industries almost seemed to be reserved for Cubans who obtained a good education. As the Cuban community grew steadily larger, Miami's banks and real estate firms, for example, scrambled to hire people who could help them connect into this lucrative new market. Other companies looked in the Cuban community for promising young recruits who, through linguistic and cultural affinity, could possibly help steer their expansion into the Caribbean and South American spheres. This caused enormous resentment among others who felt they were not getting a fair shake, including Miami's large Jewish community and its perennially neglected African Americans.

In the meantime, Cuban entrepreneurship flourished in Miami's boomtown climate. Today, there are an estimated thirty-five hundred or more Cuban-owned small businesses thriving in south Florida, many operating out of townhouses and living rooms in the Hialeah section of Miami. "It has become virtually impossible to get away with discriminating against the Cubans," says one longtime Miami resident, a federal employee who came originally from Detroit. "If a Cuban finds that an Anglo car dealer or doctor or supermarket is rude to him, he doesn't have to take it. He's always got a Cuban alternative. There's a whole Cuban economy here. They can 'buy from their own.' And that gives them tremendous economic, social, and political strength."

In the heart of an old decaying neighborhood rose Little Havana; Southwest Eighth Street became the languid but lively Calle Ocho, with restaurants featuring Cuban food, record stores with Cuban music, and clothing stores catering to Cuban tastes. One-stop shops could handle the processing of passports, green cards, work permits, tax returns, and driver's licenses, all in Spanish, and there were storefront lawyers nearby to turn to if anything went wrong. Increasingly, people from other parts of the city came to Little Havana to be part of the action. Before long, there were complaints that the Cubans were dominating, excluding, and discriminating against others, particularly poor blacks and the Haitians, Nicaraguans, and Salvadorans who poured into Miami during the late 1970s and 1980s. Part of this could be explained by the fact that the Cubans bristled at being lumped into the catchall category of Miami's colorful immigrant tapestry or of its many "Hispanics." They had seniority, they were separate, and they intended to stay that way.

Every successful Cuban, it seemed, also had to have a personal foreign policy. Families were divided, not just by where people lived (in Cuba or the United States), but also by individual views about what should be done to remove the detested Castro. Every immigrant group undoubtedly follows events in its home country closely, at least for a time, but probably none so closely as have the volatile Cubans for more than three decades. Any event anywhere in the world can be interpreted in terms of its contribution to the ultimate liberation of Cuba. Even today, heated debates take place over the tables of the Versailles (pronounced "bur-'say-less") Restaurant and Bakery, on the edge of Little Havana, over the meaning of developments in the former Soviet Union, not to mention the relative willingness of various American politicians to stand up for what is right. At lunchtime or well into the night, young lawyers, businessmen, and journalists, most of whom went to school together, linger at Versailles over countless shots of rum and cups of strong Cuban coffee to laugh and shout as they revise history and prescribe the future. They switch almost imperceptibly from English to Spanish to their own special dialect, commonly derided as "Spanglish." They have a good life in a city that their families have, in a sense, put on the map of the United States and Latin America.

MANY ASPECTS of the Cuban migration to Miami were unconventional and controversial, but perhaps none so much as the "Pedro Pan" airlift, which, in less than two years, brought almost an entire generation of children of Cuba's professional elite to the United States to "save" them from life under communism. The airlift, and the effort to help the children adjust, was the special project of Brian Walsh, then a relatively junior Catholic priest working in the pastoral center of the Archdiocese of Miami. Thirty years later—holding the rank of monsignor but still in charge of immigrant affairs at the pastoral center—Walsh delights in retelling the story of his own unusual contribution to the growth of the Cuban American community.

An Irish immigrant himself, Walsh had helped with the resettlement of refugees from the 1956 Hungarian anticommunist revolt who had first been taken in at Camp Kilmer in New Jersey, as well as the placement of Italian war orphans who had been sent to the United States. A State Department official handling refugee issues then for the Eisenhower administration taught him that popular attitudes in any host community had a lot to do with the success of the transition; in other words, "Madison Avenue had to help make the American people love the Hungarian refugees for at least three months. After that, we could have trouble."

But in Miami, notwithstanding public relations efforts, there had been a great deal of trouble and a significant backlash after the arrival of a relatively small number of Hungarians. "These people were just dumped on the community," Walsh recalls. "There were no social services at all. Even the local agencies were not contacted. Most of the time, we found out about resettlements when somebody walked in the

Havana, or for indoctrination in Eastern Europe? Was that any less traumatic? Were they better off? . . . We certainly thought we were doing the right thing at the time, and I still think we did. We were responding to parents who were absolutely desperate."

At the same time, Walsh acknowledges, the Catholic Church and various welfare agencies were willingly collaborating with an official U.S. effort, launched under Eisenhower and continued by President John F. Kennedy, to drain Cuba's intellectual resources and "to create a refugee colony in Miami that could be the basis for an overthrow of Fidel Castro." Once their children had left, of course, Cuban parents felt a greater urgency about trying to get out themselves, and visa restrictions were waived without any real consideration of the economic, political, and social impact on South Florida. "A lot of extended family of the children actually got in this way. Grandparents, aunts, and uncles. Possibly about a quarter of the Cuban refugees in Miami had the door opened to them through Pedro Pan.

"Sometime between the Bay of Pigs fiasco and the missile crisis, I think [American officials] began to reconsider" the wisdom of this open-door policy, Walsh says. "But they never really got around to discouraging Cubans from coming here until Ronald Reagan took office," after the Mariel boatlift of 1980.

As for the psychological legacy of Pedro Pan, it is still being hotly debated. Maria Domínguez was fourteen years old when she came to Miami from Havana in 1961 with her little brother, whom she remembers to have been only five at the time. A fifteen-year-old brother had preceded them by a few months and been sent to live in Delaware. "My parents were afraid that [if he stayed in Cuba] he would be put in the military and shipped off to Russia," Domínguez recalls. "They said they had to get us all out, because the communists were going to get control of the children and it was better for us to live in a free country rather than stay there and be completely controlled and dominated. I accepted that as very logical. Remember, too, that we all had the impression that we were going to go back home. Soon."

Domínguez says that her main worry at the time was for her younger brother, because boys and girls were initially put into separate camps. "I was able to see him from time to time from a distance, but he was on his own. If you think in cultural terms, for a child his age, pampered and raised in the Cuban style, it was a drastic change. I guess he couldn't understand what was happening. . . . Now that I have my own son, I realize how desperate my parents must have been to let all of us go."

In the case of Maria Domínguez's family, the emotional trauma was short-lived, because their mother immigrated the following month, and their father about nine months later. But certain families have never actually been reunited, and some Pedro Pan alumni have had to plead with Castro's government for permission to go back to Cuba for visits with dying parents or grandparents. For Domínguez, her early experiences dictated a career choice. After her husband completed medical school in Spain, they returned to Miami so that she could study law. "I wanted to be an immigration lawyer, to help poor immigrants. I wanted to give them an opportunity to assert their claim to be here, just as we had been given that opportunity," she says. Today she works for a *pro bono* immigration project of the American Civil Liberties Union, defending Central and South American, African, and Chinese people whom the INS is attempting to deport.

THE PRIVILEGED status of Cuban immigrants in the United States, and particularly in Miami, was severely tested in 1980, when a vast new wave of refugees suddenly arrived—the *Marielitos*, so known because most of them had embarked on their journey from a tiny port on Cuba's north shore, Mariel.

The bizarre crisis began late in 1979, when thousands of Cubans— many of them prospective military conscripts who feared being sent to Africa or other distant places with Castro's new expeditionary forces— crowded onto the grounds of the Peruvian embassy in Havana and demanded political asylum. Soon other embassies were similarly besieged, and it became clear that some action would have to be taken by the United States, which was where most of the people really wanted to go. President Jimmy Carter—at first reluctantly, but then more enthusiastically, as the situation began to look as if it might be milked for domestic political advantage—agreed to take them in. The news spread quickly, and thousands of others hastily prepared to leave. But Castro, not to be outdone, promptly opened the doors of prisons and mental hospitals, saying that common criminals, homosexuals, and other *gusanos* ("worms") were also welcome to leave immediately, but only from Mariel. He was not about to provide transportation, however, and so a few U.S. Coast Guard cutters and hundreds of small, privately owned craft made their way to Mariel and established an impromptu ferry service back and forth to Key West. In many cases, Cubans living in South Florida set out for Mariel in rented boats in the hope that they could find and bring back their own children or other relatives who they knew had been trying to get out; but in the chaos of this exodus, they were often disappointed and had to offer passage to others.

Over a period of weeks, what had seemed like a potential victory in one more skirmish of the endless American psychological and rhetorical war with Castro turned into a public relations disaster for the Carter administration. By the time the exit and entry gates were closed after about three months, the Marielitos came to number an estimated 125,000; although the "undesirables" among them were relatively few, they attracted a great deal of press attention (especially when they rioted in the detention camps and prisons where some were temporarily housed). The impression was widespread that Castro could dump anyone he wanted on the United States, and on his own terms. At the same time, having seen the Cuban model, thousands of Haitians got on rickety boats and headed for Miami to escape the harsh right-wing dictatorship and economic deprivation in their country.

To say that the federal bureaucracy and the social service structure of Dade County, Florida, were unprepared for this influx is a gross understatement. Ciro del Castillo, an artist who had himself been a political émigré from Cuba in 1972, worked initially as a volunteer helping to process the people who were accumulating in public parks, warehouses, a blimp hangar at the Miami airport, and even the Orange Bowl stadium. At first, the federal government seemed oblivious to what was happening. But soon, del Castillo recalls, officials in Washington recognized that "this was a crisis, so they sent in the people they thought were trained to deal with a crisis"—the Federal Emergency Management Administration (FEMA). "FEMA was prepared to deal with natural disasters, but not with refugees. These people had never seen a refugee in their life. And not one of the people they sent down here spoke Spanish," says del Castillo. The right person in the right place at the right time, he was immediately hired by FEMA (and, subsequently, by the State Department, the Office of Refugee Resettlement, and other federal agencies that had to deal with the Marielitos). The language problem was especially serious, since the vast majority of the new refugees, having grown up during the time when Castro was attempting to purge all remnants of American influence from Cuba, spoke no English.

"In the whole history of Cuban immigration to the United States during the twentieth century, no group has been discriminated against like the Marielitos," del Castillo observes. "There was not only discrimination by the government and by individual Americans, but discrimination by their own community."

The Marielitos were different. For one thing, more than 40 percent of them were black-skinned or mulatto, about the same percentage as in the general population of Cuba at the time of Castro's revolution. But the overwhelming majority of the Cubans who had immigrated to Miami during the previous two decades were white—indeed, their departure was estimated to have increased the proportion of blacks in Cuba to almost 50 percent—and if their Cuba had once been a tolerant, color-blind society, as they like to claim, many had now taken on more typically racist American attitudes toward black people. The Marielitos also tended to be less well educated and sophisticated than the typical Cuban immigrants who had come earlier, an embarrassment for some well-established Cuban Americans. The newcomers still lived more outdoors than indoors, as do most people in Cuba, sitting on lawn chairs on the sidewalks in front of their homes or congregating in large groups on park benches and street corners, and talking loudly until late at night. They showed little inclination to conform to the folkways of their new environment. Even the way they spoke Cuban Spanish seemed to be different, reflecting inevitable political influence on the evolution of the language; some old-line Cuban émigrés claimed not to be able to understand them.

And then there was the issue of the Marielitos' attitude. "A person who has lived for more than twenty years under a totalitarian regime behaves differently from someone who had that experience only for a year or so," says del Castillo. Jorge Zaragosa, a social worker for Dade County, puts it more sharply: "Some of these people were for so many years deprived of the lifestyle they felt they should have had, and now they decided they wanted to have it all at once. So they did some things that weren't so nice"—stealing cars, accepting stolen property, or engaging in other criminal behavior. Some had violent personalities, and there were many reports of rape and spousal abuse. Often, if they were on probation for a first offense, it became harder to find a decent job. All of this, of course, quickly shattered the Miami Cubans' reputation, and their self-image, as a model immigrant group. The new arrivals were suddenly the ones most noticed and talked about. (To be known as a Marielito became such a stigma within the Cuban community that some of those who did succeed learned to deny that they had come in early 1980 and invented a substitute history for themselves.)

Many of the Marielitos, having heard elaborate stories of other Cuban émigrés' legendary accomplishments, expected the streets of America to be paved with gold, and some simply pretended that they were. A phenomenon emerged in which veterans of the Mariel boatlift, eager to demonstrate that they had made the right decision, had photographs taken of themselves in front of plush houses or expensive cars and then sent them back to Cuba as evidence of their success. This happened even in the refugee camps and detention centers among people waiting to be processed. According to del Castillo, the more enterprising refugees would sell or barter the new clothes given to them by the U.S. government and make other deals, until they had enough money or goods to obtain a Polaroid camera. With this wondrous machine, they would launch a profitable business of selling other refugees photographs of themselves all dressed up and standing next to camp employees' cars in spots where the fence and barbed wire were not visible. "These guys would then put the picture into a phony letter to their family back in Cuba, saying, 'I am here, I am free, I have a job, this is my car,' " says del Castillo.

But the reality could be fairly grim for the average Marielito. One of Zaragosa's clients, a white man who said he was from a "bourgeois" background in Cuba, spoke with me late one night in his sparse apartment in Little Havana, describing with great emotion his difficulty in "mentally adapting" to the United States and his growing disillusionment with his new home. "I had a very simplistic view of what life would be like here," he said. "I thought that to grow economically in this country, it would be much easier. I also experienced rejection by various ethnic groups—by American blacks and American whites. In Cuba I lived in a neighborhood where blacks and whites lived side by side. It was a normal thing; we always identified ourselves as Cubans first. . . . And here, when I would try to explain myself in my language, it was suggested that I keep quiet. I'd be speaking Spanish with somebody in an elevator, and the people around me would become annoyed because they couldn't understand what I was talking about."

This man, who asked that his name not be used, had drifted from Miami to Houston to Detroit to New Orleans and eventually back to Miami. He was in and out of jobs and occasionally in trouble with the law for petty criminal offenses. He married a Puerto Rican woman, but soon after the birth of their son their relationship began to fall apart. Not long after he returned to Miami, he was in a motorcycle accident that nearly cost him one of his legs. Now he was trying to get his life back in order. "The essential value of this country is that it teaches you to appreciate your own worth, to be independent," he says. "But it also has its negative sides. In Latin countries, family values play a greater role. Here the family, because of economic and other problems, tends to separate. There are great opportunities here, but one can become easily frustrated."

Before long, like virtually any discussion with any Cuban immigrant, the conversation inevitably turns to politics. In 1991 this Marielito still resented the failure of the United States to provide air cover for the Cuban exiles who tried to retake their country at the Bay of Pigs thirty years earlier. He remains furious over the secret agreements between John F. Kennedy and Soviet leader Nikita Khrushchev, after the Cuban missile crisis of 1962, that kept American forces from intervening militarily in Cuba. And he denounces the "liberal and radical" *Miami Herald* as the "worst enemy" of the Cuban people. "The men who are disposed to fight for their homeland should be given all the options," he adds.

"I'm sitting here in a country that is not mine," the Marielito says with a sigh, on the verge of tears. "The Cuban people that live on the island and the ones that live here in exile are one nation. The Cuban who is here in the U.S. has maintained his culture and his roots and has never forgotten those at home. . . . I always think about returning to my country. I think ninety percent of the Cuban émigrés here feel the same way. But I'll be one of the first to go."

IN NORMAL TIMES, another hero of the endless struggle against Castro arrived in Miami almost every week. Just getting out, by means dramatic or mundane, was considered a blow against the discredited Cuban revolution. Although one might expect this to have become somewhat routine after more than three decades, everyone who made the journey was still given a hero's welcome consistent with his or her station in life. Under the Cuban Adjustment Act of 1966, virtually anyone who arrived safely from the island could still count on having a green card within a year—a privilege not accorded to any other group.

Some of the latest Cuban immigrants were disenchanted young factory or agricultural workers who lashed gigantic truck or tractor tires together to make rafts and then, alone or in small groups, set out at night from the north shore of Cuba to brave the choppy, shark-infested waters of the Straits of Florida. Rarely did anyone in Miami or in Cuba know in advance who was planning to try this when, and so no one has any reliable idea how many of these people may have perished at sea over the years. Those who did survive and wash ashore in the Florida Keys in small groups got only minor notice in the mainstream media. But on the communication network of Miami's highly mobilized Cuban community, their ordeal was recounted in detail and endlessly glorified to provide new stimulus, if any was needed, for old hard-line anti-Castro militancy.

Jesús Sanchez, thirty-four years old, was one such seafaring refugee, whom I met in Miami about fifteen months after his raft had washed ashore with him, his brother, and two friends. A former primary school physical education teacher and the organizer of a communist youth group, he had fallen afoul of the Castro regime when he resisted military service. After six years in prison, Sanchez decided he was so desperate to escape Cuba that he was willing to leave everything behind and risk his life at sea. Once he and his cohorts had stolen the tires they needed and made a raft, he says, they walked forty or fifty kilometers along the coast until they found an appropriate spot to launch themselves. It took them five harrowing days to reach Florida, but there they were rewarded for their courage with gifts of food and clothes to start a new life. Now Sanchez is proud of his job preparing airplane meals at the Miami airport and the good benefits it offers him.

From time to time, a reasonably big fish arrives from Cuba—one who can be counted upon to stir the faithful to rhetorical paroxysms, if not meaningful action. When I was in Miami, one of the latest was Alberto Grau, forty-eight years old, a large, barrel-chested man of aristocratic lineage (his uncle had once been president of Cuba) who had survived twenty-five years in Castro's prisons and labor camps and had finally been allowed to immigrate to the United States. Although he is little known to non-Cubans, Grau is a legend among his own people, especially those who have refused to compromise politically and still dream of retaking the island by force. In our conversation, Grau appeared determined to demonstrate that his will and his pride had not been weakened by his suffering. He sat stolidly and barely moved a muscle as he recounted his experiences in slow, complex classical Spanish; each time he trilled an *r*, he seemed to mesmerize the two young women who had been assigned to interpret by the Cuban-exile political and social service organization in whose offices we met.

Grau had appeared for years on the official lists of "political prisoners" being improperly held in Cuba, but he was quick to acknowledge that he was guilty of the political crime for which he had been convicted and sent to prison in 1964: conspiring to kill Fidel Castro by attacking him with fragmentation grenades in a baseball stadium. He had originally been sentenced to death, but his sentence was commuted through the diplomatic efforts of his uncle's friend, the president of Mexico. Word reached Grau in prison that Castro would be willing to let him leave for Miami anytime, but American officials repeatedly denied him an immigration visa, apparently because of the violent nature of his offense; they said he would have to complete his sentence before he could be let in.

"When I was fifteen years old, I thought that Castro was a great man, almost like Jesus," Grau recalls, as he explains his personal political evolution. "He said he wanted to build democracy for everybody, and I believed him. . . . But soon I realized that everything was a big lie. He would not permit political parties or an opposition press or radio. So I decided the only way to get rid of him would be in an armed struggle, just like the American Revolution or the Cuban uprising against Spain." When Grau was arrested, at the age of twenty-two, for taking part in what sounds like a fairly clumsy plot—one of many in the early 1960s that failed—he was visiting his elderly grandmother in the hospital.

Part of Grau's appeal on the Cuban radio circuit in Miami is his willingness to tell graphic stories of his own confinement and of the martyrdom of other Castro opponents under communism: "It's incredible how people survived, with the things that happened. Thirty or forty days in a closed cell, in isolation, without food. Just water through a pipe. Sometimes it was cut off, and we would go ten or twelve days without drinking. . . . Year after year, we worked from four in the morning until six at night. We were surrounded by soldiers with machetes and bayonets. They would beat us so we would work faster."

Sometimes, Grau says, the male political prisoners would be stripped naked and common criminals, who had been convicted on nonpolitical offenses, would be sent into their cells to rape them. One fellow prisoner whom Grau especially admired demanded a copy of the Bible and went on a hunger strike when it was denied. Finally a prison official produced a Bible on an aluminum plate and forced the man to eat part of it; he soon died. Women political prisoners who refused to wear the same uniforms as ordinary criminals were forced to go without any clothes at all for weeks at a time, and then they were mocked by the male guards as prostitutes. "When it was time to be freed, if you refused to be rehabilitated politically, they wouldn't give you your freedom. Some people were just recondemned," he says.

Grau expresses bitterness toward successive American administrations, Republican and Democratic alike, not only for failing to make a serious enough effort to overthrow Castro, but also for taking advantage of Grau and others in his situation. "I think that the United States has found it convenient to have political prisoners in Cuba," he says in a matter-of-fact tone. "If there hadn't been violations of human rights, then you couldn't have had Castro condemned by the [United Nations] Human Rights Commission in Geneva. We were pawns in an economic, political, and psychological war. . . . There are still hundreds of political prisoners in Cuba, and the United States will not let them come here, even though Fidel would be glad to let them go. The immigration people say they are terrorists, that it is not right to fight against Castro with arms."

When he was finally released from prison, on September 4, 1989,

Grau still had to wait more than fifty days for his American immigration visa. Eventually Senator Claiborne Pell, Democrat of Rhode Island and then chairman of the Senate Foreign Relations Committee, who had visited Grau in prison, exerted pressure on the Bush administration to let him in. Grau was permitted to bring seventeen other people—mostly family members—with him. During his wait of almost two months to leave Cuba, he says, he took the opportunity to speak with friends in the armed forces and the ministry of the interior and they asked him to tell Americans how eager they are to have Castro violently overthrown, if possible with U.S. military help. That is what Grau set out to do after arriving in Miami, but he found that his message was too radical for Radio Martí, the U.S. government–sponsored station broadcasting news and propaganda to Cuba. Instead, he had to seek airtime on more militant, sometimes clandestine, radio stations, in order to saturate the island with the message that it is time for an armed civilian uprising inside Cuba. "The Cuban people cannot hope that young Americans are going to die on the beaches of Cuba for our cause, unless there is a threat to the security of the United States," says Grau. "And there is no such threat anymore, so the Cubans must do it themselves."

IT REQUIRES a journey to the far south end of greater Miami, just where it seems as if the expressway is about to dead-end into the Everglades, to find one of the most powerful figures in the Cuban American community, Jorge Mas Canosa, the multimillionaire head of a huge construction company called Church and Tower (Americanized from its original Cuban name of *Iglesia y Torre*). His office is like a fortress, on the top floor of a heavily secured building behind a chain-link fence. Even the stairway leading to the office is behind a locked door, and the inner sanctum itself has no windows—just wall-to-wall framed certificates and photographs testifying to Mas Canosa's clout in Republican circles and his frequent visits to Washington. The pictures document time spent with former president Ronald Reagan, with the late U.S. senator Paula Hawkins of Florida, and even with Jonas Savimbi, the CIA-supported, anticommunist "freedom fighter" whose guerrillas faced off with Cuban troops during a long war in the southern African nation of Angola.

Mas Canosa is an intriguing case study, a small, intense man who emerged from the dark shadows of Miami's militant anti-Castro movement to a position of high visibility, from which he was virtually able to dictate the nuances of American policy toward Cuba during the Reagan and Bush administrations—and under Bill Clinton, too. He is, by all accounts, indefatigable and not easily given to compromise. If it was not his personal inspiration to launch Radio Martí and TV Martí—which infuriated Castro by appropriating the name of José Martí, one of the great patriots of Cuban history—Mas Canosa certainly helped sell the idea to Congress, lobbied for the necessary funding, and then, as a key member of their advisory board, fought to keep their broadcasts adequately hard-line. Hardly a day goes by now that he does not spend some of his time scheming and wheeler-dealing for the much-awaited transition to a free-market economy in his beloved native country.

A leader of an anti-Castro student organization at the time of the Cuban revolution, Mas Canosa was a second-year law student when he escaped to Miami in 1960. He says he left rather than face the risk of spending a lifetime in prison for political activities. After twenty years of business success (diluted only slightly by unseemly court fights with his brother, among others, over control of the construction company), he decided that the most effective way for Cuban Americans to work for change in Cuba was not to continue railing against Castro, but to find ways to "demonstrate our maturity and influence the political system of our new country, the United States." His chief mechanism for doing so turned out to be the Cuban American National Foundation, which he and some friends created in 1981, while Reagan was settling into the White House, to counter the emerging pressures on Capitol Hill for greater dialogue and more exchanges with the communist regime in Havana. It was openly modeled on the organizations that Jewish Americans had used so successfully over the years to influence U.S. policy toward Israel. Mas Canosa eventually became the main spokesman for the foundation. His critics complain that he has been arrogant and intolerant in his use of the organization—citing, for example, his occasional crusades against the *Miami Herald* for allegedly going soft on Castro—but he says they just resent his effectiveness.

Mas Canosa gloated as communism fell from grace in Eastern Europe and the Soviet Union broke apart, seemingly denying Castro his vital lifeline. Rather than building bridges to Cuba, he advocated an ever harder line: tightening the embargo and making daily life even harder. His friends in Congress, afraid that doing otherwise would have serious political consequences, dutifully followed his suggestions. After Václav Havel's democratic regime took power in Czechoslovakia, Mas Canosa flew to Prague and persuaded the authorities there that the Czechoslovakian embassy in Washington should no longer represent Cuban interests in the United States, as it had done under a long-standing Cold War arrangement. Then, as he awaited the downfall of the regime in Havana (confidently predicting that its demise was imminent each time he spoke to a reporter, only to revise his estimate a few months later), Mas Canosa entertained himself and others by speculating on the most appropriate fate for the Cuban leader: "Castro is a narcotrafficker, even worse than Noriega [the former Panamanian strongman brought to Miami by the U.S. military and tried and convicted on drug charges]. In the history of the Western Hemisphere, I don't think we've seen another guy who's killed as many people as Castro has. This is what people forget easily. I think he deserves to be in jail, and put on trial. . . . Or maybe he should be sent to North Korea and shown how to ski up in the hills there. . . . Anyway, I think he's a coward and would like to get out of Cuba before it collapses."

Cuba's future is now Mas Canosa's great preoccupation, and he says he dreams of going back "to make a contribution." Some of his rivals in Miami suspect that although he long since became an American citizen, Mas Canosa has delusions of Napoleonic grandeur and would actually like to march into Havana triumphantly, be sworn in by an octogenarian former justice of the Cuban supreme court (whom he would bring along), and take the country over in the name of capitalism and free enterprise. There are even rumors that he has already promised certain friends in Miami specific jobs in his cabinet. But Mas Canosa laughs off that scenario and says that what he really has in mind is a senior-statesmanlike role, holding on to his property and his leadership position in Miami and commuting back and forth to Havana on a new twenty-five-minute air-shuttle service to promote economic development and peaceful political evolution. "Eventually," he says confidently, in his still heavily accented English, "Miami and Havana will be so close together that each city will look like an extension of the other one."

Cuba will provide a great business opportunity for those who can move quickly, in Mas Canosa's view, and unlike Poland and other formerly communist countries trying to transform their economies, it will have the distinct advantage of a trained cadre of entrepreneurs who live close by and know what to do. "I can assure you that anyone who owns a gas station here [in Miami] knows what a free market is. Those people will go to Cuba to explore the possibility of doing business. . . . In Cuba you will need everything from toilet paper to the most sophisticated computers. And the Sanchez in Havana will be buying from the Sanchez in Miami. We will see an unprecedented era of prosperity in Florida. Everyone will be selling something to Cuba."

But where will Cuba get the funds to pay? Mas Canosa insists that unlike East European countries, Cuba will not come begging to Washington. Not a penny of American taxpayers' money will be needed to revive the economy, he says. Sitting in his office, as one of his three sons looks on impatiently, he explains: "We will be seeing a government that is bankrupt, with no credit. But in the first few months, I think we can solve the liquidity problem. There's a lot of Cuban Americans who would be willing to invest hundreds of millions of dollars; we could develop a program that would provide Cuba with between ten [billion] and twenty billion dollars, just from the private sector. We have that option. . . . In Cuba, people cannot talk about what happens after Castro. They will be jailed, or killed. So those of us in exile have a responsibility to get together, use all of our experience in the Western world, and come up with a theory that puts everything in the hands of the private sector." Indeed, Mas Canosa envisions a Cuba where there is "smaller government . . . and even more freedom than we have here in the United States. Cuba is going to be a great, great place—a serious country, with a democratic future."

But once Cuba is resupplied with everything from toilet paper to computers, what would it mean for Miami and its economy if a lot of the exiles go home? "The Cuban presence is here to stay," Mas Canosa says reassuringly. "Those who do go back to Cuba will be replaced by the new wave of immigrants from Cuba. Even if Cuba becomes a free nation, there are millions of people there who have heard so much about the U.S. that they're determined to come. So we will have a program to replace every Cuban who goes back with another Cuban who comes here. We'll work out an exchange: You send a dishwasher, you get a dishwasher. That would help tremendously, because there would be no displacement of people, no interruption of services."

If no one has yet asked the people who still live in Cuba how they feel about all this, that is not, for the moment, Jorge Mas Canosa's problem.

THE CUBAN community of Miami remains infinitely complex and extremely difficult for an outsider to penetrate or interpret. And although the vast majority of Cuban Americans tend to identify themselves as Republicans—Ronald Reagan's anticommunist rhetoric was especially appealing to them, and a street in the Cuban commercial district has been named for him—Miami Cubans are far more divided politically than people like Mas Canosa would like to admit.

In the shop windows of the now somewhat rundown Little Havana, there are still crude notices posted for "training camps" and weekend exercises conducted in remote locations by mysteriously named brigades and paramilitary organizations that ostensibly plan to invade Cuba again while Castro is still there to be assassinated. Conspiracy theories abound. People will tell you, with equally straight faces, that official declarations to the contrary notwithstanding, the CIA has never given up its material and logistical support of violent Cuban exile groups, or that Castro has at least 400 spies in Miami who are constantly inventing new subterfuges to lure his most militant, dangerous opponents into the open. (One version has it that he slipped quite a few agents into the United States as Marielitos.) It is impossible to prove any such statement true or false.

At the same time, a few lonely voices in Miami do call for a new U.S. policy of conciliation with Cuba, arguing that a peaceful transition from communism will be better for all concerned than a violent one. Until restrictions were suddenly and inexplicably tightened by the Clinton administration, one organization ran regular charter flights to Havana, which were allowed under a loophole in the tough federal regulations against commerce with the island. Another sponsored exhibitions in the United States of recent Cuban art and other cultural activities, although doing so sometimes ran the risk of violent reactions.

Orlando Padrón, one of many legendary Cuban American success symbols, knows the dangers of appearing to be too willing to deal with Castro's regime. He was dirt poor when he arrived in Miami in 1961 and still, with his son as his interpreter, tells the story of the roach-infested rooming houses where he stayed in the early days for ten dollars a night. By 1964, however, Padrón had earned enough money in menial jobs to pursue his dream of launching a factory to manufacture cigars that would be as good as the ones in Cuba. He did so well so quickly that he became nationally famous, and he was portrayed—in *Life* magazine, *National Geographic*, and children's civics textbooks, among other places—as a model immigrant. The cigars are now mostly made in Central America, where labor is cheaper, but the reception area of his company's modest storefront headquarters in Miami is still filled with testimonials to the quality of Padrón's product from the likes of band leader Mitch Miller, comedian Carl Reiner, and Polish president Lech Walesa. Forty percent of his business, he says, is by mail order.

During the late 1970s, as Padrón's father was growing old in Havana, the successful businessman became obsessed with the idea that it should be easier for the members of families divided between Cuba and the United States to visit each other. As a result, Padrón was one of the principal proponents of the so-called *Diálogo* with Castro, with whom he had fought in the Sierra Maestra mountains against the Batista dictatorship during the 1950s; so he made several trips to Havana in 1978. The most immediate result was that he was allowed to bring dozens of family members and friends out of Cuba with him, including several who had allegedly been associated with the CIA. At the end of the negotiations conducted by Padrón and other members of his delegation, Castro agreed to release more than three thousand prisoners.

When he arrived the first time, Padrón recalls, the Cuban government had his father waiting for him at the airport and also made a representative available to help him get around. "Fidel treated me with respect," says Padrón. "He had to. When he asked me what I thought of the new Cuba, I would say, 'This is not what I had in mind. This is not what I fought for.' Every time anyone else asked me what I thought about the [results of the] revolution, I said it was a disaster."

But that was not good enough for the militant exiles in Miami. In a photograph that became notorious in the Cuban community after it was published, Padrón was pictured presenting a cigar to Castro. He was immediately accused in Miami's Spanish-language newspapers and on its right-wing radio stations of selling out to communism. Several Cuban American–owned businesses declared a boycott of Padrón cigars, and a terrorist group—possibly the notorious Omega 66—bombed his headquarters. Shaken, Padrón withdrew completely from the public arena. It took years for his business to return to normal.

Padrón now refuses to discuss politics, except to offer the opinion that "the future leaders of Cuba are inside Cuba. Some of the businessmen here have lived off the pain of Cuba. If Fidel were to disappear tomorrow, they'd have nothing more to talk about." As for Mas Canosa, Padrón is concise: He is "worse than Fidel."

CUBAN LIFE in Miami is probably a unique phenomenon in the United States. It has nurtured an extraordinary loyalty in a generation whose lives it shaped. An evening with Percy Aguila, an investment banker, and Anna Lamas, a physician specializing in allergies and immunology, is instructive. They both come from elite Cuban families and have educations and experiences to match: He has worked in New York and Washington; she has her college degree from Harvard, her medical degree from Yale, and did her specialty training at Columbia and Johns Hopkins. They met for the first time during their mutual absence from Miami, but after they were married, they decided to move back home. Turning aside the opportunity for academic positions in the best medical schools, Lamas decided instead to take over the Cuban community practice of her seventy-three-year-old father, also an allergist. Aguila went to work for a local bank. He was happy to be able to be near his parents, although he does believe that the time has come when his father should stop pining over the loss of his family's sugar mills and cattle ranches in the Cuban mountains.

In their tastefully decorated home in an upper-middle-class neighborhood, where they have bought the best of everything and serve fine wines, Aguila and Lamas could be typical American yuppies anywhere but for the fact that their two-year-old daughter, Josefina, speaks only Spanish. "She's got plenty of time to learn English," says Lamas. "It's important first that she know the language, and the culture, of her people."

IN THE SUMMER of 1994 Fidel Castro—presumably believing that a new exodus would take some pressure off his country's desperate economic situation—once again eased his restrictive measures against Cuban emigration. The coastal boat patrols that used to be the nemesis of the people setting out for Florida on rafts were suddenly withdrawn. In August alone, some thirty thousand Cubans attempted to leave their country for the United States. Some died at sea, but many began to turn up in Miami, where the welcome was not quite as warm as it once had been. The media image was of another Mariel, perpetrated by Castro on another weak Democratic administration in Washington that was caught in a maelstrom of foreign policy and domestic political pressures. And this time, American ideals and the thirty-five-year-old policy of welcoming every Cuban émigré were up against a powerful surge in anti-immigrant feeling, especially in Florida.

The risk was too great. U.S. Attorney General Janet Reno, herself a former Dade County prosecutor, announced in mid-August that the welcome would finally be withdrawn. Cuban refugees would now be intercepted at sea and taken immediately to the American naval base at Guantánamo Bay, at the southeastern tip of Cuba, to await processing for their return to Castro's jurisdiction. (The government of Panama would eventually be persuaded to allow some to be held at U.S. bases there as well.) A month later, after intense negotiations in New York City, the Cuban government agreed to "take effective measures in every way it possibly can to prevent unsafe departures, using mainly persuasive methods." In return, the Clinton administration said it would process any formal Cuban applications for American immigrant visas in an orderly, expedited manner. But there would be limits, and lest anyone think the agreement was a step toward normalization of relations between the two countries, Washington instead announced a tightening of the U.S. economic embargo of Cuba, including a ban on the quarterly remittances being sent to relatives on the island by many Cuban exiles in the United States. By the following May, fearing riots in Guantánamo, Clinton relented and allowed the 21,000 Cubans held there to be processed for entry into the United States. But anyone else picked up at sea, Reno said—including political opponents of Castro—would be returned immediately to Cuba. There were no guarantees about what might happen to them there.

The change was full of symbolism. The privileged status of Cuban refugees to the United States was gone—abruptly changed by people who could scarcely remember where that status came from in the first place. These model immigrants were now, wrote Ana Radelat, a Cuban-born journalist, in the *Washington Post,* "just . . . another minority group scrambling for a piece of the American pie. . . . Cubans are facing the overt hostility that others have fought for years."

VIII
"TAKING THE FIRST STEP
TO HEAVEN":
THE POLES

CHICAGO

EVEN THOUGH the neighborhood has declined severely, the red-brick-and-stone, four-story building at the corner of Milwaukee Avenue and Augusta Boulevard, in what was once the heart of Chicago's Polish neighborhood, stands solid and imposing as ever. It was built in 1873, and when you are heading downtown from O'Hare Airport on the John F. Kennedy Expressway, a block away, you can easily read the tall letters atop the facade, proclaiming this as headquarters of the Polish Roman Catholic Union of America (PRCUA).

The PRCUA was the first of the national fraternal organizations to take root in the Polish American community in the late nineteenth century, and despite its old-fashioned, narrow-sounding name, it is still very much a going concern. It is not a particularly high-profile or controversial group, or even the largest of its kind anymore, but for one hundred and twenty years it has provided its members (now about 80,000, in twenty-four states, all of Polish descent) with economical life insurance policies, low-cost mortgage and educational loans, and other services. Today, in the richly wood-paneled offices of this building, dignitaries visit, insurance claims are settled, direct-mail campaigns and fund-raising events are planned, and decisions are made about which young Polish Americans will receive PRCUA's annual college and university scholarships. This is a quiet, conservative wing of the Polish American establishment. In concert with other similar organizations, its leaders tell public officials where they think most Polish Americans are likely to stand on the issues of the day.

Here too there are Polish-language and folk-dance classes for Chicago children. And there is an old library, a rich resource on Polish life in America, and within it the records, files, and other resources of the Polish Genealogical Society, a pacesetter in the new effort by Americans to find out more about their origins. But most of the prime space on the lower floors of the PRCUA building is devoted to the Polish Museum of America, believed to be the oldest and largest ethnic museum in the United States, and that is where the ferment begins.

For decades, the Polish Museum, staffed by elderly, poorly paid Polish Americans who got their jobs through personal and political connections, was a predictable backwater, with an obligatory anticommunist tinge. Its boldest exhibit contained the personal effects of Ignacy Jan Paderewski, the great Polish pianist and composer and the figurehead first prime minister of independent Poland, along with some pieces of furniture from the room in the Buckingham Hotel in New York where he died, in his eighties, in 1941. Hardly anyone ever visited.

The Paderewski Room is still in the museum, as are other exhibits on famous Polish actresses and patriots with some American connection. But much more attention is given these days to Polish folk art and stained glass, and to avant-garde paintings, prints, and sculpture the likes of which most Chicago Poles have never seen before and many would regard with horror. With Polish American millionaires and corporations supplementing the PRCUA as sources of funding, the museum now features Polish film festivals, concerts of Polish classical music, and provocative photo exhibits. As many as 70,000 people a year are visiting the museum or attending the events it sponsors.

These changes have been wrought almost singlehandedly by thirty-five-year-old Christopher Kamyszew, a member of the new wave of Polish immigrants to Chicago who have dared to challenge the assumptions and the habits of one of the city's most entrenched and self-satisfied ethnic communities. A tall, cultured man of aristocratic bearing, who likes to appear in white linen suits, Kamyszew became director of the museum late in 1988 and soon hired an entirely new staff. His family had been back and forth between the United States and Poland many times over the years—his grandmother was born here and his mother there—but he finally decided to settle in Chicago in 1984. The year before, because of his involvement in the underground publishing movement spawned by the Solidarity labor union, Kamyszew had been arrested by the communist authorities in Warsaw and held in prison for six months. Thus, like many other veterans of Solidarity's struggles, he came to America for political, as well as the traditional economic, reasons.

"The common assumption in this country is that Polish culture consists of the polka and pierogi," says Kamyszew, whom many powerful, established Polish Americans frankly consider an aloof, effete snob. He laughs at the idea. "I always say that the polka is no more our national dance than the pierogi our national food. We are trying here to create a more sophisticated and attractive image of Poland and its culture, to convince an American audience of our values and show them something really revealing." The alternative, he believes, would be to accept a lower status and be consigned to a life of acting out demeaning stereotypes.

Kamyszew has been accused by some of the old-line Chicago organizations of paying elaborate attention to a distant, obscure high Polish culture at the expense of their own precious Polish American traditions. "What is Polish American culture? Tell me, and I will show it," he fairly shrieks during a conversation in his dark office in the museum. "But I am opposed to inventing new folklore which has nothing to do with the country of origin. You know, these Polish jokes we experienced some time ago—these were not jokes about Polish people, they were jokes about Americans of Polish descent. . . . I don't want to be part of a very small parochial circle. I like pierogi myself, and I can dance the polka, but that's not the point. I am a citizen of the world."

Determined to resist a Polish ghetto existence and the mentality that goes along with it, Kamyszew has settled in Morton Grove, a well-to-do suburb west of Chicago where, he says, he has friends from many different backgrounds. He is somewhat estranged from his mother, a wealthy real estate investor in Chicago who he feels is "too involved in making money"—which, in any event, she apparently has not chosen to share with him. His wife, also from Poland, teaches English as a second language, but the family, despite some resistance from the older of their two children, speaks primarily Polish at home. "I re-created my life from the beginning in America," says Kamyszew in his faintly accented, upper-crust English. In his role at the museum, "I feel that I am needed and I am a part of many peoples' lives. I am important for them, and that gives me very significant satisfaction."

Although he has held on to a house he owns in Warsaw, Kamyszew has, in his own way, become a patriotic American. "In Poland, the price for idealism is very high," he says. "But I believe in the power of the individual, and here in this country, although sometimes I seem to myself a little naive, I believe it is still possible to be idealistic. I can enrich the culture of American society with my own values." His personal vision of America—and, more specifically, of Chicago—is as a place where others, from other places, will do the same and, in the process, create a more interesting, vibrant multicultural environment for all to share.

One of Kamyszew's great successes at the museum was an exhibition in 1991–92 on the golden age of Polish Chicago, from the 1880s to the 1930s. Focusing on his own definition of culture, he demonstrated that in the 1920s and '30s there were thirteen Polish-language bookstores in a short stretch of Milwaukee Avenue; many of the books they sold were published in the United States. (Today there is one such store, and very few of its Polish books are American-published.) There were about sixty Polish theater groups at the time, some amateur and some professional, and there were ambitious plans (never realized) to build a Polish opera house in the neighborhood. Kamyszew notes that the Polish Americans who visited his exhibit, "Old Polish Chicago," including everyone from congressmen to high school students, left "feeling a little better about their roots. They could see that we are all part of a very sophisticated culture."

CHICAGO IS the epitome, even the apogee, of ethnic America. By some estimates, 60 percent to 70 percent of the city's population may be bilingual, and their second language—or, indeed, their first—is the one spoken in the country their family originally came from. According to Father Joe Glab, the pastor of Saint Stanislas Kostka, the city's original Polish Catholic church, "In Chicago, you basically don't identify yourself as American. You identify yourself ethnically and by neighborhood." Glab is a young raconteur of a priest, who enjoys sitting in his office, hard by the expressway that rose some years ago next to the church, and telling stories. He has a shortened name, but he is the son of Polish immigrant parents and feasts on Chicago history at the slightest excuse. "Without these ethnic groups," he says, "there really would be no Chicago, because they were always the most industrious people here. They're the ones who made things happen, because they left someplace else to come and find a better life."

When much of the city had to be rebuilt after the great Chicago Fire of 1871, the ethnic groups then on the scene renewed and reconstructed their own unique neighborhoods, and new groups heard about Chicago as a good place to come. The word went out to various "old countries" in Europe, beset at the time by war and general mayhem, that this was a place where opportunities were to be had, so immigrants flocked in to build housing and create new jobs. Each group stuck together and found security in numbers.

Even today, much of Chicago is a patchwork quilt of ethnic enclaves. On the North Side, for example, driving west on Peterson Avenue from Lake Michigan, one passes the offices of *India Weekly* and, a bit further on, of the Seoul Travel Service, before coming to a distinctly Polish, and then a Jewish, neighborhood. In these Indian and Korean quarters, many of the businesses' signs are in Hindi or Hangul lettering respectively, each incomprehensible to anyone from a different culture. A bicyclist in Chicago can easily have a multicultural experience, overhearing conversations in rapidly alternating Spanish, German, Swedish, Greek, and African American street English, as he crosses a series of intersections. The dividing lines may be as stark as an expressway or as imperceptible as the beginning of a school-district zone, but everyone who lives in each neighborhood knows where the boundaries are and which ones it is acceptable to cross.[1]

So ethnically stratified and attuned is Chicago that international crises often resonate dramatically here, especially in the exile and émigré communities that feel emotionally engaged with events back at home. This was particularly true, as the Soviet bloc crumbled during the late 1980s and early 1990s, among people still closely attached to their roots in Eastern or Central Europe. Chicago had enough Czechs and Slovaks, for example, to conduct a high-volume public argument over whether their European homeland of Czechoslovakia should split apart and if so, on what terms. The complex civil war in Yugoslavia brought every conceivable faction out of the woodwork in Chicago and suddenly pitted Serbian Americans and Croatian Americans, blue-collar workers and professionals alike, against each other. When it was announced that anyone worldwide who could show proof that his or her father had at some time been a citizen of Croatia would be entitled to vote in the presidential election held in Zagreb in August 1992, almost one thousand people turned up at the Croatian Cultural Center and the Croatian-American Radio Club in Chicago to cast their ballots in absentia.

It is said that the first few Poles to arrive in America came in 1608, along with a small group of Germans, to help the English settlers who

[1] *The fall 1993 program guide of Chicago's Field Museum of Natural History, under the rubric of "Celebrating Diversity," included a series of three separate daylong guided field trips through ethnic Chicago. Among the areas to be visited were Little Italy, Greek Town, Chinatown, Pilsen, Ukrainian Village, Old Polonia, Little Serbia, and Germantown, as well as less formally named neighborhoods that have been or are now home to the Swedish, Belgian, Jewish, Korean, Vietnamese, Cambodian, Indian, Pakistani, Mexican, Irish, Lithuanian, African American, Arab, and Croatian communities. The three trips featured lunch, in turn, at Bohemian, Chinese, and Yugoslav restaurants.*

had established the colony at Jamestown the year before learn how to exploit the local forests for timber. Several hundred more Poles came at the time of the Revolution, of course, to fight against the British alongside the American colonists; the achievements of Generals Tadeusz Kosciuszko and Kazimierz Pulaski in that struggle are well known by American schoolchildren.

But the mass migration of Poles to America began only in 1854, when conditions were especially bad for the peasantry in Poland. The first significant Polish settlement in North America was established that year in Texas, where a group of Silesians formed the Panna Maria colony. Other Polish settlements soon followed in Michigan and Wisconsin. An estimated 2.5 million Poles arrived in the United States between 1850 and the end of World War I, and about 80 percent of them are believed to have stayed. Most came through New York, but it was in Chicago that Polish immigrants began to gather in substantial numbers by the end of the American Civil War, and here that they formed their main social, political, and religious associations. There was plenty of work to be found in Chicago's heavy industries, and a critical mass of Poles large enough to develop significant economic clout.

It is impossible to know exactly how many people of Polish origin live in the Chicago area today, but some say the number may be as high as nine hundred thousand, or even a million, if the count includes all living generations. The first-generation Polish population had begun to dwindle for a time, but the new surge of more politically motivated immigrants beginning in the late 1970s pushed it back up again. When Pope John Paul II, who originally came from Poland, visited Chicago in October 1979, a throng of well over a million people (obviously not all of them Polish) joined him for an outdoor mass in Grant Park, downtown along Lake Michigan. It is an occasion that is still remembered and talked about nostalgically in Chicago's Polish community; the only thing comparable in the lore seems to have been the visit of Lech Walesa ten years later, by then victorious over the communists.

Chicago is, in any event, commonly regarded as the second-largest Polish city in the world, after Warsaw.[2] That means it is feasible to live comfortably in the Polish community here without ever needing to speak a word of English. It is a world apart, and a comprehensive one at that.

---

[2] *According to Poland's Central Statistical Office, Warsaw's population in 1991 was 1,653,300. The second-largest city in Poland, Lodz, had 844,900 people, and Krakow followed with 751,300. The next-largest Polish community in the world after Krakow is probably found in the New York City area, with Buffalo and several other American cities not far behind. By some estimates, the total Polish American population in 1990 was about 12 million, or almost 5 percent of all the people in the United States.*

There are Polish-only radio stations, dentists, passport services, shoe-repair shops, and funeral homes—even Polish-language chapters of Alcoholics Anonymous. A *Chicago Tribune* survey in 1989 found the city had at least three dozen shops specializing in Polish kielbasa and many manufacturers that supplied them; one of the latter, Slotkowski's, claimed to produce 100,000 pounds of the sausage each week for shipment around the country.

Middle-class families have the option of sending their children to Polish-language karate lessons after school, and many families go on holidays at resorts in northern Indiana and southern Wisconsin where, on certain weekends, only Polish is spoken. For the wealthier set, the Legion of Young Polish Women has its own annual debutante ball. Billboards looming over the expressways advertise that LOT Polish Airlines has nonstop Boeing 767 service from Chicago to Warsaw; its planes are usually full.

Although many upwardly mobile Polish Americans have moved to the southwest side of the city (already the home of the "Polish highlanders," a distinct and somewhat separatist group from the Tatry Mountain region of southern Poland) or out to the suburbs, Polonia remains the spiritual heart of the community and it is the ultimate in Chicago ethnic neighborhoods.[3] It is still centered along Milwaukee Avenue, but now it begins about two miles further out from downtown than it used to. While it may not be characterized by the kind of cultural purity that Christopher Kamyszew dreams of, it is unmistakably Polish American. Here you routinely hear Polish spoken on the street, under medallions attached to the lampposts bearing the medieval crests of various cities in Poland. The distinct smell of sauerkraut and beer is redolent in the air, especially outside such spots as Wally's Polish Singing Lounge, which is down the block from a shop that caters specifically to the shipment of gift packages and the wiring of money to Poland. This is the area, even today, where most Poles who are newly arrived in Chicago feel drawn—if only to get their bearings and figure out a new life for themselves.

The nerve center of the neighborhood is the Orbit Restaurant, where Polish waitresses serve Polish food to a largely Polish clientele. I sat there in a booth over lunch one day with Roman Pucinski, an aging

---

[3] *"Polonia" is actually a term with many meanings. Strictly speaking, it refers to all Polish people who live outside of Poland—almost like a Polish diaspora—or to the Polish population within a specific country (e.g., American Polonia). But it is also used to denote Polish culture and spirit or, in the case of Chicago, a particular, well-defined neighborhood that became the center of Polish life in the city after the first wave of Polish immigration.*

ethnic politician par excellence. On the orders of the city's powerful Democratic machine, he had loyally accepted years of exile in the U.S. House of Representatives in Washington before he could get what he really wanted in life, a seat as an alderman representing a predominantly Polish ward on the Chicago City Council. Half in Polish, half in English, Pucinski, now retired, holds court at the Orbit, greeting policemen, lawyers, and businessmen as they walk into the restaurant. An occasional local celebrity stops by, too. One is Stan Borys, a long-haired, bearded Polish émigré pop-music star who draws sell-out crowds to Chicago-area concerts where he sings modern Polish rock ballads, such as "Anna" and "A Polish Man from Chicago," a tearjerker about a worker who immigrates to America and leaves his long-suffering wife and children behind in Poland.

Pucinski now serves as honorary president of the Illinois Division of the Polish-American Congress (PAC), an umbrella organization established toward the end of World War II to deal with the anticommunist political agenda of the Polish community in the United States. The PAC now claims to have about a million members; it, too, sells insurance to Polish Americans, but most of its national resources have been used to maintain a lobbying office in Washington. The organization takes credit for keeping the State Department from making any undue compromises with the regime in Warsaw during the long dark years of communist rule in Poland, and for convincing Congress to pass such bills as one that established October as Polish American Heritage Month.

At the local level, the PAC is more of a social, and social welfare, organization. The modern headquarters of the Illinois Division, on Chicago's Northwest Side, serves different needs for different people. On the one hand, it is a place where new immigrants can go for classes in practical, everyday American English. On the other, it is a kind of safe haven for one of the hardest-line factions in Chicago's Polish community, the militant World War II veterans who still feel that the United States did not do enough to oppose the Soviet-satellite regime in Warsaw during the Cold War. Even now they argue that the Polish government has been insufficiently vigilant about rooting out of its bureaucracy the remaining communists.

Many of the veterans remain organized in units that correspond to those in which they served in the old Polish army before Hitler conquered Poland, and they hold regular reunions and march in any parade that will have them (including one in Warsaw, after Solidarity came to power). During the more than four decades of communist rule in Poland, they scraped together whatever money they could to help support the anticommunist Polish government-in-exile based in London, despite its utter lack of international recognition or credibility.

Most of these veterans arrived in the United States in the 1950s, after waiting in England or France for their quota numbers to come up, and they quickly gravitated to Chicago. They followed events in Poland meticulously, and for years, whenever there was a workers' strike or other unrest at home, they turned up reliably (and often in uniform) at demonstrations in front of the Polish Consulate-General along Lake Shore Drive. Thanks to Pucinski, former representative Dan Rostenkowski, and other supporters in Congress, all veterans of the precommunist Polish armed forces living in the United States are entitled to completely free medical care at Veterans Administration hospitals around the country.

THE HISTORY of Polish Chicago is rich, insular, and intricate, and caught up always with the rise and fall of the major Catholic churches serving the community. Like many of the other people who flooded into the United States from Europe during the late nineteenth and early twentieth centuries (and especially like the Irish and the Italians), the early waves of Polish immigrants were generally of peasant stock. They came, for the most part, from impoverished rural villages where a family could barely manage to feed or clothe its children. Those children, largely uneducated, felt that as soon as they were old enough to attempt the journey, they really had no choice but to leave and seek their fortunes elsewhere. For all intents and purposes, that invariably meant America, which had a reputation as a beautiful country where everyone had a chance to become rich.

At the beginning, though, just survival would do. Father Joe Glab remembers a traditional question-and-answer, half sad and half proud, repeated often by members of his own family and others, in the United States and in Poland alike: "Why did you pick up and go to America?" "For bread" (in Polish, *"za chlebem"*). The Polish immigrants gave up what little they had when they left home, and with a reliable supply of food, they hoped, there was at least a chance of becoming independent and building a decent life.

One Catholic priest, Father Vincent Barzynski, played a key role in organizing and strengthening the sometimes embattled Polish community to deal with its competition in the rough-and-tumble world of Chicago. For a quarter of a century, from 1874 to 1899, he was the pastor of the important Saint Stanislas Kostka—at its high point, with eight thousand families, thought to be one of the largest Catholic parishes in the world—and as such, he was the dominant figure in Polish Chicago. He developed new satellite parishes, encouraged the publication of Polish newspapers, and had the idea of launching special fraternal organizations that would serve the Poles when they were discriminated against and frozen out of the mainstream institutions of the city. He had rivals in the community, to be sure, especially a few blocks away in another major Polish parish, which would eventually build Holy Trinity Church in 1905. But to the extent that the new Polish Americans were mobilized to defend themselves before the outside world, it was generally either in response to Barzynski's call or somehow in opposition to him.

"Basically, there has always been a kind of Irish rule over Chicago. Even the bishops were of Irish or German ancestry," says Glab. "The Poles are very hard to organize, and Barzynski was the only priest who was ever really successful at it. But the Poles *had* to be organized, because of their history. They survived because they were threatened, and coming from the buffer zone that was Poland, they arrived here trusting no one. The only one they really trusted was the priest."

When they wanted to save up money, many Polish immigrants, not willing to put their confidence in strangers or their banks, would actually send funds home to their parish priest in Poland to hold for them. And as for their children's education, they placed their faith totally in the priests they found waiting for them in Chicago. With the convents providing a plentiful supply of teachers who did not have to be paid very much, the diocese found it easy to establish as many schools as it needed to satisfy the immigrant demand. "The parents thought exactly like the nuns, and the nuns thought exactly like the parents," observes Glab, a later product of the same Polish Catholic parochial school system. "They were all on the same wavelength. When the nuns punished the children, they knew they would have the parents' support."

The Polish community grew steadily, reaching out, as if with tentacles, and absorbing other neighborhoods. But it was only after Polish American veterans returned from World War I, with a new sense of pride and acceptance, that Chicago's Poles began to migrate further down Milwaukee Avenue into the suburbs.[4] The real impetus, according to some, was a classic, if particularly grotesque, act of discrimination: The Polish Americans were not being permitted to bury their dead

---

[4] *It is a Chicago anomaly that one travels "down" Milwaukee Avenue even while heading northwest away from downtown.*

in the mainstream Catholic cemeteries in town, and so Saint Stanislas Kostka bought a piece of land for its own burial ground about ten miles away in Niles Township, just north of the city line. Over time, a younger generation of Poles, in effect moving to be nearer the graves of their ancestors, came to populate various parts of the corridor between the church and the cemetery.

Perhaps as much as any ethnic group in the city, Polish Americans suffered an identity crisis in the middle years of the twentieth century over what to consider, and call, themselves. One immigrants' son remembers that his mother, even though she spoke Polish at home, would object strenuously to being referred to as "Polish" in public, because she took her status as an American so seriously—and because the label could so quickly deteriorate into the epithet "Polack," usually taken to describe someone stupid or clumsy.

Roman Pucinski has a specific recollection of being embarrassed whenever his mother, a celebrity on Chicago ethnic radio, spoke Polish to him on a streetcar or in an elevator. If she wasn't speaking English, he wanted her to whisper. And he recounts, as if it had happened yesterday, his crisis of conscience when, as a cub reporter for the *Chicago Sun-Times* in the late 1930s, he was asked by a night editor whether he really wanted to use his cumbersome Polish name in his byline or come up with something crisper and "more American." Pucinski agonized but stuck with his full name during his twenty years at the newspaper, a decision that surely abetted his subsequent political career. Now, he says, he is convinced that the "melting pot" is an obsolete concept for describing Chicago, let alone America, because the city's and the country's many ethnic groups really prefer to maintain their distinct identities. Ironically, Pucinski points out, these days it is chic to speak Polish in a Chicago elevator.

But some Polish Chicagoans chose differently from Pucinski, making every effort to assimilate and integrate into the larger fabric of American society as quickly as possible. As with other ethnic groups, especially from Central and Eastern Europe, there were a fair number of Polish Americans who, during the 1950s and '60s, in effect detribalized themselves, shortening or disguising their names, making marriages to WASPs (or at least into wealthy Irish Catholic families) that would increase their social status, and falling in line with the pressures of American materialism. This was the route taken by many well-educated, ambitious children of Polish immigrants who hoped to succeed in the corporate world or to become key players in the legal or medical establishment.

It was perhaps more difficult to do this in Chicago than in other major cities—if only because here there was such a large, enveloping Polish community from which to try to escape—but those who were determined found new lives for themselves on the North Shore and in other wealthy suburbs. They did little or nothing to convey Polish culture and language to their children; on the contrary, it appeared at times as if they felt they needed to suppress this part of their background. Indeed, years later the well-heeled members of some suburban Catholic churches reacted with anxiety and even hostility when they suddenly found new parishioners arriving and demanding Masses be said in Polish and other ethnic languages. It was as if their cover were about to be blown. "The basic message seemed to be, 'If you're going to come to the suburbs, you must give up your ethnicity,'" says Glab.

Meanwhile, Polonia had no exemption from the dramatic transformation of urban neighborhoods across the United States in the 1960s and 1970s. As some Polish Americans became more mobile, their places were taken by others lower down on Chicago's socioeconomic scale. An ethnic enclave that had once encroached so rapidly on others now shrank almost overnight and became encircled by poor African Americans and Hispanics. After the first signs of white flight emerged, it was the Polish American fraternal organizations themselves that helped accelerate the decline of the neighborhood; worried about the security of their investments, they shifted the bulk of their mortgage loans from deteriorating areas of old Polonia to newer Polish neighborhoods on the Northwest Side.

Polish families virtually abandoned Saint Stanislas Kostka, which found itself in the midst of a Spanish-speaking neighborhood and, therefore, with a whole new constituency for its Masses and its parochial school. Holy Trinity, now in the heart of a dangerous black ghetto with a high crime rate, lost its traditional flock altogether, and for several years its survival was in serious doubt. The two churches are only a short distance from each other, but Mission Street forms a strict dividing line between the two neighborhoods. There were moments when Polish priests found themselves in the improbable role of attempting to mediate conflicts between black and Hispanic youth gangs.

At the large Walgreen's drugstore and other businesses along Milwaukee Avenue, in the heart of the original Polish immigrant neighborhood, the window signs advertising sale items began to be posted in Spanish, rather than English or Polish. What most upset some of the Polish American denizens was that the neighborhood became more transient; Mexicans, in particular, seemed to use it as a stopping-off point upon their arrival in Chicago, rather than as a place to settle down. Inevitably, this led to the abandonment of some grand old buildings and a further deterioration of property values. Drug dealing and other crime flourished.

POLISH CHICAGO might well have continued its decline and dispersion were it not for the new wave of immigrants who began to arrive in the late 1970s and early 1980s, largely as a result of the intense political turmoil in Poland. Many of them were still economic migrants of the classic variety—construction workers and other laborers who saw no hope for their families' future in Poland—but a significant percentage were now university-educated men and women caught up in the intellectual movement underlying the revolt launched by Lech Walesa's Solidarity labor union. Even those who were only on the margins of protest found their careers in Poland stalled. In a great reversal of the circumstances that had historically prevailed, it became more difficult to get out of Poland, but easier to get into America. Anyone with a remotely plausible claim of persecution by the communist government in Warsaw had excellent prospects for political asylum in the United States.

Bogdan Pukszta, who came from near Krakow and had a degree in American literature from the University of Silesia, left Poland in March 1982. In response to Solidarity's increasing agitation and nationwide popularity, the local communist party chief, General Wojciech Jaruzelski, had declared martial law a few months earlier, theoretically to stave off a looming Soviet invasion that could have been reminiscent of the one in Czechoslovakia in 1968. "The situation was very depressing in Poland," recalls Pukszta. "It seemed then like the system would just go on forever. Martial law would be lifted one day, but socialism and communism would just continue—at least through the lifetime of someone like myself, in his early thirties."

Pukszta should have had a certain advantage over others who were trying to leave: The previous summer in Warsaw, while things seemed temporarily better in Poland, he had married an American woman from upstate New York, and she was waiting for him in Madrid. He had expected to follow her there quickly. "But it was very hard to leave Poland at that time and difficult even to communicate with Poland from the outside world," he remembers. "You had to have permission just to travel from one Polish city to another. Getting your American visa was another story. You couldn't just enter the embassy to apply. It had to be done almost underground, somewhere quietly on the side. My leaving Poland involved traveling by train to East Berlin and being stuck on the Polish–East German border for almost a day, because they didn't know how to deal with a guy who had an American immigration visa. And then I flew Cubana, on a flight from Moscow to Havana via East Berlin, with a stopover in Madrid. That flight was a day late, but finally I managed to get out. It was a surprise for my wife when one day I showed up in Madrid."

Within a few months, Pukszta and his wife had settled in Chicago, where his parents and other relatives already lived. It was a place he had long dreamed of going, ever since he had written his thesis in Poland on the Chicago renaissance in American literature. Soon he was another all-American immigrant success story.

Before long Pukszta had a job with the National College of Education in Evanston, just north of Chicago, as a counselor for its growing population of students from Eastern Europe. In 1978 the college had established its Language Institute in an office building on Michigan Avenue in downtown Chicago, a model program intended specifically to help newcomers achieve fluency in reading, writing, speaking, and understanding English, by holding classes in a place and at times convenient to their work. After several quick promotions, Pukszta became administrative director of the Language Institute and obtained a master's degree in public policy from the University of Chicago.

In 1990, as a result of a multimillion-dollar gift from a man named Michael Louis, an executive of the Johnson Wax Company, the college was renamed National-Louis University (NLU) and began to branch out into new areas. Once Solidarity had replaced the communist government in Warsaw, Pukszta was assigned to develop new educational programs that National-Louis could offer in Poland. He became an international educational entrepreneur. Thanks to him, bureaucrats in the Polish Ministry of Education, who until recently worked for a communist government, have now endorsed an American-style undergraduate college curriculum in business administration; and officials from the Ministry of Privatization, along with bankers and fledgling businessmen, are enrolled in an NLU course offered in Warsaw called English for Business.

On the side, to promote U.S. private investment in Poland, Pukszta helped launch the Polish American Economic Forum; in 1992 he was elected its president. Since the fall of 1989, he has returned to Poland often, sometimes taking along his two American-born children so they can learn about their Polish roots. He says they find it an exotic, enchanting place. "Back in 1982, I thought I'd never see the country again. All of a sudden, it's like a dream come true," Pukszta says. But he entertains no dream of returning to live there permanently, in part because of the "huge contrasts" that he sees developing between the rich and the poor in Poland. In a number of unfortunate ways, he suggests, "Poland is becoming very much like the United States right now."

At the Language Institute, almost 55 percent of the 440 students enrolled in the spring of 1992 were Polish (followed by 22 percent Chinese and 15 percent Hispanic). They follow a standard, intensive multilevel curriculum in English as a second language. "Studies show that it takes about eleven years for an average immigrant to the United States—even more for an average refugee—to catch up economically with the rest of the population," says Pukszta, perhaps as dedicated an apostle as American capitalism has ever had. "But people who have attended our programs have needed, in many cases, only half as much time to catch up."

Despite these educational efforts and assimilative trends, the presence of so many new, relatively educated Polish immigrants has contributed to a revival of linguistic and cultural authenticity in Polish Chicago. The Polish Genealogical Society is doing a substantial business, sending a delegation every year to a five-day conference in Salt Lake City, where its members have open access to the highly developed research facilities of the Mormons' Family History Library. "I get calls every day of the week" from Polish Americans seeking help with research, says Edward Peckwas, a general contractor and operator of child-care centers who is the founder of the society. One of his associates, Rosemary A. Chorzempa, has now published a self-help book called *Polish Roots*, advising people especially on how to conduct a search of family records in Poland. Another project Peckwas recently sponsored involved cataloguing the applications and medical records of thousands of immigrants who joined the free Polish army in France during World War II. A substantial contingent of Polish Chicagoans, meanwhile, go off on the extensive annual tours of Poland sponsored by the Connecticut branch of the genealogical society.

There are, if anything, more, not fewer, Polish-language and Polish cultural institutions emerging in the city. The Copernicus Center, for example, a slick civic hall and performance arena created by Polish Americans in 1980 out of a grand old movie palace, is solidly booked with Polish-oriented entertainment, some of it direct from Warsaw or the Polish provinces. Meanwhile, its resident symphony orchestra and folk troupe practice weekly, and its meeting rooms are used by the Polish Arts Club, the Polish Heritage Club, Polish crafts classes, and a

Polish chapter of Overeaters Anonymous, not to mention the center's own English classes, which cater especially to blue-collar immigrants. Another volunteer group maintains the center's valuable pipe organ. Other ethnic communities, including Indians and Koreans, often rent the Copernicus Center for their own film festivals and other programs, and it has emerged as a favorite venue for candidate debates in hotly contested Chicago or Illinois elections. "Sometimes we're literally bulging at the seams," says Dennis Wolkowicz, the theater manager. There is a certain obvious pride in the fact that Polish Americans, once outsiders and even objects of derision, now provide Chicago with one of its busiest cultural and entertainment centers, located midway between O'Hare Airport and downtown.

To their own amazement, some of the people who came to the United States from Poland soon after World War II and struggled unsuccessfully for years to learn English now find they can get along without it after all. Even though the best jobs may still require a working knowledge of English, the standards for a successful adjustment to life in America seem to be changing, at least in Chicago. Indeed, some of the more recent arrivals, in a great reversal of American tradition and practice, are simply remaining Polish citizens. At the time of the crucial 1990 Polish parliamentary elections, after the communist regime had fallen, more than 10,000 Chicagoans were known to be holding valid Polish passports and thus were eligible to vote at the Consulate General.

ONE INSTITUTION that has survived particularly well in this environment is Chicago's Polish-language press. Poles enjoy a high literacy rate at home, and so, apparently, do those who live overseas. *Dziennik Zwiazkowy* (or the *Polish Daily News*), was founded as a weekly in the nineteenth century and has been published continuously as a daily (now just five days a week) since 1908. Emily Leszczynski, the general manager, describes the newspaper as a "welcoming institution for immigrants"—a publication where they can use the advertisements to "find jobs, apartments, automobiles, whatever they need. Plus they get all the world news, the news from Poland, and news from the community. The American papers won't report the news that affects the Polish community here in Chicago. We will."

Leszczynski, who was born to a Polish family in Germany that came to Arkansas in 1951 and then moved to Chicago three years later, acknowledges that she had relatively little to do with the Polish American community before she went to work for the newspaper. But now she cites growing circulation figures—ten thousand copies daily Monday through Thursday, twenty-five thousand on Friday—with pride, and as evidence of an increased Polish consciousness in Chicago. "It's only in the past ten years or so that this has happened, since *Solidarnosc* struck," she says. "Before that, you had to be assimilated into the American culture." Leszczynski is a portly, serious woman who rules her newsroom strictly but with a sense of humor. She seems surprised to hear herself making the comparison, but she readily draws an analogy between the Poles and Chicago's growing Mexican American population, which sustains many Spanish-language publications: "They want to keep what they brought with them—become Americans, but keep their own culture alive, too."

The recent wave of Polish immigrants has included many well-trained, experienced journalists, and so the paper has had little trouble filling its six reporter slots. (It also uses several freelancers.) In fact, the main problem that has emerged is the burgeoning competition from other publications geared to the Polish immigrants. Elzbieta Glinka, the assistant editor of *Dziennik Zwiazkowy*, worries especially about a new tabloid, *Dziennik Chicagoski*, which she labels a Polish-language equivalent of the *National Enquirer*. It has already reached a daily circulation of more than seven thousand. "They are against the establishment in Poland and against the establishment in the Polish community here. They are against everything, I might say, and that's how they have attracted readers," complains Glinka. Adds Leszczynski, "They live on scandal. They'll plagiarize a whole article. Fifty percent of their newspaper comes from papers that arrive here from Poland; they just take things and publish them as is." By contrast, she says, *Dziennik Zwiazkowy* has formal agreements with the Polish News Agency and various publications in Poland that permit material to be reprinted.

Glinka, who came from Poland in 1976 to join her mother in Chicago but has kept her Polish citizenship, believes that a key function of the Polish-language media is to make it easier for the immigrants to remain connected with the ongoing political and social debates back at home. "People here are very much involved with what is happening there," she says, especially as Poland struggles to develop a more stable postcommunist system. "Every argument there comes over here immediately." This spirit appears to have spread even to young Polish American students who may never have been to Poland, according to Glinka; she says her own children, who follow the news closely, "know everything that's happening in Los Angeles, but also everything that's going on in Warsaw." And, judging by the discussion that takes place in Chicago's Polish press, there is no excess of patriotism that leads the

Polish community in Chicago to feel they must take Lech Walesa's side on every issue. His political honeymoon is over, in American Polonia as well as in Poland.

"We print both sides of the story, Walesa's and the other side. But Walesa doesn't think for himself," asserts Leszczynski, quickly revealing her own convictions on Polish politics and speaking with the same force as she does about American domestic issues. (She says she was a supporter of independent presidential candidate H. Ross Perot in 1992.) "In Poland now, there's rampant unemployment. Everything is so expensive, you have to carry a shopping bag full of money in order to go shopping. You're afraid to go out at night. Even in the small towns, you're afraid you're going to get robbed," she says, with a nod to the reluctant nostalgia that some people feel for the economic security and physical safety of the communist years. "Poland needs somebody in power who can teach the people how to be a democracy, because they don't know. They got rid of communism and that's it. Now what do they do? They were not prepared for democracy."

For some of Chicago's Polish Catholic churches, recently on the wane, the arrival of the new immigrants has been an absolute windfall. Their huge, elaborately decorated sanctuaries are filling up once again with the faithful. Although the more educated among the newcomers may have become skeptical toward the religious establishment in Poland, especially during the period when the church seemed to have struck an ambiguous bargain with the communists, they now appear more willing to trust the priests after all. Those who have overstayed their U.S. visas, for example—and there are many, often known by the euphemism of "holiday-makers" or "long-term tourists"—may be willing to attend a lecture on immigration policies and procedures on the safely neutral territory of a church social hall, whereas they might feel more cautious, even fearful of an INS trap, in a more public setting.

Father Wladyslaw Gowin, the pastor of Holy Trinity, exudes something approaching giddiness over the rebirth of his parish as a "mission church" exclusively for Polish-speaking people. In Chicago since he arrived from Poland in 1969, Gowin still speaks English with a thick accent, but he finds it less necessary all the time to use his second language; he estimates that 80 percent of his parishioners speak only Polish. Although it is still surrounded by a black ghetto, Holy Trinity attracts a total of some two thousand Polish immigrants from around Chicago who are willing to travel every Sunday to attend its Masses at 8:00 A.M., 10:30 A.M., and 5:00 P.M., all conducted in Polish. The afternoon one, Gowin says, "is best for the cleaning people, because that's when many of them are just finished cleaning offices." Gowin also boasts that some of the mainstream Polish organizations and veterans groups are increasingly choosing Holy Trinity, rather than more fashionable spots, for their Constitution Day and other commemorative celebrations. The church has not exactly returned to the glory days when it was home to six hundred Polish weddings a year, but it is clearly back in business.

The real boom, however, is being experienced at Saint Hyacinth, an ornate parish church built in 1912, a few blocks away from the Orbit Restaurant, in a neighborhood that is being rapidly gentrified. Located further down Milwaukee Avenue, this is the new Polonia, otherwise known as *Jackowo* (pronounced 'yats-ko-vo) or the "Polish Village." According to Father Edwin Karlowicz, one of the seven priests assigned there, 10,000 people come through Saint Hyacinth's doors every weekend for its five Polish- and four English-language Masses.

But that's not all. This is a church where immigrants, as well as second-generation Polish Americans with a newly revived ethnic consciousness, send their children—almost 300 of them weekly—on Saturday mornings to study Polish language and culture. As we talk, Karlowicz reads from a list: There are the 500 children enrolled in Saint Hyacinth's full-time parochial school, plus the 150 in a dance program and 100 young adults in the "Oasis Group," a singles social club. One recent summer, he recalls, 850 people signed up for the church's English classes, so many that the Chicago Board of Education had to pitch in to contribute teachers and educational materials. The choir is bursting with recruits, and Saint Hyacinth has the honor of hosting the annual Chicago-area regional Polish American youth congress, with about 500 delegates each year.

Karlowicz was born in Chicago to Polish immigrant parents, but his own spoken Polish, he says, had become rusty until he was assigned to Saint Hyacinth in 1984. "Now it's improved a lot, with the number of confessions we hear," he says. "You have to have a good command of Polish here. If you run into five or six confessions a week in English, outside of the school children, you're doing pretty well. Most of them are in Polish." A large number of the people he sees, Karlowicz acknowledges, are in the United States illegally, and he deplores what he regards as the unreasonable restrictions that have been placed on immigration in recent years. "I don't think we're obligated to inform on any of these people. I'm in no position to do that. If things had been so difficult [for immigrants] in 1910," he says, "I don't know if my mom and dad would have made it here."

When Lech Walesa visited Chicago in 1989, Karlowicz is proud to point out, he made an appearance at Saint Hyacinth, and people were favorably impressed. In fact, he believes that the local Polish-language media have been far too rough on the postcommunist Polish government and, for that matter, on the leadership of American Polonia. "I don't think they're giving some of these people credit for what they are able to do," complains Karlowicz. "You don't know what [the media] really want sometimes."

Meanwhile, Father Joe Glab sits at the cavernous Saint Stanislas Kostka, the oldest and largest of the early Polish parish churches, offering Mass primarily in Spanish to a membership that has dwindled to about twelve hundred families. There has even been talk within the diocese of possibly shutting down this historic facility altogether, isolated as it now is from its old Polish constituency. But Glab has seen the first advance scouts of a new group coming into the original Polish neighborhood—"urban pioneers," mostly white, English-speaking "yuppies" who have decided to move back into the heart of Chicago from their suburban perches. "They think this is exotic," Glab says. "It will be like a new wave of immigration." Some of these immigrants may even be Polish Americans. But will they still be practicing Catholics, and will they be interested in the church that once took in their ancestors and organized their lives? That's what the diocese is waiting to find out.

THERE IS another, darker side to the new wave of Polish immigration to Chicago. To be sure, many of the more industrious immigrants are starting businesses, hiring one another, and contributing to the community's general economic well-being. Their children are, in many cases, the valedictorians in their parochial school graduating classes. It is the classic American immigrant model. But Father Edwin Karlowicz tells stories of established Polish American contractors and other businessmen taking unfair advantage of vulnerable newcomers, exploiting especially those in undocumented status. "I've heard of instances where an employer will just give a worker food, instead of a salary," he says. "And I've seen contractors walking around, inspecting a paint job—if he sees a few drops of paint on the floor, he may deduct two, three, or four hours' worth of pay from the individuals really breaking their backs to do the work."

According to Barbara Przezdziecka, the immigration supervisor at the Polish Welfare Association, there may be as many as 15,000 Polish immigrants in Chicago at any given time who are working illegally.

Because they are invariably paid less than others, they usually hold two or three jobs—as cleaners, baby-sitters, or construction workers—at the same time, just to get by. Even so, they tend to live several to a room, often in a basement, in the Polish Village, where they are less likely to stand out or attract attention. Sometimes they are the victims of violent crime, which they are afraid to report, lest they be discovered by the INS. In the unlikely event that they are caught, with the crowded court calendar in Chicago, it may take as long as a year before they are summoned to a deportation hearing (the results of which can always be appealed); but still a pall is cast over their lives.

Some men and women are so desperate to get a green card or find some other legal means of staying in the United States, says Przezdziecka, that they simply abandon their families back in Poland and start up new ones here. "This may seem sad to us, but to them, maybe not," she explains. "They think if they go back to Poland, they might not have another chance to come to the U.S., so they want to use being here as much as possible. Sometimes they think that they do not have anything to go back to in Poland. It's easier to live here, and they hear what is happening there, how bad the economy is."

Inevitably, there are also quite a few fraudulent marriages taking place in the Chicago Polish community. Przezdziecka, who trained as a paralegal after immigrating to Florida in 1982, says she has heard of undocumented aliens paying anywhere from $2,000 to $10,000 just to obtain a phony spouse who is an American citizen, in an effort to fool the INS. Often it works; but in the case of a woman who is attempting to remain in this country, she may unknowingly buy her way into an abusive relationship. Fearful that she will be shipped back to Poland if the fraud is revealed, she has no choice but to stay with a husband she hardly knows and endure sadistic mistreatment until at least three years have passed.

In fact, the Polish Welfare Association—founded in 1921 to deal with the fighting between Irish and Polish gangs, and supported now by federal, state, and county funds, as well as special events and donations from foundations and corporations—provides a glimpse of an underside of Polish life in Chicago that rarely surfaces in public. The association maintains a daytime homeless shelter for Polish men, with room for about twenty to twenty-five at a time, usually people afflicted with severe, chronic alcoholism. "In Poland alcoholism is enabled, by employers, by coworkers, and by family," says Agnes Kowalewicz, who is in charge of all social services at the association. "I wouldn't say that it's a worse problem than in other ethnic groups. It's similar to the Irish. But our culture tends to sweep it under the rug. These men usually arrive from Poland with an alcohol problem, and it seems the only place they can go to socialize here is the Polish tavern. They feel lonely and isolated; they don't participate in American culture." Many end up, in fact, on Chicago's Polish Skid Row.

Of the fifty-four people working at the welfare association, only three were born in the United States. Most of the rest are recent immigrants from Poland. Dealing all day every day with problems ranging from spousal abuse to job retraining to the difficulty that Polish-trained doctors, nurses, and other professionals have obtaining American licenses, they tend to be less starry-eyed than many of their compatriots. "When you come here, you think you're taking the first step to heaven," says Kowalewicz, who arrived in 1981. "When you look at America from the Polish perspective, you see that this is a free country. It takes ten years of being here to see that it's not so just and not as free as you once believed it is."

She goes on: "If you watch *Dynasty* in Poland, you presume that's the way all Americans live; then you come here and find out it's not true. The first shock is that the country is not as beautiful, not as rich as it should be. If you have any problems, there is no real backup system. People come to us and say, 'I need medical insurance because I am sick.' In Poland, it's a constitutional right of every person to be treated medically, but not here. And the money they receive here if they're unable to work is not sufficient even to support a family or rent an apartment. So people become very angry. The clash between expectation and reality is very strong."

Anna Zolkowski, the development director of the Polish Welfare Association, is American born but spoke Polish as her first language. She says that many Polish immigrants stay on in Chicago even though they are miserable in the United States. Some are unskilled laborers who work for years in menial jobs but tell their friends and family in Poland that they are doing something here that earns them much higher status. "Even as a cleaning lady, people can make more here in several years than they can make in a lifetime in Poland, and then provide things for their family. So it's worth all the risk, all the humiliation, all the stress," Zolkowski says. But there are worse cases: "We have people here who are sick and homeless, who have severe psychological problems and debilitating diseases. There is no way for them to function in this society—they don't have health benefits, they don't have anything—but they're too embarrassed to go home."

"Maybe it's because of my profession," says Kowalewicz, "but the longer I am here, the less I like this country and what it does to people."

IN THE FAR northwest corner of Chicago, set well back from the street on the west side of Cicero Avenue, is the imposing, fortresslike headquarters of the Polish National Alliance (PNA). It is an expensive piece of real estate and, in the overall context of the Polish American community, it is the real power turf. The PNA is not quite as old as the PRCUA—it was founded only in 1880—or as elitist, but it is big, and very influential. With some 300,000 members in thirty-six states, originally attracted by the life insurance policies it offered to working-class immigrants and their children for just five cents a week, the PNA can credibly claim to be a fraternal organization that speaks for a broad national constituency. When John F. Kennedy wanted to solidify his political hold on Chicago in 1960, the PNA was one of the obligatory calls he made. And it was to this slick headquarters building that Ronald Reagan and George Bush made high-profile campaign visits in the 1980s to court ethnic votes and raise political contributions.

Entire books have been written to chronicle the history of the PNA. In one of its most important symbolic gestures, it established Alliance College in Pennsylvania in 1912, to provide vocational training and education in the humanities for Polish students who were being systematically discriminated against by the mainstream American universities. It launched a Polish-language newspaper and radio station, and later it organized national bowling, golf, basketball, and other sports tournaments for Polish Americans. But from its earliest days, the organization also pursued an international political agenda: the cause of an independent Poland with secure, broadly recognized frontiers. Indeed, the PNA takes credit for putting pressure in 1918 on President Woodrow Wilson, through his friend Paderewski, to help restore Poland as a separate country after World War I.

For twenty-eight years beginning in 1939, under Charles Rozmarek, a Harvard-trained lawyer from Wilkes-Barre, Pennsylvania (who was also the founding president of the Polish American Congress in 1944 and concurrently ran that umbrella organization for twenty-four years), the PNA was an especially effective player in U.S. foreign policy during World War II and the Cold War. Rozmarek's support of President Franklin D. Roosevelt's bid for a fourth term in 1944, for example, and his later denunciation of Roosevelt and Winston Churchill for participating in the Yalta agreements that left Poland in the sphere of influence of the Soviet dictator Stalin, were both significant political events. He was substantially responsible for federal legislation that allowed perhaps a quarter of a million Polish refugees, veterans, and orphans to enter America after the war, outside the usual immigration quotas. Before he was dethroned by rivals in the late 1960s, Rozmarek also campaigned successfully for official U.S. recognition that the Soviet Union had massacred 15,000 Polish officers and soldiers in the Katyn forest in 1940—something finally acknowledged by the governments in Warsaw and Moscow only in 1989 and 1990, respectively.

Late one spring afternoon, just as the PNA's substantial staff was pouring out of the headquarters building into their large American cars for the drive home to the suburbs, I sat in the organization's vast boardroom—a plush inner sanctum decorated with plaques and crests and the portraits of various leaders of American Polonia. The PNA's current president, Edward Moskal, was much too busy that day to receive visitors, and Wojciech Wierzewski, editor-in-chief of *Zgoda*, the PNA's official in-house Polish-language publication, was deputized to see me instead. As we huddled at one end of the board's official meeting table, which looked to be at least fifty feet long, other PNA functionaries came and went. One was Adam Augustynski, a dapper young lawyer who confessed frankly that he was seeking opportunities to meet people from Washington, inasmuch as he intended to be sent there one day as a member of Congress.

Wierzewski recounted the organization's glory days and then told the uncomfortable story of its awkward relationship with the newer wave of immigrants from Poland. "A hundred years ago, it was impossible for [Polish] immigrants to survive without the PNA," said Wierzewski, a short, wiry, enthusiastic cheerleader of a man, himself a university professor in Poland who came to the United States on an academic exchange in 1980 and never returned. He had heard the horror stories of early Polish immigrant life in Chicago and other cities: "It was like life on the prairie when Americans were living in log houses. You were exposed to danger from all around, and you had to build a strong fortress to survive. Their fortress was a Polish neighborhood—with a church that had a strong cultural environment, a school, a club, a hall for entertainment. Everything was there, and there was no life outside the Polish community. You couldn't cross the street to go to the tavern on the other side, because you would be beaten up by the Germans." The PNA accumulated lots of money, and it offered a structure and a national protective network for the various Polish communities. "This organization was needed, because without it you couldn't have education or entertainment," explains Wierzewski.

Over the years, understandably, the PNA—with the PAC functioning virtually as its political arm—came to regard itself as the only, or at least the most important, game in town. It had the influence to organize and the power to intimidate, especially in Chicago; newcomers sought its favor and its friendship, if not its outright blessings (and its financing) for what they wanted to do. But not so the newer Polish immigrants of the Solidarity era. "Now," said Wierzewski with a shrug of resignation, "newcomers are looking for a place in American society. They'd like to work for the Americans. They don't need Poles." As if to prove the point, he cited his own case. As a skeptic of the old attitudes, albeit an employee of and staunch believer in the PNA, he said, "When I was coming here, I was coming to America, not to Polish America. I was looking for an American environment, an American school, an American university for my daughter. And this is the philosophy of the rest of my colleagues."

The PNA made some effort to attract the new arrivals as members and supporters beginning in the late 1970s, but it failed to rally them. There was a great age difference—most of the PNA's leadership was near retirement age—and a cultural gap, too. Actually, says Wierzewski, himself in his early fifties, "there was an attitude of incredible suspicion [on the part of established Polish Americans] toward these guys who were coming, even if they were obtaining political asylum. This organization was focused on trying to play a major role in Washington and almost turning its back on these immigrants." In any event, the well-educated émigrés and the Solidarity crowd were not interested in parades and folkloric Polish American festivals; they did not care to pay to advertise their businesses or professions in the Polish-language media; they were indifferent, if not downright hostile, about playing a role in American ethnic politics.

"They had all the answers, they knew what they wanted, and they just wanted us to support them," complains Larry Rzewski, the grandson of Polish immigrants, who is a PNA spokesman. "They had no regard for the way things are done in the U.S. You reach a point where you say, 'Well, should we be helping them? What investment should we be making? Because they don't appreciate what's being given to them.' "

The relationship became one of mutual hostility. In Wierzewski's view, "this is a result of the communist mentality." Even in the harshest days of communist rule in Poland, he says, educated people "could live quite a decent life, as long as they didn't attack the system. It was very easy." Once the intelligentsia did take on the system, they had to sacrifice many of their material comforts in Poland and, he says, they expected to be honored and somehow compensated in America for what they had given up; they wanted things to become easy again. "When these new immigrants came, many of them were ignorant and spoiled," says Wierzewski. "They treated the [Polish American] establishment here exactly the same as they did the communist regime over there— 'Old guys, stupid guys, who knows why they are up there, they should immediately give up their positions.' I am not kidding. They thought America [and especially Polish Americans] should be grateful that they got rid of communism in Poland. They came here to be paid for their fights, for their sufferings, for their time in prison, and everything else— because they were heroes. Their big disappointment was that here, nobody cares. You are on your own."

Some adjusted quickly. They became workaholics in the American style and, deploying classic immigrant ingenuity, found ways to fit into the Polish American community and to succeed and prosper in the larger world. One enterprising man launched *The Polish Phone Book*, a directory of Polish-owned or -oriented businesses and events in the Chicago area, published in Polish with occasional English translations. At first it was a thin volume, but by 1991 it had grown thick with advertising to almost four hundred pages and expanded its scope to cover Detroit and even Windsor, across the Canadian border in Ontario. It is just the right size and shape to fit on the home or office shelf with other phone directories. Selling for only a dollar a copy, it is everywhere in Chicago's Polonia, the perfect way to find a Polish-speaking real estate agent or locate a banquet hall with Polish cuisine.

But for every success story, there seemed to be a tale of displacement and discomfort, of adaptation gone awry. Perhaps 10 percent of the Solidarity-era immigrants retreated to Poland after the fall of communism in 1989. But that was not much of a solution, since once economic "reform" and capitalist values took hold in Warsaw, the small amount of U.S.-dollar savings they took with them no longer permitted them to live like royalty at home.

Some families were torn by discord. Although Wierzewski and his wife were comfortably settled and happily employed, for example, the original focus of their energies and hopes—their daughter—appeared to be rejecting everything they cherished. An only child, at nineteen she declared herself uninterested in her Polish roots and equally unhappy with mainstream American values. She is becoming a Moslem.

Meanwhile, at the PNA, Alliance College has been shut down and other long-standing programs have begun to dwindle. The organization "is not a driving force within the community anymore," Wierzewski acknowledges, "because the community does not need any support. They don't feel like second-class citizens any longer." But grandparents have been quietly enrolling their grandchildren as members, hoping that even if a generation is skipped over, the PNA will find new ways to maintain its membership and its influence in the future. At the quadrennial PNA convention in 1991, young rebels made a bold attempt to take the word "Polish" out of its title and rename it the "American Alliance" of something or someone else. They were unsuccessful.

ONE OF THE institutions that has had the most trouble charting a path through this tension is the Polish Consulate-General, still based in a luxurious old stone house on Chicago's lakefront. It must deal with many different categories and generations of Polish immigrants in representing their homeland to them and to Chicagoans in general. It has to avoid creating an unrealistic stampede back to Poland, and yet do nothing to encourage another brain drain from Poland to the United States.

For a time in the early 1990s, the office was headed by a man who, ten years earlier, as a political exile, had participated in anticommunist demonstrations on the sidewalk out front. But the toughest job of all is held by Andrzej Jaroszynski, the deputy consul general, who is in charge of relations with American Polonia. He must promote the translation of avant-garde novels while also attending ethnic bazaars. A former professor of literature at the Catholic University of Lublin, Jaroszynski found on arrival that the denizens of the PNA and other Polish American organizations in Chicago had their own notions of how the Polish government should conduct itself in the world's second largest Polish city, which did not always correspond to the instructions from Warsaw. And because he was, in a sense, one of them, albeit temporarily, he frequently had to explain that the newer immigrants were not really "less patriotic" about Poland, as was often alleged, but merely "less emotionally attached to their land, to the place where they were born." They are, as Jaroszynski likes to put it, simply "more modernized and rational, to some extent more sophisticated and more international" than the Poles who had come before.

Zygmunt Dyrkacz is one of those people. His experiences are emblematic of both the most hopeful trends and the greatest frustrations in Chicago's Polish community. Dyrkacz arrived in the United States in 1980 from the old historic Polish city of Kalisz; he had been trained as a beekeeper and had a scholarship, sponsored by the U.S. Information Agency and the 4-H Clubs, to study genetics at Michigan State University. Once he had finished his undergraduate degree in 1984, rather than returning to Poland, he and his wife migrated to Chicago. He had planned to complete a doctorate, but instead they found work as servants for a wealthy family in Highland Park, north of the city, and lived in the basement of their home. After they had a second child and the woman of the family died, they had to leave that house, and Dyrkacz became a driver for an entrepreneur on the South Side.

Meanwhile, he purchased two deteriorating four-story buildings in the old Polonia neighborhood and rehabilitated them, doing much of the work himself; within a few years, he sold them at a profit of $600,000. And so it went. Dyrkacz, a thin, energetic man with a soulful face, who sees himself as a dreamer, launched an interior-design business and also took on other construction projects. At the same time, he bought more properties, including the old Chopin Theatre, which had been a major focal point of Polish culture during the golden age of Polish Chicago. He hoped that it could serve as the nucleus for a renaissance of the neighborhood, with gentrified housing drawing in people of all backgrounds, who would learn to live together peacefully, paying special attention to the safety and the cleanliness of their surroundings.

Dyrkacz embarked on a one-man crusade for progressive political positions. He argued for strict gun-control laws, supported gay and lesbian civil rights campigns, and tried to design schemes that would permit poor people to buy and improve the substandard housing where they lived. He used the Chopin Theatre to host meetings for the neighborhood's new Hispanic congressman and to present plays candidly dramatizing the traditionally hostile relationship between Poles and Jews.

Increasingly, however, Dyrkacz came to seem like a voice in the wilderness. The neighborhood did not respond to his entreaties to clean up and make itself more secure. On the contrary, it seemed to deteriorate further. Jewish groups accused him of anti-Semitism, while Polish organizations claimed that he was deserting his heritage and becoming inordinately pro-Jewish. He rented out most of the theater's premises to a film society and began converting its basement into a cabaret for experimental theater; he opened a small coffeehouse in front, facing one of the historic intersections of Polonia. His marriage broke up. He began to feel friendless and unappreciated. "My dilemma from the beginning," says Dyrkacz, "was how to be Polish without being ethnic. I consider ethnicity to be very backward and the source of many political problems in this country. But maybe I am out of step."

IN THE SUMMER of 1993 Christopher Kamyszew was forced out as director of the Polish Museum. The leaders of the PRCUA, citing "philosophical differences" with him, declared that he had turned it into too much of an art gallery, and that this was inconsistent with the needs of the Polish American community in Chicago. He was, apparently, not "ethnic" enough. Encouraged by some of his defenders and supporters, Kamyszew decided to try again, elsewhere. He became executive director of the Society for Polish Arts.

IX
GETTING DOWN TO BUSINESS:
THE ETHIOPIANS AND THE ERITREANS

WASHINGTON, D.C.

TESFAY SEBAHTU'S story is a minor epic; it is easy to imagine it as a Third World novel or a movie. His father, a successful businessman in Asmara, a European-built city on the Eritrean high plateau in the Horn of Africa, died when Tesfay was a young child, leaving his mother in a very difficult situation. While she raised his two sisters, Tesfay was moved in with his uncle, his father's oldest brother, who had nine children of his own, mostly boys. For several years the boys all lived a grand life together in a fancy house in what had been, in colonial days, the Italian quarter of town, alongside some of the Americans who worked for the U.S. National Security Agency's high-tech listening post at nearby Kagnew Station. Tesfay attended a Catholic school, where he excelled, and he spent his summers in the countryside with his grandparents, learning the land and herding goats and sheep.

But Tesfay's childhood coincided with turbulent times in his country. Emperor Haile Selassie, the diminutive statesman who had courageously faced off against Mussolini's invaders in 1935 and made a famous appearance before the League of Nations in Geneva to defend Ethiopia's honor, was gradually losing his grip on power. The emperor had emerged from World War II with enough prestige and Western support to get away with annexing Eritrea, the former freestanding Italian colony, thereby gaining valuable access to the Red Sea. For decades thereafter, his Amhara ethnic group controlled all of the coun-

247

try's political, economic, religious, and educational institutions, through a well-heeled elite with extensive American connections. A founder of the Organization of African Unity, he was a revered symbol of the continent's aspirations to have an independent voice in world affairs. But beginning when Tesfay was a small child, Ethiopia's feudal society started to crumble. Haile Selassie, as a matter of misplaced national honor, concealed the facts about drought and famine that were ravaging some of the country's provinces, and finally a military council that came to be known as the "Dergue" forced him from office in 1974. He died a senile old inmate of one of his own prisons.

Eritrea's struggle for independence had begun in the early 1970s, and the Dergue—and especially Mengistu Haile Mariam, who emerged as its leader after killing off a number of his rivals—resisted it at least as fiercely as the emperor had. Meanwhile, the Horn of Africa also became a late-starting front in the Cold War, as the Soviet Union abandoned its political allies in nearby Somalia and switched to support Ethiopia against a Somali effort to capture another region of the country, the Ogaden desert. Even Cuba became involved on the Ethiopian side of that struggle. The United States, once a major military supplier to Ethiopia, obligingly moved over to Somalia's side and, however uncomfortably, supported and armed its dictator, Mohammed Siad Barre. Profiting from the turmoil and perceiving that the central government in Addis Ababa was growing weaker, other ethnic groups and other regions of Ethiopia mounted their own secessionist wars.

Tesfay had just attended the first day of seventh grade—the year most of his studies would switch from the Amharic language to English—in September 1979, when his mother told him they would have to leave Asmara at once. The Eritrean civil war had taken a turn for the worse, and those like Tesfay's family, who had clear sympathies on the rebels' side, seemed to be in danger. Tesfay was about twelve years old. (His official birth year is 1967, but its accuracy is in doubt; he thinks he may have been born earlier, but that it may have been embarrassing for his mother to have it known how young she was at the time she gave birth.) His uncle was already in prison, and some of his cousins had died in the fighting.

"There were a lot of Ethiopian soldiers in Asmara," he recalls, "and they looked nothing like us. It was very weird for us—the way they talked, the way they looked, and the things they did. Most of them, by that time, were from villages. They had just been conscripted, and they didn't act like city people. They were rude and always suspicious that anybody could be a rebel. We saw a lot of people get killed, sometimes in the middle of the night, just because they annoyed the soldiers. There was one couple that ran a small shop in our neighborhood, where we used to go every day to buy coffee and sugar. They were shot one night, and we saw their children crying the next morning."

Indeed, Tesfay's mother had begun to worry that out of resentment of this ragtag Ethiopian occupying army, he, like so many of his friends and relatives, might run off to the bush any day to join one of the two Eritrean liberation movements, one Islamic in its orientation and the other more Marxist. To avoid that issue, mother and son set out together on foot for the Sudanese border, leaving Tesfay's two sisters behind with their grandparents. It would be about a month's journey. "I was very scared. My mother didn't think I was going to make it. She thought she might have to rent a camel for me," Tesfay remembers gravely. But then he laughs. "We ended up renting one for her instead."

Their first stop was his mother's home village, where a cousin managed to arrange furtive passage to a point nearer the border crossing. From there, "businesspeople" charged $500 each to take them into Sudan—an illegal act at the time and a dangerous one, too, since the Eritrean Liberation Front believed it was everyone's patriotic duty to stay and fight the Ethiopians. Because they had relatives who were already established on the other side, they were able to avoid the squalid refugee camps, and soon they traveled to Port Sudan, on the Red Sea, where Tesfay's mother's youngest brother was involved with the Eritrean People's Liberation Front, the Marxist group. For nine months, young Tesfay worked in the EPLF office there; he was one of the "red flowers," the refugee children who were given "political education" in Tigrinya, the preferred language of Eritreans. But his mother feared that this indoctrination was a prelude to sending him back into the country to fight in a youth brigade, so she whisked him off to the capital city of Khartoum. There she worked as a housemaid for more than a year, while she tried to find a way to send Tesfay out to live among the Eritrean exile communities in Italy, Germany, or Saudi Arabia.

"One day we heard that the American embassy was accepting Ethiopian refugees for resettlement. I think it was Jimmy Carter who started it," says Tesfay. Because Ethiopians were now pitied for living under Mengistu's repressive, Soviet-supported Marxist regime, the United States was suddenly willing to accept them in greater numbers. "As far as the outside world was concerned, we were Ethiopians. I got up at four o'clock in the morning, and I was one of the first in line. When I went in for an interview, my mother didn't want to go. She didn't speak English, and she didn't have an education. She said I could go to America, and she would go to Saudi Arabia to work. But she thought she was going to lose me. A lot of Sudanese were saying at the time, 'If you go to America, they're going to make you a soldier and you'll never come back to your country.' But I thought America was the place to be, from the stories we used to hear and the movies we used to watch, like *The Six Million Dollar Man*." Tesfay inflated his age on his application and acted as if he were in Sudan alone, in order to maximize his prospects of getting a visa.

Before he knew what was happening, Tesfay was accepted in the resettlement program and he was one of a planeload of Ethiopians and Eritreans flying from Khartoum to Athens, and then on to New York. At Kennedy airport, the refugees were divided up among various sponsoring organizations. "A lot of them approached me," he remembers, "because I was the youngest and I was on my own. The Catholic church took me by accident, I think, because it was the only organization that provided group homes for refugees." He was brought to Washington and taken to a house in the suburbs where there were other young men, slightly older than he, who spoke Amharic. Since Tesfay knew little English, this was a relief. "There was a guy named Amin from Ethiopia. He greeted me and gave me milk and stuff. I had never drunk such cold milk before, and I couldn't drink it. So I gave it back, and they made me tea. It was August 7, 1981. I celebrate it every year as my new birthday."

Eventually there were three such houses near one another in Wheaton, Maryland, all with young Ethiopian and Eritrean refugees here on their own; nearby were several other group homes with similarly situated Vietnamese teenagers. Tesfay stayed at the house for three years, attending eighth, ninth, and tenth grades in the local public schools. In this context, he was more aware of the things that the young Ethiopians and Eritreans had in common—including language and their displacement into a totally alien culture—than of their political differences. Six months after he moved into the house, a brother and sister arrived from Rome who had once been his neighbors in Asmara. The teenage boy, who spoke excellent English, became a mentor and a surrogate older brother for Tesfay, translating television programs for him at first and later helping him with his homework and tutoring him in math and science. "We all got attached to each other in the house," Tesfay says. "We were just like brothers and sisters, although we had fights like any other family, too. We really enjoyed it. It was really good."

As far away as he was from home, the world seemed amazingly

small to Tesfay, and it was easy to believe that the problems of the Horn of Africa were at the top of its agenda. For a time, his group even had Eritrean "houseparents" whom his mother had known as refugees in Sudan. When he wrote to tell her about this coincidence, it was apparently enough to convince her not to go to Saudi Arabia after all. The night before she was due to go there, as Tesfay tells it, "something came to her mind. She didn't think it was going to work, with me here in America, my sisters in Asmara, and her in Saudi Arabia. So she sold her passport, her tickets, and everything. At that time they were all forgeries, so all they had to do was take off the picture and put in another one and send somebody else! The names didn't matter. She sold all her gold and everything else she had, to bring my sisters out to Sudan. And then I started the sponsorship papers. I finally told my social worker that my mother was in Sudan with my sisters. It didn't take that long for me to bring them all over here, just about six months."

Once his family arrived, just as he was starting eleventh grade, Tesfay moved out into an apartment with them. This was a major adjustment for him, after living with and being primarily responsible to his peers for several years. He also had to help his mother and sisters adapt to a vastly new environment, and he worked hard to support them. In the summertime Tesfay held two or three jobs simultaneously, sometimes going to the bank to deposit as little as seventy-five cents at a time. ("People made fun of me because I was a penny-pincher," he says.) With the money he saved and some from his mother, who was working as a dishwasher at a hotel, he bought a car. That contributed greatly to the family's mobility and his own popularity.

Tesfay proved to be a good student, and as a refugee he was surprised to find that he put more effort into his schoolwork than most of "the Americans" around him. He moved quickly from English as a second language into standard English classes. The one thing that gave him trouble was a public speaking course: "We had to get up in front of the class and give a speech. I used to get sweaty, and I couldn't talk. People would laugh at me, because of my accent. It was very hard, but it did help me."

After his high school graduation in 1986, he went on to a community college in Montgomery County, Maryland. There he became a math tutor and also found a large contingent of Ethiopian and Eritrean émigrés with whom he could debate politics. They went out together to reggae clubs and the Kilimanjaro, an African nightclub in Washington, but Tesfay would often slip away to the EPLF office, nearby in the Adams-Morgan section of Washington, where there were videos available of the brutal violence taking place at home. Sometimes he would bring along Ethiopian friends, in an effort to convince them that the Eritreans would eventually prevail and achieve independence. (They did, on May 24, 1991, just after a coalition of rebel forces toppled the Mengistu regime and he fled the country.)

Transferring to the University of Maryland, Tesfay obtained an undergraduate degree in electrical engineering in 1993. But he was unable to find work in that field, and at the time we met, like many Ethiopian and Eritrean refugees from all walks of life, he was driving a taxi. His mother believes it is dangerous, but being a cabdriver suits his current lifestyle, he says, allowing him to "pick up and go" whenever he wants a vacation. Meanwhile, Tesfay distributes his résumé to any passenger who will take it, hoping that one of these random contacts will lead him to an appropriate job. His mother, who had back surgery after a severe work injury, is now a street vendor, and he delivers her every morning at 6:45 to a garage where she picks up her mobile hotdog stand and then is taken to the corner of 15th and K Streets Northwest in downtown Washington. One sister has a degree in computer science from Maryland, and the other, after a stint in California, came back to enroll at Montgomery College. The family bought a house in Wheaton in 1991, just in time for a visit from Tesfay's mother's parents. (His grandfather died of complications from liver cancer during the visit, and Tesfay accompanied his body on its journey home as far as Rome.)

Now Tesfay talks about attending graduate school. But when he is not out on the street in his (or his uncle's) taxi or running some errand for his ever more extended family in America, he is often to be found at the Eritrean Cultural and Civic Center in a rough neighborhood of Washington. It is a café of sorts that was run by the EPLF during the war and has now been turned over to the Eritrean government. Decorated with tourist posters from Eritrea and photographs of the war and of planeloads of Eritrean exiles returning home after the Ethiopians had been defeated, the center is a loud, boisterous place with a billiard room and tables where young men play dominoes before large groups of spectators. Eritrean dishes are served, along with spaghetti and other Italian food and thick, authentic cappuccino. On the evening I go there with Tesfay, the only women in the place are sitting together at separate tables in a quiet spot far from the bar. Community newspapers are available to read, in Tigrinya and Arabic, and flyers on the walls announce upcoming events. In a back room sit boxes full of business envelopes with the return address of the Eritrean embassy in Washington, ready to be stuffed with announcements and mailed to the local or national exile community. Outside, the sidewalk is crowded with taxis; the D.C. police apparently grant them deference here and do not give them parking tickets.

As a man of twenty-seven (or so), Tesfay sports a moustache, a light beard, and an infectious smile, and he is clearly a frequent and favored visitor here. His natural charm seems to be composed of equal parts of Eritrean authenticity and studied American mannerisms. Sitting at a table, he quietly identifies the various minor celebrities who walk past—a body builder who once held the title of Mr. Asmara, for example, and a singer who used to pack admirers into his concerts in Eritrea but now lives in obscure exile in Washington.

Tesfay expects his mother to return to live in Eritrea someday, but he says that while he may buy a house there for retirement visits, he intends to make his life in America. He has visited cities from coast to coast and favors those in the west, like San Diego, Seattle, and Portland, which remind him of his favorite places in Europe. His dream is to marry an Eritrean woman—"I have to stick with my own kind; the minute you marry somebody else, you start to drift apart from your family"—and work for a time for an American company in London, before coming back to the United States.

He despairs, though, of ever educating Americans about Eritrea and what its people have gone through: "I pick up a lot of fares from Capitol Hill, even people who work for senators, and they ask me where I'm from. I tell them, and they say, 'Where is that? Somewhere in South America?' "

THE NUMBER of Africans who have come to live in the United States voluntarily has always been relatively small. Except for students with bona fide acceptances to educational institutions and a smattering of political exiles from places like South Africa, they have usually had difficulty obtaining immigrant visas; and the long, expensive journey was beyond the reach of most African families. Africans were far more likely to end up in Europe, especially in countries with which they had colonial ties, such as Britain and France. Africa has had a significant refugee population for decades—about a third of the 15 million refugees worldwide live on the continent, often under deplorable conditions— but American officials have sometimes seemed oblivious of that fact. The African refugees were out of sight, rarely seen on U.S. television screens, and therefore mostly out of mind.

Only with the passage of a new refugee act by Congress in 1980 did this begin to change, and Ethiopians and Eritreans were among the first in Africa to take advantage of it.[1] That year about 900 Ethiopian political refugees came to America—a paltry number compared to the estimated 125,000 Cubans who participated in the Mariel boatlift the same year (especially ironic when one considers that Cuba was a major backer of the Mengistu regime), but still a major breakthrough. Indeed, for the rest of the 1980s a substantial majority of the African refugees admitted to the United States were from Ethiopia or Eritrea; the warmth of the American public's welcome may have been vastly increased by television coverage in 1984 and 1985 of the Ethiopian famine. (By 1992, when the United States planned to admit a total of 120,000 refugees from around the world, Africa's overall allocation was still only 6,000, or 5 percent. Because of processing difficulties, even that quota may not have been fully used.)

Tsehaye Teferra, who originally came to the United States in 1971 and received his doctorate in sociolinguistics from Georgetown University six years later, runs the Ethiopian Community Development Council in Arlington, Virginia, a suburb of Washington. He explains that for educated, urban Ethiopians who spoke English and needed to leave their homeland during the 1980s for political reasons, there was really no place other than America for them to go, especially not in East Africa. "There was nothing for them to do in places like Sudan, Kenya, or Somalia," he says. "These were countries that were poorer than Ethiopia, and they could not absorb that kind of manpower. But many of these Ethiopians already had family or friends in the U.S.—teachers, Peace Corps volunteers, and so on. At least if they had to flee their country, they felt they knew something about the United States. Culturally, they would have less of a problem coming here than they would going to Sweden or Australia."

The more recent Ethiopian refugees and immigrants, however, who came in the late 1980s and early 1990s, tend to be from a totally different

---

[1] *Although Haile Selassie was one of the founders of the Organization of African Unity, Ethiopia has long held itself somewhat aloof from the rest of Africa. It claims, for example, to be one of only two countries on the continent never to have been colonized by outsiders. (Of course, this requires leaving out Eritrea, which was ruled by Italy from 1890 until 1941, administered by the British until 1952, and then federated with Ethiopia until 1962, when it was summarily annexed by the emperor.) The other African state that shares with Ethiopia the distinction of never being colonized is Liberia, in West Africa, whose coastal areas were settled by freed American slaves in the 1830s; although it functioned as a U.S. client state for many years, it was never formally a colony. Ethiopians, Eritreans, and their Somali neighbors in the Horn do have a different appearance from most other Africans—they tend to have a blend of African and Caucasian features—and they are often criticized for displaying a haughty, even hostile, attitude toward people from other parts of the continent. But there have been moments when it was politically and economically advantageous to portray themselves as ordinary Africans.*

background. Forced out less by politics than by economic deprivation and the tribal, secessionist battles that characterized the last years of the Mengistu regime, they were mostly from rural areas and may have spent their entire lives working in subsistence agriculture. They came to the United States because other Ethiopians had preceded them here. But in this case, says Teferra, they were not only illiterate in English but in their own languages. "What do you do with someone who has been farming in Ethiopia all his life" and suddenly arrives in America, he asks. "You can't make him a dishwasher, because dishwashing is especially automated nowadays. He cannot be a taxi driver, because he can't pass the test for his driver's license. Sometimes I wonder whether it is to their advantage even to bring these people here. They end up as laborers. They don't know their rights, and so they are often exploited."

According to the most reliable, albeit unofficial, estimates, there are today probably about 75,000 Ethiopian immigrants in the United States altogether.[2] At least a third of them live in the Washington area, with the rest scattered primarily in Los Angeles, the San Francisco Bay area, Dallas, Houston, and Atlanta. The tendency to congregate in the capital, Teferra believes, is merely the replication of a traditional pattern in Ethiopia: "You come from a small town, you go to school, and when you finish, you go to the provincial capital. There you complete your secondary school, and if you pass the entrance exam for the university, your next step is to go to Addis Ababa. But even if you don't pass the exam, you have to seek employment, and most of the opportunities are concentrated in the capital. So the capital has always been the center of everything in Ethiopian life—government, education, business. Maybe opportunities in Maine would be much better, but Washington is the capital, so automatically people pack up and come here. Who wants to be isolated out there in Kentucky?"

Once so many Ethiopians had gathered in Washington, they stimulated the growth of a specific Ethiopian cultural environment around them. Washington now has many Ethiopian restaurants, nightclubs, and grocery stores; there are half a dozen churches catering to the community and offering alternate services in Ethiopian languages. Visiting singers and musicians who perform in Amharic or Tigrinya pack in large crowds that include people who have traveled hundreds of miles for a reminder of home. In part because of their past travails, the

[2] *This figure likely includes some 15,000 Eritreans. They regard themselves as a distinct group, but the distinction has eluded most American government officials and social service agencies, and is regarded as politically unacceptable by most other Ethiopians.*

Ethiopians and Eritreans in Washington tend to be secretive. It is known that very few of them are on public welfare and, indeed, that there are several millionaires in the community. They often conceal their holdings as much as possible, but they can be easily identified, according to Selome Taddesse of the Ethiopian embassy. "They spend a lot of money on flashy things," such as expensive cars and large, modern houses, she says.

Ethiopians may deal with many of the same issues as most immigrant groups, and some obviously cope better than others. According to Teferra, however, there is something profoundly unsettling for all Ethiopians about the immigrant or refugee experience. Unlike the Italians, the Irish, the Jews, and other groups that have been part of the traditional American immigrant stream, he notes, "not many Ethiopians have ever been refugees in other countries. There have always been internal problems in Ethiopia—famine, drought, and so on. But people mostly moved from one region to another, in an internal migration. The very idea of being a refugee occurred for the first time in 1935," when the Italians invaded, and even then relatively few people left.

"No one ever imagined that we would end up this way, refugees in another country, displaced," Teferra says, as we speak at his office in a transitional immigrant neighborhood of Arlington, not far from Vietnamese restaurants and Hispanic bodegas. The second-floor conference room where we meet has plain white walls, undecorated except for a large map of Ethiopia, and the sign-in register downstairs indicates that recent clients of the agency have included not only Ethiopians but also Somalis, Liberians, Koreans, and Afghans.

Many Ethiopians have not handled the stress of displacement well, Teferra says, and for a long time they resisted doing anything, such as buying a house, that would imply they had made a permanent move to America. "Prior to 1978," he remembers, "people would laugh at you for buying real estate. I knew one Ethiopian who had a hobby of going around to houses to look at them; I went with him a few times, and I was really shocked by the idea that he might want to own one here. Then suddenly he dropped me in 1975; I heard nothing from him. He did not want to tell me until the next year that he had bought a house. It was like an admission that you have given up on going back to Ethiopia. Even when I bought my house in 1978, I would not admit it to people, because they would question my morality and my nationalism. They would think I had abandoned the dream of going back."

This feeling was so strong that many Ethiopian émigrés actually objected in 1980, when Teferra and others organized the Ethiopian

Community Center (ECC) in Washington. "There was real resentment. People saw us as traitors," he says, shaking his head, as he recounts the bitter feud that took place at the time. "What we were advocating was, 'Let's help Ethiopians to adjust to life here.' People were saying, 'Why bother?' In fact, they were saying, 'You are really doing a disservice by making life comfortable for these people here, so that they will not be able to return to their country.' My argument was that I was helping these people so that they will be able to help themselves. I firmly believed that it was only those people who were able to help themselves here that would be of any help to their compatriots in Ethiopia. If you can't accumulate knowledge and skills here, if you just waste your years here doing nothing, what good are you going to be to your brothers and sisters in your homeland? I believed this strongly and took it very personally."

Teferra cites "the Jewish experience" in America as a relevant model for the Ethiopians. "It is because of a strong Jewish community in this country that Israel could be a strong state," he argues. "I see a connection. If we become a very strong community here, it doesn't prevent us from returning. If we really develop skills and material wealth here, that lets us help the many Ethiopians who are suffering."

Once they did decide to settle in, quite a few Ethiopians in the Washington area enjoyed great success in business, as the owners of parking garages, taxi companies, and travel agencies, among other enterprises. And in the Washington-Baltimore area, there are now an estimated twenty-five Ethiopian and Eritrean physicians, perhaps five times as many as in an entire province at home. Despite the nostalgia they express, few have actually taken steps to return. As with many other immigrant groups, once their children are in school in the United States, they become very reluctant to leave. Yet they have a hard time deciding to become U.S. citizens; Teferra, for example, says he has carried in his briefcase for five years an application to convert his resident-alien (green card) status to full citizenship but has never found the time to fill it out.

Some successful Ethiopians have dealt with their immigrant insecurities by acquiring a great deal of property in America and indulging in an extravagant lifestyle. "It's mind-boggling," in Teferra's view. "Obviously, they have earned this money working long hours, sometimes two job shifts, sixteen hours a day. But now some carry eight or nine credit cards, and they spend lavishly. The idea of having savings is rejected. And their help to others is insignificant. There are people who have left family members—brothers, sisters, friends, and the whole community—suffering in Ethiopia, but they don't think about them. Instead they spend huge amounts here on weddings and parties."

On a single weekend in Washington in the spring or the fall, there can be as many as a dozen weddings among prominent Ethiopian families, creating a quandary for immigrants who feel they must choose which one to attend or race from one to another. If, on the same weekend, there are several more taking place out of town, with overlapping guest lists, the problem becomes even worse.

At the other end of the spectrum, the truly dependent rural people make up only about 10 percent of the total Ethiopian immigrant population in the Washington area, according to Teferra, but they require a great deal of attention. Hermela Kebede, who is now executive director of the Ethiopian Community Center in Washington that Teferra founded, estimates, for example, that there are several dozen homeless Ethiopians living on the streets of the nation's capital at any given time. "Most of them are secondary migrants who have come from other states, and they don't have anyplace to go. Some have been working for many years in low-paying jobs, and they are very unhappy, even a little paranoid," she says. "We have connections to some shelters, and we try to see if the Ethiopian restaurants can help feed them." Those who appear to have mental health problems are sent to a D.C. government "multicultural center" nearby, where there are several Ethiopian specialists.

Yosef Ford, a counselor at the community center, is himself an Ethiopian immigrant from the 1960s and a trained anthropologist. He points out that there are many other categories in the community to worry about, including highly qualified people who have been reduced to low-level service jobs, such as Ph.D.'s who are working as doormen or custodians and see no hope of improvement in their circumstances here anytime soon. Even today, he says, many of these people suffer from a "sojourner mentality," a conviction that any day things will get much better in Ethiopia and they will be able to go home and resume the life for which they were educated. Unlike many other immigrants, who dreamed of coming to America, Ford explains, these Ethiopians tend to feel, as he does, "I'm here because I'm stuck here, not because I want to be here."

Kebede argues that overall, the women among the Ethiopian refugees tend to cope better than the men. "I have seen mothers who have been able to take care of their kids, work one, two, or three jobs, and still have a life," she says. Many, though, have had to settle for being waitresses or parking lot cashiers and therefore have not had time to go out and look for other work or to take advantage of training opportunities. She estimates that "at least 50 [percent] to 75 percent of the women are overqualified for the jobs they hold. Most of them are stuck there." Kebede herself is in a different situation: She completed her undergraduate and graduate degrees at Fresno State University in California in the 1970s and worked in administrative positions at Howard University in Washington for fifteen years before becoming executive director of the center. But she too dreams of returning home one day, and she insists that 95 percent of the Ethiopians in America feel the same way. Her husband works for the Amharic service of the Voice of America, and their young daughter is being brought up to think of herself as having two countries, one of which she will have to choose at age eighteen. "I have never given up hope" of returning, Kebede says. "I have just been waiting."

The ECC, which survives on government grants and private donations from Ethiopian businesses, says that one of its most important tasks is to "promote and enhance a positive image of the Ethiopian community in the United States." But it has also taken to publishing bilingual pamphlets, in Amharic and English, on issues like "Anti-Discrimination Law" and "Health and Diet." The latter advises Ethiopians on how to modify their traditionally ultra-high-cholesterol diet and also warns of the risks of diabetes, hypertension, and HIV infection. A publication celebrating the center's thirteenth anniversary featured advertisements from Ethiopian restaurants, markets, and service agencies, along with immigration lawyers eager for Ethiopian business. Testimonial letters came from the Indochinese Community Center, Lutheran Social Services, and the Washington Lawyers' Committee for Civil Rights and Urban Affairs, among others.

MANY OF the Ethiopians in Washington, of course, come from the elite circle that once surrounded Haile Selassie, and their memories of home are of a grand and golden era of privilege. They originally gravitated to the national capital area to study, in part because they tended to have personal friends among the various American government officials and military officers who had worked in their country and now lived in or near Washington. Most had no reason whatever to believe, when they first came, that they would not be returning to Ethiopia with their American degrees to move into influential positions in the public or private sector there.

Gideon Shifaraw is an example. He arrived from Ethiopia in 1970 to attend Luther Rice College in Alexandria, Virginia, a small unaccredited school where he could work toward an undergraduate degree in business administration and marketing. Although his ancestry includes people from the Tigre and other ethnic groups, his grandfather on his father's side was a high priest of the coptic church in the holy city of Harer, and he was raised amongst the Amhara establishment in Addis Ababa. These were people, he explains, "who would count back about five or six generations to see who you are before they say it's okay to marry their daughter. If there were too many peasants in the background, then the blood is not clean. It was stupid, but that was how they were—very tight and close."

But in Shifaraw's case, there was another special factor. "My father fought in the Italian war, so he was very close to the emperor," he says with undiminished pride. "He used to tell me about the war as a child, how many Italians he killed, what he did, and what his friends did. Sometimes he'd talk to me about it until six in the morning. He was very loyal to the emperor, and one time he told me, 'If Haile Selassie asked me to kill my son, I would not ask him why. I would do it on the spot.' He used to handle imports and exports for the emperor. Then he retired from the government, and he became a farmer."

The Shifaraw farm was not exactly a subsistence operation, but a major enterprise with access to precious irrigation resources, and Gideon worked there for two years after high school. "We used to harvest twice a year," he recalls. "We had corn, grains, bananas, oranges, papaya, and soy beans." At the same time, although his grandfather on his mother's side had never been to school and could not read or write or properly count money, he was very rich—in Shifaraw's words, "one of the biggest millionaires in the country."

While he was in high school, young Gideon, like many other children of the Ethiopian bourgeoisie, participated in demonstrations against the excesses of the emperor's regime: the brutal police tactics, the crackdowns on the political opposition, and the indifference to the country's many poor peasants. He remembers that despite his family's wealth and good connections, he had to engage in the time-honored Ethiopian practice of adjusting his birthdate to make himself old enough to obtain permission to study overseas. Yet he fully expected to return and take up his place in this aristocratic milieu after a few years in the United States. However, before he finished his degree in 1977, the revolution had taken place at home. "In the seventies, we all thought we were just living here temporarily," he says. "We didn't know much about Americans and their customs. It really wasn't comfortable for us at all. Everybody wanted to go home. But then, after the military took over and Mengistu started killing people, things changed. That's when the Ethiopian people here started going into business, buying houses, and having families."

In many cases, the Ethiopian students had to settle in more completely than most, because they knew that sooner or later they would have to accommodate other members of their families who might be arriving. Mengistu's regime, in its "Red Terror" phase, executed or imprisoned many of the country's intellectuals and professionals, confiscated property, and in some regions embarked on a draconian land reform and collectivization campaign. There was a great scramble to get out alive, and the United States was the destination of choice. Shifaraw's father, a particular symbol of the old order, "was reduced to practically nothing," according to his son. "They took everything away from him. The government was giving him less than fifty dollars a week. But it was not just the money. They took away his land, his tractors and buildings. That was really insulting."

The elder Shifaraw was nonetheless reluctant to leave; like other privileged Amharas, he could not imagine having a decent life elsewhere and could not believe that things would not be set right again someday. He hung on as long as he could, surviving partly on the money that his son wired him monthly from America. "My father used to quote from the Bible, and he said I was like Joseph, taking care of my family," Shifaraw remembers. But finally he let his son bring him to the United States in the mid-1980s, when he was in his sixties.

Shifaraw himself became a U.S. citizen in 1978, soon after marrying an American woman he describes as "half-Irish, half-black." While in school, like many other Ethiopian students, he had worked as a "car jockey" in parking lots around Washington, earning $1.80 an hour. Now he got a job with Riggs National Bank. At first he was a teller and later moved up to be a loan officer (but still parked cars at night sometimes to earn extra money). For the eight years he worked at the bank, he says, he "pulled out of the Ethiopian community" and paid most of his attention to his three young children.

But then his brother and sister, who had also immigrated, opened an Ethiopian restaurant in Manhattan called the Blue Nile, and they asked Shifaraw to manage it for them. He lived in New Jersey during the week and commuted back to Washington on the weekends to see his family. "I got tired of it," he says, especially because "people kept breaking into the restaurant in the middle of the night, looking for something to steal. The police would call me at four in the morning, and I'd have to drive back in to Manhattan."

Much to the relief of his children, Shifaraw moved back to the

Washington area after several years and opened his own restaurant by the same name in Silver Spring, Maryland, just a few blocks from the D.C. line. As he describes it, this was a real family project: He installed the paneling on the walls himself, and he and his wife did all the decorating. They served a full Ethiopian menu, relying on the local business community at lunchtime and on Ethiopians who gathered there for dinner, especially on the weekends; they also catered large Ethiopian parties. On Thursday through Sunday nights, they had live music—one night reggae and on the other three, traditional dancers, singers, and bands from various regions of Ethiopia.[3]

In 1989, while Mengistu was still in power, Shifaraw made his first trip back to Ethiopia in nineteen years. He went to meet a sister there who was coming from London, where she lives in exile. "I felt like I was a foreigner. I just couldn't fit in," he says. "It was horrible. The country I thought was the most beautiful place in the world had been destroyed. Addis Ababa used to have all these trees, the streets were clean, and even the air was nice. Now it's nothing but dirt, the whole town stinks, and the buildings are crumbling. We grew up in a big house with a big garden, and everything was well maintained. Now the house is falling apart, and the garden has been destroyed. The soccer field is not there anymore. Kids I used to go to school with, who used to be rich, were begging in the street. So were a couple of my father's friends, and there was a millionaire's son who was a shoeshine boy. They destroyed the family structure, too. It was so sad. It took me almost a week to recover from the shock."

"The one good point about Mengistu," Shifaraw concedes reluctantly, "is that ninety percent of the people can now read and write. Under Haile Selassie, I'd say that eighty percent could not. But the economy is practically nil. There is no place for businessmen or intellectuals." Indeed, he claims to have spent close to $70,000 during his 1989 visit on bribes, to obtain permission to start up a business in Ethiopia. "They said everything was okay, but [with Mengistu and his military clique out of power] the people who took the bribes from me are all in jail now," he says with a shrug. Shifaraw no longer has any doubt that he will stay permanently in America. He says he will take his children home for a visit someday, "so they can know what Ethiopia is all about, that it's not just a bunch of hungry people." But then he will eagerly come right back to the United States: "One thing I like about this country is that you can be whatever you want to be. I can say

---

[3] *The restaurant closed in 1994.*

anything I want to say here. I'm always safe. I can do anything I want to do, legally. I don't have to look behind me."

ONE ASPECT of the Ethiopians' life in Washington—their tense relations with African Americans—is especially perplexing. In certain respects, says Yosef Ford of the Ethiopian Community Center, Ethiopians are drawn to this city because of its highly developed black community and its vibrant black political, economic, and social structure—not to mention its well-established black artistic and cultural circles. The population of the District of Columbia itself is estimated to be about two-thirds African American and other people of color, and so on the surface, it is less daunting than many other American cities as a place for Africans to settle.[4] "There is less of a racial issue in D.C.," Ford believes. "An Ethiopian living in a small town in Texas is much more likely to feel the pressures of race; an Ethiopian in D.C. can almost hide in the black community, theoretically." He would not ordinarily encounter the kind of overt job discrimination that is so widespread elsewhere, says Ford, given that employers in Washington are accustomed to hiring a multiracial workforce.

And yet, Ford points out, the Ethiopian immigrants "see themselves as Ethiopians first, and not as Africans or African Americans." Even in Washington, he adds, "as newcomers, they would not want to be in the position of the African American, noting that he is often on the ground floor, at the bottom rung of the ladder. Just because of their blackness, Ethiopians would not necessarily want to identify with the place African Americans hold in this society."

As a result, says Ford candidly, "relationships are not close." To the extent that Ethiopians live in neighborhoods populated primarily by the black underclass—and they would certainly try not to do so—"they would tend to stay to themselves. And if they are involved in situations of conflict, they would keep it to themselves," rather than reporting problems to the police, according to Ford. "Traditionally, Ethiopians' conflict resolution was done through the family, not external institutions." In a sense, he suggests, this is all a reflection and an extension of the cultural and physical isolation that Ethiopians experienced in Africa; thus, the Ethiopians also tend to keep their distance from other

[4] *According to the 1990 census, Washington's population of 606,900 was 66 percent black, 30 percent white, and 4 percent "other races," including Asians. Four percent of the residents, whatever their color, identified themselves as being of "Latino ethnicity." These figures, of course, do not take into account the breakdown in the Maryland and Virginia suburbs, which together have at least twice as many people as the city itself.*

African immigrants in America. As Selome Taddesse of the Ethiopian embassy puts it: "Africa is a big continent, not one big country. The guy from Nigeria doesn't eat what I eat or speak what I speak." Inevitably, the situation leads to allegations that the Ethiopians are themselves behaving in a haughty, racist manner and trying to avoid association with other Africans.

The coolness between Ethiopians and African Americans plays itself out on a practical, day-to-day working level, and it can have serious consequences. Moges Biru completed a degree in animal science at Virginia State University during the 1970s, a prelude, he thought, to returning home to work in agriculture. Instead, he used his savings from seven years' working as a parking garage attendant to buy a Shell service station in a black neighborhood of Washington. He has struggled mightily to make a go of it, putting in twelve- or fourteen-hour days six or seven days a week, and he has been startled by the hostility he feels from African Americans. "The blacks say to us, 'You goddamn foreigners, you came here, you're making money, you're taking our work,' " Biru says. "They don't say, 'you goddamn Ethiopians,' but they do say, 'you goddamn foreigners.' They don't care if we're Ethiopian or African, they just see us as foreigners. They don't know that I'm a U.S. citizen. What they see is my face. Or they hear my accent, so they know that I'm a foreigner. When they curse you, they don't ask for your ID."

Biru used to hire quite a few African Americans to work in his garage. "They were okay," he says, "but I think some of them didn't feel like working for me. One by one they left." Now he has reached the point where he hires only Ethiopian mechanics; as cashiers, he uses only members of his extended family. With his station located just a few blocks from an area that is known as a haven for drug dealers, this is, he says, an issue of trust and safety. But the fact that his staff is all-Ethiopian has probably affected adversely his business among African Americans, and, he complains, Ethiopians have not exactly flocked to his station to make up for it. Indeed, Biru laments the fact that Ethiopians are not nearly as loyal to merchants from their own community as he thinks other immigrant groups seem to be.

All of this has made Biru feel isolated and quite cynical about life in America and his own long-range prospects here. At the age of forty, he married an Ethiopian woman, a fellow exile, and they have one small child; his only vacation since he bought his business was their two-week honeymoon in San Francisco, Los Angeles, and Las Vegas. On his one trip back to Ethiopia so far, in 1985, he says, he encountered many young people, in the countryside as well as the city, who planned to immigrate. "I told them, 'It's not for you. It's not so great, not what you hear.' But they didn't want to believe me," he says. Of one thing he is certain: He does not intend to retire in the United States. "I see too many elderly people here who have no help with their lives and no family ties," he says. "When they get old, their children put them in a nursing home, or if they stay in their own house, they have no visitors. Nobody seems to care about their parents or grandparents. And if I stay here too long, everybody over there may forget me."

Another perspective on the relationship between Ethiopians and black Americans comes from John Withers, a retired diplomat who twice served in the Addis Ababa office of the U.S. Agency for International Development during the 1960s and 1970s, the second time as chief of mission. "I didn't find a generalized racial attitude" among Ethiopians, says Withers, who is himself an African American, "except that they wanted to be sure that any black who served in the capacity of mission director was fairly worthy and well thought of and would have the ear of headquarters here in Washington." Many of the Ethiopian friends Withers and his family made were associated with Haile Selassie and his regime and now live in the Washington area, where the Withers family sees them often. These people come primarily from the Amhara elite and, as Withers puts it, they "stress education as the means toward upward mobility. There is enough left of the family structure that has not been shattered by the American experience. They seem to have a much larger percentage of their youth going to college than does the American black middle class, where it is hard to control the youth, who are influenced by the downward pull of the underclass."

One of the reasons Ethiopian men, even from the elite group, have a much harder time adjusting to life in America than the women, Withers suggests, could be that "some of the odium that attaches to the young American black male may, just through skin color and appearance, attach to the Ethiopian male." This feeling may have been exaggerated, he adds, by "the drop in social status" that many Ethiopian men experienced in coming to the United States, even if they are still economically well off here. "To be a dean, or president, of Haile Selassie University, or a government minister in Ethiopia, raised you to a certain level. Even though you may have a much higher salary at the World Bank [in Washington] or at an American university, your status is less here, because there are many people at the same level. It's a very nice middle-class level, but it's not the high status that the ruling classes had" in Ethiopia.

Ethiopians in business here prefer to hire their own compatriots, Withers says, in part because there is a "natural tribal identification and an affinity for their own people. They can speak Amharic together." Furthermore, he says, Ethiopian employees tend to have a different relationship from American blacks with their employers: "Ethiopians are much less critical of those who work for them and more subservient to those for whom they work. The tensions and problems of obedience and status just simply don't exist [within a circle of Ethiopians]. It's much more hierarchical, and they accept their role more readily than do American blacks, who are often hostile simply because they have to work for another person." This tension is understandably more severe, in Withers's view, if one is working for "a foreigner, and a black foreigner at that, who is doing very well and owns the business." He regards this as a milder form of the hostility that has been seen to develop between Korean immigrant businessmen and their black employees and customers.

Unlike the Koreans, says Withers, Ethiopians are not especially fearful of African Americans, but they may be "contemptuous" of many of them. This is an issue not of race, but of class, he insists. "Ethiopians, not having had the experience of American racism, react differently to what they find here. They think in terms of class to a much greater extent than most Americans. They would show respect to a black of a certain class but would not respect a white who is not doing very well in life."

No CONVERSATION, or even casual encounter, in Washington's Ethiopian and Eritrean communities can go very far without becoming enmeshed in home-country and Horn of Africa politics. Taxi drivers, at the slightest provocation, harangue their passengers about the latest developments in Addis Ababa or Asmara or, worse still, in the bowels of the State Department. The parking lot attendants seem to operate a kind of underground telegraph, spreading the word when it is time to hold a demonstration or otherwise mobilize the community. In the restaurants along Columbia Road and Eighteenth Street, in the Adams-Morgan section, long after the other customers have moved on, feverish debates rage into the night over *injera* and *wat* and other hyper-spicy delicacies, best eaten with the fingers. Meetings are held on the weekends in the auditoriums of local high schools, where poets and politicians stir adoring crowds to outrage, while souvenir flags and sweatshirts and coffee mugs are sold in the corridors to raise money for the cause. All of this goes on without any special notice by the media or the larger community.

Certain controversies seem impossible to put aside. Moges Biru, for example, still remembers the day when Somalia got its freedom from the British and the Italians, while he was in elementary school, and immediately laid claim to a large swath of Ethiopia. "They wanted to fight right away," he recalls with enduring resentment. But as a perennial hot topic, nothing quite matches the issue of Eritrea's independence from Ethiopia. Immigrants discuss the subject with a vehemence reminiscent of debates over the Bolshevik Revolution that must have taken place among Russian exiles in New York and Paris during the 1920s. Some Amharas argue fiercely that the Eritreans have fooled sentimental liberals in the United States and Europe by claiming to be a separate ethnic group when, in fact, they are just the ambitious, aggressive residents of a region of Ethiopia who have taken advantage of the chaos and the weakness of central authority in Addis Ababa to chop off a strategic piece of territory. They point out that many Eritreans who grew up in Addis Ababa are indistinguishable, culturally and physically, from other Ethiopians; many carry the same names. And they claim that the new leadership of Ethiopia, while ostensibly dominated by Tigreans, has really turned the country over to Eritreans. (The Eritreans and the Tigreans are ethnically related and speak the same language.) The tail, they say, is wagging the dog.

Hailu Fullas Hailu is a man of Oromo and Amhara background, an accomplished linguistics scholar who worked with the Mengistu regime on its literacy campaigns for several years but then left the country as a result of disputes with Marxist intellectuals. Having worked in Washington as a telemarketer and a drugstore clerk, he now teaches communications courses at the University of the District of Columbia. At the time we met, the new regime in Addis Ababa was negotiating the arrangements for the referendum in Eritrea that would lead to the province's independence, and Hailu was so angry over this that he had canceled his first trip home in fourteen years.

"Nobody would say that injustice has not been done to Eritrea," Hailu acknowledges, "but we have every right to own the port of Massawa," on the Red Sea, which had been a key outlet for Ethiopia. "My friends here don't want to see us have any kind of dependence on any other power." He said he was convinced that if he were to return to Ethiopia and express such views, he would risk immediate assassination. It is a painful conclusion for him, since he grew up believing that "Ethiopia is God's country. In my childhood, there were two divisions in the world—Ethiopia and everyplace else." And it is only politics, Hailu insists, that prevents him, his French Canadian–born wife, and their three children from returning to live in the paradise he remembers.

But the Eritreans in Washington, who tend to have a lower socio-economic status than many of the Ethiopians, feel triumphant that their country and their culture have achieved official international recognition after years of repression and subjugation by the Amhara establishment. Negusse Ketem grew up in a farm family in a rural area of Eritrea and worked for thirteen years as chief clerk for the prisons department in Asmara, where he had an opportunity to observe many abuses of power. After years of scratching out a living as a security guard in Washington, he finally achieved his dream of becoming a taxi driver in the late 1980s. Ketem complains that after the more subtle abuses committed by Haile Selassie in Eritrea, Mengistu "just burned and destroyed everything. There was no choice but to separate and live as neighbors in peace." When he first came to the United States through Sudan in 1979, Ketem says, he had many Ethiopian friends, because they shared a common refugee plight and could understand each other more easily than they could communicate with outsiders. But now, he explains, they have been driven apart by events at home. "The Ethiopian people who are living here have not done anything wrong, but their leaders have killed my people, and it is hard to talk about it together. We manage to say hello to each other, but we don't discuss politics."

Thus, the Eritreans in Washington increasingly spend their time separately from the Ethiopians, at their own cultural center or in the few Eritrean restaurants that have recently opened to serve their own distinct cuisine. Ketem, who has managed to buy a house and to give a small church wedding for his oldest daughter, is proud of the Eritrean Americans' solidarity. "Living here is hard. But we have a very good system, a very good culture," he says. "If someone has something good happen, we all share it. If someone has trouble, we collect money from everyone to help."

Meanwhile, the decline—and, according to some, persecution—of the once-powerful Amhara elite in Ethiopia has provoked a profound response among the émigré community in Washington, which has raised a great deal of money to support the new All Amhara People's Relief and Development Association (AAPRDA) back home.[5] On the Memorial Day weekend of 1994, some 2,000 Amhara exiles and immigrants gathered in a vast Masonic temple hall in Fairfax, Virginia, for a fund-raising party that began at five in the evening and went until well past midnight. The parking lot outside was full of taxicabs, and long-lost

---

[5] *More than half, and perhaps two-thirds, of the Ethiopians living in the Washington area— excluding the Eritreans—are estimated to be of Amhara background.*

friends milled about, catching up with one another. Celebrating the second anniversary of the AAPRDA (which was formed to protest the Amharas' recent exclusion from the governing circles in Ethiopia), the well-dressed crowd listened to a taped message from the embattled president of the association in Addis Ababa, ate food donated by local Ethiopian restaurants, and danced and shimmied to traditional music played by five different bands. Tickets cost twenty dollars, dinner was five, and there were plenty of drinks and souvenirs for sale. Some of the singers had the red, yellow, and green colors of the Ethiopian flag draped around them. Hardly a word of English was spoken. This was a classic, all-American ethnic solidarity festival, combining a militant political rally with a wild party, affordable to all social strata.

But contrary to Ketem's generous attitude toward them, some of the Ethiopians who have made their home in Washington are thought by others to have done things that were very wrong indeed, and the controversies swirling around them have led to new fissures in the community. There is Goshu Wolde, for example, who played a key role in Mengistu's regime and was his foreign minister for three years during the 1980s; he has now established a D.C. office of an Ethiopian political party that promises "to wage armed struggle" against the new government of Meles Zenawi in Addis Ababa, which enjoys nominal American support. Wolde denies that he had anything to do with Mengistu's "Red Terror," but his critics, including officials at the Ethiopian embassy, insist that he is personally responsible for many deaths. In an interview with the *Washington Post*, he dismissed these allegations as "propaganda," saying, "I don't kill people. I love people." Still, he is regularly denounced in the Ethiopian community.

Another person accused of committing atrocities while working for the Mengistu regime is Abera Yemaneab, who appears to have walked straight into a trap set for him by the Meles government. A tall, handsome, graying man familiar to many in Washington from his years as a taxi driver, Yemaneab was a key figure in the Coalition of Ethiopian Democratic Forces (COEDF), an umbrella group of opposition parties and organizations that pressed for Meles to invite other political forces and ethnic groups into his transitional regime. According to Yemaneab's wife, Alemtsehay Gebru, he was one of the first people Meles met with during his visits to Washington before taking power. In fact, she says, much of the planning for his warm welcome among Ethiopian exiles in Washington took place at the red-brick row house in a rough part of town where Yemaneab lived with his family and maintained the COEDF's Washington offices.

In December 1993 several hundred Ethiopian activists converged on Addis Ababa from Europe, North America, and other parts of Africa for a conference they said would discuss peace and reconciliation—a public effort by COEDF's leaders to confront the Meles government on human rights and other issues. They wanted to know, for example, why the regime was imprisoning journalists and firing university professors who were critical of its policies. But seven of the activists, including four from Washington (who had received clearance for the trip from the Ethiopian embassy), were immediately arrested by security police at the airport and taken to jail. Two months later, all were released except Yemaneab, who, the government said, would face charges of "crimes against humanity" for allegedly killing dozens, perhaps hundreds or thousands, of people while serving Mengistu.

Gebru, who has been able to use her job in the advertising department of the *Washington Post* to attract a fair amount of press attention to Yemaneab's case, says these charges are outrageous. She portrays her husband as having merely helped organize farmers' associations and urban development cooperatives during the Mengistu regime. Indeed, she describes a harrowing period in 1979 when their family at first went underground in the southern part of Ethiopia and then escaped to Somalia, because the Mengistu government was so displeased with Yemaneab. When they finally managed to get to Rome, after being held under house arrest in the Somali capital of Mogadishu for several months, they obtained visas for the United States. At first, Gebru says, Catholic Charities settled them in Dallas, where they felt very isolated; but they soon made their way to Washington, where they could find jobs and dabble in exile politics. She eventually took American citizenship, while Yemaneab insisted on remaining an Ethiopian, which may have been his fatal mistake. It made his arrest less of a risk for Meles.

Yemaneab's fate immediately became the new cause célèbre in Washington's Ethiopian community, especially among Amhara. His fourteen-year-old son, Terefe Abera, faxed President Clinton almost daily before going to school, pleading for the U.S. government to intervene on his behalf. "The people in power in Ethiopia are not at all democratic people; they will not even listen to anyone who has any ideas which are different than their own. So people like my father and my mother are forced to live in exile," he said in one typical letter to the White House. Meanwhile, in the living room of her neat and well-organized row house, Gebru, herself of Tigrean origin, churns out press releases and letters to members of Congress and holds court on the tragedy that has befallen her family. "It's ridiculous that the U.S. is helping this undemocratic government [in Ethiopia]," she says, with tears in her eyes. "They're using my tax money. I'm an American now, so I can say that!"

State Department officials, for their part, say quietly (and not for attribution) that notwithstanding any human rights abuses it may be committing, the Meles regime is a relative improvement over Mengistu's—and that however difficult his family's circumstances may be, they are tentatively impressed by the allegations against Yemaneab, which must be resolved in the Ethiopian judicial system, along with other cases involving officials from the brutal Mengistu era. Most of the disputes within the Ethiopian and Eritrean exile community, they suggest, have an overlay of ethnic rivalry that is virtually impossible for uninitiated Americans to understand or help resolve.[6]

SELOME TADDESSE, a woman in her early thirties who was an émigré just a few years ago and is now the press and information counselor at the Ethiopian embassy in Washington, has ridden a roller coaster through her country's recent history, and she surveys the scene with a certain detachment. She finished high school in Addis Ababa at the peak of Soviet influence over the Mengistu regime and received a scholarship to study journalism in Minsk. In ideological trouble with the Ethiopian "youth association" there, she faked mental illness in order to get an exit visa. Eventually, with seven compatriots, she escaped to West Berlin and applied for political asylum in 1984. Two years later, having learned German, she made her way to the United States and studied on another scholarship at Mount Holyoke College in Massachusetts.

After spending a year helping Ethiopian refugees resettle in Boston, Taddesse came to Washington and did the same work with Teferra's Ethiopian Community Development Center in the Virginia suburbs.[7] Her dream of graduate school in international affairs evaporated, as her siblings began to arrive and had to be supported. After Meles took over, she was invited to come back home and work for the government; but the time she spent in Addis Ababa, while attending a two-month seminar given by the ministry of foreign affairs, left her in a state of culture shock. She found it hard, for example, to get used to the idea that people

[6] *After the original charges against Yemaneab were dismissed by an Ethiopian court in April 1994, the Meles regime nonetheless kept him in prison, saying that other charges might be filed. His case was then taken up by Amnesty International and other human rights groups.*

[7] *As ethnic rivalries have intensified among the Ethiopian exiles in Washington, mirroring events at home, Teferra's center in Virginia has become a principally Tigrean institution, while the ECC in Washington serves mostly Amhara.*

dropped in to visit unannounced at any hour of the night or day. "I was happy to be home, but I felt like a foreigner," Taddesse says. "That was sad. Here, whenever something happened to me that I didn't like or I was unhappy about, I always said, 'Oh, it doesn't matter, I have a home where I can go.' That always kept me going. But once I was there, I felt like a foreigner. I'd meet Americans, and I felt like I had more in common with them than with Ethiopians."

Taddesse came around and saw the importance of rebuilding Ethiopia but was greatly relieved to be assigned as an embassy official in Washington. She still lives like a refugee (earning less than she did as a resettlement counselor), but she goes to work every day in the posh Kalorama section and behaves like a diplomat. She has given up her green card and now talks of "building bridges" between the Ethiopian immigrant community and an embassy that was off-limits to it for almost two decades. And she tries to persuade people—especially "if they have education or money"—to go home. Someday, she says, she will do the same.

X
CHOSEN TO LIVE
AT THE FLASHPOINT:
THE KOREANS

LOS ANGELES

IF THERE WAS ever an Irene connected with Irene's Liquor Store on Figueroa Street deep in the South Central neighborhood, no one seems to remember or speak of her now. These days the dark, dank little shop with a big sign is owned and run by Yung Ho Kim, a man of broken dreams who is afraid to come to work and afraid to go home, but has no other choice.

Kim, who has advanced training as a metallurgical engineer, arrived in California from Korea in 1971 with high hopes for a prosperous new life in America, where he heard that so many of his countrymen had succeeded. But he soon found there was no market for his technical expertise and that, in any event, his total lack of English-language skills greatly inhibited his prospects for achieving his own American Dream. Desperate after a couple of months of being unable to find work as an engineer, he accepted a job as a janitor, and for a time he was consigned to cleaning bathrooms in a building near the Los Angeles International Airport. Eventually, he moved on to a machine shop, and then into a job as a welder. Kim kept getting fired, however, because of his lack of familiarity with the equipment and his basic inability to communicate. He did manage to stay in one factory job for seven years, but finally quit in 1986, when he used his savings to buy Irene's from its previous owner, a black attorney who no longer wanted to do business in the neighborhood.

He was frightened right from the moment he became the proprietor

273

of the liquor store, Kim tells me in English that is, more than twenty years after his arrival, still barely comprehensible. And if anything, the situation in this tense neighborhood, just a few miles away but a world apart from the glitter of Hollywood and Beverly Hills, has deteriorated in the last few years. It is an area known for drug traffic, stolen cars, and clashes between gangs. Yet the streets seem eerily quiet, except when police cars, fire engines, or ambulances, their lights flashing and sirens screaming, converge on the scene of some incident—an occurrence common enough to keep people permanently on edge.

Stocked with cigarettes, snacks, and basic food items, as well as a broad array of beer, wine, and liquor, Irene's nonetheless has an empty, tentative look. It is open from seven in the morning until ten at night, seven days a week, 365 days a year. Kim's one employee, a Mexican immigrant, generally unlocks the door and minds the store alone for the quiet, early-morning hours. Kim himself gets in at about ten o'clock, after a sixty-minute drive from his home to the south in safe, suburban (and conservative) Orange County. He immediately stashes his sleek Acura Integra behind a tough metal fence, where no one can get to it, and begins his twelve-hour vigil. It concludes with a furtive dash through the darkness and back into the car for the long drive home every night. In between, customers come and go, but the shop is never really crowded. Kim has relatively few conversations in the course of a typical day. At the time of my visit to Irene's, he said this had been his routine for more than five years, without a single day off.

The menace comes, Kim says, not only from local youths who are often drunk and may be selling or using drugs but also from Korean gangs that sweep through occasionally and demand "protection" money —not a subject he cares to discuss in detail. He readily acknowledges that he keeps a handgun behind the counter near his cash register but says that he rarely takes it out. Instead, if he catches a theft in progress—and he says there are many, especially of beer—he politely asks for payment and threatens to call the police. Sometimes it works, and sometimes he gets mugged; so far, nothing worse has happened. Seldom does Kim actually turn to the police; if there is trouble in the neighborhood or suspicious characters seem to be hanging around his store after dark, he is more likely to lock himself inside and wait until the perceived danger passes or it looks safe enough outside to leave for home. Mostly, he just assumes that a certain amount of his merchandise will be stolen, and he readily admits that he jacks up his prices on everything to try to make up for that. Some of his patrons "have no money, but they still have to drink and eat," he says with a shrug. "They're going to steal."

Kim's wife, a real estate saleswoman, often helps on weekends, but he says he is bothered by the fact that she, and anyone else who pitches in, constantly has to ask him for the correct prices on some items. He is both proud and annoyed to be the indispensable manager of his own haunting, meager domain.

During my visit to Irene's, I encounter Kim's sixteen-year-old son, Arnold, who has come along to work in the store on a weekday during spring break. He is a tall, all-American-looking suburban high school student. He is stocking the shelves and, with a bemused look on his face, watching customers walk in and out. In contrast to his father, Arnold insists that he is not at all frightened to come to South Central. "There's occasional fights and verbal arguments over prices," he says in his own unaccented Southern California inflection, "but the people are really friendly, so I don't worry." Indeed, he has formed casual friendships with some peers in the neighborhood, and he says he actually feels more comfortable here than he did on the two visits he has made to Korea. "I wasn't really welcome there," he feels, "because I was born in L.A. and I'm really an American. I don't carry on a lot of Korean traditions." In fact, it is only since his grandmother, who speaks no English at all, has come to live in the Kim family's house, that Arnold has begun to develop a bit of a Korean-language vocabulary. Yet Arnold Kim's life is one big paradox. He may feel a hundred percent American, but, as he puts it, "when you look at me, the first thing you would say is that I'm Korean."

KOREANS BEGAN coming to the United States in significant numbers only in the 1970s. The South Korean government enacted a law facilitating emigration in 1961, hoping to ease the country's serious unemployment problem and earn valuable foreign exchange, while also sending people overseas to learn technology that they might later bring back home. The exodus was slow at first, but by 1973, about 100,000 Koreans were leaving each year; that number had doubled by 1977. Among those who arrived in America—the other favorite destination was Japan—most were motivated primarily by the desire to obtain a quality education and a better life for their children. What made them different from so many other waves of voluntary economic immigrants to the United States during the twentieth century was that they came not from the countryside, but from the crowded cities[1]; and they tended to be from

---

[1] *Seoul, the South Korean capital, with an estimated population of 10.7 million people in 1990, is one of the largest cities in the world. Hundreds of thousands of people were drawn there during and after the Korean War, when other parts of the country were devastated, and most never left. The country's belated but intense postwar economic revival and its subsequent industrial boom exacerbated the internal migration to the cities, where, for many years, it became difficult to guarantee decent housing and other essential services.*

an educated upper- or middle-class, rather than a peasant, background. Many had grown impatient with the apparent limits on what they could attain in Korea and begun to chafe under the old Confucian principles of their rigidly hierarchical culture. A large number were ambitious professionals, much favored at the time under U.S. immigration law.

The big cities on the West Coast of the United States, with their orientation toward the Pacific Rim, were an obvious place for Koreans to settle, and whatever the overall numbers at any given time, about 25 percent of all Korean Americans have consistently lived in Southern California. That was true in 1980, when the Census Bureau counted more than 350,000 Koreans nationwide, and still in 1990, when the official figure was up to almost 800,000.[2] Although the rate has recently slowed, for a long time the commonly accepted assumption was that 30,000 or 40,000 Koreans were arriving in America each year. There are many more working-class people among today's arrivals than before. But a considerable percentage of all the socioeconomic groups obviously chooses to remain in the Los Angeles area, which now has the largest concentration of Koreans outside of Asia.

During the same period, Los Angeles has become an attraction for many other immigrant communities, large and small. In this respect, among others, the once-stodgy L.A. has sprawled and emerged as a true rival to New York City. Increasingly a mecca for Mexicans and Central Americans, it is now home to the largest community of Salvadorans outside of San Salvador. In addition, the city welcomed many Soviet Jews and other refugees from communism during the final years of the Cold War. Hundreds of thousands of Vietnamese and other Southeast Asians have settled in Southern California, and the movie industry has continued to attract restless people from all over the English-speaking world, and elsewhere, too. Like New York City, Los Angeles is a place where many visit and simply decide to stay, but it seems somehow more open and flexible. Although it has the usual complement of ethnic enclaves, including authentic Hispanic *barrios*, Los Angeles is also notable for multicultural neighborhoods and schools where an eclectic mix of people who never would have known one another elsewhere are suddenly thrown together.

---

[2] *Some observers believe that the census significantly undercounts Korean Americans, and that the total in Southern California alone may be as high as 300,000; certain activists claim it is 500,000. (It is well known that many Koreans refuse to respond to the census, because they feel it asks questions that are invasive of their privacy.) But there is general agreement that about 40 percent of all Korean Americans live on the West Coast (including Seattle and San Francisco, as well as the Los Angeles and San Diego areas). Other large concentrations are in New York, Chicago, and Philadelphia.*

According to the Reverend Cecil Murray, pastor of a large African American church on the fringe of South Central, there are "one hundred forty-six different nations" in the city, many of whose contributions to its development have never been fully appreciated. The 1990 U.S. census said that English was still the first language in only 54.6 percent of the homes in Los Angeles County, Spanish in 31.5 percent, "Asian languages" in 8.3 percent, and "other" in 5.6 percent of them. "Other," in this case, has to be a broad category, since Jeff Beckerman, the official demographer for the City of Los Angeles, estimates that more than a hundred different languages are spoken in the city. Mike Woo, a Chinese American who was the first person of Asian background to serve on the city council (and later ran unsuccessfully for mayor), counted forty separate languages and dialects in his district alone. Statistics from the California Research Bureau indicate that nearly a third of the county's residents in 1990 were foreign born (compared with 21.7 percent in the state overall, and 7.9 percent in the whole United States). This represents a dramatic change from 1960, when only 9.1 percent of the people in Los Angeles County were counted as having been born in another country. The demographic shift became dramatically clear in the early 1990s, when Asian Americans began to outnumber whites in the entering freshman class at UCLA, the city's great intellectual institution of upward mobility. What is uncertain, amidst these trends, is whether L.A. will have more success than New York City in discouraging the white middle class from fleeing en masse to the distant suburbs.

Despite the reputation of Los Angeles, and of California, as the new frontier where all would be generously and equally welcomed, some groups have the numbers and the style to become insiders rather quickly, while others seem condemned to be perennial outsiders. Koreans had an early taste of the xenophobia that later became much more commonly recognized. "I can speak flawless English without a foreign accent, but I am still seen as a foreigner," says Marcia Choo, of the Asian/Pacific American Dispute Resolution Center, who arrived with her parents in 1970, when she was five years old. "I am Korean American. I am an American citizen, I vote in every election, I pay my taxes, and I contribute to the society and participate as fully as I am able to, or allowed to. But I will never look like a white American, and that's how a lot of people still define what an American is." The hostility is equally bad, Choo says, whether it comes from "the stupid jerk on the street who calls you a 'chink' and tells you to go back home" or it surfaces "when I go to corporate board meetings and people are amazed at how wonderfully I speak English and want to know where I learned it." One can only imagine what the reaction might be if more people in Los Angeles realized that, as some experts estimate, about 30 percent of the Koreans here at any given time are undocumented aliens (a statistic that is apparently either unknown, or regarded as unimportant, by the INS).[3]

Initially, many Korean immigrants to Los Angeles were drawn to work in the burgeoning local garment industry. As the Korean American community and economy grew, there were considerable opportunities for Korean businessmen, doctors, lawyers, accountants, and the Korean-speaking staff they felt they needed to do their jobs. Before long, there was an explosion of Korean restaurants, nightclubs, pool halls, communal baths, herbalists, acupuncture clinics, travel agencies, and even banks. They were identified to the public with signs almost exclusively in Hangul, the Korean alphabet. With substantial investment pumped in from Seoul, this exotic-looking "Koreatown" came to occupy a larger and larger area of the Wilshire business district, until entire tall buildings were taken up with Korean-related offices and enterprises. Indeed, Cho Huh, secretary general of the Korean Chamber of Commerce in Los Angeles, acknowledges that he keeps "a list of tycoons in Korea" who are looking for major real estate investment opportunities in Los Angeles. In the process, other ethnic groups, especially Latinos, have sometimes been squeezed out of commercial space they had come to regard as their own. (Ironically, most of the overnight residents of Koreatown are still Latinos; the Korean businessmen generally go home to more affluent neighborhoods.)[4]

After a time, of course, many of the middle-class Korean professionals who arrived found themselves blocked from making full productive use of their training and credentials in Los Angeles, either by the unwelcoming white establishment or by other Koreans who had come much earlier and had no desire to share their turf. The typical syndrome was for an immigrant who could not make a living in his own field to

[3] *After the devastating earthquake that hit the Los Angeles area in January 1994, many local politicians—taking a cue from Governor Pete Wilson, who was by that time supporting Proposition 187, to deny health and education benefits to undocumented immigrants—sought to restrict the amount of federal relief aid that could be provided to people who are in the country illegally, in this case mostly Latinos from Mexico and Central America. Indeed, acting at the behest of California congressmen, the House Appropriations Committee approved an amendment to President Clinton's earthquake relief package, explicitly denying undocumented aliens equal access to federal housing vouchers.*

[4] *The Koreans were not the only ones to arouse controversy on this account. So many buildings in downtown Los Angeles were purchased by Japanese interests in recent years that a black member of the city council introduced a resolution to forbid the sale of property in the city to foreigners. Buried as an embarrassment, it was never voted on. A related issue arose in Monterey Park, east of Los Angeles, where the city council tried to require newly arrived Chinese shopkeepers to put English-language signs in their windows.*

work in a service job long enough to save money to open his own shop.[5] But Koreatown was soon saturated with small businesses, and the newer arrivals had to look for other avenues and other neighborhoods where they might practice their entrepreneurial skills. Invariably, a large number of them, like Yung Ho Kim, became the owners of corner groceries, liquor stores, and convenience stores, often in areas undergoing a transition. Indeed, by the early 1990s, some 40 percent of the small, independently owned grocery and liquor stores in the Los Angeles area were in the hands of Korean immigrants. In the inner-city neighborhoods populated primarily by poor African Americans, the figure was closer to 70 percent. Because the major supermarket chains and drugstores have closed most of their outlets in those sections, the Koreans often became the only reliable, nearby source of food and alcohol. The pattern was repeated in most other cities around the country with a substantial Korean population.

"There are many reasons for this," says Yumi Park, former director of the California regional office of KAGRO, the Korean-American Grocers Association of the United States, which has become a very substantial and influential trade association.[6] "You can get into the grocery business without really having much knowledge about the products you carry. It's not like a gas station, where you have to know about certain types of technical things. It has a better cash flow than the dry cleaning business, and it's easier to run. It's basically pretty easy to get into, and it requires less capital than a lot of other businesses. It's also very steady and is not too much affected by the economy; it doesn't matter whether the U.S. is in a recession. And it's a business you can usually run with your family members; you don't have to hire any extra people or outside help. You can keep it on a small scale." In effect, there is very little overhead cost.

For those willing to put in the time—hours like those worked by Yung Ho Kim and worse—the rewards can be substantial. "Some grocers really struggle and barely get by," insists Park. But after a relatively short period of time, many Korean grocers have been able to buy large houses in distant upscale suburbs. (Even before they could afford

---

[5] *According to the* Wall Street Journal, *approximately one in ten Korean American adults is believed to own a business, compared to one in fifteen whites and one in sixty-seven blacks.*

[6] *KAGRO was founded to try to achieve some political and economic unity in a Korean American business community that is often plagued by disputes and disharmony. It is a national organization, with even a Canadian branch, but there are 3,500 members in California alone. The dues are only $100 a year, but many of the estimated 6,000 Korean grocers in the state refuse to pay. Among other functions, KAGRO saves its members money by acting as a consortium to buy many items in bulk.*

the houses, some will have rented apartments there, so that their children would have an address that qualified them to attend better public schools than are available in the heart of Los Angeles.) Given their work schedules, they never spend much time in those houses, but typically travel back and forth in a Mercedes-Benz or other luxury car. If their children do exceptionally well in school, as many do, they are even able to afford the tuition to send them to Stanford or an Ivy League college in the East. Says Yumi Park, all of this—a spacious home, a prestigious car, and an elite education for their children—would have been "impossible if they had stayed in Korea."

Before long, Korean immigrants had a higher average per capita annual income than Americans generally. It is statistics like that which stirred rumors in the black community of Los Angeles that Asian immigrants, and especially Koreans, benefit from special favors when they arrive in the United States. "A large group in the African American community believe strongly, as a truth, that Korean Americans are given loans, if not grants, by the U.S. government to buy up property and take over small businesses in low-income areas," says Marcia Choo. "One gentleman told me he knows for a fact that Koreans get seventy-five thousand dollars from the American government as an interest-free gift, which is simply not true. And there is a belief that Koreans are favored in bank loans, which they are not. We have just as difficult a time getting a loan from Bank of America as everyone else."

In fact, the easiest part of entering the retail grocery and liquor business for Korean Americans was that most of them never had to go near a bank, or otherwise apply for credit, in order to buy their stores. They were usually able to benefit from one form or another of the traditional Korean system of *kye,* a kind of community self-help savings plan that eventually yields a major windfall for everyone who participates. In its simplest variation, a group of families (as few as ten or as many as several dozen) get together every month or so for a big supper; each contributes the same amount of money each time to a central account. The total collection of funds, which can ultimately run into hundreds of thousands of dollars, is invested somewhere to earn interest. But each month—or each year, depending on the precise ground rules the particular group has agreed upon—one family, often selected by lot, gets to redeem its share for use in starting or expanding a business (or perhaps to fund a major family event, such as a wedding). Those who are lucky early on must promise to continue attending the sessions and making contributions, and possibly even extra amounts, at least until everyone has had a chance to win once. (The last ones to draw from the pot may receive more, in order to make up for their wait.)

Kye is a meaningful and practical custom for Koreans to have brought to the United States, says Im Jung Kwuon, a journalist and social commentator who writes about the Korean American community in Los Angeles. "It promotes saving, which can be a difficult task" for immigrant families, she says, "and you have this immediate bond with other people who are supporting whatever you are doing." Besides, she adds, it has given a fresh and prompt start to thousands of Korean entrepreneurs who would ordinarily have had to wait much longer to obtain conventional bank loans. There are many possible permutations, and even manipulations. Some shrewd businessmen, who enter more than one such group at a time, manage to coordinate their payouts in order to obtain a very substantial sum—a quarter of a million dollars or more—just when they need it. They are, in effect, beating both the American and the Korean systems.

Of course, many of the grocery and liquor stores that were available to be purchased at an attractive price in the 1970s and 1980s, in Los Angeles as in other major cities, were in deteriorating inner-city neighborhoods. In L.A. they had been owned, in many cases, by first- or second-generation immigrant Jewish or Mexican families, who moved out in fear after the urban upheavals of the 1960s. In the aftermath of the 1965 riots in Watts, for example, many shops sat vacant for years. Despite special incentives intended to help blacks invest in their own communities, few could put together the financing necessary to start a business. Many of those who did soon failed, in part because of the same hazards of crime and theft that faced everyone else before or since. It was into this vaccuum, and a hotbed of hostility, that the Korean immigrants stepped. The standoff that evolved was historic in its proportions.

"The Koreans see this as a land of opportunity, of freedom and equality," explains Yumi Park, "but a lot of them simply don't realize that African Americans had to fight for their freedom during the civil rights movement of the fifties and sixties. They think this is the way it's always been; they didn't know that blacks had to ride in the back of the bus and could not vote." Meanwhile, she notes, "the blacks see the Koreans as intruders from outside who come into their community, take all their money away, and then go live in a nice neighborhood. And they complain that the Koreans treat them with disrespect. . . . It's true, a lot of the Korean retailers are rude. But they're not just rude to blacks, they're rude to everybody. When I walk into the stores, they're rude to me. It's just the way Koreans are. They don't smile very much, and they don't like to touch people."

In the early 1990s, concerned about the tension that was developing between Korean shopowners and their black customers, KAGRO took several African American leaders from Los Angeles on a familiarization trip to Korea. "One gentleman came back," relates Park, "and said he understands the situation much better now, because he suddenly realized that in Korea everyone seems to be rude to everyone else!"

The Korean storekeepers, for their part, have the general perception that many of their black customers not only dislike them but also routinely steal from them. "That's the number-one complaint," explains Park. "They say, 'How can I be nice to people who steal from my store all the time?' Some of them claim that one out of two people who come in steal something. I think that's a little high." One local African American researcher, however, did a survey of black customers entering Korean-owned stores in South Central; to her surprise, she found that 18 percent of her sample admitted openly that they had stolen merchandise from the Koreans at some point, and she concluded that the figure was probably low.

But many of the most serious problems revolve around, or can be traced to, language difficulties. The black customers "don't like the fact that most of these Koreans don't speak English," Park says. "I know a lot of Americans get insulted when Koreans speak only Korean among themselves, in front of a non-Korean person. But I don't think Koreans realize it's because they don't speak English that there's all this tension. A lot of [the Korean shopkeepers] are trying to learn, but for some of them, learning a foreign language is very, very difficult," especially given their age and the number of hours they work. Park points out that it took her four full years—even though she was of junior high school age and had already traveled widely with her military family when she arrived in America—to become comfortable in her new tongue. She recites a litany of particularly egregious miscommunications that she has heard about in the grocery and liquor stores, all growing out of Koreans' ignorance of everyday idioms in the neighborhoods where they do business. They are a mixture of tragedy and comedy:

- "A young boy came into one place and said, 'Hey, man!' We know that's like saying, 'Hello!' But the Korean man felt very insulted and said, 'How dare you call me "hey man"?' So he got all upset and had a fight with the guy, and the boy threw rocks at him from outside and ran off. He didn't understand that what he thought was an insult was a friendly gesture."
- "A customer walked into a store and said, 'Give me five!' The

owner thought he was asking for money, so he pressed his alarm to call his security company. And the police came."

• "At another store, a robber came in with his gun wrapped in newspaper. He pointed it at the owner and said, 'This is a stickup.' But the guy didn't know what 'stickup' meant, so he just looked at the man with the newspaper and said, 'Newspaper over there. I have Seven-Up, but no stickup.' "

Meanwhile, young blacks are frustrated that they cannot even get hired to work in the Korean-owned stores in their neighborhoods. The Korean Americans, says Yumi Park, are "too stingy. They'd rather work from 8 A.M. until midnight than hire someone else. Or if they can afford to, they'd rather hire a cousin; then at least they won't have trouble communicating with their help. They also say, 'Well, blacks don't work as hard as Koreans.' Hardly anyone does, since the Koreans are workaholics. But I think Asians overall are probably more prejudiced than other people. The Japanese are very supremacist, and Koreans are the same. I cannot deny that."

The tensions boiled over in March 1991, when Latasha Harlins, a fifteen-year-old African American girl, was shot dead by Soon Ja Du, fifty-one, proprietor of the Empire Market on Figueroa Street, just a few blocks away from Irene's. The incident was recorded on a security camera in the store: The black teenager approached the Korean woman, who was alone behind the counter, with two dollar bills in her hand. Du accused her, in broken English, of stealing a bottle of orange juice priced at $1.79. Harlins showed her that she did have the juice in her backpack but waved the money in the air that she was intending to use to pay for it. As they quarreled, Harlins threw the juice down on the counter. Du grabbed for the backpack to look inside, but got the girl's jacket instead. Harlins, who towered over the Korean woman, reacted angrily and slapped her hard. Du reeled backward, but once she regained her balance, pulled out her .38-caliber revolver from under the counter and fired at Harlins, who had turned her back and begun to walk away. Harlins fell forward as the bullet hit her in the back of her neck.

A videotape of this event—like another, depicting the police beating of black motorist Rodney King that took place just two days earlier—was shown repeatedly on television in Los Angeles. As part of an altercation involving a bottle of orange juice, Du's action seemed outrageous. But subsequent coverage of the case highlighted the fact that the incident occurred in a nasty thirty-two-block area where 936 felonies had been reported the previous year and merchants felt they had to be constantly on guard against trouble. The Korean American community, convinced that Du had not intended to kill Harlins (and that, as an inexperienced shooter, she had no reason to believe she would ever do so), pleaded for understanding. Indeed, Du, whose son was a victim in one of the 254 assaults reported in the neighborhood that year, came to be portrayed in the media as a struggling immigrant, bewildered by the hostile environment where she earned her living and exhausted—perhaps even mentally unbalanced—as a result of her fourteen-hour days in the store. When Du was convicted of voluntary manslaughter several months later, a white woman judge sentenced her to four hundred hours of community service, a $500 fine, reimbursement of Latasha Harlins's funeral expenses, and five years' probation. Her store was shut down, but the black community in Los Angeles was furious that the system had pronounced the life of one of its children to be worth so little.

Yet Koreans insist that the Harlins case is really the exception to the rule. They point to countless other incidents across the country, many of them never widely reported, in which hardworking Korean merchants are the victims of violent crime and justice is seldom done. In various parts of New York City, for example, stores owned by Korean immigrants have been subjected to lengthy boycotts because of perceived slights to black customers, a failure to hire black employees, or arguments with neighboring non-Korean businesses. Others have been the targets of arson, armed robbery, and nighttime break-ins followed by binges of looting. At one shop in Manhattan, some ten thousand pairs of high-priced sneakers were taken in just a few hours during a nighttime break-in; there, as elsewhere, the uninsured owners were left penniless. In Washington, D.C., where they may have been specifically singled out because of their vulnerability, several Korean American shopkeepers were murdered in 1993 as they worked in their grocery markets or dry cleaning stores. Rarely have arrests been made and the perpetrators punished in any of these cases.

Yumi Park estimates that it will take years for the problems between the Korean merchants and their black customers to ease, at least until more second-generation Korean Americans who are fluent in English begin to take over the stores. But many of the Korean shopkeepers' children, with their high-priced educations, are unlikely to want to succeed their parents in the retail grocery and liquor business. Already, Park says, the lists she has seen from the state of California of people buying convenience stores are beginning to include names that look Vietnamese, Laotian, or Middle Eastern. And unless they do better than the Koreans on the language front, they, presumably, will have their own problems.

K. W. LEE is a short, scrappy fellow, full of restless energy and armchair profundity. He is also a rather unusual specimen, in that he left Korea for the United States in 1950—after World War II, but before American intervention in the dirty conflict between the communist North and the capitalist South that ripped the northeast Asian peninsula apart and became the emblem of the Cold War. He had been a student activist in Seoul but felt there would be no future for him under what he correctly foresaw as a succession of dictatorships in his native country.

Lee arrived in America by boat at the age of twenty-one as part of a group of ten students. Since he was the only one in the group who was not sponsored by a church, he had raised the money for his passage from his brothers. At the time, there was certainly no place he could go in the United States to settle in a Korean community. Indeed, Koreans were virtually unknown to Americans. Most people who looked at him and heard his "oriental" accent assumed he was Chinese or, worse yet, Japanese and, given their postwar prejudice, probably not to be trusted. This was especially true in the small towns where Lee studied and worked. He went to college at the University of Illinois in Champaign-Urbana, where his mentor, the great communications scholar Wilbur Schram, urged him to pursue a doctorate. But Lee felt that journalism was his calling, and he plunged right in, penetrating a profession that was not especially welcoming to immigrants at the time.

After a year of looking, Lee found his first job at a small paper in Kingsport, Tennessee, but then moved on after a few years to the *Gazette* in Charleston, the capital of West Virginia. Shortly after his arrival there, while he was working the police beat, he met an emergency room nurse who proved to be a good source. "She was a girl from Virginia," Lee says. "I married her within three months. There were no Asians." In fact, he was the only minority group member on the newspaper staff, and before long the *Gazette*'s crusading publisher assigned him the formidable task of investigating the institutions in the city and the state that still practiced illegal racial segregation. "It was like being in the civil rights movement, going in and opening places up," Lee recalls with a broad smile and, still, a trace of an accent. "West Virginia was like another country. It was isolated. Then, in the sixties, the VISTA workers showed up from Harvard and Berkeley, and the way of life began to change. It was an incredible experience."

After twelve years in West Virginia, Lee moved on to Sacramento,

California, where for two decades he worked as an investigative reporter for the *Union* and the *Bee*. There, among others, he took on Ronald Reagan, who, as governor, "was dismantling the government." "I had a ball," Lee says, "because California was in such a constant state of flux." But when he retired from daily reporting in 1990, Lee, who had become the classic assimilated immigrant, finally decided he wanted to do something more authentically Korean. Having failed once before when he tried to launch a weekly newspaper in Los Angeles for the growing Korean American community, he now accepted an invitation to start up a specialized English-language paper here, with the same name and under the ownership of the *Korea Times*, one of Seoul's leading national newspapers. Leaving his family (including three grown children) in Sacramento, he began a biweekly commute by car to "start all over again." Once he installed himself in Los Angeles, it was as if he had returned home after years in exile, and he found himself newly angry and impatient with the mainstream world where he had been so successful.

"You cannot apply the conventional wisdom of acculturation in America to the new immigrants from Asia," Lee believes, "because they come from independent, viable cultures. Their lives hardly touch each other. During my first half-year here in Los Angeles, I had occasional contact with some Chinese newspaper people, but I never met a single Vietnamese person. What kind of common ground do we have with Cambodians? We are separated by thousands of miles and thousands of years of history." Notwithstanding the standard census categories and commonly accepted terms of reference, he insists, there is no such thing as an "Asian American."

Just within the Korean community, Lee points out, "there are mosaics and layers of different people from different times and different places. These are the realities that the Anglo media don't understand. What I see among my colleagues in the media here is a dangerous combination of arrogance and ignorance. I hate to use the word racism; it's more cultural ethnocentrism." At the time he launched his local weekly English edition of the *Korea Times*—a moment of extreme tension in Los Angeles between Korean immigrant merchants and other ethnic groups, particularly blacks—Lee felt that no one was making a serious effort to decipher the majority culture for the Koreans or, in turn, to explain the Koreans' concerns and needs to the broader community. There were, for example, only two reporters with a Korean background on the staff of the *Los Angeles Times*, and they were relatively junior people with little influence. Except in moments of crisis, like the shooting of Latasha Harlins, it would be easy to read the *Times* and be utterly unaware of the Korean community's existence.

"The Korean predicament," says Lee, "is that, unlike the Chinese and the Japanese, we come here without an infrastructure built by prior generations, without the sophistication of a history in America. The Koreans have no time to orient themselves to American culture. They come with wives and children and even grandparents. Many of them are highly educated, but what do they become after they get here? Entrepreneurial proletarians. They have absolutely no support. They can't get on welfare, they have no civil rights groups to represent or defend them, and they have no interpreters. They turn into urban warriors, because they have no alternative." Typically, language problems increase their distance from everyone else.

Indeed, Koreans are, in many respects, the least known and most poorly understood of the major postwar immigrant groups. Like the Cubans who flocked to American shores after Fidel Castro came to power, the Koreans who came to the United States were politically appealing in Cold War terms: They were from the anticommunist south, and most brought with them a fervent attachment to capitalist, free-market values, not to mention a gratitude for the American role in the Korean War.[7] But for all their exposure to U.S. troops of every ethnic background, even today the realities of life in America can throw them for a loop. "This whole concept of multiculturalism is foreign to Koreans," points out Marcia Choo. "We come from five thousand years of a monocultural, monolingual society. We don't have to deal with race relations, really, in Korea," she says, because there are no minorities present.

Those who believe that the Koreans have been a model of success in America, Choo says, have no idea of the degree of human tragedy just below the surface. "People don't see the pain, the domestic violence, the child abuse, the drug abuse, and alcoholism. That's all prevalent in our community. We are number one when it comes to the people who go through the criminal justice system for spousal abuse," she says.

Choo describes a syndrome common in many Korean families:

---

[7] *There were allegations at various times that the communist government of North Korea was attempting to infiltrate the Korean émigré community in the United States, particularly in Los Angeles, but no such instance was ever publicly revealed. It does seem clear, however, that for many years operatives of the KCIA (a South Korean agency modeled after its American namesake) had free rein to investigate— and possibly to interfere with—the South Korean opposition's political activities in the United States. This was especially true when opposition leader Kim Dae Jung, while in exile in Boston and Washington, used his American base to denounce the military regime in Seoul and to speak in favor of the reunification of North and South.*

"When people come over here, the father, the head of the household, often loses his status and his stature. That causes a lot of tension in the family circle. He begins to feel inadequate because he can't provide for his family like he used to and now he has to send his wife to work. Often, though, the women adjust more quickly. They learn English faster, and that's another source of frustration for the man. He's too proud to take these low-paying jobs. And so his wife is passing him up in terms of gaining newfound freedom and experiences and friends and language acquisition. And then you lose control over your kids, because nobody's home to watch them; they're prone to join gangs. You begin to lose touch with your family. You're discriminated against because you don't speak English or you speak English with a foreign accent. You're treated as less than human by the rest of the world. So what do you do? You lash out at the people close to you, the most convenient targets of your anger."

As a result, the divorce rate has soared among Korean immigrants, according to Tong Sung Suhr, whose Wilshire Boulevard law practice includes a growing number of marriages gone awry. Traditionally, many immigrants have sent their children back to Korea to find an appropriate spouse; Suhr says the couples are much less likely to succeed when it is the American-raised young woman who goes husband hunting in the old country than when it is the other way around. "Girls who are brought up in Korea tend to be submissive," he explains. "But the girls that grow up in the U.S. tend to be more assertive, which doesn't sit well with a traditional Korean male."

K. W. Lee, driven by a passionate need to connect with these alienated Koreans who have joined him in America—to be their long-sought English-language interpreter, to each other and to the confusing, often frightening, netherworld of Los Angeles and beyond—assembled a staff of ambitious young Korean American reporters for his experiment in the new community journalism. In a large, low yellow-brick building of 1950s vintage on Vermont Avenue, just on the fringe of Koreatown, a dour publisher sent over from Seoul watched the finances, while the reporters created a frenzied, messy all-American newsroom. There, like other ethnic journalists all across the country, they turned out a combination of news from home and news of their community. Lee was their pied piper, and they, like him, were inevitably in one stage or another of figuring out what it really means to be Korean in America. Sometimes the process can be painful.

There is Kay Hwangbo, for example, a 1983 Harvard graduate who migrated west from her home near Washington, D.C., to work through what she herself calls "an identity crisis." First she freelanced and wrote for a suburban daily in the San Francisco Bay area, before responding to K. W. Lee's invitation to come to Los Angeles. "She's a brilliant kid," says Lee proudly. "She could have gotten a job with the L.A. *Times* or the *New York Times* or anywhere, but instead she came here. She wants to feel that contact with some authentic reality."

Hwangbo immigrated with her family in the mid-1960s from Taegu, South Korea's third-largest city, when she was only four years old. Her father, who came on his own at first, originally intended to obtain his Ph.D. in engineering at the University of Connecticut and then return home, but after a year, he sent for his wife and children, and soon the couple decided to stay and enjoy the economic opportunities that presented themselves. They settled in the Washington area when Hwangbo's father got a job there as an aerospace scientist, and Kay sailed through her public high school in Rockville, Maryland, as an academic star. "I was the one who studied all the time, the nerdy Asian," Hwangbo recalls with a laugh. Thus it was natural for her to aspire to attend a prestigious university. "Koreans see things in a very stratified way; it's very clear to them what's the first best, the second best, and the third best," she notes with a trace of sarcasm. "They like Harvard. They like it more than Yale or Princeton. It's a little bit better known, the first among equals."

Ironically, although Harvard is the ultimate nonethnic mecca for high achievers, it was there that Hwangbo began to feel more of a Korean consciousness. It had been awakened during the summer before her senior year in high school, when she traveled to South Korea for two weeks on a program sponsored by the Ministry of Education in Seoul. "It's a propaganda thing, but it really works," she remembers. "There were about two hundred fifty or three hundred [Korean American] high school kids, and for me, having grown up in Washington, seeing all these Koreans was really exciting. For the first time, I met West Coast Koreans, who seemed a lot more hip than us bookworms from the East." At Harvard she found that there were almost 200 Korean American undergraduates from various parts of the country, and she discovered both that she had a great deal in common with most of them and that she no longer stood out from the crowd. "Both the men and the women were welcoming to me. It's a very liberal, experimental atmosphere, and I felt more sought-after there than anywhere else," she says.

But still, several years out of college, Hwangbo saw that "all of my friends were white, and I had a very Western attitude about everything." On a second trip to Korea, this one lasting three weeks, "I had a really wonderful time. When I came back, I thought, 'I really should learn more about Korean [language], and what being Korean means.' And then K.W. called me. . . ." In her role at the *Korea Times,* she says, she was able to pursue her interest in writing about social issues and public policy problems as they affect "a disenfranchised population— the Koreans."

"As I get older, I feel more and more race-conscious," observes Hwangbo. "I can see how there are some white people whom I've come in contact with who are racially insensitive. I used to think it was my problem—like, 'Well, too bad I'm Asian'—but now I see it as their problem." Gradually, her life has become "more Korean." Before she had been at the *Korea Times* very long, she and a young man she had met, a UCLA alumnus who was working as a business consultant, started up an organization for young Korean American professionals. This thrilled her mother, Hwangbo says, because "her main concern is that I get married. I know she's happy about my coming to Los Angeles, because there are more eligible Koreans here. She's like a Jewish mother, but even more so. She's very predictable."

Yet the identity questions still haunt her, Hwangbo admits. "One day I was sitting around, and I felt kind of stricken. I don't know why. I guess it's that you're constantly having these talks with second-generation [Korean Americans] because you're interviewing them, and all these issues keep coming up. I suddenly thought I had to decide what my loyalties were. 'Am I an American? If I had to choose between being an American or being a Korean, what would I do?' I felt like I had to know where I was and where I stood." After ruminating for some time, she says, "I think that I chose being an American. And then I immediately felt a little bit bad, like, 'Why are you doing this to yourself?' "

Such conflicts may be more poignant for Hwangbo than for most, because her father has now chosen to return to Korea. In order to accept an opportunity to head up the South Korean government's new satellite program, he went back to Seoul in 1990, took a substantial pay cut, and resumed his Korean citizenship. With Hwangbo's sister enrolled at Stanford University and her American-born brother at the University of Chicago, her mother stayed on as a consumer safety official at the U.S. Food and Drug Administration. It proved difficult, in any event, to sell their expensive home in Potomac, Maryland, during a serious economic recession. "We had never been really close," says Hwangbo of her relationship with her father, "so when he moved to Korea, I thought it would be no big deal to me. He expressed some doubt, and I said, 'Dad, go for it. You've worked very hard here, and this is your chance to do something really exciting.' But once he left, I felt very alone, very isolated. I'm getting adjusted to it. He comes back every three or four months to visit. But it's hard on my mom. Now she expresses regrets" that the family ever came to live in America.

Sophia Kim, whom I found sitting across from Kay Hwangbo in the *Korea Times* newsroom, has her own issues to deal with. Her father came to study journalism at Brigham Young University in Utah in the late 1950s but found himself unable to master written English satisfactorily. Soon he migrated to Los Angeles, where he worked for a time on a Korean-language community newspaper, but eventually he set himself up as a businessman to support his wife and four children. Among his specialties was selling wigs to Korean Americans and others. "When I was in junior high school," recalls Kim, "the Koreans in L.A. were in the forefront of the wig business. And I used to spend a lot of weekends and summer days being very much a part of that business. It started out of our house. We had one room that was occupied with boxes and boxes of Korean-made wigs. And I used to really resent it, because I didn't have my own room. On my free days, I was dragged along by my father in our station wagon. He would go to different wig stores and bargain and sell. I ended up waiting in the car, guarding the wigs. The greatest reward for me was that I got a scoop of ice cream at this coffee shop when the day was over. As an immigrant child, to me that was such a big treat."

Kim's family lived in a Japanese-American section of Los Angeles when she was a child—an awkward situation, given the mistreatment of Koreans under decades of Japanese colonial rule and the mutual suspicion of the two nationalities toward each other. "It was really kind of a traumatic, difficult experience for me," she says, "because I was raised with a lot of anti-Japanese sentiment. These were second- and third-generation [Japanese American] kids. I always felt they hated me because I was Korean and they were Japanese and they were supposed to be superior. But the real reason was that I was an 'F.O.B.' ('fresh off the boat'). I had an accent, and I dressed differently."

At Hollywood High School and Scripps College in Claremont, California, Kim was ostensibly more integrated into the Anglo world. As she puts it, she learned "to be assertive, to speak out and be independent," rather than being "obedient and submissive like the traditional Korean female."[8] But, like Hwangbo, she developed a need to learn more about, and return to, her roots. After internships at other "American" newspapers, Kim signed on with K. W. Lee. "I really love

---

[8] *A number of Korean Americans I met cited to me a traditional Korean proverb regarding the role of women: "When you're born, you live for your parents. When you marry, you live for your husband. When you get older, you live for your children." Korean women have been taught for centuries that they must never live for themselves.*

ethnic journalism," she says. "There is immense emotional satisfaction in covering this big, growing community. It's history in the making. I think we do very fair, objective coverage, but we also do a certain amount of advocacy journalism, too. When the mainstream newspapers blow a story up or are exploitative, we can put things in perspective and maybe let others see what the Korean side is, to be fair. And I don't think that means compromising on our ethics and integrity."

Complicating her own identity struggle further is the fact that Kim married an Ethiopian political refugee, an electrical engineer who defected from the former Marxist government in Addis Ababa while in the United States for advanced naval training. Their two young daughters, she speculates with a chuckle, "may be the only Korean-Ethiopians in the United States." They draw constant compliments for their unusual attractiveness. But she adds, "I am concerned about my children's future. Will they be accepted by a Korean culture where interracial marriage is not accepted?" Judging from the record in her own family, they are not off to a great start: Although Kim's mother, after an initial reluctance, came around and developed a strong attachment to her first grandchildren, at the time we spoke, her father still had not agreed even to see them, because they are half-African. Meanwhile, Kim says, when her husband drives around their primarily Hispanic and white neighborhood in the San Fernando Valley in a beat-up old sports car, he is occasionally stopped by the police and asked what he is doing there. "But he's real nice to them and he has that real cute [Ethiopian] accent, so they leave him alone," she explains.

Ultimately, says Kim, hers is a "limbo generation" of Korean Americans, caught between two worlds. "Korea's not our home, we're not accepted there. They can tell right away where we're from, because of what we wear and how we walk in an assertive way. And I don't speak perfect Korean anymore." She pauses. "Yet we're not one hundred percent accepted here either. But even if this is not perfectly home, the way I want it to be, it is home. I really can't imagine living anywhere else, or in any part of the country other than Southern California."

ON APRIL 29, 1992, four white Los Angeles police officers were acquitted of all charges of criminal wrongdoing in connection with the brutal beating of black motorist Rodney G. King more than thirteen months earlier.[9] It had been a dramatic case, watched nationally and internationally for its revival of old issues of police brutality and equal treat-

---

[9] *Later, two of the officers were convicted in federal court of violating King's civil rights.*

ment before the law of all Americans. As a result of a change of venue, the trial took place in the largely white suburban community of Simi Valley, north of Los Angeles proper. Within two hours of the jury verdict, which they considered unfair and insensitive, outraged mobs of blacks and Latinos were in the streets in many parts of town, overturning cars, setting fires, breaking store windows, looting, and otherwise attacking any symbol they could find of the more privileged establishment. The smoke was so thick at first that planes had to be diverted from Los Angeles International Airport, and much of the rioting could be seen live on television across the country and throughout the world. Governor Pete Wilson called out the National Guard, but it soon had to be supplemented by 4,500 federal troops sent by President George Bush (who said he found the root cause of these civil disturbances in the liberal social programs of the 1960s and '70s).

By the time the 1992 Los Angeles riots finally subsided five days later, they had broken all records and become the worst in American history, with 58 people dead, more than 2,000 injured, and at least 12,000 arrested. The official overall cost estimate was $717 million; more than five thousand buildings were damaged or destroyed, and three thousand businesses were affected.

When the dust had settled, it became clear that the primary target of looters and arsonists during the uprising was not so much the Anglo establishment as businesses run by Korean Americans, especially in Koreatown and the South Central district. They sustained nearly half of the total damage in the city. According to KAGRO, 535 Korean-owned grocery and liquor stores suffered significant losses, along with hundreds of flea market stalls, clothing stores, auto repair shops, and other enterprises—more than two thousand Korean businesses in all. Despite the hardships many of the Koreans experienced in their own daily lives, they were obviously perceived by the truly dispossessed as being among the privileged few and, therefore, singled out for especially harsh treatment. Yet one reason they were hit so badly was that the police seemed to ignore the threat to the Korean businesses in favor of areas where more influential people lived and worked. Indeed, the toll might have been worse had not Korean vigilantes decided at one point to patrol Koreatown themselves, armed with shotguns and other weapons. Some shop owners in South Central took up positions on the roofs of their stores with automatic rifles and, if their warnings were not heeded, dispensed quick justice against the rioters. (At Irene's Liquor Store, Yung Ho Kim stood his ground. He chased away would-be looters and stayed in the store day and night until the riots had subsided.)

So severe was the situation that, in a great role reversal, family and friends back in Korea began raising money to send to the immigrant merchants here to help them get back on their feet. The South Korean foreign ministry announced in Seoul, with rhetorical flourish, that it would seek "reparations" for the damage done to Korean and Korean American property in Los Angeles. Even those not directly affected by the violence found that their businesses suffered during the severe local recession that followed the riots.[10] Banks reported a doubling of the delinquency rate on Korean Americans' loans, and dozens of businesses took advantage of the $999 "bankruptcy packages" offered by law firms serving the community.

These were sobering developments—new evidence, if any were needed, of the frailty of some immigrant success stories, and of the uniquely bad relationships between Koreans and other ethnic minorities in Los Angeles. One immediate response was militancy, a determination to turn Koreatown into a self-sustaining fortress that would not be so vulnerable in the next riots. If their turf effectively becomes off-limits in times of disorder, argued some Korean American conservatives, then the bands of marauders would have to head elsewhere, perhaps even to Beverly Hills and other truly wealthy areas.

But there were also bridge builders who emerged and began to speak up for different, more collaborative approaches. One of the most visible was Angela Oh, a criminal defense lawyer who has never been to Korea and cannot read or write Hangul but strongly identifies herself as a Korean American. By the Korean American community's special form of reckoning, Oh is considered a member of the "second generation."[11] As the cocounsel (along with a black lawyer) of a special California State Assembly committee looking into the causes of the riots, she achieved a high national profile in appearances on *Nightline* on ABC and other television programs to explain the Korean point of view.

Oh feels very strongly that Korean Americans should speak up

[10] *One of the institutions that suffered the most after the riots was the English-language* Korea Times. *"It was devastated," says K. W. Lee, by a decline in advertising and circulation—reduced to a monthly, instead of a weekly, with only a skeleton staff. (A daily Korean-language edition was still published in Los Angeles, however.)*

[11] *According to what the Koreans consider the "European" system of reckoning, Oh, as the American-born daughter of immigrants who came to the United States after the Korean War, would be regarded as a first-generation American. But in the Korean community, that term is reserved for adult Korean American immigrants; their U.S.–born children are known as the second generation. People who immigrated with their parents at the age of eight or ten but grew up in the American system are called "1.5"s. If they were in their late teens when they came, they are "1.25"s, and if they were born in Korea but arrived at a very young age, they are "1.75"s.*

more aggressively on their own behalf and end their self-imposed isolation. She argues, for example, that Koreans, African Americans, and Latinos have all been common victims of the white Los Angeles power structure's indifference. "We have to think about how to modify the system to make it responsive to our needs, and to what people really want," Oh tells me during an interview at the offices of the blue-ribbon Anglo law firm where she is a partner. "Whites are sitting back right now, pretending that they don't have a role in [the search for solutions to ethnic conflict in Los Angeles]. And of course, they're the ones who are going to have to give up some power. They will not concede that easily. I'm sorry if they don't like the idea of having to help out in a situation they don't believe they helped create. But I think the reality is they did help to create it. That's the message that hasn't gotten across. White flight is what caused redlining and left these neighborhoods in the condition they are in."

"Really, when you get down to it," Oh continues, "everybody wants the same thing. They all want to be able to survive for their kids, they want to have a decent place to live, and they don't want to be fearful about walking from point A to point B. These are not race-specific things."

Studiously avoiding an overdeveloped sense of ethnic solidarity, Oh has not hesitated to criticize Korean financial interests when she thinks they have done something wrong—for example when a Los Angeles hotel owned by investors in Seoul broke a union and fired 175 Latino workers the day after Thanksgiving. This is just the kind of "immoral" action, she says, that contributes to a negative stereotype of Koreans and damages their relations with other groups. But in the period following the riots, Oh, as the incoming president of the Korean American Bar Association, put public pressure on the other "Asian/Pacific Islander" communities in Los Angeles, some of them quite comfortable and self-satisfied, to understand the need to make common cause with the Koreans. "There's a real resistance to coalition building," even amongst various Asian groups, she complains. "Korean Americans have never asked for the Japanese Americans, the Chinese Americans, or the Filipino Americans to stand with us on anything. They have no history of ever having supported us before. In fact, [some of them] have a history of having oppressed us. If you look at what they've done in politics here, it's been nothing to really help us. It's for their own narrow interest."

One obvious solution would be for more Korean Americans to become involved in conventional politics themselves. Yet informal studies show that they are slower than many other immigrant groups to take U.S. citizenship, even after they have met all the requirements, and that a relatively low percentage of Koreans actually registers to vote. (In Los Angeles County, fewer than 40,000 Korean Americans were registered to vote in 1991, according to Jerry Yu, president of the Korean American Coalition.) The Los Angeles neighborhoods where the Koreans live are dispersed over a broad geographical area, negating any prospect that they could influence local government by voting as a bloc even if they were registered in larger numbers. The places where they conduct most of their business are divided among several different city council districts, and so those who can afford it find themselves giving money to, or raising it for, a variety of African American, Latino, and Chinese American council members, hoping that overall their interests will somehow be protected.

Occasionally, organizations like the Korean American Coalition mobilize the community on issues that seem to affect them significantly—intervening, for example, to oppose California's proposed "English-only" law and to persuade the Los Angeles Police Department to preserve its Asian Crime Task Force. But as for "community empowerment," Yu says, the Koreans are far behind most other groups. Mike Hernandez, a Los Angeles city councilman, agrees. The Korean Americans, he says, "don't have a voice."

It was Jay Kim, a "first-generation" civil engineer turned politician, who scored a significant breakthrough in 1990. He became an instant legend that year, as the only Korean American serving in an elected public office in the United States. To find him, I drove out to Diamond Bar, a wealthy suburban city of some 75,000 people at the far eastern end of Los Angeles County, almost thirty miles from downtown, where he was a Republican member of the city council.

Kim, who immigrated to study at the University of Southern California in 1961, married a fellow Korean but did not return to visit his native country for the next three decades. His three children (one of them a neurosurgeon) have all made pilgrimages there to get in touch with their roots, but for him it has never been a concern. Indeed, in the council election that sent him to office by a landslide just three years after he moved to Diamond Bar, Kim's ethnic origins were not an issue. He ran as a successful businessman with 140 employees across the state of California, someone who understood how to build freeways, clean up toxic waste, and design prisons. His campaign strategy was simple: "I laid out a piece of paper and listed my strengths and weaknesses. Then I looked at it every day and figured out how to highlight the strengths and how to bury, or at least mitigate, the weaknesses. After that, I did some research on the city's needs." In an area full of immigrants, his slight accent, with an occasional missing definite article or a verb that did not agree with its subject, was not a liability.

Before long, Kim was promoted to mayor. Then, in 1992, at age fifty-three, he was elected to Congress from a conservative Southern California district—another first and, in his own words, another American Dream fulfilled. He had become an unstoppable Korean phenomenon, with a simple political and economic philosophy: Taxes should be held down and many traditional government functions, such as building bridges, privatized. In an interview with the *Washington Post* on the day he was sworn in as a member of the House of Representatives, he joked that maybe one day he would run for president. National Republican figures did not quite appear to promote those dreams, but in 1994, Kim was reelected to Congress with 68 percent of the votes in his district.

Whenever Kim's name came up, the Korean Americans I spoke to expressed pride that one of their own now walks the corridors of power. Like politicians from other minority ethnic groups, he apparently benefited from substantial contributions from people who cared more about his name and his origins than his political affiliation or views. In a conversation before he went to Congress, Kim himself said he felt some obligation to promote the prospects of other Korean candidates for public office. "But I wouldn't do that blindly," he cautioned. "I would have to look at anyone as an American first and then as a Korean. If he's a liberal, I would have trouble with that. But again, blood is thicker than water, and we need some more Korean politicians." The lesson that was not lost on many observers, however, was that Kim's success was based in part on his becoming, and acting, as un-Korean and all-American as possible. And while he was an important symbol, his day-to-day actions and decisions had little to do with the wrenching problems faced by Korean Americans on the firing line in the inner-city neighborhoods of America.

FOR AFRICAN AMERICAN activists and civic leaders in Los Angeles, the period after the 1992 riots provided a new opportunity to invoke an old principle: a community's right to assert control over itself and its circumstances. And as the issue played out, it had a profound effect on Korean Americans' ability to recoup their losses and reestablish themselves in business.

At the cavernous First African Methodist Episcopal (AME) Church on South Harvard Boulevard, an influential institution on the edge of

South Central with some 8,500 members, the Reverend Cecil Murray took on the combined role of problem solver and angry community spokesman. At one point during the riots, he actually interposed himself and some of his parishioners between a line of police and a mob of people trying to throw rocks at them. "Perception is everything," he insists during our long conversation in his office, as he tries to explain the neighborhood's hostile attitude toward the Koreans. "If you talk to a hundred South Central blacks, ninety-nine would say [of the Korean merchants], in the language of the streets, 'they dissed us—disrespected us.' They never looked at you, they never greeted you when you walked in the store. They threw the change at you. They gave you that hard look that says they think you are filth. That by itself would be tolerable, if not ethical. But then they take the hard-earned money given them, whether it's for a loaf of bread or a pint of whiskey, and they invest not one cent in that indigenous community. They take it all to their community, where a dollar turns over eight times. In the black community, it is turned over once, into [the Koreans'] hands, and out. That is an inequity."

What made things worse, says Murray, is that the Koreans did not "invest emotionally" in the communities where they had their stores. Speaking as if he were addressing a hypothetical Korean American shopkeeper, he says, "You work with none of the clubs, you sponsor not one Little League team, you give not one scholarship. By and large, you do not offer jobs, because your business has tended to be a family business, as you were getting on your feet. Your family slept there in the shop, or upstairs or downstairs; you worked like Trojans. Wonderful. But when you take my money and cannot or will not hire me, will not invest in my community, do not teach me, and yet treat me with contempt, and I am still poor . . . then there comes a trigger. The gun is already loaded, cleaned, and primed, and an incident like the Rodney King fiasco puts pressure on the trigger finger."

The Koreans, Murray concedes, may have found themselves accidentally "at the flashpoint of an historical event," but he insists they still must share in the consequences. Murray is in the forefront of an effort to reduce drastically the number of liquor outlets in South Central, where "down-and-outers, people with no work ethic, and self-destructive people congregate. Without all these liquor stores, they would be somewhat dispersed." According to Mark Whitlock, a former title insurance company executive whom Murray has hired to work with the church on community programs, "We have more liquor stores in South Central than the entire state of Rhode Island, and seventy-five percent as many as Connecticut. The liquor business in our community has enhanced crime and contributed to juvenile delinquency. If we choose not to have the liquor stores reopen, that is our right."

Under the traditional system in Los Angeles, a license to operate a liquor store, once granted by the state of California, was difficult to revoke but easy to sell, along with the business, to a new owner. No special hearing or clearance was necessary, and the city had no control over the placement of the retail outlets. But at the urging of ministers like Murray and black members of the L.A. city council, new laws were passed after the riots, requiring a community review and a public hearing before any store could be opened (or reopened) to sell liquor; clearance from the zoning and planning commissions was also to be obtained on each site.

The focus was especially on "problem liquor stores" where, according to police records, there was a history of citations for loitering, public drunkenness, and prostitution, or that had been the scene of murders, rapes, and other violent crimes. Many would be allowed to reopen only under stringent conditions, including a new restriction on their hours of operation. "Some of these liquor stores are right next to schools or churches," complains Dora Leong, a Chinese American who is a legislative assistant to Councilman Mark Ridley-Thomas, an African American, "and they're open from eight in the morning until two in the morning. There's really no reason for a liquor store to be open at eight o'clock in the morning and to have people waiting at seven-thirty for it to open, who are already not in good shape to begin with and are pestering little children walking by."

Korean merchants and civic groups cried foul when the new, tougher licensing procedures were put into effect. Indeed, by early 1995 only 23 out of the 176 Korean-owned grocery and liquor stores in Los Angeles that were closed after the 1992 riots (not to mention the hundreds of others that were damaged) had been able to reopen. Only 35 percent of the Korean American small-business owners in Los Angeles are estimated to have had any insurance on their property, and many of those policies were with unlicensed, fly-by night companies that were unwilling or unable to pay substantial damage claims. The owners of many shops, having struggled with these insurance problems and spent money on reconstructing their property, found that they were still hopelessly mired in red tape and legal proceedings.

Ryan Song, who succeeded Yumi Park as executive director of KAGRO's California branch, says he accepts the importance of educating residents of these neighborhoods about the risks of alcohol consumption, but he complains that the small retailers are twice-punished victims who have become scapegoats for larger frustrations. "They've elevated the issues to a degree that it's the liquor store that's causing all the harms or woes in the community," he says with obvious skepticism. Song points out that most of the shopkeepers rely on many sources of income to survive, including food stamps and money orders, along with grocery, cigarette, and liquor sales. As long as the shops damaged in the riot are prevented from reopening, he says, liquor consumption is not necessarily being reduced, but "other surviving stores are getting a windfall." Song adds that it would not be adequate to allow stores to reopen without restoring their permission to sell alcohol: "In a small market, if you just sell the groceries, you can't make a profit. Because of the demand, if you don't sell the liquor, people will go to another store where they can shop for the grocery items and the liquor items at the same time."

Angela Oh, for her part, argues that however much the new licensing policy is legalistically cloaked as an implementation of community control, it has begun to look like "a race issue," with Koreans as the targets. "I don't think there should be that many liquor stores out there either," she says. "But the reality is that they did exist there, and this is not how we get rid of them. It's just wrong, morally. You don't just destroy a person's livelihood and say, 'Too bad, we don't want you anymore.' You compensate them, or you give them incentives to go elsewhere. The fact is, it comes down again to money, and how are you going to get that?"

Even as Oh spoke, the Los Angeles Black-Korean Alliance, a relic of the city's efforts to achieve racial harmony during the 1980s, formally disbanded. The membership had dwindled steadily, and, as Marcia Choo, one of the original Korean members, puts it, "It's really tough out there right now. The problems are overwhelming. I don't know if just a handful of people committed to bridge building is going to make that big of a difference at this stage. People are facing foreclosure on their homes because they can't make the payments. So nobody wants to talk about race relations. That's the last thing on their minds. One of our colleagues called us the lunatic fringe, because in the midst of all this, we were still trying to work toward building multiethnic coalitions. I was even called a communist [by some Korean Americans] because I advocated joining hands with people who [in their words] 'tried to destroy our community.'" Events like Korean American–African American prayer breakfasts to celebrate Martin Luther King's birthday, once sponsored by Councilman Mike Woo, are a thing of the past.

Meanwhile, Korean-Latino relations also needed attention. As Carlos Vaquerano, a Salvadoran who works at the Central American Refugee Center in Los Angeles, puts it, "In the past, when we talked about Asians, we always called them *chinos*, because of the way they looked. Culturally, it's been a great experience for us to get to know that not all people from Asia are Chinese." After the 1992 riots, Vaquerano says, the Koreans seemed to become more sympathetic to Central Americans, because "they began to see that we are both minority communities with social problems who are discriminated against." In many neighborhoods of the city, notes Antonia Hernandez, general counsel of the Mexican American Legal Defense and Educational Fund, Latinos and Koreans need each other to keep their businesses going; in the "swap meets," the flea markets that occupy old drive-in movie lots, they often operate stalls side by side. But, she warns, "the Latino community has the same concerns as the African American community: They don't want the liquor stores."

AFTER THE COMBINATION of the riots and the severe 1994 earthquake in the San Fernando Valley, a small number of Korean families left Los Angeles. Some were reported to be moving to Bakersfield and Fresno, in California's Central Valley, and others to Colorado. But in Seoul, the South Korean government, which keeps careful statistics on such matters, noticed a more profound phenomenon: that the number of Koreans immigrating to the United States was declining steadily, and the number returning, while still relatively insignificant, was going up each year. Compared with 1988, when 24,000 Koreans left to live in America, there were only 11,000 who did so in 1992 and 8,000 in 1993. Whereas only 3,000 Koreans returned home permanently from the United States in 1988, that figure was up to 6,500 in 1992.

Admittedly, the circumstances in Korea changed quite dramatically during this period. Through the late 1980s, Koreans were emigrating not only for economic reasons, but also because of the human rights abuses committed by their authoritarian government and the constant threat of war with North Korea. By the early 1990s the standard of living had improved considerably, a transition to a seemingly stable democracy was underway in South Korea, and the tensions on the Korean peninsula had eased somewhat.

In a government survey of 5,914 Koreans who gave up permanent residence status or citizenship in America to return to their home country in 1993, 44.8 percent said they had "failed to overcome the language barrier and cultural frictions" in the United States. Another 19.6 percent said they had "failed to find proper job opportunities or failed in business," while 14.1 percent returned for personal reasons, such as divorce or marriage. (The rest came back for educational and other miscellaneous reasons.)

The Korean government claims that it neither encourages nor discourages its citizens from going to live in America. "The homogeneity of Korea is now a weak point. We need to know the outside world better and make our country more open by international standards," admits Ju Hum Lee, an official of the foreign ministry in Seoul. "The government position is that we want Korean Americans to become good American citizens and good neighbors of other ethnic groups. But we hope that they and their descendants will keep their identity as Koreans. The only tragedy is if they marry Caucasian Americans."

IM JUNG KWUON spills out her story matter-of-factly. It is a Korean American soap opera. Her childhood was chaotic, because her father, who had brought the family from Korea to America, could not decide whether to stay and if so, where. Business in Los Angeles was bumpy. They tried Chicago, but it was too cold. He got three deportation letters. They took a farewell tour around the United States in a station wagon, but then never left, because things were too unstable at home in Korea. The movers packed them and soon unpacked them. Back in Los Angeles, Kwuon was trained to be "the number-one marriage-market eligible female daughter," complete with instruction in Korean language, history, piano, dance, and tae kwon do. After two years at UCLA, she dropped out of school, moved out of her parents' house, and went to work. Instantly, her father disinherited her. "I didn't have a diploma and wasn't going to be an intelligent mother, so the only prospect left was that I would be a prostitute! That's what my father thought, this was it." For ten years, he never visited her apartments, lest he be thought to acquiesce in her status as an "independent single woman."

For Kwuon, there were therapists and suicide attempts and more therapists. The Asian ones could not seem to understand Kwuon's need to rebel; finally an Irish American one, who also happened to be a tae kwon do instructor, helped her get back on her feet. Kwuon returned to school and got her degree. The good news was that she decided to get married; the bad news, from her father's point of view, was that her fiancé was not Korean, but Polish American. She was told never to mention his name in her father's presence, nor to bring him home. Several Thanksgivings were spent apart. But after three years, just as they were about to put on their own wedding, Kwuon's father relented. He paid for the festivities. All lived happily ever after, sort of.

Kwuon earned a master's degree in psychology and counseling, with the goal of helping people like herself. She began writing a column for the *Korea Times* about all the Korean immigrants' unmentionable problems—language, alcohol, smoking, sex, incest, child abuse—and how to get help. "With most of my Korean friends," she says, "what happened to us in our twenties, we followed the profession our parents picked, we married the person our parents picked. And by our thirties, quite a few of us are either divorced, or not happy in our jobs, or we are married but not really living together, having separate households or separate sexual, emotional lives. And we share children. We sort of bring these children up, but it's not a bonded relationship between mother and father. So maybe after a divorce and unhappy relationships, they will find out what went on with their parents, and then figure out what cultural values they brought over and readjust."

In virtually every Korean American family, it seems, a deeply sad story like Kwuon's can be told. There is an ethic of suffering among Koreans, says Angela Oh, the high-profile criminal lawyer. "We even have a word for the concept: *han.* Wherever we go, there is tragedy," says Oh. "People ask, 'Why us?' " They are the Irish of Asia, some say. Or is it the Italians of Asia? Or the Jews of Asia? It is a peculiar twist on the concept of the chosen people—in this case, chosen for anguish and unhappiness.

K. W. Lee, the editor, agrees: "The Koreans are the people of *han.* It is the underpinning of the Korean psyche. Koreans have nurtured these smoldering, unquenched woes for centuries. Grudges and woes produced by external invaders and internal rulers. Any Korean who spent his adolescence in Korea has in his DNA this gene called *han.* It's a very exquisite, indescribable feeling. When Koreans arrive in America with *han,* then through the next generations they want to have it requited. Revenged. Fulfilled. It's such a cosmic sorrow. We are condemned to repeat the mistakes of other minorities because we lack the memory. I call it the American tragedy."

XI
"WE KNOW WHO WE ARE":
THE MASHADI

KEW GARDENS, NEW YORK

FROM THE OUTSIDE, Shaare Tova could be a synagogue like any other in America, albeit on the modern side. It is made of red brick and decorated with a large steel menorah. At sundown each Friday or on the evening of any Jewish holiday, people converge hurriedly on this middle-class neighborhood in Queens from every direction—on foot, by car, or on the Long Island Railroad from Manhattan—to worship there, or just to celebrate together. There is an upbeat bustle about the scene, as friends and relatives greet one another and exchange their latest news. Children coming from home hug their fathers, who arrive directly from work; grandparents beam at their grandchildren and turn aside to boast a bit to anyone willing to listen about how they have grown and what they have done.

Once inside, people jam the hallways as they funnel into the large sanctuary or one of two smaller chapels. Shaare Tova turns out to be a highly observant place. Although there are slight variations among them, the several services are conducted entirely in Hebrew and, as in most Orthodox congregations, the women sit separately from the men, either in the balcony or behind a rail on the main floor. But some people, soon after arrival, head directly down the staircase to the social hall in the basement, to help prepare for the festive events that will follow. Those events will be truly joyous and cacophonous, as hundreds of people who know each other well get together for dinner and dancing.

Meanwhile, during the services, in the evening or the next morning, while the more devout or patient generations remain at prayer, there are often separate clusters of young boys and girls gathered in front of the low-rise edifice (the boys with their heads covered, some still wearing their *tallith*, or prayer shawl), passing the time.

But this is not really a synagogue like any other—not, for example, like the more sedate-looking Kew Gardens Synagogue just across the street. A plaque on the wall, just to the right as one enters Shaare Tova, explains why it is special, in both English and Farsi. The English version reads: "This entire building has been constructed with the financial help and effort of the Mashadi Jewish community of New York and abroad, 1980–83."

Indeed, Shaare Tova is out of the ordinary not just because it follows the Sephardic (or "Spanish") tradition of Jewish worship, as distinct from the Ashkenazi (or "German") tradition practiced across the way; although a definite minority, there are many Sephardic congregations in the United States, especially in the New York area.[1] What distinguishes this synagogue most is that all of its seven hundred families, with perhaps only one or two exceptions, trace their origins to Mashad, the fourth-largest city in Iran, in the northeastern part of that country, near its borders with Afghanistan and the central Asian part of the former Soviet Union (now the independent republic of Turkmenistan). The Mashadi make up not so much a separate sect as a unique Jewish community that has maintained itself intact through centuries of extraordinary adversity.[2] Now they are one of America's smallest, and yet least absorbed, immigrant groups, and they are struggling against the dreaded threat of assimilation.

[1] *The Sephardim, who constitute about a 20 percent minority in the world Jewish community today, include the descendants of people who lived in Spain and Portugal from the Middle Ages until their persecution and expulsion toward the end of the fifteenth century. Most other Jews, especially in the United States, are considered Ashkenazim, a term that originally applied to those from the Rhineland valley and France, who migrated to the Slavic lands after the Crusades and later, after their persecution in Eastern Europe, came west again. The two groups, which are represented roughly equally in Israel despite the imbalance elsewhere, differ in their pronunciation of Hebrew, cultural traditions, and synagogue liturgy. Ashkenazi Jews are often said to follow the "German" ritual, and Sephardic Jews the "Spanish." The* Misrachi, or "Oriental" Jews, *who, after the Babylonian exile, settled in Iran, elsewhere in the Middle East, and in North Africa, had no known historical ties to Germany or Spain but long ago fell under the influence of "Spanish" Jews and adopted the Sephardic rite. (Generally speaking, there is only one form of Sephardic worship, whereas Ashkenazim are divided among Orthodox, Reform, and—in America—Conservative synagogues.)*

[2] *Because of imprecision in its transliteration from Farsi, the name of the city is rendered in various ways in English, including Meshed. I have chosen to use the more common spelling of Mashad, and of Mashadi to describe its people (rather than Mashhadi or Meshedi).*

•

Mashad is a city of particular importance to Shiite Muslims. Its name translates as "place of the martyr," and it is there, according to legend, that the Imam Ali Reza, eighth in the line of descent from Ali, the son-in-law of the prophet Mohammed and the founder of the Shiite faith, died from eating poisoned grapes and was buried many centuries ago. Over the years, the revered imam's elaborately decorated tomb has become a shrine that is frequently the object of pilgrimages and sometimes the scene of fanatical displays of piety, including bloody self-flagellation. As the story has been handed down, when Nadir Shah, the Sunni Muslim who ruled Persia from 1736 to 1747, conquered central and south Asia as far east as India, he established his administrative capital in Mashad, thus building a coalition with his rivals and winning broader religious sanction for his political and military accomplishments.

In about 1740, Nadir Shah ordered various ethnic groups living under his domain to send representatives to settle in Mashad, in order to build up his capital as a center of business and trade. Among the recruits were forty Jewish families from Kazvin, a city seventy-five miles northwest of Tehran, who supposedly enjoyed a particular reputation for honesty and therefore were given the delicate assignment of helping protect the spoils that Nadir Shah had brought back from India. As in many parts of the world, the Jews, excluded from most other fields, tended to be merchants. (According to another version of the scantily documented history, the Jews were actually dispatched to Kalat, another one hundred fifty miles north, for other duties, but were diverted by civil strife and found themselves stranded in Mashad, not considered an especially welcoming environment for non-Muslims.)

The Jews had barely established themselves in Mashad when their patron, Nadir Shah, was assassinated in 1747 by Shiites who were angry that he had confiscated some of their clergy's land. Nonetheless, the Jews prospered in business and benefited from an atmosphere of relative tolerance. Their numbers grew slowly as additional families migrated from other cities to join them in Mashad, and they created their own comfortable quarter, remodeling and connecting their houses to each other and retreating behind a locked gate every night. But in March 1839, at a time when local religious leaders had a great deal of authority because the central government of Iran was weak and corrupt, the Shiites of Mashad suddenly turned on these strangers who had arrived in their midst ninety-nine years earlier. Reacting to a rumor that a Jewish woman had grievously insulted the Shiite community on one of the holiest days of its calendar, a mob attacked the Jewish neighborhood, sacking its synagogues, destroying the sacred Torah scrolls, and killing dozens of people. It was the Iranian equivalent of the pogroms that were so common in Russia at the time.

During the assault, a few Jews escaped through the rear gates of their compound and appealed to the local imam to intervene and stop the violence. He said he would, but only on the condition that all the surviving Mashadi Jews agree immediately to convert to Islam. On the strength of that promise—that a few Jewish families would go to the mosque each day to profess their faith in Allah and Mohammed until the conversion was complete—the mob relented and the rest of the community was spared.

On the surface, the conversion of the Mashadi Jews was prompt, efficient, and thorough. Knowing their lives depended on it, these *jedid el Islam,* or "new Muslims," steeped themselves in the Muslim prayers they were expected to say and the new customs they would have to observe. By all accounts they attended the mosque regularly (ultimately building their own) and sent their children, whom they now gave Persian names, to special religious schools to study the Koran. Many of the men made the *haj,* or pilgrimage, to Mecca and Medina and on their return, in devout Muslim fashion, added *el hajji* to their names. This apparent enthusiasm brought them considerable acceptance in Mashad and further success in business. But the Jews still lived together in their own quarter, and there they entered into a secret pact to preserve their original beliefs and traditions. Underground—literally, in their basements—they celebrated the Jewish Sabbath and holidays and, with lookouts posted on the street, privately conducted ceremonies that were no longer officially tolerated. Young children were sworn to secrecy, and in order to avoid the risk that they might later be asked, or tempted, to marry genuine Muslims, their parents arranged betrothals, and eventually marriages, to the children of other Mashadi Jews at a very early age. (This did not arouse particular suspicion, since it was entirely consistent with the Persian custom of pledging their young children to each other.)

Within a couple of years, divisions emerged within the Mashadi community, and a large contingent of the most observant people moved across the Afghan border to settle in the city of Herat, where they believed they could practice Judaism more openly among less militant Sunni Muslims. But Iranian soldiers captured Herat in a battle in 1856 and marched the Jews back to Mashad under harsh winter conditions. The community was permitted, in effect, to purchase back those who survived the journey and reaffirmed their conversion to Islam, and the Mashadi settled on a long-term strategy of renewed accommodation. They were like the "Marranos" of Spain and Portugal, who had been forced to convert to Christianity but maintained their Jewishness in secret.

This double life continued in Mashad for more than seven decades. Rather than serving as artisans or craftsmen who might have to work for others, the Mashadi were now almost universally merchants; this helped them preserve their freedom to practice their own religion, albeit on the sly. Jewish-owned shops were kept open on Saturdays, but with young boys left in charge, with instructions to explain to customers that their fathers were unavailable. Public weddings conducted according to Muslim regulations were followed a few hours later by private ceremonies that adhered to Jewish tradition. Occasionally, rumors spread that the *jedid el Islam* were not very devout Muslims after all, and according to Mashadi historians, sometimes bribes had to be paid to keep the secret safe. A few Shiite leaders apparently suspected the truth but helped conceal it in order to avoid civil unrest that could disrupt Mashad's lucrative religious tourist trade.

Some Mashadi migrated to Russia for a time and carried on their businesses there. But after the Bolshevik revolution of 1917, they came rushing back to their secure, predictable lives in Mashad. When the Pahlavi dynasty came to power in Iran in 1925, Reza Shah decreed that Iranians were free to practice any religion openly, and the Mashadi Jews finally abandoned their charade. They once again began to follow Jewish customs publicly. During the rise of fascism in Europe, however, there were parallel developments in Iran. Once again fanatical Shiites began to launch raids on the Jewish quarter in Mashad, especially during Jewish holidays. Reza Shah, calculating his geopolitical position on the basis of the long-standing mutual hostility between the Persians and the Russians, sided with Hitler against Stalin.

Although Iranian Jews were spared any of the organized persecution and genocide of the sort conducted by the Nazis, there was an ominous growth of anti-Semitism in the country, and especially in places like Mashad. Soon after the end of World War II, the Mashadi, by now several thousand strong, took a collective decision that it was time to leave the city where their families had been for more than two hundred years. Gradually, so as not to attract undue attention to what they were doing, they packed up and migrated to Tehran through the late 1940s and early 1950s. A number of the younger people went directly to Israel, where some Mashadi had been settling for many years, including people who had completed their sham pilgrimages to Mecca during the nineteenth and early twentieth centuries with a visit to the Islamic holy sites in Jerusalem and stayed on in what was then known as Palestine.

In Tehran, where many other Jews lived, the Mashadi continued to keep mostly to themselves. Still prosperous in the businesses they had brought along with them, they settled in several different parts of the sprawling capital but constructed four synagogues of their own within a three-mile radius. Whether because of their unusual history and the Islamic influences they had absorbed or because of their status as smaller-town provincials, they did not mix well with the seemingly more sophisticated, flashy Tehrani Jews. The Mashadi dressed differently, and they had their own cuisine, influenced by their contact with Russia and Afghanistan. They had their own dances for festive occasions, in which the women played a key role. Their children generally studied French as a second language, after Farsi. A few independent-minded young Mashadi did "intermarry," as the practice came to be known, with Tehrani Jews of their own choosing, but not many. Most continued to follow old courting and betrothal rituals, accepting the marriages their parents arranged for them among their own narrowly defined group and otherwise following the unique folkways that had evolved in Mashad.

The various Iranian Jewish communities—there were others based in Shiraz, Isfahan, and Tabriz, for example—thrived, especially during the modernizing reign of Reza Shah's son, Mohammed Reza Pahlavi. He was first installed in power by the World War II allies when they removed his father, and later, in 1953, after Iran experienced a brief interlude of leftist revolutionary rule, he was restored to the Peacock Throne by the U.S. Central Intelligence Agency. The shah came to be seen as an important American ally in the turbulent Middle East. Although the fundamentalist Shiites who fomented discontent in the bazaars and mosques were harassed and tortured by his secret police (and some were eventually deported), the Iranian Jews were full participants in the shah's effort to develop the country quickly with its burgeoning oil revenues. There was also a great deal of overt and covert commerce between Iran and Israel, which saw the shah as a benign counterbalance to radical Arab leaders like Iraq's Saddam Hussein. The shah permitted, and sometimes openly encouraged, Iranian Jewish immigration to Israel.

When the tables turned in the late 1970s and the shah was overthrown by the Ayatollah Ruhollah Khomeini and his radical Shiite entourage, the vast majority of Iranian Jews tried to get out as quickly as possible, and the Mashadi were no exception.

So it was that after another period of relative security, this one lasting no more than twenty or thirty years in most cases, almost all of the Mashadi immigrated, en masse, to Israel or to New York, where many had relatives or friends who had already begun to establish themselves in business. By the time the militant Islamic Guards took over the U.S. embassy in Tehran in November 1979, the Mashadi were gone.

Most of those who left during the revolution had to leave all their possessions behind; some women tell of departing with thirty or forty pounds of jewelry concealed on their bodies and in their clothes. Caroline Kordmany, whose father had a privileged appointment under the shah as the influential commissioner of imports and exports for the city of Tehran, had her eighth birthday during the revolution. She remembers that she and her brother, a year older, treated it all as an adventure for a time, rushing out of their luxurious home across from an international bank to watch spellbound every time the demonstrators paraded by. The amusement ended with the terrifying sound of gunshots and teargas grenades that would wake them in the middle of the night.

"Everyone was waiting for things to get better, but once we heard the shah was leaving, that was the end of it," she recalls with sadness in her eyes. "We were told we were going for a short time and we'd be back when the revolution was over. I could come back to my dog and all my things, but I could only take a suitcase with me. We got whatever visas we could and took a Pan Am flight from Tehran to JFK. I remember it was snowing when we arrived, and the snow was up to my head," says Kordmany, now an English major at Queens College and a diamond dealer on the side. "We had a beautiful summer house on the outskirts of Tehran. The state took over everything."

Several years earlier, a number of Mashadi families, anticipating the shah's downfall, had sent their teenage sons to live with cousins, or on their own in groups, and attend high school in Kew Gardens. Thus, they were established in time to receive their parents.

In Kew Gardens the Mashadi who had come earlier received the influx of refugees enthusiastically, but the Kordmany family lived at first "in a horrible, little tiny apartment." "Still, I felt much more secure being in my small room in Queens with my parents than I did in Iran" at the end, she says.

It was a cruel irony, but when they first arrived, many Mashadi were vilified and discriminated against in Queens as "Iranians"—the very people who were humiliating the United States before the world. "It was like a curse to be called an Iranian in 1979 and 1980," remembers one Mashadi businessman. "I used to say that I was Persian and hope that people wouldn't know it was the same thing."

Today, according to the most reliable estimates, the Mashadi Jewish community numbers only about 16,000 or 17,000 people in the entire world. About 9,000 live in Israel, perhaps 2,000 in London, and another 1,000 in Milan, Italy. (Mashadi business communities were established in London and Milan early in the twentieth century.) Several hundred found their way to Hamburg, in northern Germany, after World War II,[3] and about 200 Mashadi—out of some 20,000 Iranian Jews overall—are believed to have remained in Iran after the Islamic revolution (but only one family in Mashad itself, where they care for the Jewish cemetery and the abandoned synagogues). The other 4,000 are in the New York area, mostly in Queens or Nassau County, Long Island. Some of those in Israel have mixed freely with the larger Jewish community (although even there, separate Mashadi synagogues have been constructed), but the other Mashadi, especially in New York, remain fiercely independent.

THE AVERAGE person meeting Mashadi for the first time would say that they do not really stand out from other Americans in their appearance. They look far more mainstream, for example, than some Orthodox Jewish groups with roots in Eastern Europe, such as the Hasidim, many of whom intentionally set themselves apart by wearing long curly forelocks and untrimmed beards, long black coats, and wide-brimmed black hats. It has been remarked by outsiders that both Mashadi men and women of a certain age are endowed with a haunting, distinctive Persian handsomeness, but their children look uncannily like everyone else. Yet most Mashadi, once they get beyond the pleasantries in a conversation, will insist that they can spot each other in an instant (for one thing, they all seem to know one another) and that they are a people truly distinct from everyone else. They do not generally put it this way, but one soon gets the impression that the Mashadi feel, on some level, that having endured as much as they have, they are implicitly superior to all other Jews, if not all other people. And the less they mix with others, they seem to believe, the more likely they are to maintain their superiority.

---

[3] *So isolated were some of the Mashadi from other Jewish communities around the world that they had little or no information about the Holocaust in Europe, even after World War II had ended. "The news media were always censored in Iran, so we only knew what the government wanted us to know," one Mashadi woman told me. She explained that her family emigrated from Tehran to Hamburg in 1978 for business reasons, without any real knowledge of the genocide that had taken place under the Nazis a few decades earlier. She has now become a fervent advocate of educating Mashadi children about the Holocaust.*

The Mashadi are surely among America's strongest believers in group identity and what have come to be known in modern American politics as "family values." Divorce is almost unheard of, and they tend to be very conservative on social issues, adamantly opposed to abortion and worried over the general permissiveness in modern society. Yet the Mashadi generally shy away from involvement in the larger society's institutions and politics. Some attribute this to their having been outsiders in Iran, an experience that left them believing it safer not to be noticed.

According to Abraham Dilmanian, whose father was a renowned historian of the Mashadi, most of them still live in America as if "in a special bubble. They do business primarily with each other. They say 'hi' to their neighbors, but they have no real contact with the outside world, except as their children grow up and sometimes bring non-Mashadi friends home." They make a particular effort to speak Farsi at home, and to teach the language to their children if they do not already know it. In some cases, this inhibits the adult immigrants from developing their idiomatic English skills and reaching out. Their social contacts are very narrow. Many of the adult Mashadi I interviewed said they had never met an African American, a Hispanic, or an immigrant from the Far East, except in passing; most have had little or no contact with Ashkenazi Jews, whom they view as a potentially corrupting influence on their children.

Horror stories circulate routinely among the Mashadi about what can happen to people who do not stay resolutely in the fold. "In our community, nobody drinks very much, there's hardly any smoking, you don't find drug problems or crime," insists one Mashadi leader. "These things never happen, because of very positive peer pressure. There was one possible incident of AIDS. It wasn't actually confirmed, but the guy was completely away from his family for the last twenty years. Probably he was a drug addict. About three years ago, some people saw him in Manhattan driving a taxi, and finally last year he passed away; but it was never confirmed."

"I am comfortable with the lifestyle I have chosen," says Bernard Livi, a diamond dealer in Manhattan who studied electrical engineering at San Jose State University when he first came to the United States from Iran in 1971 and later obtained a master's degree in business administration. Now thirty-eight years old, he took some time to come back into the fold, but he is very happy that he did. "I enjoy spending Saturdays with my parents, my brother, my sister. We get together every Saturday for meals, with my wife and my sister's children, and her husband, and my brother's children, everybody. The kind of food we eat is exactly what we had back home—rice mixed with different kinds of stew, made with kosher meat. Every Shabbat we spend together, the entire family. I enjoy that a lot, and I couldn't have done it if I lived by myself in California. I would miss that immensely. In San Jose, you had to drive fifty miles just to buy some kosher meat. Here it's easy; in every block you have it."

Sarah Karmely has spent much of her life doing a tour of the Mashadi communities around the world. Born in India, where her father was in the rug business, she was taken to England as a young child. At seventeen, she was matched up with a young Mashadi businessman visiting from Italy. "His parents knew my parents," she recalls. "At first, I said no way would I do this, because I was modernized and very British. But of course, what is meant to be . . . we believe very much in fate. After two days together, we decided to get married. And we did, within six months. I was so young." After living in Milan for many years, they came to New York just at the time of the Islamic revolution in Iran, so they had the benefit of all the services being offered to the immigrants settling in Kew Gardens. For a time, they moved to the more upscale Forest Hills with their three children, but then quickly returned to be nearer to Shaare Tova.

On the one hand, Karmely concedes, the Mashadi necessarily give up a great deal of privacy by living within their community. "Everyone can tell you what a person's late grandfather had for breakfast," she says with a laugh, in her British accent. "There are no skeletons in the closet. You know everything." (Bernard Livi puts it more bluntly: "Parents become very careful about which girls they want their sons to go out with. They want to know the background, whether the father is a crook or not, whether he's honest, trustworthy, and religious.") But on the other hand, Karmely notes, in "unfortunate circumstances"—as when her daughter-in-law died, leaving her son with a four-year-old child—"people are enormously supportive, loving, helpful, and caring. The community rallies around you and shares in your pain. This is something I'll never forget."

When the Mashadi first arrived in force in Kew Gardens, they rented space in the basement of the Ashkenazi-run Kew Gardens Synagogue for their own separate Sephardic services; as their numbers grew and the basement became too small, they moved to the auditorium of a nursing home and then to other temporary quarters. Very soon, however, after the donation of a piece of land and a successful fund-raising drive, construction began on Shaare Tova (which translates literally from the Hebrew as "gateway to kindness"), and it quickly became the rallying point for the community. It was the center of Mashadi life, the place where people with a similar background could gather routinely for practical advice on everything from prenatal care to income taxes, and could count on hearing a sermon every Saturday in Farsi. The synagogue's sexton, Faizollah Zabih, a former rug dealer now in his eighties, who worries aloud that there is "too much freedom" in the United States, has kept everything very much on the traditional Mashadi track. Indeed, the synagogue's leaders—elected in very old-fashioned style, with only men having the right to vote—have come to wield a powerful influence over the evolution of Mashadi life in America.

Abdolrahim Etessami, for example, is a key figure. An international carpet dealer who was president of the Mashadi community for almost two decades in Tehran, he had been preceded to the United States by his wife and three sons. Intercepted by them on the telephone during the Iranian revolution while he was on a business trip to India, he agreed only reluctantly to fly directly to New York rather than stopping at home to pick up some things he wanted to bring along. Once he was settled in Queens, however, he soon moved into a similar position of authority here. Etessami organized the building of the synagogue (as he had previously done in Tehran) and was later responsible for the controversial decision to divert a substantial sum of money raised in America, along with funds donated by the communities in London, Milan, and Hamburg, to construct a nursing home for the Mashadi in Israel. Now over seventy years old, he is involved with a project to build another synagogue in Great Neck, Long Island. There are, however, suspicions that other American Jews who live there, not so eager to have more Iranians in their midst, have worked behind the scenes to make it more difficult to obtain all the necessary permits. ("Why do you have to have your own synagogue?" they are reported to have asked a delegation from Shaare Tova. "We have quite a few synagogues in the neighborhood already. Why can't you join ours?")

Sitting in his office on East Thirty-first Street, just off Madison Avenue, on a summer afternoon, with his son Kamran looking on and an immense roomful of rugs in the background, Etessami explained to me his strongly held view that the Mashadi around the world must "stay under one umbrella" in order to "keep our heritage." This is not so much a political position, he says, as an historical imperative. His statistics may not be entirely reliable, but he speaks with the authority of someone who is accustomed to being taken seriously: "We are known all over the world for our honesty, and for staying together. We could always trust each other, but not trust anyone else. We've married together and become one big family, and this remains. During 250 years, maybe we have had ten divorces. There have been some marriages, maybe ten or twenty, between our children and other Iranian Jews or Ashkenazim in America. It's not forbidden, but we prefer to stay in our own community, because we know who we are. Everyone knows what happened in the past in each family. We look at the family character and background, the mother and father, how they live together and how they treated each other."[4]

Kamran Etessami, a dark-complected man with an angular face who also works in the family rug business, grins and nods in assent as his father speaks. He is pleased to report that he and his brothers have helped keep the family pure Mashadi, although no one can predict what the next generation may bring. "There's a proverb in Persian," he notes. "The pigeon with the pigeon, and the dog with the dog. It's better to stay with the same background."

Obviously, the question arises whether the Mashadi have run the risk of serious genetic damage by marrying so consistently within their own relatively small group. This is not a favorite subject for public discussion, but it is widely accepted now that, as Sarah Karmely puts it, "it's not so healthy genetically for cousins to marry each other." Dilmanian, for his part, says that he has heard of Mashadi families who have been warned by doctors that they must be more careful on this account, lest they produce children with serious genetic disorders. As one woman explained, "If you're concerned, you just learn to stay away from those families."

Unlike the children of most modern, upwardly mobile immigrant groups in America, and unlike the mainstream of twentieth-century Jewish immigrants in particular, very few young Mashadi have drifted toward the professions. Rather, they have concentrated themselves in a few areas of business that their ancestors practiced in Iran; by Dilmanian's estimate, about 50 percent in jewelry, 30 percent in carpets, and 20 percent in other areas, including the garment trade. "There are several people with Ph.D.'s, but most of the youth go right to work in

---

[4] *Every conversation with the Mashadi comes around quickly to the importance of family, and the stories are legion about the unhappy parents who nobly stay together for the sake of their children, rather than take the easy route of divorce followed by so many "Americans." There are persistent rumors that Mashadi businessmen who travel to Bangkok are sometimes unfaithful to their wives. "This was allowed for men under traditional Jewish law, and even under Muslim law," says one Mashadi woman. "We close our eyes to it. But I'm sure that all our men do when they get to Bangkok is to have a massage. That's not so terrible."*

business. And we have only a few practicing M.D.'s," he says woefully. Dilmanian (who is himself a rarity in the community because he trained as a physicist and remained a bachelor into his forties) recently chaired a committee that raised scholarship funds to encourage Mashadi college students to consider medicine as a career, but he ended up being disappointed by the materialism that tends to steer the most promising young Mashadi in other directions. "It's a very competitive community," Dilmanian notes. "So it's a difficult battle to convince young people to go into professions, because the competition is for the girls of the community. The young men want to get a nice young wife, and the condition, according to what they understand, is that they have to be young and rich, able to buy a big house right away." The cherished model in most families is still to marry young and have a large family as soon as possible. "And you can't really achieve that goal quickly enough by going to medical school," Dilmanian adds.

Now that the Mashadi community is well established and feels relatively secure in America, a larger percentage of the youth are at least attending college. But because of the taboo on moving out of one's parents' home before getting married, the choice of institutions that are considered acceptable is rather narrow. For example, although Lobat Hakim graduated second in her class from Manhasset High School on Long Island in the late 1980s, she had no real option of going away for her further education. Indeed, her father would not even permit her to commute into Manhattan to attend Columbia University or New York University, lest she have to be away from home on her own at night. So she settled on Hofstra University, near her family's house, where she happily graduated with honors (and, soon thereafter, got married and became pregnant).

Inevitably, Shaare Tova and the Mashadi community around it have become something of an island in Kew Gardens, which is one of those American neighborhoods that seems destined to be home to successive waves of immigrants. It is now a more mixed area, as one can tell immediately from the restaurants just near the synagogue. The Kosher Kettle, for example, coexists across the street from Ali Baba's Heat It in a Pita. There is a pizza parlor down the block, along with Chinese and Thai restaurants; many of the people who come and go at the nearby 7-Eleven speak to each other in Spanish.

The most significant migration has been westward to Great Neck, just across the Queens border, in Long Island's Nassau County. There many Mashadi have bought or built very large houses and stirred complaints about their ostentation. Certain *dorehs,* or cliques, which are positioned at the top of the informal but widely acknowledged Mashadi social hierarchy, set the tone for the community's extravagant lifestyle there. The weddings and bar mitzvahs, some Mashadi of more modest means complain, have gotten completely out of hand, with the guest lists sometimes swelling beyond a thousand names and the expectations for gifts becoming unreasonable.[5]

While awaiting the construction of the new synagogue, a group of observant Mashadi have taken a long-term lease on the banquet room of a hotel just across from the Great Neck station of the Long Island Railroad. There they hold their own regular Shabbat and holiday services, as well as a morning and evening minyan every day, within walking distance of many of their homes. The banquet room has been decorated to resemble a synagogue, and even railings have been installed to separate the women's seats from the men's.

A few blocks away, in a converted warehouse, the Mashadi Youth Committee (officially still a part of Shaare Tova but increasingly impatient with the synagogue's authoritarian leadership) has opened a spiffy new suburban headquarters, with freshly painted and carpeted rooms that can be used for lectures, classes, and recreational activities. Most of the programs conducted here relate to the Holocaust or to Israel, including a subsidized project that sends fifty young Mashadi there every summer for a crash course in Zionism. "We don't really have any country of our own right now," explains Behnaz Dilmanian, secretary to the youth committee and coordinator of its programs. "But we are Jewish. So if we should decide we had to leave here, at least we could have Israel as our country, because we don't want to go back to Iran. Nobody wants to go back." She pauses, and then adds, "No one will ever go back. It's for sure."

This office also publishes the youth committee's monthly publication, *Megillah,* which contains articles in both Farsi and English.[6] A typical issue carries birth, bar mitzvah, engagement, and marriage announcements, along with a communiqué from the Mashadi community in Israel, announcing the election of new officers and members for its Central Board and Ladies Board, and an occasional poem. There are

[5] *It is said that in the typical Mashadi family, among the generation now getting married, just the first cousins of the bride and groom, with spouses and children included, number at least 200.*

[6] *The megillah is the unusual-looking scroll that contains the story of Queen Esther, a young Jewish woman who supposedly saved her people from extinction in ancient Persia when she was selected to marry King Ahasuerus and thereby neutralized his evil chief minister, Haman, who had planned to murder the Jews. The story, which is read every year on the Jewish festival of Purim and accompanied by great merriment, has special significance for Iranian Jews, since it takes place in the Persian city of Shushan.*

columns with health tips alongside advertisements for Farsi-speaking doctors, dentists, car dealers, mortgage bankers, and boutiques.

But *Megillah* has also become the forum where challenges can be raised to the Mashadi conventional wisdom. In the January 1994 issue, for example, a number of soul-searching English-language articles took up controversial questions being debated in the Mashadi community. One complained that the perpetuation of nine traditional "marriage-related ceremonies involving much expense" had created an unreasonable burden for many families. Its authors also suggested, among other things, that the Mashadi community discourage "unnecessary meddling and rumors" relating to young couples and consult "sociologists and other American experts in this field" about how to simplify marriage practices. Another article asserted that "the cost of birthday presents and the frequency of birthday parties have grown out of proportion," with the result that young Mashadi children are being taught "values we may not want them to learn."

BAHMAN KAMALI has never seen Mashad, but he is an ardent Mashadi. He was born in Tehran in 1951, and—according to what he was told as a child—he was one of the first ten Mashadi babies delivered after the community's migration to the capital. After high school, he came to the United States in 1969[7] to study at the University of Buffalo, obtaining both his bachelor's degree in mathematics and his master's in statistics and probability within four years. During the academic year, Kamali, whose nickname soon became Bob, lived in the dormitories and mixed mostly with other Iranian students. In the summertime, along with hundreds of other young Mashadi who would converge from the universities where they were studying around the United States, he would come to Kew Gardens, share a group apartment, and work as a waiter to help finance his education. "Even though our parents were wealthy enough, we didn't like to bring money from Iran to spend here," he explains. "It was worth ten times as much there."

[7] There were very few places available in Iran's universities, compared to the large number of people graduating from high school, during the period of the shah's modernizing reforms—perhaps two thousand spots for 10,000 applicants each year. The only alternative for most young men not admitted to a university was military service, but beginning in 1969, the shah liberalized the rules governing permission to study overseas. Anyone who could pass an English examination and could afford to go applied to an American university. The shah apparently felt this would ease some of the pressures in Iranian society, while building a cadre of well-trained young people who would return home and help develop the economy. But one unintended side effect was that it also created a vocal, well-educated Iranian opposition overseas, especially in the United States. Whether opposed to the shah or not, very few of the Iranian Jewish students who studied abroad returned home to stay.

Just as he was beginning to study toward a doctorate, Kamali had an opportunity to become involved in the oriental rug trade. A cousin in New York who was going back to Iran for a visit one summer gave him rugs on consignment to sell in Buffalo, and he enjoyed considerable success. Soon he had dropped out of school and, in a business he established with his older brother, Barry, who had preceded him to America, he was traveling across the country, buying up used rugs from transient American households for resale in the European market.

By 1977 Bob Kamali was in a comfortable enough position to return to Iran (for only the second time since 1969) and look for a wife. As a successful twenty-six-year-old entrepreneur, he would be regarded as a good catch. Indeed, he left for Tehran in June and returned to New York with Ruth, his nineteen-year-old Mashadi bride, on August 25, after a quick honeymoon in Europe. This was a business transaction of sorts, and it took place according to the time-honored Mashadi guidelines. They became engaged soon after they met, and were married a week later. "At that time, each of the boys in my age group who went back had about ten or fifteen choices of girls to marry," Kamali recalls. "Ruth was recommended to me by a few different people. I stopped in London on the way, and a Mashadi there even told me about her. I had never seen her before, but I knew her parents and family. I even knew her grandfather." In fact, the couple's great-grandfathers had been brothers and, as in most Mashadi marriages, the families were well known to each other. (On a family tree prepared by his grandfather-in-law that goes back 240 years, Kamali says, he is personally acquainted with "99 percent" of those who are still alive.) About 650 people attended their ceremony in a Mashadi synagogue and the lavish party that followed in a Muslim club on a Tehran mountaintop—by all accounts, a small affair compared to the Mashadi weddings that now take place in America.

Back in New York, as the rug trade dwindled (in part because of the Iranian revolution), Kamali and some of his uncles, who had arrived in the 1979 wave, started up a leather business on Manhattan's West Side. In 1984 they began importing cowhides from South America and processing them for the manufacturers of clothing, belts, handbags, and shoes. Their fifth-floor office on West Twenty-ninth Street is a warren of cubicles where employees (mostly Asians) pore over stacks of purchase orders and budget printouts. In a large open area at the back stand tall piles of brightly colored leather pelts that have been shipped in by subcontractors in upstate New York.

Kamali, a bald, heavyset man who moves and speaks quickly, and his wife Ruth, who wears an eternally optimistic expression, now have four children. These days they put much of their time and energy into the Concerned Mashadi Parents Association (CMPA), an organization Bob Kamali started with his brother Barry and four other men out of concern that as Mashadi children become more Americanized, they will reject their religious and historical legacy. The group has proposed building a Mashadi community center on Long Island where there would be organized social and athletic activities for various age groups. Many Mashadi parents feel torn about which of two school systems— yeshivas, or religious schools, run by Ashkenazi Jews or secular, public schools—would be a more appropriate place to send their children. Because some believe that both are inadequate, the CMPA has talked about starting its own religious school system specifically for Mashadi youth.

In the meantime, the group holds "parent effectiveness training" workshops and sponsors lectures by psychologists about how to handle growing parent-child conflicts that the Mashadi tend to blame on the permissiveness in American society. "Growing up in an autocratic society back in Iran makes it very difficult for us to understand how our children are behaving sometimes," says Barry Kamali, who immigrated in 1965. "We have to educate ourselves about democracy here, and mutual respect." Ruth Kamali, his sister-in-law, agrees: "We judge our kids a lot. In Iran, you raised your voice to a child, and that was it, because they didn't see any other options. Here, because of the liberal rules, they see other options. They say, 'I'm going to leave the house.' And parents feel, 'I must keep them in the family, but how?' We cannot use the same methods that were used in Iran. We have to find new ways to handle the situation, and it's not easy. It takes a lot of reading and support and reminding."

Bob Kamali's favorite model of a Sephardic group that has kept its values and maintained its solidarity is the Halabi Jewish community, most of whom came to the United States from the Syrian city of Aleppo before tougher immigration quotas were enacted in the 1920s. Far more numerous than the American Mashadi (perhaps 30,000 today) but equally obscure, they are still concentrated in Brooklyn and have experienced relatively few defections from their close-knit ranks.

Kamali has led delegations to spend Sunday afternoons in Brooklyn with Halabi leaders, in order to try to understand their success. Like the Mashadi, they tend to live near each other and to do business together, in their case mostly in electronics and textiles. But Kamali has come away convinced that "certain measures" taken by the Halabi have made the difference among their children: separate schools, an exclusive community center, and a rabbinical proclamation, which he calls "a most wonderful thing," that the Halabi elders first issued in February 1935. Kamali, who acknowledges being somewhat obsessed with these issues, waves the blue document in the air before showing it to me. It declares straightforwardly that anyone who marries a non-Jew will be immediately expelled from the Halabi community; in the strictest Halabi families, unmarried children are still required to reaffirm their commitment and sign a copy of it every year.[8] In an era when, Kamali claims, "we see fifty-seven percent assimilation overall between Jews and non-Jews," he believes the Mashadi should consider implementing something similar.[9]

In retrospect, Bob Kamali finds it frightening how close he himself came to abandoning his traditions in his youth. If he had not gone back to Iran to marry, or if five or ten more years had passed before so many of the Mashadi came to America, he speculates, "I would have been established here, and I would have been definitely lost, because I didn't care so much at the time. I could have easily stayed in Buffalo for the rest of my life. I loved Buffalo. I had friends there, and I got used to it." He finds comfort in the continuity that preserves the bonds of the Mashadi from one generation to another. "Some friends I have today, our children are in the same class, and our fathers were in the same class in Mashad," he notes. "So when you know your fathers were friends and your children are friends, that kind of gives you a special closeness to each other."

IF SPLITS are looming among the Mashadi, as inevitably they are, the grounds are not the usual ones that might be expected among American immigrant groups. It is one thing that some of the younger people, who have learned to respect democracy, object to the fact that Shaare Tova

[8] *Efforts to convert to Judaism, says the original 1935 Halabi declaration (taking a much harder line than most other Jewish communities or congregations), are "absolutely invalid and worthless." It goes on: "We have therefore bestirred ourselves to build and establish an Iron Wall to protect our identity and religious integrity and to bolster the strong foundations of our faith and religious purity which we have maintained for many centuries going back to our country of origin, Syria." A subsequent "clarification" issued in 1946 stresses that a "convert" or anyone married to one is not entitled to attend services in Halabi congregations or to be buried in the community's cemetery. The proclamation was reaffirmed again in 1972 and then at a special convocation in 1984, when it was signed by representatives of some thirty-five synagogues, schools, and organizations "of the Syrian and Near Eastern Jewish communities of Greater New York and New Jersey."*

[9] *Numbers that purport to measure the rate of assimilation among ethnic and religious groups in America are approximate at best. According to the Jewish Information and Referral Service, Kamali's estimate is high and the actual figure is closer to 52 percent.*

does not bother to hold elections for its board every three years, as its bylaws seem to require. (At one point, the sitting board apparently kept itself in office for seven years without elections, and it was said that some members actually controlled more than one vote on controversial matters. Among the signs of unrest is the fact that another new organization, the Mashadi Outreach Association (known as MORA, which means "teacher" in Hebrew), was formed to promote more intensive education in the community around the general Jewish heritage, traditions, and practices, rather than just retelling the heroic Mashadi story.

But far more significant is the emergence of a sizable dissident group of Mashadi, mostly young people, who feel that the older generation and the community's establishment are not religiously observant enough. Indeed, the issue most likely to provoke a heated debate within any group of Mashadi today is how fully the sabbath (or Shabbat in Hebrew) must be honored. Although the Mashadi in Tehran followed Sephardic patterns and practices that essentially correspond to Orthodox Judaism, they routinely drove to the synagogue and ate meals in their favorite restaurants without worrying excessively about dietary restrictions; the same has generally been true of the Mashadi in America. But the young people who have become *shomer shabbat,* or more strictly observant of the Shabbat, believe, for example, that religious Jews should never ride or otherwise travel on Saturdays or important holidays. They refrain even from turning on electricity on those occasions, and at all times they insist on eating only food that can be certified kosher. There is talk that some have found even their own parents' homes and practices wanting, from a religious point of view. Skeptical elders trace this attitude to a particular Ashkenazi-run yeshiva in Queens that many young Mashadi women have attended.

For Caroline Kordmany, this has become a major concern. As a young child and the daughter of the shah's import-export commissioner in Tehran, Caroline lived in a very secular, assimilated environment; in fact, she attended a Muslim school, studied the Koran, and learned Arabic. Having attended a yeshiva from the time she arrived in America, she is now very devout about respecting the Sabbath. Because she lives in Great Neck, she refuses to travel to Shaare Tova for weekly or holiday services, and she will not eat at the restaurants patronized by many of her peers. "That means I can't hang out with them on Saturdays, and the guys just don't go for that," she says. It is a subject on which she can be quite emotional: "They think I'm too observant, supposedly. But at least I can almost ensure that my kids will be Jewish, for another generation. Their kids, I can almost guarantee, will not be

Jewish. These people will become totally assimilated. Their children will lose all traditional values, and they're bound to intermarry."

But Kordmany says she feels terrible conflict over the issue. When she spent a summer in Israel, as a children's counselor in a program for religiously observant Ashkenazim, she says, "I felt really out of place. I wondered, 'Why am I here? What's my future?' For some reason, I understand the Mashadi people better. If they tell me small things, or hint at something, I just get it right away. It's like one huge family. But I think they're losing their values, in a way, their sense of identity. They're trying to be much more Americanized than before. They're not thinking of the future. They're thinking of the now-and-here, and it's comfortable for them, because they're being accepted by the outside world. They're living in Great Neck and driving their Mercedes, and they're fine. But that's not going to secure a future for their kids. Certainly not as Mashadi Jews—I'm not sure as Jews, even."

As separate as the Mashadi may seem to an outsider, it is not separate enough for Kordmany and some of her friends. What they would like to do is to keep the Mashadi together by bringing more of them in their own, more deeply religious and observant, direction. "What's wrong with being separate?" she asks. "Everyone's trying to make us part of the melting pot. But why be a part of this system that is called America? We're fine citizens, we're okay, we vote, we're not dangerous or anything, so I think it's okay to have some sense of identity in our community. Of course, it takes more effort because you're going against the trend. It's going to be hard, but I hope the fruits will make it worthwhile."

But in an article she called "Truth or Dare," in the "youth supplement" of the January 1994 issue of *Megillah,* Debbie Hakimian, a Mashadi teenager, took a different view and, in the process, confronted a number of delicate discontents felt by some of her peers. "Being part of a community has always reassured me that even when I'm on my own I'm not alone. It's the backbone of our existence. Growing up as Mashadi teenagers gives us a feeling of structure, security, and shelter that not many teenagers have," she wrote. But she went on: "Unfortunately, the community has changed from a comforting, familiar environment to a group of clones. If the youth of our community were all robots, life would be perfect. . . . But we are human beings and cannot be trained to think and feel a certain way. . . . No one knows how much ingenuity could be hidden in the minds of Mashadi youth. Unless we are allowed to grow, no one will ever know." By pushing their children into their businesses, she said, "Our parents are not only depriving us, but also society, of our possible achievements. It is not an injustice for our parents to attempt to remain uniform, but it is an injustice to force us to follow in their footsteps."

"The Mashadi community views its female youth in a very backward way. Women are treated as if they cannot take on any responsibility," Hakimian argued. "These male dominating views are not only backward but also detrimental to the mental well-being of modern Mashadi girls. They are taught in school that women and men are equal and then come home to a household with different sets of rules for the two sexes." She also took on the issue of materialism: "The Mashadi community has placed so much value on wealth that it has lost sight of the people behind the dollar sign. What is more important to us, love or money? . . . We must learn to choose our friends based on who they are, not what they're worth. Simply being set financially doesn't insure a lifetime of contentment."

Worrying in print that her views would be dismissed as those of a "rebellious teenager," Hamikian insisted it was "love for the community" that had caused her to speak out. "I want the community to thrive and [I] know that it won't, unless our parents compromise their values and acknowledge the fact that we are not only Mashadis, but also Americans. . . . You can either move on through life, pretending not to see what is right in front of your eyes, or you can do something to try and adapt our community to the contemporary needs of a generation of American-born Mashadi teenagers."

How these tensions are handled will have a great deal to do with the future of the Mashadi in America. In the long term, Abraham Dilmanian predicts sadly, "the community will be divided into two groups. Those who become completely observant will be easily absorbed into the Orthodox Ashkenazi community, and those who are not so observant face the danger of eventual assimilation with non-Jewish people. Their children go to public schools, and they will drift away. It will take many generations and it will happen gradually—there will be some groups that stay together—but the Mashadi community will eventually disappear."

THAT BREAKUP of the Mashadi community hardly seems imminent, judging from a visit to Shaare Tova on the evening of Purim, the quintessential Iranian Jewish festival, when three or four generations of many families came together for a gala celebration. Here I easily found people in their twenties who unquestioningly accepted the community's practices and rules, including some who told stories of being almost "born-again" Mashadi, of finding new meaning in their lives through loyal adherence to the group's traditions.

Avisar Levy, for example, twenty-seven years old, was born in New York, the first of four sons of a Mashadi couple who emigrated from Israel to Kew Gardens, where they became part of a very small, early Mashadi community in the 1960s. He says, "I grew up basically with Americans"—a term he uses to refer to the Ashkenazi Jews with whom he went to a yeshiva. "I always knew I was different because I was Sephardic, but I didn't know what it meant to be Mashadi. I knew it was a Persian heritage of some sort. But around the time Khomeini came into power, all of a sudden there was an influx of relatives I had never seen before." He found their history and traditions meaningful, their closeness and warmth quite appealing. Now, having graduated from Queens College, Levy works with two of his brothers in his father's diamond business (the fourth son is still in high school), and he says he spends almost all of his spare time with other Mashadi.

Unlike many of his more Americanized counterparts, Levy still lives with his parents while he looks for the right Mashadi woman to marry. "I just didn't move away, because I had no reason to," he says. "I enjoy myself, I enjoy my friends and everybody around me." He explains in a slightly confidential tone that most young Mashadi couples, while they may continue to pretend to let their parents arrange their marriages, actually exercise far more judgment of their own today than they used to. "We tend to go out more, meet more girls, and try to get to know each other a little bit more" before making a decision, he says; but then they usually allow their parents to call the shots about the ceremonies and the rituals. He adds that, "I'll always consider myself Mashadi. I don't know if I'll always live amongst them, but I do know that I hold the community very dear to me."

"I'm possibly the least Mashadi person you'll come by," says Jonathan Aminoff, who feels self-conscious about the fact that at twenty-one, he is just beginning to learn Farsi and to socialize with people in the community of his own age. He grew up in Forest Hills, the child of Mashadi immigrants from England and India, but in his deeply religious schooling, he says, "I was always around Ashkenazis and Americans. I didn't know any Mashadi children, and I didn't realize the values my parents were passing on to me were actually Mashadi values." Pressed to define those values, he says they include being "very family oriented and never disrespectful to your parents. Being around your parents, talking to them, and always eating dinner together is very important—doing special things with them, going out together with your family to events sometimes." Now that he has been drawn into the Mashadi circle and met more people of his own generation, he says, he has found "a very bonding friendship. It's hard to explain, but there is a greater warmth than with my American Ashkenazi friends." He appreciates the way Mashadis speak —"they use their hands and their eyes," he says—and what he perceives as their more complex ways of expressing themselves than other people. He insists that "you have to dig deeper to understand what they mean." His only worry is whether he will be able to find an appropriate "Mashadi girl" to marry when he is ready.

Aminoff, who plans to become a stockbroker after graduating from Queens College rather than entering his father's jewelry business, has given virtually all of his free time for several years to Hatzolah, a volunteer ambulance service for New York City staffed entirely by Orthodox Jews. In order to be accepted as a Hatzolah volunteer, he explains, "You have to be religious and a Sabbath observer. You have to know what you can and cannot do under Jewish law—how to treat a woman and preserve her modesty, what guidelines can and cannot be violated on the Sabbath. Of course, we do operate on Saturdays. Judaism states that to save a person's life is the most important thing." Aminoff is proud of the fact that although the Mashadi have not tended to participate in such projects in the past, they recently donated a $100,000 ambulance to Hatzolah. He hopes now that he can help persuade them to become more involved.

And so went the refrain. Neda Behnam, twenty-seven, immigrated to New York from Iran with her mother early in 1978, catching up with her father, who had come two years earlier, and a grandmother who had already been in the United States for several decades. Her husband is in the jewelry business, but she has branched out, with her sister, into making and selling gift baskets. Some 80 percent of their customers are Mashadi, and they filled 120 orders at the Purim celebration alone. Behnam says that her mother-in-law objected strenuously at first to her departing from the traditional Mashadi woman's role of homemaker but has finally come around. ("She said, 'You don't need to work, so why do it? It doesn't look nice.' She didn't understand that working is not just for making money, but also for satisfaction.")

"I enjoy being part of this community," Behnam says. "It gives me a good sense of belonging. There were times as a teenager when I was ashamed of being Persian, with all the things that were going on in Iran, but I was never ashamed of being a Mashadi. Many Tehranis and other people envy how united we are, the way we get along together."

Gabriel Livian, also twenty-seven, was born in Italy and came to Kew Gardens in 1980. He buys and sells emeralds in his family's business. Still living with his parents, he goes on Sundays to play basketball and volleyball with an exclusively Mashadi crowd at a gym on Long Island reserved especially for them during certain hours. "I'm proud of being Mashadi," he says matter-of-factly. "My parents want me to marry a Mashadi because it's more secure. The community likes to stay together. They feel safer, especially now with AIDS and all that."

Even Jackie Kamali, Barry's son and Bob's nephew, has well-formulated views on this issue at age sixteen. Although he goes to Great Neck South High School with a great mixture of people from different backgrounds, he says he spends almost all of his free time with other Mashadi. "I think it's understood that I have to stay inside the community all my life," he says. "But I don't think there's any reason why I shouldn't. I like the friendly atmosphere. Everyone's very close, everyone knows each other. Our family sees each other very often, and I like it. My American friends, they don't have a community that they belong to. They just live their own lives, and they're not very close with their families. I feel obligated to stay with the community, but it's a good obligation."

Jackie's dilemma now is whether to go away to college, as he is tempted to do, and perhaps to go as far as Chicago. "If you're gone for four years, it's like everyone's inside the community and you're not. You can start being kind of like an outcast. Being away for four years would be a long time."

FOR AN OUTSIDER, the attitude of the Mashadi Jews and the far more numerous Tehrani Jews in the United States toward one another is at once incomprehensible and almost comical. Saeed Amirian, known commonly as "Steve," is a non-Mashadi who came from Tehran in 1969 to study in the United States and stayed; he now owns a silver-plating company in Manhattan. It does not take much to provoke him into complaining about the Mashadi. "It is a known fact," he says, "that they are less attractive physically, compared to non-Mashadis. This comes about because they have been marrying amongst themselves for the past two or three hundred years." Furthermore, he insists, Mashadi are uncouth—"they speak very loudly, and they don't have basic, fundamental society etiquette. In Great Neck, they double park their cars just to talk to each other. They stop traffic. They have no regard for normal society, for the law of the land."

Amirian says he admires the Mashadi for their generosity to each other and to outside groups in need, but he resents the fact that they seem to hold themselves aloof from and above other Jewish groups. "They don't want to mingle with us, or let our children marry their daughters or sons. They look down at us. We are not worthy enough for them," he says, insisting that Tehranis would probably be refused membership at Shaare Tova if they were to apply. He tells the story of a wealthy young Mashadi man who refused to marry a Mashadi woman but was denied permission by his parents to marry any non-Mashadi Iranian Jew. In protest, according to Amirian, "he married a Swedish girl. You see what can happen."

A young Mashadi woman—who preferred to be quoted anonymously—acknowledges that Mashadis may be unconsciously rude to others when they get together in large groups, but she insists that it is really the Tehranis who cause problems. "I feel like the Tehranis are a little jealous of us, because they are not as pretty as the Mashadis. We have fairer skin, and we're more elegant people," she says bluntly. "They are loud and tacky, in the way they dress and the way they carry themselves. They're less natural, with a lot of makeup and dyed blond hair. We dance similar dances, but when we dance, we are more graceful." She goes on: "The Teheranis probably find us very dry and icy, cold, without emotion, because of the way we are. We're very lacking in sensuality, I guess, for them. But for me, looking at them, I see them as showy and loud, just too tacky. I have some Tehrani friends that I like, but overall, I dislike them."

Amirian, who has never been to a Mashadi wedding or other celebration, believes that it is time for the various Iranian Jewish groups to try to have more of a dialogue, and he has become involved with an ecumenical organization called the Sephardic Heritage Alliance, Inc. (SHAI). "We say, 'Let's be together, we are in America, we have one common enemy—American culture!' " he explains, raising his voice. Thus far, the Mashadi have not been terribly responsive.

Occasionally, a new recruit actually manages to penetrate the Mashadi community. Take Sam Ahronoff, for example, whose parents' Russian Jewish families were expelled by the communists from Tashkent, the capital of Uzbekistan, in the 1920s. As he puts it, "they walked over the mountains and when they came to Afghanistan, they stayed there for forty years." During that time they were merchants in Kabul, until they immigrated to the United States in 1968, when Sam was eleven years old. He lived in Queens as a boy, but after high school and college, he moved into Manhattan. There, he says, "for many years I was completely out of the religion." But then Ahronoff made some friends who got him interested in Judaism again and introduced him to a Mashadi woman. Apparently, he checked out fine. They were married in the late 1980s, and by that time, he says, he had become Orthodox in his beliefs and practices. Now he works (in a family business importing colored stones from Thailand, India, and Sri Lanka) and lives almost entirely among the Mashadi, who he says have warmly welcomed him into their community. "I just got lucky. I guess you can say it was love, and being in the right place at the right time," says Ahronoff with a good-natured smile. "The Mashadi are very hardworking people. They're shrewd and smart. Unity is important to them. And I feel very much like an insider."

And then there are insiders who feel smothered and try to get out, or at least to live as individuals on the fringe of the Mashadi community. That is the situation of Behrooz Hakimian and his daughter Sheida. Up to a point, their story is like many other Mashadi sagas: He came to study at the University of Illinois in the late 1960s and later went back to Tehran to take a Mashadi wife who met his family's requirements. But rather than moving to New York, they settled in Saint Louis, Missouri, where there was a retail branch of the Hakimian family's carpet business and his older brother, married to "an American" of Ashkenazi Jewish background, was already living. As Sheida, who was born in 1971, puts it, her parents "integrated, but they didn't assimilate. They didn't compromise who they were." The family lived in a wealthy Saint Louis suburb but spoke Farsi at home; they attended an all-American Conservative synagogue.

Sheida, the eldest of three sisters, recalls a childhood fraught with conflict and stress. At school, during the Iran hostage crisis, she was called a "terrorist." Meanwhile, at home every Friday night an extended family of thirty or so people would gather for Shabbat dinner. "At the end of the night, the men in the family would gamble, play poker for money," she recalls. "I had a neighbor who would come over, and I sensed that she was afraid of it all. She heard people talking a different language, and she saw us kissing each other on both cheeks and showing our emotions a lot." Sheida eventually made friends in the larger world, and after high school she went off to study at Boston University. During her first year away, her mother died of leukemia at the age of thirty-nine.

A year later, Sheida's grief-stricken father moved with his other daughters to New York, so they could have the support of his late wife's family. They settled in a Long Island neighborhood where many other Mashadi lived. Now, when Sheida came home from college and after she graduated, she was suddenly surrounded by Mashadi, who had their own ideas about how a young woman should lead her life. In dealing with her mother's death, she had come to accept some of the more secular-oriented principles of Reform Judaism. "As far as going to the synagogue and being religious, it was all out the window," she says. And she did not care to be told what she could wear to the grocery store. As a member of a prominent, respected Mashadi family, she was stunned to receive phone calls asking whether she would consider marrying men she had hardly met.

Today Sheida helps her father run the Global Rug Corporation, the wholesale part of the family business, on Manhattan's far West Side. She is launching an export operation to Mexico, where she has traveled alone, despite the disapproval of extended family and friends. A second daughter has gone off to college on her own. Even worse, Behrooz Hakimian is dating a Tehrani woman, whom his daughters appear to like. "The problem is," says Sheida, "there's no in-between. You're either in all the way, or you're out. They won't accept you for just half the time." There are many things she still admires about Mashadi customs, she insists, including the persistent family closeness and the abnormally low divorce rate. "But there's so many things I want to do, so many dreams I have, and if I don't marry somebody outside the community, I won't have the opportunity to do those things. I want to travel, have my own business, and work on Shabbat, but these things just aren't acceptable," she adds. "I'm proud of my culture, my language, and my people. But if they can't accept me for who I am, I don't want to compromise my beliefs and conform just for the sake of everyone else."

Sheida Hakimian, age twenty-two, looks out from her father's office over a sea of rugs made in India and Pakistan, and she sighs deeply. "Change is inevitable for the Mashadi, it's like a law of nature," she says. "But I don't think it will happen in my lifetime."

PART FOUR

THE POLITICS OF IMMIGRATION

AMERICA IS constantly reinventing and redesigning itself. That is supposed to be part of its charm. But in the area of immigration policy, the order of the day is more often confusion. Congress, in particular—usually in response to lobbying by various special interests, but occasionally on its own—is forever changing the rules and fixing the problems it created the time before. In the 1980s and 1990s, many new categories of immigrant were created. There were now special visas for rich people who wanted, say, to leave Hong Kong before the British turned it over to the Chinese. Because they were thought to be in short supply among native-born Americans, certain professions were favored—until, that is, they came to be in greater supply than seemed desirable. Students could stay on for "practical training." Others might come as au pairs. The Amerasian children of GIs who served in Vietnam obtained a special preference.

And then there was the visa lottery—at once the most charming and confusing innovation of all—designed to help rediversify the immigrant stream by admitting nationalities regarded as desirable but who had not been coming in such large numbers anymore. In Chapter XII, I describe the experience of one especially favored group, the Irish, with the lottery.

Concurrent with these attempts to loosen the rules, a new anti-immigrant sentiment has emerged in various sectors of American politics and society. Conservatives worried about the threat of multiculturalism and bilingual education are in a tacit alliance with African Americans who have become convinced that many immigrants succeed only at their expense. I describe this unusual coalition and some of its historical precedents in Chapter XIII. Finally, in Chapter XIV, I offer some of my own observations about the moral and practical implications of the recent hysteria over illegal and legal immigration and suggest a few changes in policy and enforcement.

XII
PLAYING THE ODDS:
THE VISA LOTTERY AND
THE LUCK OF THE IRISH

EVERETT, MASSACHUSETTS

ON A THURSDAY evening in September, the lights are burning after hours in the 1950s-era city hall, and it is not because of some contentious city council meeting. On the contrary, about half a dozen activist city employees have stayed on and, joined by other community volunteers, are helping with a "visa clinic" sponsored by the Irish Immigration Center in nearby Boston. In a large open room stands a long table with a row of electric typewriters spaced a few feet apart. Behind each typewriter sits an impromptu counselor and across the table a folding chair. On another table off to the side are coffee, tea, and doughnuts. The photo-copying machine is humming away nonstop, and there is an extra large supply of white business envelopes and first-class postage stamps.

The clients for this service have all taken numbers, and they form an orderly line that snakes down the corridor and out into the street of this bedroom community. They are mostly Irish—but also, in a few cases tonight, Italian, Argentine, or Lithuanian—and they all have one thing in common: They are applying for U.S. permanent resident visas (green cards) under a special lottery to be conducted a few weeks later by the State Department and the INS under rules dictated by Congress. These are known, in the vernacular of the immigration business, as "Morrison visas" (for Bruce Morrison, a former Democratic representative from Connecticut who sponsored the legislation establishing this exercise), as distinct from the "Berman visas" and "Donnelly visas" (for Congressmen Howard Berman from California and Brian Donnelly from Massachusetts, respectively) that were the prizes in prior lotteries. The idea this time is to make available forty thousand extra immigrant slots a year for three years to people from thirty-four "adversely affected countries and areas" whose citizens used to come in large numbers to live legally in the United States, but due to changes in the law and in migration patterns, no longer do so. With a few notable exceptions, the winners will be mostly white, reasonably well educated people from places other than Mexico, Central America, the Caribbean, Asia, or Africa. There is nothing subtle about the discrimination inherent in this process; it is a candid effort to dilute the current immigrant stream with some more traditional participants. Only people from certain countries may apply.[1]

But there is another kicker here: extra special treatment for the Irish, who, thanks to their friends and fellow ethnics on Capitol Hill, are guaranteed to receive fully 40 percent—or sixteen thousand—of the "Morrisons." Whereas people from Ireland once made up a very substantial and consistent percentage of American immigrants, they seem recently to have had a harder time gaining legal status, with fewer being admitted under special employment categories or as family members of U.S. citizens. This is an official opportunity to begin making up for that disadvantage and deficit.

Not that it would be any easier to win this lottery than the Irish Sweepstakes. Even from the limited list of eligible countries, hundreds of thousands, if not millions, of people will apply. Boundaries and jurisdictions mean a great deal in these matters, so it is not clear whether applicants from Northern Ireland, which is officially part of the United Kingdom, will enjoy the same extra break as those from the Irish Republic. And the procedures, in any event, are complex, confusing, and ever shifting. At first, for example, every applicant had to produce in advance a letter from an American employer guaranteeing him or her a job of at least a year's duration. The requirement of the letter, eminently vulnerable to fraud and corruption, has recently been eliminated, although evidence of a job offer will still be necessary to finalize a Morrison visa for anyone lucky enough to be selected.

---

[1] *The official list of countries and territories whose citizens were eligible to apply in the 1991 lottery included Albania, Algeria, Argentina, Austria, Belgium, Bermuda, Czechoslovakia, Denmark, Estonia, Finland, France, Germany, Gibraltar, Great Britain, Guadeloupe, Hungary, Iceland, Indonesia, Ireland, Italy, Japan, Latvia, Liechtenstein, Lithuania, Luxembourg, Monaco, Netherlands, New Caledonia, Norway, Poland, San Marino, Sweden, Switzerland, and Tunisia.*

There is no limit on how many copies of the same application can be submitted by a single individual in different envelopes, but to have a chance at being successful, any envelope must get to a particular post office box address in the Virginia suburbs of Washington, D.C., and arrive only between two specific dates in October a week apart. Those that come too early or too late will be thrown away by the outside contractor hired by the government to manage the affair. It is commonly assumed that when the magic moment does arrive, all forty thousand special visas available will be spoken for in a matter of a few hours, if not minutes. But then, some wonder: Might all the applications be held for a week, and then forty thousand drawn at random, in true lottery style? How would duplicate winners be replaced? Will the odds be improved if one mails multiple copies of an application from different locations in the same city, or from different cities, or only from the Washington area? If someone from Northern Ireland does get lucky, must she go all the way to London to pick up her visa, or could she get it in Belfast, or even Dublin? These are the kinds of questions being asked at the clinic, but no one seems to have definitive answers.

Theoretically, as Congress intended it, most of the applications for these visas would come directly from Ireland and other points overseas, where deserving individuals had presumably been frustrated by a years-long backlog and had tired of standing in endless lines at American consulates with no result. Surely some of the people entering the lottery would actually fit that profile, but the nasty little secret, known by all who think about it (including those who drafted the legislation), is that the overwhelming majority of the Morrison applicants would almost certainly be people already in the United States, either illegally or on student or other temporary visas that offer no long-term security.[2] Vast numbers of men and women living in the shadow of the law throughout America suddenly perceive a chance, however remote, to solve their problems with unanticipated ease but are baffled by the tangle of regulations they must follow. Thus arises the need for workshops like this one. Here they will get lots of advice and possibly a bit of comfort, all for the price of the stamps and the photocopying.

Even if no applications at all came in the mail from overseas, there would be plenty of Irish applicants from within the United States to soak up their own generous quota in the lottery several times over. By the most reliable estimates available to the Irish Consulate General in

[2] *In the end, the State Department reported that 75 percent of the applications had been mailed from within the United States, but many of those may have come from people living overseas.*

Boston, with unemployment in Ireland reaching 18 percent, there were close to 40,000 undocumented Irish workers in the United States at any given time in the early 1990s, the bulk of them living in New England (with a special concentration in the Boston area) or New York, and still more coming all the time. They have jobs—at least in good economic times—on construction sites and in factories, restaurants, bakeries, offices, and private homes. They assiduously avoid welfare and other forms of public assistance, lest they be labeled "public charges" (who are automatically excludable under immigration law). Some are married and have children in public or parochial schools. These people are, for the most part, already well settled into American life and would find it materially and psychologically difficult to return to live in Ireland. Indeed, going home to stay is not even an option they seriously consider.

They might not fit most people's standard image of illegal aliens, since they so resemble the physical stereotype of the ordinary, average white American, but the daily lives of many of these young Irish men and women have much in common with those of, say, undocumented Mexicans in Los Angeles. They tend to work on the margins of the official economy and are sometimes exploited. They live in difficult, occasionally overcrowded conditions, and often feel they must go about their business furtively, in order to avoid detection. They are intimidated, and yet impudent and sometimes imprudent, too. But they are, for the most part, law-abiding members of their community. And they have to worry that if they try to go home too often to visit their family, one time they may not get back in, and thus would be denied their only forseeable livelihood.

"THIS IS a very unusual situation for Irish people," says Lena Deavy, director of the Irish Immigration Center, in her own thick brogue. A nurse by training, she is a member of the Sisters of the Assumption, an antiestablishment religious order that works in poor communities in Ireland and abroad. While studying for a master's degree in education at Harvard, she became interested in the problems of the young undocumented Irish in Boston. Eventually, on the strength of her own temporary work visa, she decided to stay on and try to help them. "For the vast majority, probably the only offense they ever committed was to run a traffic light," Deavy says, "and suddenly they're living in a position where technically they're breaking the law."

The obvious expectation is that Boston, home of the Kennedys and countless other successful Irish American families, would be a hospitable place for anyone arriving from Ireland—all the more so because the Irish once suffered such severe discrimination there at the hands of Yankees and other patricians. But, says Deavy, "some Irish Americans have a vision of Irish people that is very outmoded. They think of Ireland as a conservative and Catholic country, where young people grow up and dress a certain way and the girls act like nice innocent Irish colleens. I would say it is a vision of what Irish people were like about fifty years ago. [Those whose families have been here a long time] have difficulty understanding that Irish young people today have many of the same struggles, aspirations, and hopes as young people growing up in this country or in any other Western community. While it's still con- servative in many ways, Ireland has become much more open to influ- ence from America, England, and Europe."

In a word, Deavy says, there is a classical "generation gap" between the young Irish immigrants and the well-established, church-connected but sometimes haughty Irish American denizens of Boston, generally people whose families left Ireland in the mid- and late-nineteenth cen- tury. The newcomers—irreverent, quite likely countercultural in their orientation, and often boisterous—are seen as something of an embar- rassment by the more straitlaced old Boston Irish, not least because they are "illegal." They may even be lumped together as troublemakers with the people who do clandestine fund-raising for the terrorists of the Irish Republican Army. Therefore, they usually do not get much help from the Irish American establishment.

Jeffrey Keating, vice consul at the Irish Consulate General in Boston (which helps fund Deavy's center), sees the problem as even more com- plicated. He also perceives serious tensions between the young Irish im- migrants and another group of émigrés who left the same economically desolate areas of western Ireland after World War II, and especially in the 1950s, and have now achieved middle-class or lower-middle-class status in the United States. They are traditional-minded and very con- cerned to preserve what they have accumulated; they do not want to be confused with upstarts who live "illegal," and possibly even "immoral," lives. "The new Irish tend to be better educated, more cosmopolitan and sophisticated, even left-wing," Keating says. "They don't have a lot in common with the people who've been here for thirty years or so. They have different views on contraception and, to a lesser extent, abortion. And they're also more mobile. They've kept their connections at home much more successfully; they like to travel back and forth, to the extent that they can get away with it."

Keating observes that the young undocumented Irish workers seem more willing than earlier generations to mix with people from different backgrounds. "I do think that some older Irish people, especially Irish Americans, tend to be quite racist. They still make statements which surprise me," he says. "My impression is that the young Irish people who come here do not have as many hangups about color or race." If that is true, it certainly should make it easier for them to get along in the multiethnic communities around Boston where they tend to live.

Actually, says Lena Deavy, some of the Irish have it better than many other undocumented workers because they live at least a modified version of the idealized, all-American life of the "white and bright." She worries that "we Irish can be used to hold places, to prevent certain jobs from being given to people who don't speak English or who are not white." In hard economic times, the result can be conflict—potentially volatile and violent conflict—between the Irish and the Hispanics and African Americans who are essentially occupying the same socioeconomic niche.

Still, Deavy has a veritable catalogue of horror stories about the bad treatment some undocumented Irish workers receive—of contractors, families, and even volunteer agencies in the Boston area that take on vulnerable immigrant employees and eventually refuse to pay them, or pay them far less than originally agreed. Typically, an employer bent on exploitation never asks such a worker for a Social Security number or other documentation until several weeks have passed, and then feigns surprise upon being told that the person's papers are not in good order. This is usually followed by a refusal to pay the worker his anticipated salary, on the grounds that something has changed since the original agreement was made and that the employer is now at risk for hiring someone illegally. If the worker protests too vigorously, Deavy says, there may be "abusive phone calls and a whole process of intimidation. The employers assume that because the workers are undocumented, they have no rights and they won't report the situation. They play on their fears and threaten to turn them in to the INS." Meanwhile, the workers' rent and other bills may go unpaid.

In Massachusetts, however, there are legal protections for such workers, even those hired illegally. Through an organization called Immigrant Rights Advocacy, Training and Education (IRATE), Deavy and others involved with similar public-interest groups have sought to settle such disputes privately and amicably or, when necessary, have taken the offending employers before a state tribunal to force them to pay up. "In most cases," she says, "we've been successful in getting the money—but not before the [immigrants] have suffered a lot of stress."

It is the stress, in the end, that most preoccupies Deavy. "If people are in an undocumented state that lasts for three to five years, it has very serious psychological and emotional effects," she observes. "The first year can be like an adventure, especially for young people. There's a certain excitement about it, a certain kind of novelty. You're in a new country, the weather's much nicer, the lifestyle's better. And there's much more opportunity, in comparison with being unemployed in a very quiet rural area in Ireland. There's a great freedom."

But after a time, those who would like to settle down in America may find it difficult to do so, especially if they lose one of their several jobs. When they have extra time on their hands, Deavy says, they often head for "a place where there's a certain security for Irish people—the pub. One of our weaknesses is drink. When they're under stress, other people may turn to other things, but Irish people can more easily revert to drink. It's a way of dealing with their loneliness." As a result, there is a serious problem of alcohol abuse among the young Irish immigrants, just as there might be among the same people had they never left Ireland.

One of the most dreaded moments in Deavy's sixth-floor office near the Boston Common is getting the news that some undocumented Irish workers have been "lifted" by the INS. One day when I visited her, the center received an emergency call advising that agents had raided a factory in Maine where several young Irish men had been working illegally. The caller was immediately put in touch with a legal services center in Boston that could provide someone to explain to the arrested people about their rights under U.S. law. "If we can get to them in time, we tell them that they don't have to give information, that they can remain silent until they get an attorney," Deavy says. "And we advise them to take 'voluntary departure,' because that means they'll be able to come back again." Under the terms of voluntary departure, the immigrants must leave as soon as possible and pay for their own air tickets back to Ireland. The alternative is a formal deportation hearing before an immigration judge; if they lose in that proceeding, they may get a free ride home one time but are likely to be permanently banned from the United States.

MOST OF the people attending the Everett visa clinic seem utterly stable and securely employed or self-sufficient. Their stories are disarmingly simple. "I first came here on vacation in 1986," remembers Adele C., a twenty-seven-year-old woman from County Kerry in the southwest of Ireland, trying her luck in a visa lottery for the third time. "There's no jobs at home. I lived eight miles from the nearest town. All the young people try to leave, even those who graduate from college, because there's nothing there. I liked it here, so I came back to live in 1987. I came in on a tourist visa and just overstayed. They were giving out multiple-entry visas then, so it was easy. I went home once, and I was questioned for two hours on my return, but they couldn't prove that I was coming to work."

But work she did, first as a baby-sitter and then as a housekeeper. Now Adele is in business for herself, in the great American tradition, and she dispatches various people to clean houses around the Boston area. "We're already making a contribution to this country," she says with a grin, describing herself and her friends. "We're doing jobs that a lot of American people wouldn't do. They wouldn't lower their standards to baby-sit or to clean—things like that—but we're quite happy to do it." In her case, she is convinced, her income is no less than it would be if her status were normalized. One thing would be different, though: She says she would register her business with the Internal Revenue Service and pay the appropriate payroll taxes. "How can I pay taxes now," she asks rhetorically, "when I'm not really here?"

"There's nothing to fear about living this way, not unless you're pushing drugs or really being a nuisance to society. They don't bother you," says Adele. "It's been a great experience, really. It has broadened my mind. This is my first experience of being on my own. I had never lived away from home. Now I live in a Portuguese community in Somerville, and it's so different from Ireland." The only reason she keeps trying the visa lottery, she explains, is that "I'd be more comfortable with legal status, and knowing I could go home when I want to."

With Adele at the clinic is Claire C., a friend from Northern Ireland, who has also been in the United States without a legal visa for four years, working first as a waitress and then as a nanny for a Boston family. Her own family in Ireland has little objection to what she is doing, Claire says, because her father has long been in Boston in undocumented status himself. She has, in a sense, followed in his footsteps. (In fact, he is now applying for a visa in the same lottery.) "My mother is at home praying and lighting candles in the chapel," she says, "hoping that one of us gets a Morrison, so we can both become legal and go back to visit." (With a green card, either one, father or daughter, could then legally sponsor the other for permanent residence and, eventually, citizenship. Claire's mother, apparently, has no desire to immigrate but just wants to be able to visit, or be visited by, her family without having to fear the consequences.)

Then there is James Sheils, also twenty-seven, a university graduate from Dundalk, who has virtually lost his Irish accent during five years in the United States working in biotechnology laboratory and sales jobs. He is perfectly legal but has gone from one special work visa to another, until he has tired of the instability. "I'd love to get a green card," he says. "I'd love it more than life itself. I'm looking for a new job now, and if I find one, I'll have to apply for another H-1 visa to go with it. If I had a green card, I could do whatever I wanted—multiple jobs, whatever. I wouldn't be looking over my shoulder, waiting for my H-1 to run out and wondering what's going to happen. I'd like to stay here; I'm happy and I have a pretty good lifestyle. Australia's the only other option I've entertained, and I think I'm too old to start out there now."

James Whitmore, a clean-cut young man from Wexford, also enjoys the temporary security of a work visa that comes with his job as an English teacher in a Catholic school in Everett. But he too is trying for a Morrison, because he faces the constant worry of what would happen if he lost his job or decided he did not want it anymore. "I've made a good effort to stay legal," he says, "but to go home . . . there are no teaching jobs at all there."

By nine-thirty in the evening, the Everett city hall is quiet. David Mooney, deputy director of the Irish Immigration Center, counts up records on sixty-eight people who came for help—a disappointingly smaller turnout, he says, than at a similar, earlier clinic in Quincy, south of Boston. Yet he pronounces himself satisfied. Each person has gone away with nine copies of his or her application, plus nine preaddressed, stamped envelopes, with a home country clearly marked on the front, and instructions about when to mail them. A tenth copy of each application has been left behind for Mooney to send from Washington, when he travels there just before the actual lottery takes place. He and his volunteers turn out the lights, load their material into their beat-up cars, and head for an Irish pub in Dorchester to celebrate a small success within and yet against the system.

ON A SUNDAY morning a few weeks later, I catch up with Mooney again in Virginia, at a Quality Inn a mile or so from the post office where the lottery applications would be processed. With some Irish and Irish American helpers, he has brought down a very large quantity of mail from Boston and he is now participating in a kind of weekend-long festival of young immigrants, would-be immigrants, and their friends and sympathizers. At breakfast time, it is difficult to hear over the Irish-accented din in the hotel coffee shop. A jocular, charismatic figure,

Mooney cheerfully greets any member of his flock who comes by, and he joins in the latest uninformed speculation on what the lottery results will be. While he waits to lead a group on a tour of Washington's monuments, he cannot resist telling me the story of his own adventures settling in America.

"Before I came over, I had what was considered a decent job in Dublin, as a claims adjuster for an insurance company," says Mooney, who has a high school degree but never bothered to start a university education. "I just got bored with it. With the recession in Ireland, there's no hope, really, of promotion or changing jobs. Most people sort of accept the fact that when you get out of school and go into a company or a job, you stay there for the rest of your working life. I could see myself in Ireland, getting married, buying a house in the suburbs, having kids, growing old, being bored. I wanted something different. . . . I had planned my departure for a year. Then a friend of mine who'd lost his job said, 'I'm getting out of here, I'm going to America.' I had been to the States on holiday before, visiting my sister who was living in Seattle, so I decided to come along."

Mooney and his friend arrived in February 1986, settled in Santa Cruz, California—a choice they made purely on the basis of climate—and were immediately hired to work in a Mexican fast-food restaurant. When asked for a Social Security number, Mooney says, he jotted one down from a "wanted" poster in the local post office and just changed a few digits. "It was absolutely no problem," he recalls. "You didn't have to show a Social Security card or anything like that. As far as they were concerned, we had green cards. The average American doesn't understand the immigration system. It's foreigners who are the experts." (His friend later used three different Social Security numbers— all false—for a single job and never suffered any consequences.)

After nine months, the two Irishmen decided to go south, traveling in a broken-down old van they had bought in California for five hundred dollars. En route, Mooney learned an important lesson about stereotypes in America. "We were driving through Texas, when we were pulled over. We thought it was an agricultural checkpoint, where they want to see if you're transporting any food that could have medflies. We had no license, no insurance, no nothing." But the man in uniform turned out to be from the Border Patrol. "The guy asked us, 'Are you U.S. citizens?' We said, 'Yes.' 'Where are you going?' 'New Orleans.' 'Fine, go ahead.' It was all very low-key. We'd been in California, we had our tans. If we had looked Mexican, we would have been in trouble. But they weren't looking for white Europeans [to be here illegally]. And they didn't expect to find them in Texas."

Following a stint together in New Orleans, his friend returned to Ireland disenchanted, and Mooney was on his own. He headed straight for Boston, the legendary Irish American haven, and within two days he had found two jobs as a waiter, one by day and one by night. "I made more than enough money to live on," Mooney says, and, by then more respectful of official formalities, "I paid my taxes. There's a special code the undocumented are entitled to use on tax returns instead of a Social Security number. It just goes through as normal, no questions asked. There's no communication between the IRS and the INS." Never mind the fact that an Englishman had long since left the United States for Ireland using Mooney's name and the return portion of his air ticket (which Mooney had sold him); as he left, the Englishman had also turned in the stub of Mooney's U.S. tourist visa, thus eliminating any formal evidence that the young Irishman had overstayed the legal limit.

Working in Boston restaurants and living in group houses, Mooney made many American friends. At one point, he was asked to train a rookie waitress from New Hampshire, a young woman whom he discovered to be of Czechoslovakian, French Canadian, and Irish background. The next Saint Patrick's Day they were married in the function room of a hotel where she was then working. Four months later, Mooney had a provisional green card, valid for two years; once he could prove to the INS that his marriage had lasted that long and was not an immigrant's "marriage of convenience" of the sort fabled in the movies, he was entitled to a permanent visa and could begin the process of becoming a U.S. citizen.

Mooney took up immigration work himself after he was charged two hundred dollars for a one-hour consultation with a lawyer he had gone to see about applying for his green card. "That really pissed me off," he recalls, "so I decided to do it myself. I called the Irish Immigration Center for advice, and when they helped me, I thought, 'Hey, it would be good to volunteer for these guys.' I got more and more involved in the fund-raising end of things, and I found I had a bit of a knack for it." When the restaurant where he was working closed down, Mooney wrote a grant proposal to create an "outreach coordinator" for the immigration center. By this time a master of the American method, he got the grant and got the job.

Mooney now does something he believes in for a meager salary (which he supplements by working as a banquet waiter and doing housing-discrimination testing for a civil rights organization), while his wife earns a more substantial income as special-events coordinator for a Boston department store. He hopes to move on eventually to a career in politics. "Basically, I want to see what happens," he says. "In Ireland,

I know what would happen. I could tell you where I'd be in ten or twenty years. Here, it's constantly changing."

For now, "I am, in a way, trying to help people beat the system," says Mooney. "There is such a lack of education. At the time of the Donnelly visas, people thought it was some sort of INS trap, that if you sent in your name and address, the INS would come and get you. That's what I thought. . . . This time, one guy who was going back to Ireland gave me five hundred copies of his application to mail for him. The post office is making a fortune, and we're dealing with questions like whether you have to write 'USA' on the envelope."

AT THE APPOINTED MOMENT in October, there was an avalanche of entries in the lottery from the Irish—and from everyone else eligible—with plenty of jockeying for competitive advantage, real or imagined. Back in Ireland for a funeral, Lena Deavy actually persuaded the postal workers union to suspend a national strike for a day, just to let the lottery mail get out on time. Notwithstanding the implied damage to Ireland's national pride, anyone who makes it to America and stays is still regarded as something of a hero by those left back home.

On the night when the processing of applications was to begin, David Mooney and thousands of others with a similar mission converged on the Merrifield post office, on Prosperity Avenue in Falls Church, Virginia. At 7:00 P.M. there was a huge surge, and all that one could see was envelopes being thrown over the heads of a crowd estimated at 75,000 people, as three postal workers screamed at them in vain to form an orderly line.

The next morning, there was a party atmosphere in the sunshine on the rich green lawn in front of the post office—and a substantial police presence. By now people were standing in line, both to put mail into the post boxes and to use the portable toilets that had been brought in. Most carried backpacks, and many looked as if they had spent the night outdoors. They lounged in beach chairs or took photographs of each other to record their presence on this historic occasion. The INS, if it had decided to attempt a roundup of "illegals," could have had a field day (or risked a serious riot); but this was the immigrants' party, and no one was about to get in their way.

WHEN THIS PARTICULAR lottery was finished, the State Department reported that 9.3 million valid applications had been received during the official application period; another 7.5 million that arrived at the post office box too early and 2 million more that got there too late were automatically disqualified from consideration. This meant that the overall chance that any single envelope received between October 14 and October 20, 1991, would contain a successful application was 4.3 tenths of 1 percent; the chance for any envelope mailed at any time was 2.1 tenths of 1 percent. Most people, of course, submitted multiple copies of their applications. The average number submitted by each visa seeker from Britain was calculated to be 459. One particularly eager person claimed to have submitted ten thousand copies. (He did, in fact, win his visa.)

The Irish were indeed the biggest winners in the first lottery for Morrison visas, with 20,000 of their applications selected (followed by just over 12,000 for Poland and some 6,400 for Japan). But 27 percent of the Irish who were selected never claimed their visas, and so only 14,617 received permission for permanent residence in the United States. Even among them, an unknown number stayed on in Ireland, with no immediate intention of actually immigrating to America. "We've got people who use the visas just as security, to fall back on," says Marie Keegan, of the Center for Emigrant Advice in Dublin. "There are so many thousands of undocumented in the States who are desperate for these visas; it's just not right."

But Liam Donohoe, who has a doctorate in mathematics from Brown University and is one of the lottery winners who stayed in Ireland with his green card, explains that he would never leave for America without "a decent job" and that, in any event, he is reluctant to leave his elderly parents. He cautions Americans against believing that the Irish are "dying to get out," as they were during the potato famine of the nineteenth century and later political turmoil. Most, he says, would prefer to go to England, if they can find work there, because the adjustment is so much less daunting than in the United States.

Investigating why more than a quarter of the Irish who were offered visas failed to follow through, Keegan found that for some, "by the time they win, their circumstances have changed. They're doing something else, or they're in a relationship." Another group, she says, including the "long-term unemployed," simply does not have the money for the processing fees and the flight across the Atlantic. And still others cannot manage from a distance to organize the job offer that remains a requirement for receiving a Morrison visa.[3]

The experience with the first year of Morrisons brought a number of reforms in the lottery procedure for the subsequent two years. Most

---

[3] *Winning the lottery does not, in any event, guarantee a visa. They are issued on a first-come, first-served basis to those who respond in a timely manner to their notification that they have been selected. But the usual restrictions—against people with certain communicable diseases, with a criminal or terrorist record, or who have committed previous immigration fraud—also apply.*

importantly, multiple entries from a single person were banned, and a computer made all of the selections of winners randomly from among all qualified applications received during a monthlong period earlier in the year. (Some 200,000 entrants in 1992 and 230,000 in 1993 were disqualified because they submitted extra copies of their applications.) Stampedes at the post office became unnecessary.

In the second year, 25,000 Irish applications were selected in order to try to fill their special quota, and in the third year 32,000. In the end, another 14,000 Irish people were declared eligible to immigrate legally to the United States in 1993, as a result of the 1992 lottery; and in 1994, more than 21,000 became eligible because of participating in the 1993 sweepstakes. But still, at least 10 percent of the Irish who were selected and then completed the required paperwork did not take advantage of their eligibility. With Canada added to the list of eligible countries in the 1992 lottery, it slipped immediately into third place, but still well behind Poland.

For subsequent years, Congress did away with the Morrison visas and established a new category of "diversity immigrants," also to be selected by lottery. This time, however, citizens of countries that had sent more than 50,000 legal immigrants during the previous five years would not be eligible to enter, and no one country would be permitted to have more than 7 percent of the visas. Ireland thus lost its special privilege. The Irish could apply now only in a category with other citizens of the European Community.

XIII
THE BACKLASH:
CLOSING THE DOOR TO
"THE COUNTRY OF SUNSHINE
AND FREEDOM"

ONE NIGHT in the early 1980s, on the streets of Denver, Richard Lamm had what he now considers a transforming experience. He was on his way to pick up his daughter from an evening activity when he spotted an automobile, driven by someone obviously impaired by alcohol or drugs, weaving down the road and smashing into one parked car after another. He quickly hooked up his siren and his flashing lights—he happened to be governor of Colorado at the time—and, after a brief chase, pulled the driver over. Several city policemen responded to his radio call, arrested the man, and took him off to jail.

The next day, when Lamm's state police security detail followed up on the case, they discovered that the drunk driver was an illegal alien from Mexico and that the Denver police, having no address for him and finding no basis for holding him, had simply set him free. Lamm was furious. To him, the incident highlighted a special lawlessness that was gripping America, implying an inability to assert control over the nation's future. Before long, this became the impetus for a new crusade by this freewheeling Democratic politician who enjoyed rattling the establishment. Lamm had reacted with embarrassment and anger when a president from his own party, Jimmy Carter, seemed powerless to head off the Mariel boatlift from Cuba in 1980; now he decided he would try to make a national issue of the need to control immigration more strictly.

Soon he published a book on the subject, *The Immigration Time-Bomb*, took to the lecture circuit, and became a stalwart of the immigration-control group FAIR (Federation for American Immigration Reform).

"I think we have to take a very hardheaded view of immigration," Lamm told me as we talked in his law office on the forty-seventh floor of a Denver skyscraper several years later, after he had left the governorship. "We have to ask ourselves how many people we can absorb and assimilate into our culture. Who should they be, and how should they be chosen?" Leaning back in his chair, his cowboy boots propped up against his desk, Lamm gestured toward the Rocky Mountain foothills just beyond his panoramic, wraparound window. He spun out a forboding scenario: Hordes of undocumented Mexicans, arriving furtively from the border towns to the South, disappearing daily into the Hispanic neighborhoods of Denver and then, if they do not soon find work, moving on to other cities in the West.

Lamm's concern is not limited to illegal immigrants, but also extends to those who come in legally. "I don't think we have the luxury of bringing in unskilled workers anymore," he says in a voice mellowed by years of practice at political persuasion. "In the early 1900s, we could perhaps get away with that, and it did work. But not now, with twenty-seven million people already essentially existing outside the world of work" in the United States. In Lamm's view, the continued admission of very large numbers of people, just because they want to come or happen to be related to others who are already here, threatens to aggravate the country's serious social and economic problems. Noting that under the amnesty provisions of the Immigration Reform and Control Act of 1986, the government had "legalized over three million people who had an average of a fifth-grade education," he warns that "we're growing two underclasses in America. We haven't solved the problem of the black underclass, and now we're creating a Hispanic underclass. Our first duty ought to be to our own poor."

Unless a clear signal of greater restrictiveness is sent out soon, Lamm argues, people from all over the world will eventually swamp the United States. "You take a poll in Korea, and seventy percent of the people want to come to the U.S.," he claims. "Take a poll in Mexico, and fifty percent of the people want to come. Ten percent of El Salvador now lives in the U.S. Well, El Salvador's not a very nice place to live, and if I lived there, I might try to get out, too. I'm not blaming them for wanting to come. I'm blaming us for letting them in." He goes on: "Believe me. America is a land of opportunity, and it is very clear that more people want to come here all the time. You can let in three million people a year, and then someone's going to say, 'Well, why don't we bring in the fourth million?' There are two billion people out there in the world with a standard of living below the American poverty level. We can't take two billion. . . . The Golden Door is so magnetic, so attractive to people, that we have to make some harder choices."

Lamm advocates limiting immigration to 500,000 or 600,000 people a year overall, and those people should be selected, he says, "for their skills and what they can do for this country." He also believes that the principle of family reunification, a major pillar of immigration policy, has been taken too far. "There's no reason why an immigrant should be able to bring in their cousin, or even their brother or sister. I think it ought to be limited to immediate family—children, wife, and parents," he says.

Moreover, Lamm would also exclude those skilled people of whom the United States already appears to have an ample supply. "We've got more engineers now than we need. And we clearly don't need any more doctors or lawyers. The estimates are that we have seventy thousand surplus doctors right now in this country. And we're still bringing in something like fifty percent of the graduating medical class of the Philippines, where they desperately need doctors. It's crazy. It doesn't help us, and it doesn't help them. If I were in Pakistan and went through medical school, I'd want to come and live the good life in America, too. But every surplus doctor in the U.S., I think, accounts for something like five hundred thousand dollars worth of billing." That, he suggests, only adds to another problem by forcing up the cost of medical care and health insurance.

The precious supply of immigrant visas should instead be reserved, Lamm suggests, for "any skilled machinist, physicist, or any kind of research person or professor in any kind of science. You would be looking for different things at different times in our history; it depends on what the labor market is telling you."

A former civil rights lawyer, Lamm now advocates a much tougher effort to distinguish between political refugees, who have a well-founded fear of persecution in their country of origin, and economic migrants, who simply seek a better life. He acknowledges that his own grandparents were economic refugees, on one side from Germany and on the other from England. His family's is, he recognizes, "a typical immigrant story" of poor people finding fulfillment in America: His father's father was a brick mason, and his mother's father ran an ice house. "But the fact that our grandparents came under one set of circumstances does not necessarily mean that the same applies today," he says. "The biggest thing in public policy is to know when the world has changed and when you ought to react to it. The single most important thing is to understand what the new realities of your society are."

Some of the people who are most understanding about the need for limits on immigration, Lamm contends, are the immigrants themselves. "There's a big dichotomy between the Hispanic leadership and the average Hispanic," he says, with the former arguing the case in political terms and the latter forced by economic circumstances to be more realistic. "The vast majority of Hispanics want less, rather than more, immigration. A guy that goes out to work every day and works very hard worries a lot about the fact that just as he's starting up the economic ladder, all of a sudden a whole bunch of illegal immigrants come in and take his job." And Lamm deplores the fact that "there are whole linguistic ghettos growing up in the United States. It's no longer necessary, as it was for our grandparents, to actually learn English. You can listen to the radio station and the TV station in Spanish and read a Spanish newspaper. You can live your whole life in Spanish—you don't have to assimilate anymore." This, he says, even encourages the formation of separate Hispanic youth gangs.

It is only the "intelligentsia," Lamm believes—in this case, a well-intentioned but insidious coalition of people brought together from the right and the left of the political spectrum, with varied motives—that still pushes for increased immigration. "I reflect the average American viewpoint," he insists.

THIS IS FAR from the first time in modern American history that there has been a widespread populist backlash against immigration, and it will certainly not be the last. The most sustained episode in the twentieth century dates back to the period before, during, and just after World War II, when domestic economic circumstances and a particularly narrow definition of "Americanism" combined with other political and social currents to help exclude those who were most desperate to come to the United States. Nowhere can this be traced more poignantly than in the Indianapolis archives of the American Legion, the veterans' group that exercised extraordinary influence over national policy on immigration and refugee issues in that period.

One letter in the files tells a great deal of the story. It was written on November 26, 1938, soon after the Nazis had occupied parts of Czechoslovakia, by two brothers, Ernest and Erwin Waldmann, Czech Jews who had served in World War I and were now on the run. They had somehow found temporary refuge for themselves and Ernest's family in Zagreb, Yugoslavia (now the capital of independent Croatia), but were inevitably turned away when they approached the American consulate there for visas to enter the United States. Penned on four sheets of Erwin Waldmann's small personalized stationery in an elaborate, cultured European script and with labored English syntax, the letter was addressed to "The Organization of American War Veterans (Soldiers of the Great War)" in "Indianopolis [sic] U.S.A.," but, because it must have been one of many such missives at the time, found its way easily enough to Legion headquarters.

The Waldmanns' note began by saying that they had read in the newspapers of a resolution recently passed by the Legion's National Executive Committee, expressing a general sympathy for the large number of racial, religious, and political refugees in the world at the time. "We all were much touched by the noble stand you took up [in Indianapolis] on behalf of Civilization and Humanity," they said. Then came their pathetic appeal:

> You know the present conditions of hardship which has befallen certain people which is unic [sic] in the history of our days & the world & which have no precedent.
>
> As there is nobody in America we know or are acquainted with, we herewith appeal to you *as old soldiers of the Great War* & beg you as colleagues for your kind intervention & help thus enabling us to go to USA by letting us have affidavits or any other permits to go & stay in USA, in the country of sunshine & freedom.

The U.S. consulate in Zagreb, they said, "will give you if you so desire full information that we are honest people," and then they listed their birthdates and credentials: Erwin, born in 1892, "teacher of languages, designer of publicity, wall painter—has learnt chicken-farming . . . etc."; Ernest, born in 1896, "cinema operator, cinema worker, useful for everything"; Ernest's wife Margaret, born in 1902, "cook, teacher of musik [sic], housemaid & lady's companion"; and, in much larger letters, clearly the greatest object of their concern, "THEIR DAUGHTER VERA ALICE WALDMANN, 6½ years old."

"Will you be good enough & do all you can in order to get us on the list of Immigration thus enabling us to get to the States at once," they went on. "You can do it by sending us affidavits. We feel sure that we are not appealing to you in vain, althemore [sic] as we shall be *no burden* to you in America. God will bless you for your kindness & your good deeds & so we trust you & hope soon to hear from you."

The archives in Indianapolis contain a carbon of a curt and businesslike answer to the Waldmanns, typed and dated December 20, 1938, from H. L. Chaillaux, then director of the Legion's National Americanism Commission and the organization's point man on immigration for several decades. "Your letter of November 26 has been received," he wrote to the return address in Zagreb that had been added to Erwin Waldmann's stationery, hastening to point out that the National Executive Committee's public expression of sympathy for refugees was not to be overinterpreted. "The American Legion is not in a position to assist in bringing into this country those who in their homeland are at the moment oppressed," said Chaillaux, a postal worker in California who was himself descended from a French immigrant family, as he launched into what sounded suspiciously like a form-letter reply. "Our first obligation is that of attempting to find jobs for several hundred thousand of our own unemployed World War veterans. You can readily see that that is rightfully our first duty."

The Legion official went on: "We must further refrain from active participation in the field of activity which you have suggested because of the fact that our National Convention in Los Angeles, California, which was held in late September, 1938"—even as the Western powers were preparing to sign Czechoslovakia over to Hitler at the Munich Conference—"passed a resolution directing the Legislative Committee of the Legion to support legislation in the coming session of Congress which would close the door of the United States to immigration for a period of ten years. This resolution was deemed advisable because of the fact that we have some ten to twelve million of our own Americans who are and have been for the past five or six years unemployed. We cannot, therefore, justify the continued policy of adding to this unemployment by the continuance of or the extension of the present immigration quotas."

In what reads now like a particularly callous conclusion to his letter, Chaillaux added, "While we have the most profound sympathy for the plight of those who are oppressed in the nations of the world by policies which do not prevail in the United States, we must abide by the will of the majority of our organization as expressed through Convention action and long-established policy." He closed with an expression of "sincere good wishes for your well being."[1]

[1] *Other correspondence in the Legion's archives indicates that throughout the 1930s and during the early 1940s, Chaillaux endorsed the arguments of "patriotic" organizations that opposed efforts to relax restrictions in order to admit German Jewish children and other victims of Nazism to the United States. When a Legion post in Oklahoma wrote in 1940 to complain that "about fifteen thousand Jews a month are entering the United States," Chaillaux replied with a barrage of statistics. Many aliens, he said, "came here from countries which no longer exist and are not now deportable. We can do nothing about it but keep them. These are the so-called refugees. This is the loophole through which hundreds enter on every boat as visitors." He also complained that "refugee children from Spain, Hungary, Poland, and what-have-you who went to England . . . are now being dumped on us in order that England may provide better protection for her own children. After those parentless children arrive in the United States, our immigration laws are such as to then make it possible for the parents of the poor orphans who are here to come in. We will, therefore, shortly have the entire families, and the adults will be replacing Americans on jobs and the Americans will be going on relief rolls."*

It is impossible to know whether the Waldmanns actually received Chaillaux's written lecture on unemployment in the United States—or, indeed, what the fate of this one frightened family, among hundreds of thousands of others, might have been in a Europe haunted by the Nazis—but there are many other such exchanges in the Legion files. And there is plenty of additional evidence that this powerful organization faithfully acted upon its members' virulent anti-immigrant and antirefugee attitudes. Dozens of bills in Congress, for example, were supported—and, in some cases, apparently written—by the Legion, with a view toward stemming the immigrant flow. One, offered by Senator Robert R. Reynolds, Democrat of North Carolina, in 1936, was styled as an effort "to further reduce immigration, to authorize the exclusion of any alien whose entry into the United States is inimical to the public interest, to prohibit the separation of families through the entry of aliens leaving dependents abroad, and to provide for the prompt deportation of habitual criminals and all other undesirable aliens, and to provide for the registration of all aliens now in the United States or who shall hereafter be admitted."

The Legion was not at the ramparts alone, of course. One of the most active anti-immigrant spokesmen of the period was John Cecil, president of the American Immigration Conference Board in New York City. During the late 1930s, he initiated citizen petitions to Congress (all bearing prominent proof that they had been printed by union labor) urging passage of Reynolds's and other exclusionary legislation; each person who signed was required to donate a dime to the cause. "The paramount issue in the United States is jobs!" declared one petition. The language that followed was like a forecast of the debate to come many decades later:

"The 1939 session of Congress will determine if American jobs DO belong to Americans, or if they are to continue to be given indiscriminately to NEW immigrants. Protest against continuing to make America the dumping ground—of all Europe—for surplus labor and the political agitators—and their victims. No other nation permits citizens of the United States or any other country to enter and take jobs and relief belonging to Nationals, regardless of what the excuse for migrating may be. Only America fails to protect its jobs and relief from foreign usurpation."

In a section especially intended to scare, and to tap into the deep vein of American anti-Semitism, the petition warned, "OPPRESSED MINORITIES OF ALL THE WORLD NOW SEEK AMERICAN ASYLUM AND JOBS. There are in Europe about seven or eight million human beings who must migrate because of political, economic and social disturbances. These include . . . practically the entire Jewish population of Europe with the exception of those in Great Britain. These include hundreds of thousands of Spanish people. . . . Refugees are coming to our ports by the shiploads and are being rushed into employment with as little delay as possible. They are coming under the quotas. They are coming under the permits of temporary visitors, the number of which has no legal limit. These temporary permits are extended time after time, for the benefit of aliens who hold American jobs. More refugees have settled in the United States in the last year than the number who permanently settled during this period, in the rest of the world. Refugees are at work everywhere in America and everytime a job is filled by one of them, an American is thrown out of work." (Emphasis in original.)

A strategy memorandum sent by Cecil to his supporters noted that "five splendid immigration and deportation bills" had been passed by the House during the first session of the Seventy-sixth Congress, and that more good legislation was still awaiting action. One bill was being opposed by a senator from Washington state, he said, who was "depending upon the same old crowd of reds, pinks, fellow travelers and New Dealers, aided and abetted by the Labor Department."[2] What was at stake, Cecil said, was nothing less than "the protection of American Institutions and traditions from an invasion of a horde of aliens intent on destruction of the American Republican form of government. . . . For the most part, we have financed a winning fight with dimes, given by people who still believe that America belongs to the Americans; people whose forefathers made this nation great, and gave it a Republican form of government; people who still believe that American jobs and American opportunity belong to Americans, and to the sons and daughters of Americans. Thank God for the Christian men and women who so willingly have worked and sacrificed for this victory, which is now in sight."

The campaign brought Cecil an obsequious telegram of congratulations from Senator Reynolds. "I consider these petitions of sufficient importance that I respectfully urge you to double your efforts to enlist patriotic Americans everywhere to stand up and be counted on this paramount issue," he wired Cecil in New York. In his telegram, Reyn-

---

[2] *Notwithstanding the popular swell of anti-immigrant feeling, several U.S. government agencies did actually promote immigration—and respect for immigrants—at the time. The Office of Education in the Interior Department, for example, sponsored a weekly Sunday afternoon program on CBS Radio, entitled* Americans All, Immigrants All. *It was, said the department, "dedicated to all the men and women who have come to the shores of the United States since early times, to give of their brain and brawn, and to share its freedom and its greatness."*

olds, who was having trouble getting some of the bills out of committee, said Cecil's American Immigration Conference Board should "secure greatest number signatures possible and have them ready for filing when I wire you that it is proper time to present them to the Senate in order that my colleagues in the Congress may know the attitude of the American people."

The American Legion maintained its militant policy against any increase in immigration long after the end of World War II, and indeed well into the 1960s. The organization fought relentlessly for approval of the McCarran-Walter Immigration Act, which was sponsored by Senator Pat McCarran of Nevada and Representative Francis Walter of Pennsylvania, both Democrats, and passed over President Harry S Truman's veto in July 1952; the "Counter-Subversive Section" of the Legion's National Americanism Commission issued broadsides in its favor, essentially labelling all opponents of McCarran-Walter as communists. Most public attention was focused on the bill's provisions that sought to exclude "subversives" from the United States, but the legislation also maintained the ethnic and racial makeup of the country as revealed by the 1920 census as the basis for immigration quotas—rather than substituting the 1950 census, as many of McCarran-Walter's opponents advocated.[3]

In *Firing Line,* the Americanism Commission's newsletter, the Legion kept up a steady Cold War drumbeat against "unrestricted immigration" as "a major security problem." A special edition dated May 20, 1957, warned that "dangerous and deceptive amendments" to soften the impact of McCarran-Walter, sponsored by liberal Democrats and then pending in Congress, were on the verge of approval. "This year, because the Communist campaign has been so vigorous and the Red tactics so deceptive, patriotic legislators can no longer hold off the enemy without powerful help from the voters," warned *Firing Line.* The McCarran-Walter Act, it said, had the objective of ensuring "that citizens of the United States—whatever their ancestry—will form a true nation, not a hodgepodge of unassimilated minority groups," whereas

[3] *To change the standard to the population as reflected in the 1950 census, as advocated in "leftist proposed amendments" to the McCarran-Walter Act, would unacceptably increase immigration quotas, argued the American Coalition, a Legion-allied "patriotic organization" based in Washington. It also opposed efforts to transfer unused quotas from certain countries to others where the demand to immigrate to the United States was greater. "The net effect [would be] to transfer the unused portion of the large quotas for natives of Northern and Western Europe to orientals and to natives of Southern and Eastern Europe," complained the coalition. "This would emasculate the national origins immigration system which seeks to preserve the basic cultural composition of the United States."*

the proposed amendments would "bring in a flood of immigrants sufficiently huge to actually change the cultural character of our population" and "permit actual enemies of the American form of government, criminals and Communists, to enter the United States in unrestricted numbers."

By the late 1960s, after public opinion had forced abolition of the national-origins quota system and immigration law had been substantially liberalized, the American Legion found itself in a defensive posture. When a November 1967 article in *Look* magazine highlighted the fact that the Legion had ardently opposed an effort in Congress in 1939 to enact legislation that would have admitted ten thousand child victims of the Nazis—ultimately unsuccessful, in part because President Roosevelt refused to take a stand on the bill—an internal Legion memorandum advised that "the best defense is to point out that the nation was at that time operating in a climate colored by the experiences of a ten-year depression." Also, said the memorandum, "isolationism was at that time a very strong sentiment throughout the nation, and obviously also quite strong within the ranks of The American Legion. . . . This isolationist sentiment lent itself to a desire not to become involved with the problems being created by Nazi activities in Germany." It concluded that "what The American Legion would do with regard to similar legislation today may be an entirely different matter from what was done in 1939." It was unfortunate, wrote the Legion's national adjutant a few months later, in response to a letter of protest from a woman in Massachusetts, that the author of the article in *Look* "did not include reference to the action of The American Legion in later years when [it] was in the forefront of the movement to admit 400,000 refugees" from World War II to the United States.

IN THE HARD economic times of the late 1980s and early 1990s, many American politicians once again began to define immigration as a major national problem and to use the issue to great rhetorical benefit. There was a rebirth of an old, familiar demonization of immigrants, as Congress voted, for example, to prohibit entry into the United States by travelers and potential residents infected with the virus that causes AIDS. Movements sprouted up that were dedicated to preserving "American culture" from an ominous multicultural threat, and some states approved legislation to make English their official language.

As if to follow in the footsteps of his predecessor Pat McCarran, Senator Harry Reid, a Democrat from Nevada, introduced an Immigration Stabilization Act in 1993 that would drastically cut the quotas for legal immigration from 800,000 to 300,000 a year. His proposal would also make it more difficult to obtain political asylum in the United States, increase the criminal penalties for smuggling aliens into the country, double the size of the Border Patrol, provide for immediate deportation of aliens convicted of crimes, and remove the option of automatic U.S. citizenship for the babies of women who were in the country illegally at the time they gave birth.

"Our federal wallet is stretched to the limit by illegal aliens getting welfare, food stamps, medical care, and other benefits, often without paying taxes," said Reid as he introduced the measure. His language was reminiscent of the pre–World War II era: "Safeguards like welfare and free medical care are in place to boost Americans in need of short-term assistance. . . . These programs were not meant to entice freeloaders and scam artists from around the world." Pointing to the February 1993 terrorist attack on the World Trade Center in New York, Reid complained that "Americans have seen heinous crimes committed by individuals who are here illegally."

But few people became as emotionally engaged in the immigration debate as the governors of states with the largest influx of undocumented aliens. They went far beyond anything Richard Lamm had imagined proposing when he became involved with this issue in Colorado. Republican governor Pete Wilson of California, who estimated that two million out of his state's thirty million people were illegal immigrants (a figure the INS disputed as an exaggeration), went further than most. He not only supported the Proposition 187 ballot initiative, denying public benefits to anyone who could not prove he was in the country legally, but also suggested an amendment to the U.S. Constitution denying citizenship to some people born on American soil. As his 1994 campaign for reelection heated up, Wilson made frequent visits to the border, in San Diego and in El Paso, Texas, where an INS experiment in tougher enforcement was underway. At one point, he appealed directly to the government of Mexico to stem the flow of people coming across, only to be told by the foreign ministry in Mexico City that it preferred to conduct its official relations with the United States through Washington, not Sacramento.[4]

Various governors filed lawsuits against the federal government to recover the high cost to the states of illegal immigration, including the expense of imprisoning some immigrants charged with crimes or await-

---

[4] *Some observers felt that Wilson's hard line on the immigration issue was intended to strengthen his prospects as a possible Republican presidential candidate in 1996 or beyond. It failed.*

ing deportation. Wilson claimed that California was spending $1,600 per person per year to provide undocumented aliens with public services—a price it could ill afford in view of the decline of the state's defense-related industries and which, in any event, it could not predictably budget for, never knowing how many people might arrive in any given year.

For his part, Governor Lawton Chiles of Florida, a Democrat, struck a deal with the INS in 1994 to release illegal immigrants from his state's prisons (most of them serving sentences for drug-related crimes) with clemency, on the condition that they accept immediate deportation to their home countries and agree never to return, as well as waiving any pending legal challenge to their convictions. Chiles, who claimed it was costing Florida $60 million a year to keep 2,700 aliens in prison, said he needed the space for dangerous homegrown criminals, who were routinely being released because of prison overcrowding. However, his lawsuit seeking $1.5 billion from the federal government to cover education, health care, and other routine services for illegal immigrants was thrown out by a federal judge in Miami who said he had no authority to force U.S. authorities to pay.

President Bill Clinton, as a former governor of Arkansas himself, was openly sympathetic to the states' actions and promised to pursue remedies to ease the burden of immigration on their strained budgets. Not only did he authorize tougher controls at the Mexican border but he also explicitly excluded undocumented aliens from the original health care reform proposal he submitted to Congress. Under the Clinton plan, illegal immigrants were not to be provided with the "health security cards" intended to guarantee affordable medical care to all citizens and legal residents.

Indeed, few national or state politicians dared to speak against the conventional wisdom that unchecked illegal immigration—and possibly the legal flow of refugees and immigrants, too—was causing the United States great economic and social problems. Even liberal Democrats with a reputation for standing up for the underdog rushed to get on the anti-immigrant bandwagon. One of the few exceptions was Ann Richards, the Democratic governor of Texas, who, while she joined the effort to obtain supplementary funding from the federal government, took a more moderate approach to the immigration issue. In Texas, where public social services are less highly developed than in California, the annual costs per illegal immigrant were estimated to be about half as much, and in 1994 there were thought to be only about a fourth as many undocumented aliens in Texas as in California. Perhaps more importantly, however, Texans are far more accustomed to living with Hispanics on both sides of the border, and they tend to see the immigrants as promoting trade and economic growth. (Richards was defeated for reelection in 1994, but her Republican successor, George W. Bush, also seemed to hold back from exploiting the immigration issue.)

IN RECENT YEARS, some of the strongest and most emotional opposition to immigration has emerged among the indigenous minority communities in American cities, and especially among African Americans. There is a widespread impression, particularly in the poorer inner-city neighborhoods, that some newly arrived immigrant groups can count on special benefits that are simply not available to blacks who have spent their entire lives in the United States. The main focus of the resentment, as discussed in Chapter X, is the Koreans who have bought up so many of the neighborhood convenience stores that serve as the principal suppliers of food, beverages, and other daily necessities to many black families. Although Korean immigrants are not all that numerous—and relatively few of them enter the United States illegally—they seem to attract a disproportionate amount of the negative attention.

Echoing the complaints heard so often in Los Angeles and related to the 1992 riots there, the Reverend Timothy McDonald, pastor of Atlanta's First Iconium Baptist Church, an overwhelmingly black congregation in a poor neighborhood, asserts that the Koreans "take resources out without putting resources back in. They do not hire our people; they only hire their own." While he insists that he does not condone violence or theft, McDonald says he finds it understandable that Korean-owned grocery and liquor stores are among the first targets of attackers and looters when racial tensions arise in Atlanta. "The perception is that the Koreans get benefits that we do not—that they come from overseas and get all these subsidies, and that's how they can go into business. This is partially true, but not totally. I realize Koreans have always been entrepreneurs, and they know how to pool their resources. I think they're smart economically, and there are some things we could learn from them. But if we had those same opportunities, if we could get those same loans and interest rates, then we could buy the stores. I believe there's definitely some truth in that; the opportunities are just not as available for us."

Rhonda M. Brown, who comes from the other end of the black economic spectrum in Atlanta and is chief executive officer of her own office-systems company, agrees with the complaint that emerges from the inner city. The Koreans "don't understand us, and we don't understand them," she says. "They see everything still as Martin Luther King and the civil rights movement, that kind of thing from thirty years ago. And we don't know anything about Koreans, other than the Korean conflict of forty years ago. There are not even conversations going on, because we can't understand their dialect and they can't understand ours. So people just point at each other to save their lives. The only things we've begun to talk about are public safety issues."

Far more significant in numbers, and more immediate in their impact on African Americans' lives, are the Hispanic immigrants, and especially those coming from Mexico (who have only recently become more numerous in Atlanta than the Cubans who used to migrate north from Miami). In Atlanta, which was one of the last big cities to receive a major influx from south of the border, black-Hispanic relations are, on the surface, calmer than those with Asian immigrants. Organizations in the two communities have developed "a working relationship," says Brown, despite widespread fears that sophisticated Mexican and other Hispanic immigrants will, in effect, hijack minority-enterprise programs originally intended to stimulate self-help and business ownership among African Americans. Meanwhile, at the lower end of the market for services, where few Atlanta workers are unionized, she believes that blacks have clearly been pushed aside. "At one point, all the people who cleaned hotel rooms here were black," Brown says, citing a highly visible example. "That was the norm. But it's not the case anymore; now you find more Hispanics than blacks. That's just the kind of shift we anticipated and feared when the laws changed to let more people in."

The Hispanic labor force is exploited in Atlanta, just as it is elsewhere, in the view of McDonald. "They are industrious. They want to work, and they'll do any type of work," the minister says. "So they are undercutting the labor force in this city. Not that they are doing it deliberately to hurt blacks. They're only doing it to survive, and yet they're being blamed for it. This has created some tension, because they will work cheaper than African Americans. Compared to where they came from, this is heaven, they are getting a tremendous increase [in their wages]. And many of them are skilled—they are artisans, bricklayers, and carpenters. Of course, in south Georgia, they are used a lot in the fields. It is like slave labor. It's criminal."

Indeed, according to Teodoro Maus, the diplomat in charge of a newly expanded Mexican consulate general in Atlanta, the number of Mexican immigrants arriving in the southeastern United States has grown substantially in recent years, precisely because the word spread that plentiful work was available in rural agriculture there. Many of those who came, he says, were secondary migrants, who had become victims of the economic decline in the late 1980s and early 1990s in such states as California, Texas, and Louisiana. By Maus's conservative estimate, about 60 percent of the Mexicans in the Southeast are in the country legally, and the other 40 percent are undocumented. As in the case of Mexican immigrants elsewhere in America, they tend to come to Atlanta from particular states and regions in Mexico, after getting the message that others from those same areas have been able to earn their livelihood and build a new life there. In this case, the people usually hail from the states of Michoacán, Zacatecas, and Guanajuato.

Echoing his government's official position, Maus says, "We are against our people coming here, because we want to keep them in Mexico. We want to export products, not people. The fact is that some of our best and most industrious people are the ones who leave. They are very good people, who want to find a job and make some money." The great problem, he adds, is that whenever a typical undocumented immigrant goes home, voluntarily or otherwise, "he will never say that it was bad, that the work was horrible and he was exploited. He will say that it was great and he made a fortune. Then he may spend all the money he took a year to save—besides what he had been sending home—in a night or two in a *cantina*, inviting everybody in the village and buying them drinks. So then there are six, eight, or ten more people from the village who will say, 'I'm going. I want to have the same experience.' And they do. But they have a pretty rough time."

Given the economic growth of Atlanta in recent years, Maus says, his office "constantly gets calls from construction companies, asking us, 'Do you have any Mexicans who could work for us?' For some reason, we have a reputation as good workers in construction." But more likely, the Mexican immigrants, along with a growing number from rural areas in Central America, end up working in the chicken-processing industry or in areas of agriculture where they are badly abused and poorly paid. Maus tells the story of four farmers who kept a group of twelve Mexican workers in chains as they transported them from one work site to another. Even in a case like that, or in others where U.S. labor laws have been flagrantly violated, he says, it is difficult to prosecute the offenders, because the workers "will not accuse them directly. They are scared that they will be deported, and they are afraid that the government will close the factory or the farm and they'll be out of a job." In a particularly cruel irony, some of these same workers become targets for the Ku Klux Klan, which is still strong in some pockets of south Georgia. The

Klan, says Maus, is adept at setting various groups against each other, warning the blacks in speeches and leaflets that the Mexicans "are taking away your jobs, your women, and everything else."

According to Reverend Timothy McDonald, what happens in the city is not dissimilar, just more sophisticated. He blames "the white power structure, the chambers of commerce, and the *Fortune* 500 folks who are here" for using the immigration issue to stir up tension between Hispanics and blacks in Atlanta. "They like to keep the underlings fighting among themselves," he says bitterly. As we sat talking in the office at his church, McDonald received a telephone call from a man who owned a carpet business and needed several people for a few days of heavy labor. He thought the pastor might be a good source of referrals. "He said, 'If you don't call me back right away, I'm going to find some Mexicans for the job instead. They've got a good attitude, they work cheap, and they're dependable,' " McDonald reported after hanging up the phone.

One issue that has stirred growing sympathy in the African American community toward certain immigrants is the widespread perception that Haitian refugees have been significantly less well treated, and made to feel less welcome, in the United States than most other groups. This concern is especially strong in Southern cities like Miami and Houston, both of which have served as detention centers for Haitians thought to have entered the country illegally or who are waiting for a decision on their request for political asylum—and both of which are influenced by a strong Hispanic subculture. An early explanation for the bias against Haitians was that a large number of them were believed to be carriers of the human immunodeficiency virus (HIV), which causes AIDS. But increasingly, the primary motivation for keeping Haitians out of the country—even though they were fleeing a repressive government, like those who came from Cuba—has appeared to be racial.

Valerie Michaud, an African American who is an accountant for the Exxon Company in Houston and is married to an educated, upper-middle-class immigrant from the Haitian capital of Port-au-Prince, has made the Haitian refugees' plight in her city a special cause. "Truly, I don't want to see Haitians come to America anymore," she says, because she has become convinced that some of them—especially the rural, unskilled poor who speak no language but Creole—"are treated worse here" than by the military and the ruthless police brigades at home. According to Michaud, many of those who turn up in Houston (where there are believed to be several thousand Haitians living at any given time) say that while they were being held in INS detention camps near Brownsville and other Texas cities along the Mexican border, they were taken out at night and brutally beaten by Hispanic guards. "I guess Haitians rank even lower" than everyone else, she says. "It seems like in our culture, someone always has to be the underdog."

But to her dismay, Michaud has found African Americans' sympathy for the Haitians to be short-lived and superficial. "I have discovered that there is a lot of bias within the black community against black immigrants who come from any other country," she says. She relates that when her husband, who works at a Houston bank, was promoted to a supervisory position, "he had more problems from black Americans than from anybody else, because he's Haitian, he has an accent, and he speaks differently. But also because he has a very different work ethic from not just black Americans, but Americans across the board." Indeed, among the poor Haitian immigrants she has counseled in Houston, Michaud has found that "they want to work. It's the first thing they tell me. They don't want to sit around watching TV. They've been dumped in an apartment complex full of refugees from all over the world, and they get assistance. They get food stamps. But they want to work, they don't want food stamps."

The same experience is described, Michaud says, by Nigerians, who have also begun to migrate to Houston in substantial numbers and tend to display a strong entrepreneurial spirit. "People say, 'Why do they work so hard?' They don't understand that the immigrants want to be independent. And what we don't understand, we fear. So we fear that these people are going to take things from us that we could have had ourselves, if only we had the same mindset."

The misunderstanding is compounded, Michaud suggests, by the fact that in the view of Haitian, Nigerian, and many other black immigrants, "black Americans don't really have a country." Whereas the black people who have come to America more recently can take the high moral ground of choosing where to live, she says, "Our ancestors did not come here willingly. And we have people who remind us of that every day."

Wanda Coleman, a black American poet, summarizes the tension in these words: "Immigrant populations expect rational behavior from blacks driven mad by poverty and racism. Blacks expect immigrants to empathize with our plight the minute they set foot on our turf." Neither side has any chance of getting its way anytime soon.

XIV
THE FUTURE OF IMMIGRATION
AND THE NATURE OF AMERICA:
REDISCOVERING OUR VALUES

THE UNITED STATES is still a nation of immigrants, and, by its very nature, it will always be one. The failure to appreciate that fundamental fact, and the flawed assumption that one day the country will have assumed its fully developed state and will no longer need or want any more immigrants, are at the heart of many misunderstandings. It is the welcome that has always been extended to new people, and the assumption that they will invariably add something beneficial to the nation, that have made America different from everyplace else in the world. To be Japanese, say, or French implies a certain homogeneity of background and acceptance of cultural norms. To be American means being part of an ever more heterogeneous people and participating in the constant redefinition of a complex, evolving cultural fabric.

The principles and values involved in this concept are too basic, too fundamental to the soul of the country, to be thrown out for the sake of short-term political expediency or cyclical economic panic. In America, it is not possible to say, in effect, that the lifeboat is full and the ladder is going up, that we do not have room for anyone else. If that had been said at various critical moments in history, many of us would not be Americans today.

We sell our country hard—through the Hollywood movies, television programs, music, clothing styles, soft drinks, and fast food that we export. We gloss over the violence and poverty and social strains in our midst and market our political and economic systems as if they were the best ever devised by humanity. Indeed, every day we send out the message, none too subtly, that anyone in the world in his or her right mind should want to live in America. It is hardly surprising, then, that so many people try to come. That they sometimes receive such an ambivalent welcome is nothing new, even if it is often profoundly disappointing. The fact that immigrants may be easier to pick out today than at some earlier time—because of skin color, language, and various cultural features—does not make them any less eligible to contribute to the country they have been persuaded to choose.

Luckily for those of us already here, and contrary to much conventional political wisdom, new immigrants almost always add something to this country. As the stories told in this book make clear, not every immigrant succeeds or leads a happy, fulfilled life in America any more than every person born in this country does so. There are communities, some of them described here, where immigration has been associated with serious crises. But one study after another has shown that overall, immigrants still have a positive economic impact. As economist Gregory de Freitas of Hofstra University has put it, they "help expand the demand for labor and increase the number of jobs, which tends to outweigh any negative effects they may have. . . . The question always seems to be phrased in terms of immigrants taking jobs from Americans, when lots of Americans have jobs because of the impact of immigrants on the economy. . . . Immigrant restaurants and businesses pay taxes, and their workers buy clothes and food and homes in neighborhoods that were formerly dead." Indeed, the reports from the U.S. Department of Labor at the end of 1994 and the the beginning of 1995 were that the economy was expanding and millions of new jobs being created—just at the time when immigration, legal and illegal, was said to be reaching crisis levels and provoking political unrest.

The Urban Institute has found that wages actually rose faster during the 1980s in those parts of the country where immigrants settled than in those where they did not and that immigrants help create more jobs in urban areas than does the native population. And, debunking one of the most prominent myths, the Federal Reserve Bank of New York discovered in 1991 that the male immigrant "faces on average significantly higher rates of average taxation than do natives."

In recent years immigrants have helped revive—and, indeed, in some cases, save—American cities. As de Freitas pointed out, they have resettled and improved decaying neighborhoods, bringing them to life with a new and varied generation of restaurants and shops. Their children have kept schools open and teachers employed. From 1980 to the mid-1990s, immigrants have doubled their rate of home ownership, according to a Harvard University study, to the point where some 55 percent of them now own the places where they live. The increase is particularly pronounced among Hispanics and Asians, who not only have arrived in larger numbers but also have bought into the all-American goals of getting an education and purchasing a home. This is a far cry from the stereotype of the illegal alien who comes to take unfair advantage of American hospitality.

There are other positive effects of immigration, harder to quantify or even to describe adequately. In an era of crass materialism and widespread, growing cynicism, immigrants help renew, enrich, and re-discover the values of America. They stand for entrepreneurship and originality; they believe in, and live daily, many of the precepts that have become meaningless slogans to others—for example, that hard work will bring its rewards. Just as they always have been, they are the valedictorians of today, the concert pianists and rocket scientists of tomorrow, the writers, poets, artists, and musicians working at the frontiers of creativity.

Immigrants bring us new foods and original ways to look at old problems. They remind us of ideals too often forgotten, except in empty political dialogue, in America today: the value of family, respect and care for our elders, kindness and compassion for a larger community of interest. Because some of their lives have been so dramatically trans-formed by coming to the United States, they sometimes seem to believe in the country more genuinely and more meaningfully than some of our most obsequious super-patriots. The immigrants are often genuinely guided by the deep spirituality and faith that other self-proclaimed "real" Americans brandish primarily as a demagogic prop.

Nonetheless, one must recognize that what worked in the late eighteenth and early nineteenth centuries, when the United States desperately needed imported labor to build its economy, will not necessarily work in the same way today. And no country likes to feel it has lost control over its borders and its fate—least of all the United States, so accustomed to being a "superpower" in the post–World War II era, and now the only surviving one at that. It seems only logical and reasonable to suggest that there must be a way to honor the country's founding ethic and overwhelmingly positive experience of immigration without potentially surrendering entirely to the whims, and the timing, of all the people around the globe who are unhappy where they are.

The current system of controlling and regulating immigration clearly does not work, and therefore is easily—almost universally— mocked and defied. The issue now requires more thought and less rhetoric. Toward that end, after several years' experience with immigrants and their daily lives, I offer a few modest recommendations:

• While there is clearly a need to calibrate and control to some extent the flow of immigrants into the United States, the number officially and legally admitted should more closely approximate the number who actually come each year. This would not just be more generous, but also more realistic. At the Mexican border, in particular, the regulation should be left far more to natural market forces than to ceilings artificially determined in Washington.

Economic studies have demonstrated—and my own anecdotal observations have reinforced my conclusion—that a large percentage of the immigrants from Mexico and Central America do not necessarily intend to stay permanently in the United States, but would prefer to come and go as the potential for earning money dictates. "These people for the most part are migrating for labor, and when the jobs are not forthcoming, there is a strong tendency for return migration," says Douglas Massey, a sociologist at the University of Chicago. Indeed, many of the illegal immigrants I observed at the Mexican border seemed to feel a panic that they had to get into the United States right away—and try to bring their family with them—because it might become more difficult to do so later. They were probably right, given the Clinton administration's effort to strengthen border controls even further in the wake of the plunge in the value of the Mexican peso. If the people now crossing the border illegally could come and go seasonally or according to the economic cycle—obtaining permits to stay for fixed periods of time—fewer would bring their families. The inescapable conclusion, therefore, is that if it were easier to enter the country, there would be fewer people who would choose to stay and a lower level of permanent immigration from the south. In effect, the problem would be decriminalized.

In any event, it is absurd to put so much emphasis on new police measures along the southern border, when the INS itself knows that the largest number of immigrants illegally in the United States today entered routinely through airports and simply overstayed their visas. Everyone, including the immigrants themselves, realizes that the INS makes no effort whatsoever to track down and deport such people. Most of them lead normal lives until they can find a way to become legal residents through marriage, special work arrangements, or by winning one of the visa lotteries.

• While some form of credible enforcement is needed at the border, by now it should be clear that bigger, better, and more fences, or the introduction of more Border Patrol officers in a kind of human wall, do not really do the job. Law enforcement at the nation's frontiers should focus on issues that really matter, such as drug interdiction, which requires a far more sophisticated approach than is now being taken.

Otherwise, the biggest need is to monitor people at the border for the diseases they may be bringing into the country. This is equally true of airports and boat docks, as well as land crossings. The federal funds now wasted on ineffective enforcement at the border would be better spent on monitoring, and possibly even immunizing or treating, people for certain diseases which present a real threat to the health of Americans. Among them are illnesses easily and silently communicated to others, including tuberculosis, some sexually transmitted diseases, and intestinal parasites and bacteria. The children who cross the border, at least, could be inexpensively provided with certain immunizations that are standard in the United States, including those for such diseases as polio, diphtheria, pertussis, tetanus, measles, mumps, rubella, hemophilus flu, and hepatitis B.

• The Immigration and Naturalization Service is, by common consensus, one of the worst-performing and least-effective parts of the federal bureaucracy. Tales of its insensitivity and indifference toward perfectly legal refugees and immigrants—in most cases, productive, law-abiding people who are future U.S. citizens—are legion. Human Rights Watch and other humanitarian and civil rights organizations have documented horrific abuses at the Mexican border. And while many of its officers are well-intentioned, the Border Patrol is perhaps the least well trained law-enforcement organization in the country, even as it has become the fastest growing. When the INS has been in the news recently, it has not been for its new successes in doing its job, but, for example, for its failure to collect and deposit the user fees added to airline passengers' tickets, for its reluctance to punish high officials found guilty of sexual harassment and other abusive conduct, or for a lawsuit filed by Hispanic agents charging discrimination.

A major review of the INS and its various components is urgently needed, with a priority on simplifying and rationalizing the way asylum cases and other common problems are handled. This review could be accomplished with the leadership of appropriate committees of Congress, aided by outside experts. A smaller Border Patrol, trained to the standards of the Federal Bureau of Investigation or the Secret Service, would be one desirable outcome.

• Just as it has had to do in other periods on other issues, such as civil rights in the 1960s, the U.S. government and significant private institutions must conduct an overview of immigration policy and its implementation to be sure that it meets certain commonly accepted standards of fairness and decency. The differential that currently exists between the treatment of black and white potential immigrants, for example, is a racist blot on the record of a free society. Similarly, few observers are fooled by the distinctions currently drawn between acceptable political refugees (who generally come from countries whose leadership or prevailing ideology we do not like, such as Cuba) and the economic ones (who usually come from countries whose governments we support, such as El Salvador). In the real world—and in American history—there is little in the way of true distinction between the two categories.

• It is fair and reasonable for the federal government to help the states with any economic burden imposed on them by unexpected immigrant flows. That said, however, some of the policies now being enacted—such as California's Proposition 187—are not only inappropriate on a human level but also potentially dangerous for the nation as a whole. The courts will ultimately decide the constitutionality of these measures, but there is no indication that Proposition 187–like laws will actually dissuade illegal immigrants from entering the country. On the contrary, the most immediate impact after the November 1994 vote in California was to deter U.S. citizens and legal immigrants with Hispanic surnames from taking advantage of facilities and services they were fully entitled to use. Common sense would seem to dictate that, expensive though it may sometimes seem, it is far wiser to keep the children of illegal immigrants in school, where they will potentially gain practical knowledge along with exposure to American values, than to turn them out onto our city streets to be educated in a life of crime and delinquency. Similarly, to deny basic public medical care to all undocumented aliens creates the risk of serious epidemics of tuberculosis and other diseases and further burdens on the public.

AFTERWORD

Events in California, and in a few other states where the impact of illegal immigrants has been especially noticeable in recent years, have had a profound effect on the national political dialogue about immigration. It became fashionable once again, in the last years of the twentieth century, to target immigrants as the scapegoats in national political and social debates, especially in the context of America's search for new directions and goals in the post–Cold War era.

The phenomenon was especially pronounced during the buildup to the 1996 presidential election. Pat Buchanan, the populist conservative who ran against the Republican mainstream establishment in his quest for the party's nomination, made anti-immigrant invective a key element in the standard stump speech he used to rouse angry crowds across the country. "If we can send an Army halfway around the world to defend the borders of Kuwait, can't we defend the national borders of the United States of America?" Buchanan entreated, as he proposed instituting a five-year total moratorium on legal immigration and building a much stronger fence—a virtual wall—along all two thousand miles of the U.S.-Mexican border to prevent illegal entries. He employed rhetoric that seemed calculated to stigmatize not only immigrants but also many native-born members of minority groups, including Jews and Hispanics, as outsiders who were enjoying unfair advantages. He struck an especially responsive chord among white working-class men looking for someone to blame for what they perceived as a loss in status and power. The strong implication was that "José," as he sneeringly singled out the typical Hispanic immigrant, and the other foreigners being coddled by the Democrats did not belong in Buchanan's

America. Indeed, the polls indicated that his views on such "social issues" as immigration and abortion played a more significant part in Buchanan's appeal than his proposed economic policies that would weaken big business along with big government.

Former senator Bob Dole, the eventual Republican presidential nominee, may have considered taking the highroad on immigration, but he obviously abandoned that idea upon sensing the anti-immigrant feeling that was sweeping the nation. Dole had never made immigration a matter of special legislative interest, even after he became Senate majority leader, and as a Kansan, he was not known for strong views on the subject one way or the other. Now he took his cues on the issue from California's Governor Pete Wilson and, in the final desperate phase of his campaign, lashed out vehemently. "Why are you paying millions in taxpayer dollars to provide drug rehabilitation for illegal immigrants?" he asked a cheering crowd in Riverside a few weeks before the election. "And worse, why are thousands of Californians the victims of violent crimes committed by people who should have been stopped at the border before they so much as stepped foot in the United States of America?" Dole accused President Bill Clinton of forcing changes in an immigration bill "to allow illegal aliens to stay in public housing for up to 18 months" and "so that illegal aliens afflicted with AIDS cannot be denied taxpayer-funded medical treatment, no matter how high the cost." His vice-presidential running mate, Jack Kemp, a former congressman from Buffalo, New York, and a cabinet member during the Bush administration who had long been known as a free-market defender of immigration, found it necessary to undergo a weekend conversion before the GOP convention in San Diego to secure his place on the ticket. Then he, too, plunged into the anti-immigrant rhetoric of the campaign without any sign of hesitation or discomfort.

Further reinforcement, if any were needed, came from Richard Lamm, the former Democratic governor of Colorado who had become active in millionaire businessman Ross Perot's Reform party. In trying to wrest the presidential nomination away from Perot—who had certainly influenced the political dialogue as an independent candidate in 1992 but seemed doomed to lose again—Lamm revived the anti-immigrant themes that had served him so well as a public figure out of office before he veered off into such issues as his complaint that too many resources were being devoted to medical care for the elderly. Lamm failed to budge Perot from center stage, but he managed to give a little extra nonpartisan energy to the movement to restrict immigration. Those who failed to see the light, he implied, were condemning their children to live in a very crowded, greatly changed country.

The Clinton administration, on the defensive on so many fronts during the final months of its first term, could hardly stand aside. It promised "new border enforcement technology": the automated processing of illegal aliens, faster fingerprint identification of those arrested, better "infrascopes," new lights and radios, higher and longer fences, extra Border Patrol agents, and more. When the U.S. Commission on Immigration Reform proposed cutting the quotas for legal immigrants and refugees, the Democratic White House quickly and enthusiastically endorsed the recommendations. But that was not enough for the conservative Republicans who had taken control of the House of Representatives in the 1994 midterm elections, vowing to enact their radical "Contract with America." They argued, among other things, that America's burgeoning problems with drugs and terrorism were inextricably related to historically high levels of immigration. Some, foreshadowing Buchanan's tactics, advocated a total moratorium on admitting any new people into the country, and many were prepared to revoke the fundamental constitutional principle that anyone born in the United States is automatically entitled to citizenship. Working with some long-term critics of immigration in the Senate—including Alan Simpson of Wyoming, who became chair of a key subcommittee when the Republicans achieved majority status in that body at the same time—and joined by Democrats who wanted to stay ahead of the anti-immigration curve, the House Republicans did produce a substantial body of restrictive legislation before the 104th Congress adjourned in the fall of 1996. It was easier to do so in part because in the post–Cold War era there were fewer categories of immigrants, such as those from Central America and Southeast Asia, whose presence remained explicitly connected to U.S. foreign policy.

The complex new provisions were contained in the Illegal Immigration Reform and Immigrant Responsibility Act of 1996 and in sections of a "welfare reform" law that was the subject of much election-year controversy. There were new penalties for people caught overstaying their valid visas or entering the United States without formal inspection by the Immigration and Naturalization Service (for example, by crossing on foot from Mexico or Canada between authorized checkpoints). An unlawful six-month stay would result in a three-year ban on reentering the country, and a year-long one in a ten-year ban; even a day's overstay on an authorized visit under a multiple-year, multiple-entry visa could cause the visa to be automatically canceled. Anyone arriving with false documents could be summarily excluded without a hearing and sent home on the next plane.

One of the most dramatic changes was to tighten the process for evaluating applications for asylum in the United States. Convinced that the traditional American welcome for the legitimate victims of religious and political persecution was being abused by specious and frivolous claims, Congress ordered that all asylum-seekers be sent immediately to a detention center and interviewed within forty-eight hours. If they could not persuasively establish their case with an asylum officer (without any help from attorneys, interpreters, or family members), they were to be deported immediately. Appeals, which had come to consume a year or more (during which the asylum applicants were able to work and travel freely and sometimes disappeared), would be severely restricted. Those already living in the United States intending to make belated applications for asylum were now required to do so within a year, and if they ultimately failed, they would be deported, even if they had already established themselves here. Similarly, long-term lawful permanent residents convicted of a serious felony would be instantly expelled. By some interpretations, immigrants would now be subject to the arbitrary judgments and actions of the INS, instead of enjoying full due process when their status is challenged.

Most egregious, in the view of many commentators, were provisions that sanctioned new forms of discrimination against legal immigrants. As of the date the welfare reform law was enacted, newly arriving immigrants became ineligible for food stamps, even if they otherwise would have qualified; those already in the country and receiving this benefit were given a few extra months before being cut off. A year later, many legal immigrants, including senior citizens and those who became disabled after arriving, were to be kicked out of the Supplemental Security Income (SSI) program, which provides cash assistance for basic needs to those unable to work. Overall, immigrants were to be banned from receiving any federal, means-tested benefits during their first five years in the United States. After that, any eligibility would be determined by evaluating the immigrant's own circumstances and "deeming" all of the original sponsor's financial resources to be available to the immigrant. Any citizen or legal resident sponsoring an immigrant, including a family member, now had to sign an enforceable affidavit demonstrating income high enough (at least 125 percent of the poverty level) to guarantee that the immigrant would not become a "public charge" and require government benefits; the affidavit would remain in effect until the immigrant became a citizen or was legally employed for ten years. If the immigrant was caught using public assistance, the sponsor could be prosecuted for repayment.

Some of these provisions were softened or refined in subsequent legislation and regulations (and several states decided to continue certain benefits with their own funds). Still, the clear effect was generally to apply different and tougher standards to noncitizen immigrants—even those who had lived legally in the United States for an extended period of time—than to native-born Americans.

The reaction of many of the people affected was to rush to obtain citizenship. In huge ceremonies around the country, thousands were naturalized, where once there might have been just a few hundred. An all-time high of 1.8 million legal residents were expected to apply for citizenship in 1997. Others responded with despair, and at least five suicides were reported that seemed to be connected to the new cutoffs of benefits. In one case, Ignacio Muñoz, a seventy-five-year-old immigrant from Mexico, shot himself in Stockton, California, after receiving notice from the Social Security Administration that he might lose his monthly disability check of $440. The Urban Institute estimated that about 40 percent of immigrant families earn too little to meet the new threshold for sponsoring family members; the result, predicted the demographer Jeffrey Passel, might be to "encourage illegal immigration."

With an increase in the well-publicized INS raids discovering undocumented immigrant workers in sweatshops and on construction sites, Congress also moved to tighten employment restrictions. The number of documents that prospective employees may use to establish their identity and their authorization to work was reduced; even U.S. citizens were no longer able to use a simple birth certificate or a certificate of citizenship to establish their eligibility. Four-year pilot programs were to be established in at least five states with high estimated populations of illegal immigrants—probably California, Florida, Illinois, New York, and Texas—to confirm every individual's eligibility for employment. But in a victory for business interests, while participation in the programs was made mandatory for workers, it remained voluntary for private employers, the very people who often hire undocumented workers in a deliberate attempt to flout the law and save money by paying them lower wages. To the extent the programs succeed, they will depend on whether the INS and the Social Security Administration establish reliable databases that can be drawn upon by using a toll-free telephone confirmation system.

Despite a plea by the INS that it could realistically recruit and train no more than seven hundred new Border Patrol agents a year, Congress ordered that the agency increase the force by one thousand a year for five years. At the same time, it authorized an increase of three hundred investigators a year for three years to probe alien smuggling and the unlawful hiring of undocumented immigrants. Stiffer penalties were enacted for document fraud and for smuggling people into the country illegally. (The discovery in the summer of 1997 of a smuggling ring, apparently nationwide in scope, that brought deaf Mexicans to sell trinkets on the streets of

American cities while being kept in slavelike conditions seemed to strength-
en the demand for stricter enforcement.) The new law also mandated the
construction of a triple-layer fence and a complex system of roads to enhance enforcement of border controls in the San Diego region, with an
automatic and permanent waiver of environmental and endangered-spe-
cies statutes that might ordinarily come into play.[1]

Some of the most extreme measures were rejected during congressional debate, partly because President Clinton adamantly opposed them. For
example, the Republicans were forced to abandon a proposal, championed
by Congressman Elton Gallegly from Ventura County, north of Los Angeles, to federalize California's Proposition 187 and encourage all states to
remove the children of illegal immigrants from public schools. The Gallegly
amendment to the immigration bill lost ground quickly after every major
law-enforcement organization and many influential chiefs of police came
out against it, arguing that it would do much greater harm to the country
to deny these children an education, thereby putting them into the streets.
Cuts in legal immigration—especially of the family members whom immigration reformers blame for the "chain migration" that they say has become
such a problem—were also avoided. In their original form, both the House
and Senate bills debated in 1996 covered legal as well as illegal immigration issues, and they would have forced a reduction of at least 30 percent
in the quotas used by American citizens to bring in their spouses, parents,
children, and siblings and by business to obtain special visas for workers.
They also would have sharply cut the number of refugees admitted each
year for humanitarian purposes. As the debate proceeded, however, both
houses were persuaded that they should deal separately with the two broad
categories of legal and illegal immigration—that anger over illegal immigration did not necessarily justify sweeping new policies restricting legal
immigration. One turning point came when Bill Gates, the head of the
computer giant Microsoft, contended in a speech at the National Press Club
that cuts in legal immigration could make it more difficult for America's
high-tech industries to compete internationally.

---

[1] All the talk of enhancing the fence along the southern border caused a Texas correspondent for the New
York Times to calculate the costs of a two-thousand-mile project using various materials. He found that
a standard twelve-foot-high chain link fence running the entire distance could be constructed for as little
as $166.8 million; a heavier gauge with "razor ribbon" at the top would run $251.9 million, and elec-
trification would cost another $362 million. A basic concrete wall fifteen inches thick and twelve feet high
would cost $1.4 billion; making it a full two feet thick would cost an extra billion dollars, and painting
it two coats on both sides would cost another $507.9 million. To build the equivalent of the Great Wall of
China, which is what the task might require, the Times reporter estimated an expenditure of $45.2 bil-
lion. (Sam Howe Verhovek, "A 2,000–Mile Fence? First, Get Estimates," New York Times, March 3,
1996, Section 4, Week in Review, p. 1.)

The situation was sufficiently confused, however, that with the approach of April 1, 1997—the well-publicized date when many provisions of the immigration and welfare reform bills were scheduled to take effect—many immigrants feared, mostly erroneously, that they faced imminent deportation. Crowds gathered outside INS offices, not entirely sure whether they were seeking help or protesting their fate, and many individual immigrants found themselves vulnerable to unscrupulous operators offering quick fixes to their problems for a price.

For certain people, including some 300,000 Nicaraguans, Salvadorans, and Guatemalans who had been allowed to enter the United States as refugees during the 1980s because of civil wars in their countries and were now living mostly in south Florida, there was legitimate cause for concern. Their asylum cases had dragged on for a decade or more, and with new efficiency and zealousness the INS was trying to clear the decks by ruling there was no longer any justification for them to stay—in effect, seeking to apply the strict new asylum rules retroactively. Lawyers for 50,000 of the Central Americans argued in a lawsuit that these uniquely vulnerable immigrants had been misled by the U.S. government into believing they were eligible for "suspension of deportation" but were now having the rules changed on them. At the very least, the bureaucracy seemed unwilling to recognize that they had started new lives here and that their children, who were citizens by virtue of having been born in the United States, were in school and otherwise living normal American lives. The "homeland" to which they would be deported might be unrecognizable or, in the case of the children, completely foreign. Ironically, many of the adults might feel forced to try to remain in the United States illegally if they wanted to avoid being separated from their children. "Seldom if ever has such a dramatic, heart-rending, and powerfully persuasive case of irreparable harm to literally tens of thousands of human beings been presented to this federal court," wrote Judge James King of the U.S. district court in Miami in June 1997, temporarily blocking their deportation and scheduling a full trial on their lawsuit for 1998.

Immigrant advocacy groups reacted to the tough new legislation and the hostile climate by urging people legally in the United States to become citizens and participate fully in the political process as soon as possible. The INS announced in June 1995 that it was adding a thousand staff members just to handle applications under its Citizenship USA Program, but that was hardly enough to handle a surge that was just beginning. A later investigation revealed that the agency hastily naturalized some 180,000 applicants in 1996 (out of an overall total of about a million that year) without going through the usual criminal background checks, including verification of their fingerprints. According to the audit by an outside accounting firm,

16,400 people in that group had had at least one felony arrest, and almost 5,000 should have been denied citizenship either because they had criminal records or because they lied along the way. Although Republicans claimed that the abuses were part of a partisan Democratic effort to produce reliably loyal voters in time for the 1996 election, INS Commissioner Doris Meissner and other Justice Department officials insisted it was really a matter of inefficiency and poor accountability in the agency—problems that could be fixed relatively easily. The INS promised to initiate procedures to revoke the citizenship of those who did not deserve to have it, but there was serious question whether everybody who had slipped through the net could be identified and located. Meanwhile, the backlog of legitimate applicants for citizenship waiting to be processed continued to grow.

Stung by the uproar, the INS announced that it was suspending the practice of encouraging voter registration at naturalization ceremonies. New York politicians, however, accustomed as they are to seeking immigrant votes, were outraged. Republican senator Alphonse D'Amato and a Democratic challenger, Charles Schumer, both claimed credit for getting the agency to reverse its policy only days after it had taken effect.

Pressed by Congress to become more effective at policing the borders and preventing fraud, the INS said it would open thirteen new offices in Europe, Asia, Africa, and Latin America to thwart illegal trafficking in would-be immigrants. But the agency's credibility was seriously undermined by a number of cases involving internal corruption. For example, the head of the INS operation in Honduras, who was touted as one of the agency's experts on Chinese smuggling, was arrested when he arrived in Hong Kong in July 1996 with five blank Honduran passports, allegedly destined for an immigrant-smuggling syndicate. Eight months later, the chief American immigration officer in Hong Kong was also detained there, along with his wife, for questioning by special anticorruption police on charges of visa fraud. It was unclear just how many INS officials might be involved in the multibillion-dollar trade in which Chinese migrants have been known to pay as much as $40,000 each to be brought illegally into the United States.

The principal advocate in the House for restricting legal immigration, Republican representative Lamar Smith of Texas, chair of the immigration subcommittee, promised to return to unfinished business when the 105th Congress convened in January 1997, but he ran into unexpected difficulty. Many Republican legislators had encountered an electoral backlash over their votes for the stringent measures the previous year; in a number of states, newly naturalized Hispanic voters tipped the balance in favor of Democratic candidates. That was exactly how Representative Robert Dornan of California, one of the most conservative members of the House, lost his seat to a Hispanic woman; he insisted it had been stolen. Even in Florida, Bill Clinton, now seen as a president relatively sympathetic to immigrant needs, attracted enough support from the Cuban American community to carry the state. In the Senate, Alan Simpson was succeeded as chair of the immigration subcommittee not by a restrictionist from Arizona, as expected, but by Spencer Abraham of Michigan, a member of a Lebanese immigrant family. Abraham made clear that he felt cuts in legal immigration would be bad politics as well as bad policy.

The immigration debate in the new Congress thus centered on efforts to "fix" some of the excesses of the previous year. When Clinton and the Republican congressional leadership reached a budget compromise in July 1997, they agreed to spend $11.4 billion over five years to restore SSI and Medicaid benefits to certain legal immigrants, especially the disabled and refugees, who had lost them. Food stamp aid to noncitizens remained on the taboo list, however, and Republicans said they had established the important principle that future immigrants would be denied a retirement income at public expense. Indeed, the final balanced-budget compromise reached in the summer of 1997 permanently excluded from the SSI program anyone who arrived in the United States after August 22, 1996, and subsequently reached retirement age or became disabled.

Meanwhile, much of the anxiety over immigration was again expressed through the language issue. Just as Benjamin Franklin had once warned that early German immigrants' insistence on speaking their own language threatened the status of English and the fabric of the nation, there were now horror stories about the menace of Spanish. Every politician seemed to have heard the tale, perhaps apocryphal, of a case in California, New York, or Florida where a fine, upstanding citizen had gone to renew her driver's license but could not find a clerk on duty who spoke English. A growing number of state legislatures have thus enacted laws making English their "official" or "only" language. The empty symbolism of the issue was underlined by the fact that most of the new recruits to the cause—such as Montana, New Hampshire, South Dakota, and Wyoming—had few immigrants in their states.

At the federal level, the bill to make English the official language for all states was actually named for a deceased congressman, Bill Emerson of Missouri, who had once championed it. Having been passed in the House by a very substantial majority in 1996 but having gone nowhere in the Senate, it was now reintroduced with 110 cosponsors. House Speaker Newt Gingrich, a Republican from Georgia, was on the record warning that unless the country took this step, it might experience "decay of the core parts of our civilization," and he held up the strife in Canada as an unfortunate result of efforts to institutionalize bilingualism. (It was actually Quebec's insistence on legally enshrining French as a mother tongue and primary language, close observers said, that caused a great deal of trouble in that province; there special police had been sent through commercial districts to ensure that the signs in French were larger than those in English. The requirements suggested on behalf of English in some versions of the legislation pending in the United States were not far removed from this.) With unclear signals coming from the Supreme Court on the issue, the debate seemed sure to continue.

But the arguments about language ultimately reflected larger anxieties over the future makeup of the country. A survey done by Harvard University, the *Washington Post,* and the Henry J. Kaiser Foundation and published in 1995 revealed that white Americans—the frequently misnamed "Anglos"—tend to overestimate the proportion of the country's population represented by various minority groups, including African Americans, Asians, and Hispanics. Indeed, the study showed that many whites believed they themselves were already in the minority, which is far from true. These misconceptions, combined with the publication of frightening statistics about the number and percentages of foreign-born residents in the country and with projections of the nightmare scenarios that lie ahead, are obviously enough to exacerbate the scapegoating of immigrants. They also help explain new waves of insidious discrimination against people who look or sound different from the proverbial "average" American, without regard to their actual legal status.

One study after another has appeared in recent years to refute the conventional wisdom about immigration. A report from the Public Policy Institute of California, for example, said that perhaps half of all Mexican immigrants, legal and illegal alike, move back home within two years of their arrival in the United States. Since many of them are young and single, the Public Policy Institute found, they come to earn money but feel few ties to this country; only 20 percent of them stay for five years or more. Contrary to the assertions of many U.S. politicians, the availability of social welfare programs actually has little to do with the young Mexicans' decisions, according to the study, and thus they are likely to keep coming even if California's Proposition 187 and other similar laws are ever put into effect.

More important, the National Academy of Sciences (NAS), in a two-year, $800,000 study funded by the federal Commission on Immigration Reform, found that "immigration benefits the U.S. economy overall and has little negative effect on the income and job opportunities of most native-born Americans." Far from being the much-lamented drain on the country's resources, immigrants make a net annual contribution of $10 billion, according to the study. "While some have suspected that blacks might suffer disproportionately from the inflow of low-skilled immigrants," it added, "none of the available evidence suggests that they have been particularly hard-hit." As has always been the case, immigrant labor permits some goods and services to be produced more cheaply, the study said, and as it expands, it will help support a growing population of retirees. Taking the long view, the NAS study rejected any association of immigration with high crime or social strife. Despite the scare stories about the prospective racial makeup of the U.S. population by the middle of the twenty-first century, it suggested that because of the current levels of intermarriage, "the social meaning of ethnic and racial lines will become increasingly blurred."

There are important and worrisome trends, of course, but they may be different from the ones that ordinarily get attention in the narrow discussion over immigration. Highly skilled Asian immigrants, for example, newly impressed with economic and political developments in their native countries and distressed by events in the United States, including the anti-immigrant backlash, have begun returning home in larger numbers. (The investigation into potentially illegal fund-raising activities on President Clinton's behalf in the 1996 campaign by a few Asian Americans may also have brought about a distasteful upsurge in discrimination against the larger, undifferentiated group.) For the first time, there is talk of a "brain drain" *from,* instead of to, the United States, but the policymakers seem oblivious.

Indeed, the defense of immigration as a fundamental building block of American culture and society has become almost entirely the province of people outside the political system. "No one is 'more American' than anyone else," writes the columnist Jon Margolis in the *Chicago Tribune,* stating a simple truth that suddenly sounds radical. "Every citizen is equally a citizen, either by becoming one through naturalization or by being born here."

Michael Leven, the hotel executive who helped organize the Indians and other Asians who have become a major force in his industry, puts it more baldly. "If someone had not been willing to give my immigrant grandparents a break when they came to Boston, I probably wouldn't be here," he says. "People have always been afraid of newcomers, but we have to get over that. . . . There has never been any real basis for opposing immigration but racism, in one form or another. That is not what America is supposed to be about."

SOURCE NOTES AND
BIBLIOGRAPHIC REFERENCES

PROLOGUE

Like many American immigrant family histories, mine is retold differently by different people, depending in part on when they first heard the details themselves, how old they were at the time, and who was doing the telling. But although some of my many cousins on one side or the other may disagree with some elements of the story, I have attempted to present here what I believe to be a consensus version of events. It was, in any case, endorsed by the last living member of my parents' generation, my uncle, Leo Ungar, who reviewed a draft and suggested changes during his own last days. My visit to my father's birthplace, the village of Tusice, in eastern Slovakia, near the Hungarian, Polish, and then-Soviet borders, took place in March 1988.

INTRODUCTION

The conference on Environmental Challenges and the Global South was held on April 13–14, 1992, under the auspices of the School of International Service at American University.

The classic study of how well immigrant groups did or did not truly assimilate in America is Nathan Glazer and Daniel Patrick Moynihan, *Beyond the Melting Pot: The Negroes, Puerto Ricans, Jews, Italians, and Irish of New York City* (Boston: The M.I.T. Press, 1963). "The notion that the intense and unprecedented mixture of ethnic and religious groups in American life was soon to blend into a homogenous end product has outlived its usefulness, and also its credibility," Glazer and Moynihan argue in their preface. "In the meanwhile the persisting facts of ethnicity demand attention, understanding, and accommodation. The point about the melting pot . . . is that it did not happen. At least not in New York and . . . in those parts of

America which resemble New York." In an assertion that many might quarrel with today, they go on to say, "This is nothing remarkable. On the contrary, the American ethos is nowhere better perceived than in the disinclination of the third and fourth generation of newcomers to blend into a standard, uniform national type."

A useful, and more recent, historical overview can be found in Roger Daniels, *Coming to America: A History of Immigration and Ethnicity in American Life* (New York: Harper & Row, 1990).

Two other interesting perspectives on these issues are to be found in Michael Novak, *The Rise of the Unmeltable Ethnics: Politics and Culture in the Seventies* (New York: Macmillan, 1972), and Ted Morgan, *On Becoming American* (Boston: Houghton Mifflin, 1978). For a more recent discussion that includes compelling case studies, see Louise Lamphere (ed.), *Structuring Diversity: Ethnographic Perspectives on the New Immigration* (Chicago: University of Chicago Press, 1992).

I: WE CALL OURSELVES AMERICANS

The individuals whose stories are told in this chapter were selected from among the hundreds I encountered over a period of more than four years. There are many others I would have liked to include but could not for reasons of space.

I visited and interviewed Alan Patel in Pensacola, Florida, in August 1993, and Michael Leven in Atlanta, Georgia, in August 1994. My Le Bartram was interviewed in Rittman and other nearby towns in Ohio in February 1991. I first met Alix Cantave in his office at the Somerville, Massachusetts, city hall in August 1991, and spoke with him again at his home in the Roslindale section of Boston in April 1994. Michel Laguerre's statistic on the number of people of Haitian ancestry living in the United States comes from "The Invisible Immigrants," by Joel Dreyfuss, in the *New York Times Magazine*, 23 May 1993, pp. 20–21, 80–82.

Anna Moscicki was interviewed in Dubois, Wyoming, in June 1992, and Mohamed Arabi in Houston in December 1993. I interviewed Po Wong in San Francisco in March 1991, and the Mwalimu family at their home in Silver Spring, Maryland, in September 1994.

II: LIFE ON THE FRONTLINES OF IMMIGRATION: PARADISE LOST

My interviews for this chapter were conducted in and around Temecula, California, in July 1992, and later by telephone. Clippings from the *Riverside Press-Enterprise, Los Angeles Times,* and other Southern California newspapers were helpful in filling in details of the accident resulting from the Border Patrol chase and its aftermath, along with other similar incidents. The record of hearings held by a subcommittee of the U.S. House of Representatives on the incident and on general Border Patrol pursuit policies was also a useful source on the history of the region and of INS involvement there. *(Immigration and Naturalization Service and U.S. Border Patrol: Agency Mission and Pursuit Policies.* Hearing before the Government Information,

Justice, and Agriculture Subcommittee of the Committee on Government Operations, House of Representatives, 102d Congress, 2d Session, July 30, 1992. Washington: U.S. Government Printing Office, 1993. ISBN 0-16-041674-4.)

III: LIFE ON THE FRONTLINES OF IMMIGRATION: TROUBLE ON THE BEACH

Interviews for this chapter were conducted in Revere, Massachusetts, and Boston in September 1991 and subsequently by telephone. Clippings from the *Boston Globe,* the *Revere Journal,* and other local newspapers were also helpful, and I am grateful to Amy Sessler of the *Globe* for her assistance with my research.

IV: COPING WITH DIVERSITY

The report on the Reverend Tyng's sermon can be found in "News Clippings, Hayes Administration, Mexico & China," Volume 107, 1877–81, page 191, a scrapbook in the Rutherford B. Hayes Presidential Library in Fremont, Ohio. There is no precise date on this particular clipping, but from the context, it would appear to have been published in the *New York World* during the first week of February 1881. Hayes's controversial veto of the anti-Chinese immigration bill of 1879 is discussed in Ari Hoogenboom, *The Presidency of Rutherford B. Hayes* (Lawrence, Kansas: University Press of Kansas, 1988).

Leon F. Bouvier's book, *Peaceful Invasions: Immigration and Changing America,* was published in 1991 by the Center for Immigration Studies (1815 H Street NW, Washington, DC 20006-3604). The portions quoted here are from the acknowledgments and preface (pp. ix–x and 1–8).

The economic arguments in support of immigration are drawn from Julian L. Simon, *The Economic Consequences of Immigration* (Cambridge, Massachusetts: Basil Blackwell, Inc., in association with the Cato Institute, 1989), which pulls together his work of many years on these issues. For the broad view, see especially Chapter 17, pp. 337–46.

Statistical information in this chapter is drawn primarily from *Statistical Yearbook of the U.S. Immigration and Naturalization Service for 1988* (#PB89-193932), published in August 1989, and from subsequent annual editions of the same publication through 1992, all available through the National Technical Information Service of the U.S. Department of Commerce (5285 Port Royal Road, Springfield, VA 22161), and from various reports of the results of the 1990 census. Notable among the latter is Sam Roberts, *Who We Are: A Portrait of America Based on the Latest U.S. Census* (New York: Times Books, 1993), my review of which was published in the *Washington Post* Book World on April 10, 1994. Also useful was the *Refugee and Immigrant Resource Directory, 1990–91,* compiled by Alan Edward Schorr and published by the Denali Press (P.O. Box 021535, Juneau, AK 99802-1535). For information about the quota system and other aspects of the history of immigration policy, I relied upon *U.S. Immigration Law and Policy: 1952–1986,* a report prepared by the Congressional Research Service of the Library of Congress for the Subcommittee on Immigration and Refugee Affairs of the Senate Judiciary Committee (S. Prt. 100–100, 1988).

For the Palmer raids and related matters, see Sanford J. Ungar, *FBI: An Uncensored Look Behind the Walls* (Boston: Atlantic–Little, Brown, 1975), pp. 40–45. Garvan's reference to "alien filth" is from Curt Gentry, *J. Edgar Hoover: The Man and the Secrets* (New York: W. W. Norton, 1991), p. 77.

The material on public attitudes toward immigrants is drawn from "Public Opinion on Immigrants: National Polls, 1937–1990," Chapter Three in Rita J. Simon and Susan H. Alexander, *The Ambivalent Welcome* (New York: Praeger, 1992). The quotations from newspaper columns are from unpublished papers by the same authors.

The authoritative biography of Walter Lippmann, where his attitude toward his own heritage is discussed extensively, is Ronald Steel, *Walter Lippmann and the American Century* (New York: Vintage Books, 1981). For his comments on Hitler and Nazism, see especially pp. 330–33.

A particularly useful, concise overview of the changing racial and ethnic balance in the United States can be found in "Beyond the Melting Pot," by William A. Henry III, the cover story in *Time*, 9 April 1990, pp. 28–31. On the New York City schools, see "Immigrants Jam Schools, Invigorating a System," by Joseph Berger, *The New York Times*, 26 April 1992, sec. IV, p. 6.

V: ON THE BORDER

My reporting along the border in Texas, in the area of Brownsville and Harlingen, and in Matamoros on the Mexican side, took place primarily in October 1990. I visited Mexico City and Monterrey in July 1992. My interviews and observations along the border in California, and in Tijuana, are mostly from visits in July and September 1992. A number of valuable books and articles about the border, and life along it, have been published in recent years; among them is William Langewiesche, *Cutting for Sign* (New York: Pantheon, 1993), an expansion of his series that appeared earlier in the *Atlantic Monthly*.

There has been a great deal of thoughtful newspaper and magazine comment, before and since the passage of Proposition 187 by California voters in November 1994, about the relative attitudes toward illegal immigrants in Texas and California. Especially useful is the coverage of the issue in the *Los Angeles Times*, *San Diego Union-Tribune*, and *Dallas Morning News*. See also Sam Howe Verhovek, "Texas and California: 2 Views of Illegal Aliens," *The New York Times*, 26 June 1994, p. 12. For a revealing description of the tactics used by some supporters of Proposition 187, see Elizabeth Kadetsky, "Bashing Illegals in California," *The Nation*, 17 October 1994, pp. 416–22.

For a discussion of the backlash against Mexican workers during the Great Depression, see T. H. Watkins, *The Great Depression: America in the 1930s* (Boston: Little, Brown, 1993), pp. 68–70.

VI: MANIPULATED BY HISTORY

Most of the material in this chapter is based upon interviews conducted during a visit to Minneapolis and Saint Paul in August 1990. I was assisted particularly by Ruth Hammond, a freelance journalist in the Twin Cities who has written extensively about the Hmong and has also taught English to Hmong immigrants. See especially her two series: "Strangers in a Strange Land," *Twin Cities Reader*, 1–7 June 1988, p. 1 ff; 15–21 June 1988, p. 1 ff; and 22–28 June 1988, p. 1 ff; and "Rumors of War," *Twin Cities Reader*, 25–31 October 1989, p. 8 ff, and 8–14 November 1989, p. 8 ff. She is also the author of "The Great Refugee Shakedown," *The Washington Post*, 16 April 1989, p. B1, among other articles.

A recent, authoritative background source is *Hmong: History of a People*, by Keith Quincy (Cheney, Washington: Eastern Washington University Press, 1988). *The Hmong Resettlement Study* (Volume I, Final Report), prepared by the Northwest Regional Educational Laboratory in Portland, Oregon, and published in April 1985 by the Office of Refugee Resettlement of the U.S. Department of Health and Human Services, provided an illuminating evaluation of the Hmong experience in various parts of the United States after nearly a decade, complete with recommendations for how it might be improved upon. Other useful sources include Bruce T. Downing and Douglas P. Olney (eds.), *The Hmong in the West: Observations and Reports* (Papers of the 1981 Hmong Research Conference at the University of Minnesota), (Minneapolis: Southeast Asian Refugee Studies Project, Center for Urban and Regional Affairs, University of Minnesota, 1982); and Henry T. Trueba et al., *Cultural Conflict and Adaptation: The Case of Hmong Children in American Society* (New York: The Falmer Press, 1990). The bibliography in the Quincy book suggests many other useful places to look for detailed background on the history and culture of the Hmong.

VII: A LONG VACATION

Most of the interviews for this chapter were conducted in Miami during January 1991. Adis Vila was interviewed later at the Department of Agriculture in Washington, while she was serving in the Bush administration.

Several useful books about Miami, and the Cuban influence there, have been published in recent years. They include two books by David Rieff, *Going to Miami: Exiles, Tourists, and Refugees in the New America* (Boston: Little, Brown, 1987) and *The Exile: Cuba in the Heart of Miami* (New York: Simon & Schuster, 1993), as well as T. D. Allman, *Miami: City of the Future* (New York: Atlantic Monthly Press, 1987) and Joan Didion, *Miami* (New York: Simon & Schuster, 1987).

VIII: "TAKING THE FIRST STEP TO HEAVEN"

The interviews for this chapter were conducted in the Chicago area in May 1992 and August 1993. The Polish community in Chicago has been prolific about documenting its history. Two of the more interesting works are Joseph John Parot, *Polish Catholics in Chicago, 1850–1920: A Religious History* (DeKalb, Illinois: Northern Illinois University Press, 1981), and Donald E. Pienkos, *PNA: A Centennial History of the Polish National Alliance of the United States of North America* (Boulder, Colorado: East European Monographs, 1984; distributed by Columbia University Press, New York).

IX: GETTING DOWN TO BUSINESS

The interviews for this chapter were conducted in the Washington, D.C., area over a period of several years. Coverage in the *Washington Post* of various controversies concerning the Ethiopian and Eritrean exile communities was also helpful. See especially Phil McCombs, "Ethiopia's Potomac Politics," *The Washington Post*, 18 February 1994, p. 61.

X: CHOSEN TO LIVE AT THE FLASHPOINT

The material for this chapter was gathered primarily during visits to Los Angeles in March 1991 and September 1992. Information from the South Korean government was obtained during a trip to Seoul in November 1994. There have been many good books and articles in recent years on Los Angeles as a magnet for immigrants; see, for example, David Rieff, *Los Angeles: Capital of the Third World* (New York: Simon & Schuster, 1991).

XI: "WE KNOW WHO WE ARE"

I conducted interviews with the Mashadi in Manhattan, Kew Gardens, and Great Neck, New York, in June 1993 and February 1994. Bahman Kamali and his family were particularly generous in helping me arrange access to members of a very closed community. For the history of the Mashadi in Iran, I relied upon information from these interviews, especially with Dr. Abraham Dilmanian, whose father was a renowned historian of the Mashadi, and Ida G. Cowen, "The Secret Jews of Meshed: Marranos Who Came Back," *Hadassah Magazine*, February 1981, pp. 12–31. I also benefited from access to various unpublished memoranda and correspondence in private circulation within the Mashadi community.

XII: PLAYING THE ODDS

My interviews with Irish participants in the lottery for Morrison visas took place in the Boston and Washington areas in the fall of 1991, with the particular cooperation of the Irish Immigration Center. For the rules and regulations and outcome of the lotteries, I relied on the Bureau of Public Affairs at the State Department.

XIII: THE BACKLASH

My conversation with Richard Lamm took place in Denver in October 1990. His book, coauthored with Gary Imhoff, is *The Immigration Time-Bomb: The Fragmenting of America* (New York: Truman Talley Books, E. P.

Dutton, 1985). My discussion of the anti-immigration policies and attitudes of the American Legion and other "patriotic" organizations is based on correspondence and other material found in the Legion archives in Indianapolis, which I visited in August 1990. The interviews in Atlanta were conducted in October 1992, and in Houston in December 1993. The quote from Wanda Coleman appeared in "Remembering Latasha: Blacks, Immigrants and America," *The Nation*, 15 February 1993, pp. 187–91, and was cited in draft testimony on "Immigration and Community Tensions" prepared by Thomas Muller for presentation to a hearing of the Commission on Immigration Reform on October 1, 1993.

XIV: THE FUTURE OF IMMIGRATION AND THE NATURE OF AMERICA

The quotations from Gregory de Freitas, Douglas Massey, and studies by the Urban Institute and the Federal Reserve Bank of New York are in Larry Rohter, "Revisiting Immigration and the Open-Door Policy," *The New York Times*, 19 September 1993, Section 4, p. 4. The statistics on immigrant home ownership are from an annual analysis performed by the Joint Center for Housing Studies at Harvard University, cited in H. Jane Lehman, "Immigrants Add to Rising Pool of Home Owners," *The Washington Post*, 2 July 1994, p. E1.

Amidst the recent political controversies surrounding immigration, a number of works have appeared that contribute usefully to the dialogue. Several important recommendations are set out in *U.S. Immigration Policy: Restoring Credibility*, the 1994 interim Report to Congress of the U.S. Commission on Immigration Reform (1825 Connecticut Avenue NW, Suite 511, Washington, DC 20009). Articulate arguments over immigration issues can be found in Vernon M. Briggs Jr. and Stephen Moore, *Still an Open Door? U.S. Immigration Policy and the American Economy* (Washington: American University Press, 1994); John J. Miller (ed.), *Strangers at Our Gate: Immigration in the 1990s* (published in 1994 by The Center for the New American Community at the Manhattan Institute, 1010 Massachusetts Avenue NW, Washington, DC 20001); and Nicolaus Mills (ed.), *Arguing Immigration: The Debate Over the Changing Face of America* (New York: Touchstone, 1994).

ACKNOWLEDGMENTS

I AM GRATEFUL to many people for their help with this project, but none so much as the hundreds of immigrants and refugees I met and interviewed along the way. Many of them trusted me beyond all reasonable limits—in part, I suppose, because they were so eager to tell their stories. Although some had come to America from countries where it could be very dangerous indeed to talk to strangers, especially those bearing notebooks and tape recorders, they confided in me, opening up their hearts (and, in quite a few cases, their homes) and sharing their fears and aspirations without any way of knowing what the result might be. We met in offices, shops, social service centers, churches and synagogues, parks, hotel lobbies, cars, and restaurants—not to mention living rooms and kitchens—and often we talked until I thought I would drop. I always came away knowing something new or understanding it better.

Inevitably, it was not possible to describe all of these people's adventures and insights, or even to mention some of their names, in an already very long manuscript, and that is one of my few regrets about the whole enterprise. But I will long remember, for example, a madcap visit to the home of Hungarian immigrant Irene Ray in rural Smithville, Ohio, one cold February night, when she served me dinner amidst flashing Christmas decorations and pressed a lifetime of tales upon me. Then there is the lingering warmth of a nighttime session with the family of Duong Dinh, a Vietnamese immigrant in Pensacola, Florida, who played in a rock band, designed his own house on a computer, and had flown to Denver just to see the Pope. I have a vivid image of the Pentecostals from Ukraine who huddled in the basement of their Full Gospel church in the Midwest and told me that their main puzzlement with this country was over why Americans waste so much glass. And of the brown-bag lunch at Child and Family Service in Honolulu, where a collection of Samoan, Thai, Chinese, Filipino, and other Asian and Pacific Islander immigrants sought to convince me that someday the entire United States would have to become just as multicultural as Hawaii.

To all these people and many other immigrants, including those I watched bravely crossing the border into Texas and California, I offer

393

thanks for their cooperation. I only hope I have done justice to them and their stories.

THIS WAS AN ambitious project that seemed logistically and emotionally overwhelming at times. My agent, Robert Lescher, one of the wisest people I know, pushed me to take it on in the first place and then kept me going whenever my energy lagged. Alice Mayhew, my editor, once again proved to be both perspicacious and patient, and the book has been improved by her astute, worldly suggestions. Her assistants, including Eric Steel, Liz Stein, Sarah Baker, and Lisa Weisman, were enormously helpful; Roger Labrie sprinted with me to the finish line in a manner both able and indulgent. As usual, the copy editors, designers, publicists, and lawyers at Simon & Schuster have also proved to be consummate professionals.

During the entire time I worked on this book, I have served as dean of the School of Communication at American University in Washington. There I have been blessed with wonderful colleagues on the faculty and staff and stimulating students. I have benefited greatly from the intellectual companionship and reliable friendship of so many in the school and at the university; but nothing compares with the privilege of working closely year after year with Glenn Harnden and Patrick Martin, who have become like brothers to me. Their support has been invaluable.

Greg Pearson designed a research system for this book that enabled me to hit the ground reporting all across the country; he made wise and careful choices on my behalf. Tony Berlin, David Gately, and John Zollinger were among the graduate fellows in the School of Communication who, using Greg's methods, later helped me plan my travels and target my efforts. Other students who made valuable contributions to the research or cleaned up after me at various times included John Mies, Sandy Wurz, Susan Caskie, Doug Reardon, Stacy Tobin, Zivo Feit, Terry Martin, and David Lefort.

But I would have been nowhere without the network of family and friends who frequently called my attention to immigrants and immigration issues on their minds, to new twists on perennial topics. Chief among them was George Pollock, my father-in-law, whose depth of knowledge and breadth of interests rival any computerized database I've yet encountered. I was also glad whenever I spotted an envelope in the mail from, among others, Jim Baughman or Vivian Cotchen; it meant more clippings and new leads. In addition, my colleague Chris Simpson and various employees of the Immigration and Naturalization Service and other government agencies, who shall remain nameless here, passed along useful information.

Rita and Julian Simon shared generously their academic knowledge of my subject. Additionally, for their own particular contributions at various stages, I am grateful to Priscilla Labovitz, Henry Ferris, Roscoe Barnes, and Claudia Medina. Luke Seaward preserved my sanity by getting me into the water, and George Vicas, my producer and mentor on various visits to Czechoslovakia, indulged the visit to my father's home village that raised my immigrant consciousness in the first place. I have also benefited greatly from having close friends in far-flung places, including David Denoon, Jack

Fuller, Karen Greenberg, and Goran Rosenberg, with whom it is still possible to discuss ideas.

My sister Mimi Fredman, always on call for late-night consultation, has played a major role in yet another phase of my life. Along with my other sister, Yetta Kahn, my uncle Leo Ungar, and my cousin Fred Grossman, Mimi also helped assure the accuracy of my prologue. Beverly Pollock, my mother-in-law, was among the few people I was willing to risk sharing the early drafts of some other chapters. This project truly became a family affair.

As I traveled, I benefited from the hospitality, the contacts, and/or the good will of many people, including Marilyn Glassberg and Marc Csete in Miami; Beverly and George Pollock in Chicago; Victor and Carolyn Dix in Wooster, Ohio; Ruth Hammond in the Twin Cities; John Ruffner in Temecula, California; Alex Kafka in Corpus Christi and Becky Thatcher in Brownsville, Texas; Amy Sessler in Revere, Massachusetts; Bahman and Ruth Kamali in Kew Gardens and Great Neck, New York; Daniel Pollock and Sally West in Atlanta; Raph Pollock and Lesley Newton in Houston; and Michael Schnorr, Jorge Hinojosa, and Adolfo Davila in San Diego and Tijuana. Yeshi Imagnu helped me find new paths into the Ethiopian community in Washington.

Only Wendy Lanxner, with her musical ear, sharp wit, and total fascination with the subject matter, could have deciphered the accents on my hundreds of hours of tapes and produced such clean transcripts. Denise Brinker and Pablo Coirolo helped me sort out intractable, mostly self-inflicted computer problems; the people at the American University Computing Center Hot Line also rescued me more than once, including the time when I accidentally deleted the entire revised manuscript of the book from my hard drive. Darrell Capwell, Anne James, and Lisa Holt managed to minimize the chaos and maximize the good times in my office, while all this was going on—and other things, too.

My wife Beth, to whom this book is dedicated, has been my personal think tank through all the years I have been working on it. A careful reader and a sharp critic, she has made time to give me fresh ideas and constructive feedback at every step, notwithstanding all the other demands on her time and energy. My extraordinary children, Lida and Philip, have had to cope with this book for what must seem like most of their lives; there has been no such thing as a vacation where I did not find an immigration angle to pursue, hardly a night or a weekend when the project did not tug at me. Still, they have shown interest and involvement as if it were the equivalent of their soccer games and band concerts, and that's pretty good. This family of four means everything to me, and it is my highest calling to make my partners in it proud and happy.

THERE ARE TWO people who I especially wish could see this book, and I pause here to remember them. Tillie Landau Ungar, my mother, was an immigrant girl who taught her entire family, and everyone else she took under her wing, to appreciate the best of America; she knew what this country could and should mean to those who struggled to get here. She died, two months before her eighty-ninth birthday, just as I was starting to work on this project. The loss of my mother made me draw even closer to my Uncle Leo, my late father's brother. For years he had followed my work, but this was his favorite thing I had ever done. He too sent me clippings about immigration issues, and he loved to hear, in person or on the phone, how the book was coming along. When he died at ninety-one, he missed holding it in his hands by less than a year.

That entire generation of my immigrant family is gone now, but this book, in a sense, is their legacy. They knew that America always needs fresh blood to keep it going.

Washington, D.C.
July 1995

In preparing the paperback edition of this book, I have had inestimable help from Jennifer Jose, Devin Wilson, and Wendy Belzer. Frank Sharry and his colleagues at the National Immigration Forum are the most reliable sources for day-to-day developments in the debate on these issues, and I thank them. The editors at the University of Illinois Press have been sensitive in allowing me to bring the book up to date. I am also grateful to the people across the United States who have been willing to keep an open mind on immigration in the midst of a cacophony of misinformation and disinformation, not all of it well-intentioned. Especially notable are the wonderful TESOL people (Teachers of English to Speakers of Other Languages), who are doing extraordinary work on the frontlines of the social and cultural integration on which this country depends. I greatly appreciate them and the others who have educated me and listened to me during the past two years.

Blue Ridge Summit, Pa.
August 1997

INDEX

Abera, Terefe, 270
African Americans, 14, 38n, 46, 109, 198, 229
  Ethiopians' relations with, 263–65
  Haitians' relations with, 39–40, 364–65
  Koreans' relations with, 279, 280, 282–85, 297–300, 361–62
  new immigrants vs., 94, 95, 188–89, 263–66, 278n, 280, 282–85, 297–300, 333–34, 361–65
African immigrants, 19, 22, 50–52, 97
  Ethiopians and Eritreans, 104, 174, 247–72, 292
aging, aged, 52, 265
agriculture, Mexican immigrants employed in, 55, 64–65, 363
Aguila, Josefina, 216
Aguila, Percy, 215–16
Ahronoff, Sam, 328–29
AIDS (HIV infection), 37, 166, 358, 364
Albanian immigrants, 98
Albanian language, 113
Alexander, Susan, 108–10
Alien Act (1918), 106
Alien Registration Receipt Card, 112n
All Amhara People's Relief and Development Association (AAPRDA), 268–69
Alliance College, 240, 243
Alpert, Geoffrey P., 68
Amerasian children, problems of, 35–36, 98
American Civil Liberties Union, 203

American Coalition, 357n
American Immigration Conference Board, 355–57
American Legion, 352–55, 357–58
American Refugee Committee, 178
Amharic language, 248, 250, 266
Aminoff, Jonathan, 325–26
Amirian, Saeed, 327–28
amnesty, 93n, 103, 109, 135, 166
anti-Semitism, 111, 245, 306–7, 308, 355–56
  Holocaust and, 13, 14, 17, 18, 111, 311n, 317
Arab American Communication Service, 45
Arabi, Mohamed, 44–47
Arabic language, 45
Arab immigrants, 44–47, 107
Aristide, Jean-Bertrand, 40
Arizona, 115, 116, 117, 162n
Army, U.S., in World War I, 12
Army Corps of Engineers, U.S., 145
arson, in Revere, Mass., 73, 85
Arthur, Chester A., 92
Ashkenazi tradition, 305, 313
Asian-American Hotel Owners Association, 31
Asian immigrants, *see specific ethnic groups*
Assad, Hafez el-, 46
assimilation, 14, 20, 42, 140–41, 174, 228, 311–15
  Tyng's view of, 91–92
Association for the Advancement of Hmong Women of Minnesota, 186–87

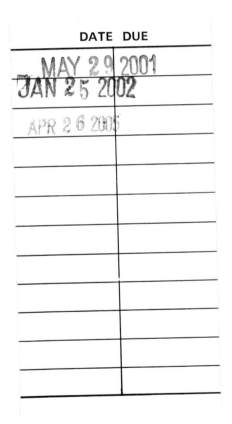